FRANCI'S WAR

ABOUT THE AUTHOR

Franci Rabinek Epstein was born in Prague, Czechoslovakia, in 1920. She attended French and German schools before dropping out to apprentice in her mother's haute couture salon. In 1942, Franci and her parents were deported to Terezín. She remained there for over a year and a half and was then deported to Auschwitz, then to forced labour camps in Hamburg, then to Bergen-Belsen. After liberation by the British army, she returned to Prague an orphan and a widow, re-established her fashion salon, and married Kurt Epstein. In 1948, after the Communist takeover of Czechoslovakia, the couple immigrated to New York City with their eight-month-old daughter. Franci supported the family by establishing another salon on the Upper West Side. She died of a brain aneurysm in 1989.

FRANCI'S WAR

A TRUE STORY

Franci Rabinek Epstein

AFTERWORD BY HELEN EPSTEIN

MICHAEL JOSEPH
an imprint of
PENGUIN BOOKS

MICHAEL JOSEPH

UK | USA | Canada | Ireland | Australia
India | New Zealand | South Africa

Michael Joseph is part of the Penguin Random House group of companies
whose addresses can be found at global.penguinrandomhouse.com

First published in the United States of America by Penguin Books 2020
First published in Great Britain by Michael Joseph 2020
001

Copyright © Franci Rabinek Epstein Estate, 2020
Afterword copyright © Helen Epstein, 2020

Grateful acknowledgment is made to the following:
Page 219 (bottom): Photo courtesy of Ronnie Golz
Page 221 (top left): Photo courtesy of Doron Leitner
All other photos courtesy of Helen Epstein

Map by Virginia Norey

The moral right of the author has been asserted

Set in Adobe Garamond Pro
Designed by Cassandra Garruzzo
Printed and bound in Great Britain by Clays Ltd, Elcograf S.p.A.

A CIP catalogue record for this book is available from the British Library

HARDBACK ISBN: 978–0–241–44104–6
TRADE PAPERBACK ISBN: 978–0–241–44110–7

To Helen, Tommy, and David
In memory of their grandparents

CONTENTS

Map of Franci's Route   xi

Photographs   217

Afterword   225

Editorial Note   243

Acknowledgments   249

Timeline   251

Notes on the Concentration Camps   255

FRANCI'S WAR

FRANCI'S ROUTE, 1939–1945

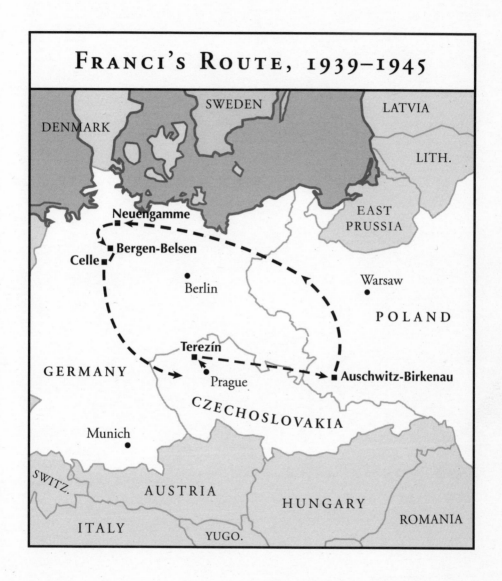

1

It was a hot day in the first week of September 1942, and the Industrial Palace of Prague was teeming with people. Most were lying or sitting on the loose straw on the floor; others were wandering around in a stunned daze. Gone were the shiny displays of Czechoslovak industry that had given the place the air of a happy carnival.

I had often come to the Industrial Palace when I was a child and my father's electro-technical firm, Korálek & Rabinek, had a booth.* It had always been a treat. I returned home with free samples, balloons, and stacks of glossy catalogs. This time I would not return home because the Industrial Palace had been converted to the assembly point for the deportation of undesirables, i.e., Jews, by edict of the Nuremberg race laws.

None of us should have been surprised. The trap had been closing

---

* Editor's note: The assembly point was then called Radiopalác Pražských vzorkových veleterhů.

for three years by then, but the systematic humiliation and brainwashing had been gradual and only partially successful. Our humanity was still intact. Our situation had somehow not fully registered until now. It was quite a shock to be suddenly treated like so much cattle.

I was twenty-two and lying with my head in my mother's lap in a sort of stupor. I had just had a tonsillectomy. I had not eaten for a few days and was having trouble breathing the air that was filled with straw dust. My mother kept stroking my hair and trying to make me drink a little water. My father was walking around from one acquaintance to another, hoping to find out what was in store for us. Groups of SS men were storming in and out, yelling orders and rounding up groups of Jewish men to clean the latrines. They made a point of picking out the most distinguished-looking older men in the crowd, the men wearing glasses. My father was one of them.

When they told me in the hospital that my parents and I had been called up for a transport, the nurse, who was a friend of ours, said *We can get you out of it because of the surgery.* I thought this over for a few minutes and then said *I'm not letting them go alone. They're too old and they don't have anybody else.* My mother was sixty and my father was sixty-five. I couldn't visualize those two people going alone anywhere. And there was a little egotistical motivation too. My husband was already gone. I would have been left all alone. Besides, by September 1942 I was so fed up with all the restrictions in Prague that I thought any change of scene would be a relief, no matter what was waiting on the other end. I was always like that, unfortunately.

Hitler invaded Czechoslovakia on March 15, 1939, a bit over two weeks after I turned nineteen. My interest in politics was nonexistent, and I was only vaguely aware that all four of my grandparents were Jewish. A year earlier, I had become the owner of my mother's *haute couture* business. I was carefree, slightly spoiled, and mainly interested in dancing, my business, flirting, and skiing, in that order.

My father, Emil Rabinek, was born a Jew in Vienna in 1878. He was the youngest son in a family of Austrian civil servants and a firm believer in assimilation. At the age of twenty, he had converted to Catholicism in order to circumvent the *numerus clausus*—the Jewish quota—at the University of Berlin. Emil Rabinek had fought with the Austrian army during the First World War without much enthusiasm, and welcomed the formation of the Czechoslovak Republic in 1918. He had lived in Prague for many years. While he remained—emotionally and culturally—an Austrian, he saw the establishment of the Czechoslovak Republic as a new experiment in social democracy, a sort of Switzerland in the heart of Europe with equal rights for all minorities. He chose to be a Czechoslovak citizen.

The next twenty years justified his choice. My father lived as a member of the German-speaking community of Prague, patronizing German clubs, theaters, and concert halls. One of his favorite statements was *I am a Czechoslovak citizen of German nationality.* He never learned proper Czech. Our extensive library was almost entirely German, with translations from French, English, and Russian literature. He led me to admire everything German or, at least, filtered through the German language. There was not one Czech book in the house until I was in my teens and began to buy them for myself.

Though my father had had plenty of warning about Nazism, he dismissed the news that came from Germany as propaganda. He believed in German decency, justice, honor, and civilization. He was also absolutely certain that Czechoslovakia was a strong country, its sovereignty guaranteed by its French and British allies. Not even the occupation of Austria in March 1938 had shaken his convictions, and he considered his cousins who had fled Vienna to be cowards. His eldest sister, Gisela Rabinek Kremer, and some of her children had remained there. That gave him further evidence that it was a mistake to panic and run.

There were, in addition, financial considerations. In February 1920, when I was born, my father had been a rich man—co-owner of a shipyard and an electro-technical wholesale house. Following the American Crash of 1929 and the depression years, his wealth had shrunk. We still had our beautiful apartment, with all its books and paintings, and were living very comfortably. But by the time the Germans occupied Czechoslovakia, our income came mostly from my mother's and my *haute couture* business, which, in earlier years, he had considered the caprice of a liberated career woman. Now, my father kept busy as its bookkeeper. Business was good, but most of our capital was tied up in it, and not readily available to convert into foreign currency on the black market. My father often said *At our age we are not emigrating without capital*.

Unbeknownst to me and in spite of all his brave talk, my father was writing letters to his cousin in England with the purpose of getting me out of the country. Nothing ever came of it, and only twenty-five years later did I learn from this guilt-ridden relative how my father had pleaded with him to do something, anything, to save me. He must have done it under pressure from my mother, who felt that a major catastrophe had befallen the Czech nation in general and our family in particular.

My mother, Josefa "Pepi" Sachsel, spoke excellent Czech and had a very deep allegiance to the Czech people, although she, too, was born in Vienna. Both her parents had died when she was nine, and in 1891, she and her two older brothers were taken in by Aunt Rosa, her father's sister, and moved to the Czech town of Kolín.

Rosalia Sachsel Lustfeld, according to my mother, was desperately poor and deeply pious. A regular at Kolín's synagogue, she preferred to discuss the Talmud with itinerant Chasidim to running her used clothing store. The brothers soon ran away: Emil Sachsel joined the Austro-Hungarian Navy and eventually settled in Bratislava; Rudolf Sachsel became a peddler and eventually a rich wholesaler in Prague. Pepi, being a girl and only nine, remained in Kolín, learned Czech, attended grammar school, and was stuck with Aunt Rosa's overpowering love, religious fervor, and rigidity. This combination of traits managed, over the years, to sour my mother's connection to observant Judaism and turn her into an agnostic.

The Hilsner Affair was also a factor. In 1899, when Pepi was seventeen, a Czech Catholic seamstress was found dead in a pool of blood during Passover. A Jewish vagrant named Leopold Hilsner was the chief suspect and accused of ritual murder. My mother told me there had been pogroms all over the country, including in Kolín. And another factor that soured her on Judaism: her first love had been a wealthy Jewish boy in Kolín, and his parents had shipped him out of the country to prevent him from marrying a poor orphan.

Aunt Rosa had taught her niece how to assess used clothing and how to sew. At twenty, Pepi followed her brothers' lead and left Kolín. She moved in with her brother Rudolf in Prague and found a job at one of the city's best-known dress shops, Moritz Schiller. Within two years, she became its *directrice* and buyer. My mother had no wish to marry, but to allay Aunt Rosa's fears for her virtue in the big city, she married a former Kolín schoolmate, and became Mrs. Oskar Weigert.

During that first decade of the twentieth century, Pepi traveled to Paris every year and became a sophisticated businesswoman. But her marriage was miserably unhappy because Oskar had syphilis, then an incurable disease. In 1908, she had a nervous breakdown. Her boss conferred with Aunt Rosa and Pepi's prosperous brothers, and they were able to get her marriage annulled on the grounds that it was never consummated. Josefa Weigert moved into a boardinghouse, where she met electrical engineer Emil Rabinek. After a decade-long affair, and the death of Aunt Rosa and his mother, Fanny Rabinek, they married in December 1918.

Emil Rabinek did not object to Pepi's career, but did not want her to work for anyone else. So she opened her own *haute couture* house, Salon Weigert, in a space adjoining their apartment on 53 Spálená in Prague. My mother was equally at home with Czech and German clients, perhaps leaning a little more to the Czech side. Many of them adored her and were often friends as well as customers. She had excellent relations with her Czech employees. I was born in February 1920, and as I grew up, she balanced my father's Germanophilia quite nicely.

My own allegiance was entirely with the Czechoslovak Republic. I was, after all, a child of the Republic, only two years younger than the state itself. I considered myself a Czechoslovak citizen. My parents tried to bring me up as a citizen of the world. German was spoken at home, Czech was spoken everywhere else, and I was sent to Prague's French school, baptized a Catholic, and attended church and confession. I knew I had Jewish family members because I visited Aunt Rosa's grave in the Jewish cemetery once a year with Mutti (my mother). But religion did not interest me very much. By the time I was thirteen, I began to question Catholic dogma and soon afterward asked my father to have my papers changed to read "without religious affiliation."

Those were the kind of Jews I and my parents were when the Germans occupied Prague on March 15, 1939.

3

In April, a tall, sandy-haired man with a Prussian crew cut had appeared at our door and identified himself politely as the commissar appointed by the Reichsprotektor to "aryanize" our Jewish business. After inspecting our records and watching how the workroom operated, he must have come to the realization that our salon was entirely dependent on the taste and work of its owners and their relationship to its customers—not a potential gold mine for him. Hinting broadly that his wife needed new clothes, he advised us off the record to sell the business *pro forma* to one of our employees and perhaps stay on as hired help. After he left, Mutti and I went into the workroom to discuss the situation with our staff. Our seamstresses and one tailor were all under thirty, and our belief in their loyalty was so strong that it never occurred to us to worry about a possible leak to the authorities about the proposition we were about to make to them.

They did not seem to be surprised. This sort of thing was going on all over Prague, but somehow none of us had expected it so soon. A lively discussion began about who should become the *pro forma* owner. We decided to sleep on it. My parents had misgivings about putting our livelihood into the hands of an employee—no matter how loyal—while I thought the idea simple and brilliant. Actually, we had no choice. We could close the business completely, but that would entail living on our savings for an unforeseeable length of time and also deprive more than a dozen people of their jobs.

The next day Marie, who had been working for us the longest, offered to be part of the transaction. A secret contract was drawn up by a reliable attorney and member of the Czech underground who had arranged more than one similar transfer. Marie and I would draw the same salary and divide the profit in half. To make the transaction plausible, the lawyer made a loan to Marie, enabling her to buy the business from us. We repaid him. The contract was buried on the grounds of the attorney's country house. A sign painter changed the names over our entrance door.

After this, life went on more or less unchanged, except that the staff began to call Marie "Miss Marie," instead of by her first name. Our customers, including the German customers, accepted the situation without much comment. Some inquired discreetly whether my mother was getting her fair share.

Then the systematic harassment of the Czechs in general and the Jews in particular began. First came the definition of who was considered a Jew: anyone with at least two Jewish grandparents. I discovered that I had four. Then Jews were barred from public places, and signs to that effect were put up at all restaurants, coffeehouses, playgrounds, swimming pools, theaters, concert halls, etc.: JEWS UNWANTED. Only the river was still accessible to us.

Jews were dismissed from all the universities; Jewish doctors were allowed to treat only Jews, and their offices were confiscated one by one. Eventually all Jewish-owned businesses were aryanized and the National Bar Association disbarred all Jewish lawyers. But some Czech organizations and businesses procrastinated. The Czech Philharmonic resisted the longest, almost one year. The national gymnastic association, Sokol, complied, but a large number of regional groups let it be known privately that its Jewish members were as welcome as before.

We were ordered to wear a yellow star with the word JUDE in the middle. This had to be sewn on the left side of every outer garment, over the heart. Anyone circumventing this order was subject to immediate arrest. My father and I considered this the ultimate insult; Mutti accepted it much more philosophically, maybe as a punishment for our disregard of our ancestry.

Next came the confiscation of all jewelry, which had to be brought to appointed places in person. Then radios. Then Jews were only allowed to ride in the last car of the tram and only allowed to sit in the event that no Aryan was standing. The following year, only Jews who worked and had a special pass could ride the tram. The ones who did not have a pass had to walk everywhere.

There were certainly some Czechs who sympathized with the Germans and who were quite happy about the persecution of the Jews. But most of the Czechs I came into contact with resented these edicts. Some made a point of giving up their seat in the tram to let a Jewish woman sit down. These well-meant gestures led to embarrassing situations at times. Prague was full of Germans in civilian clothes. There were altercations in trams or buses that ended in fistfights if only Czechs were involved, but could get much more unpleasant if a German was present. Meanwhile, the oppressed tried to fight back as best as they could. Uninsured jewelry got stashed away with Aryan friends. Large radios were moved to the homes of non-Jewish neighbors and friends, and smaller, older ones were turned in instead. Many a yellow star was hidden on the street by a strategically carried book or handbag, or often not worn at all.

I did that for a long time and, as an added precaution, decided to get a nose job. My father and some of my Jewish friends had always teased me about having a so-called Jewish nose. I was an avid moviegoer and the prohibition on Jews attending cinemas was one of the hardest for me to bear. If my nose were a different shape and I didn't wear a star, I reasoned, I could pass without much risk. I had the operation and wound up, after four weeks of headaches, looking like my mother with her straight, slightly turned-up nose, but never actually got to go to the movies because she got hysterical every time I even mentioned the idea.

4

In June 1939, my parents and I were arrested by the Gestapo—because of my boyfriend's mother's jewelry. My boyfriend was Pepik "Joe" Solar. His mother had stashed some of her jewelry with a Major Z., who had been Joe's commander in the Czechoslovak Army. Because they were looking for Joe, they arrested us.

This was my first contact with the Gestapo. They arrested my parents first without telling them the charges, and me a few hours later, when I returned home from an errand. They interrogated us separately for twelve hours, with my parents totally unaware of what this was all about. Compared to what would happen later in the war, I was not mistreated during those long hours. I was even offered chocolate and cigarettes, alternating with threats of shooting me or my parents if I didn't talk. That night, I was put in a car with my parents and two Gestapo men. We were taken to Pankrác prison and lined up, facing the wall, with some fifty other people.

My parents were on either side of me. Behind our backs, a few guards were marching up and down. After a while, my father turned toward me with a questioning look. Instantly, he was knocked down by a guard, his glasses flying off his face. I bent down automatically to help him up, but a shouted order stopped me, and I realized that it was better to keep still. By midnight we were all led off to different cells. I was put in with two middle-aged ladies to whom I announced that this was all some terrible mistake and that, clearly, I would be going home in the morning. One of them seemed to find my announcement very amusing, while the other just waved her hand, too depressed to argue with me.

The first woman was named Marianne Golz. She was very attractive, with flaming red hair and the self-assurance of an actress, which it turned out she had been. The second was Ludmila, the wife of a high officer in the Czechoslovak Army and a functionary of Sokol, who had fled the country to join the free Czech soldiers abroad. Ludmila had been imprisoned for the previous three months and repeatedly questioned about the network that enabled Czech men such as her husband to slip out of the country under the noses of the Germans.

My two cellmates could not have been more different from each other. Where one was flamboyant and witty, the other was dignified and quiet. Where one's moral attitudes seemed to be at least questionable, the other had been married for twenty-five years to the same husband with rocklike love and devotion. These involuntary roommates had more in common than I at first understood. They both were instantly protective of me and took it upon themselves to give me an elementary education in the ground rules of German detention.

The first rule of the game seemed to be not to let your interrogators know anything they did not already know. Never admit anything, they told me, especially not the truth. Never volunteer information, no matter what the promise of reward.

To my nineteen-year-old eyes, Marianne seemed like an adventuress and *demi-mondaine* with great sensitivity and compassion for others, an enormously courageous daredevil. Ludmila's courage manifested itself more in quiet passive resistance to her captors. I believe that neither of them ever implicated another person during the entire time they were detained. I learned that Marianne was an early anti-Nazi and a Christian who had been married to a Jewish journalist in Vienna. He had fled Austria in March 1938. Marianne had stayed behind in Vienna, obtained a quick divorce on racial grounds, and went to work to help her friends.

She smuggled their money and jewelry into Switzerland, while carrying on an affair with an SS officer in Vienna. This affair allowed her to cover her tracks and make a fair number of useful connections in the high echelons of the SS, in and out of Austria. It had all worked beautifully until the day when the gentleman was transferred to more important duties. At that point, Marianne prudently decided to move her activities to Prague. Here, she became involved with the Czech Resistance. Unfortunately, one arrest had led to another, someone talked too much, and Marianne wound up as Ludmila's cellmate. Despite all her connections to the SS, she was unable to get word out that she was being held in Pankrác prison.

Fascinated by Marianne's stories and personality, I listened closely to what she reported about the experience of the Jews in Austria and the methods used by the Nazis. We had plenty of time and nothing else to do since day after day went by without any of us being called in for questioning. Marianne explained to me the mechanics of the system of confiscation, humiliation, and—finally—deportations, which had already started in Vienna.

Marianne did not know where exactly these people had been taken, but she did know that the weight of their luggage was limited to fifty kilos, and that everything else one owned had to stay behind. She tried to convince me to try to escape if and when I got out of this prison. She *did* convince me that it was foolish for my family to remain in an apartment adjoining the business where I was employed, not only because of the risk to Marie but because our apartment was large and modern, and would be confiscated sooner or later. We would then be forced into one room in another "Jewish apartment."

All this useful information was spiced with quite incredible stories from her life, some of which caused acute embarrassment to Ludmila, who did not consider them fit for my nineteen-year-old ears. But the two women adamantly agreed that the Nazis were monsters who had to be fought on every level. I began to believe every word they said. Every day, I looked for my mother during the twenty-minute exercise march in the prison yard, but never saw her.

Two weeks later I was called for interrogation and released half an hour later. Much later I would learn that Marianne was released a few weeks after me, when one of her SS friends returned from a trip and did not find her home, but rearrested in 1943, when her luck ran out. She was beheaded in Pankrác prison that year. I never learned what happened to Ludmila.

5

I came home to our empty apartment. My first stop was my
father's desk. I opened the top drawer, and found—to my
horror—a list of *my* mother's jewelry with Major Z.'s address.
I also found a suspicious-looking vial without a label that contained little pills. Then the doorbell rang and I stuck it into my
pocket. It was my boyfriend Joe, who filled me in on what had
happened while I was in prison.

Joe had contacted a Czech lawyer with access to the Gestapo to
find out why we had been arrested. He learned that his brother
Paul was suspected of dealing in foreign currency and that two
Gestapo agents had searched his apartment. There, they found a
slip of paper with Major Z.'s name and address, and notes about
jewelry, and locked the brother's family up. Then they interrogated
Paul's mother and asked about Joe's whereabouts. She told them
that Joe was probably-visiting his girlfriend—i.e., me. They arrested us, confronted Major Z., and let him go with an admonition
to stop being a Jew-lover. We were released from Pankrác for the

sum of twenty thousand Czech crowns, a ransom delivered in a plain envelope, stuck into a copy of *Mein Kampf.* My parents were indeed released a few hours after me.

Each of us reacted to that first imprisonment in a different way. My father was furious at my boyfriend, and ranted about keeping lists that implicated uninvolved others. He stopped only when I produced the list I had found in his desk. Joe drew the conclusion that the Germans could be bought and that his newly found connection to the Gestapo might prove useful in the future. Mutti was happy to see me all in one piece, and ready to forgive everything and everybody.

I told them what I had heard from my cellmate Marianne. They listened but considered me naive: Marianne might have been an *agent provocateur* put in with us to acquire information. Nonetheless, I insisted on discussing her suggestion that we give up our large, centrally located Prague apartment, move the business to a separate location, and look for smaller, less attractive living quarters that would not invite German requisition. My idea was to move to the suburbs, far from the center of town, where raids and other surprises were less likely. It took months to convince my parents, but I stood my ground and we eventually did just that.

When the Second World War officially began on September 1, 1939, my father retreated into a dreamworld of his own, never doubting an Allied victory. He walked six miles every day to listen to the broadcasts of the BBC in the home of one of our employees where our radio was parked. He had maps all over the house with flags pinned into position where the Germans claimed to be and where the BBC said they were. The situation looked bleak, but once the war started, my father's optimism soared sky-high. That Christmas, Joe gave me a puppy. Tommy soon became the center of my family's attention, and a faithful companion during my father's news-gathering walks.

In the beginning of 1940, with the war going into high gear, my boyfriend became deeply involved with the Resistance's clandestine smuggling of former Czechoslovak servicemen out of the country to enable them to join the anti-Nazi military effort abroad. Joe had been discharged from the army only a short time before the occupation. While serving, he had been a happy-go-lucky guy, never taking the army very seriously. After the German occupation, his attitude had changed completely. He felt guilty sending other men off, and by the end of April, he had decided to join the growing units of volunteers.

The exit route had been tested many times before and was considered fairly safe. A patriotic ranger led groups of five to ten men through the woods across the border to Hungary. From there they made their way to Yugoslavia and eventually to Palestine and England, where a Czechoslovak government-in-exile had been formed. There was a long and tearful leave-taking at our house, with even my father moved to sniffles, and Joe left without forgetting to arrange for two baskets of flowers to be delivered the following day for Mutti and me.

After three days without news we were convinced that he had made it safely and felt happy and proud. Then, when I returned home from work a week later, Mutti told me that I had a visitor in the dining room. There was Joe, with a week-old beard, smelling of sweat and manure, a picture of utter misery. Something had gone wrong and his group had been intercepted by a German patrol. Some were caught, some were shot, but Joe and a buddy had escaped and made their way back to Prague on foot, getting rides and food from sympathetic farmers. They had covered about four hundred miles over back roads and fields. There was no way of knowing whether the Germans were looking for them, and it was dangerous to stay at his mother's or even my house. He was even dangerous to the Resistance.

For the next few weeks he disappeared into different mountain cabins owned by his friends, constantly changing his location. Before he left, we decided to get married. I felt terribly sorry for Joe, and also, he now seemed something of a hero to me. I had always liked him for his marvelous sense of humor. No matter how bad things looked, he could always make me laugh. He was my favorite playmate. Besides, Jews now had a curfew of eight p.m., and my parents and the puppy were just not enough company for the twenty-year-old woman I now was.

6

When I broke the news to my parents, my father flew into a rage, accusing Joe of stealing me away from him. Mutti, on the other hand, liked the idea of our getting married, thinking it was good for me to be with another young person in this difficult time. After Joe came out of hiding and returned to Prague, we finally decided to move out of the center of Prague. Our landlord was delighted: this enabled him to rent our apartment quietly to new Czech tenants.

We found a tiny place—just two rooms and a kitchen, with no central heating—on the outskirts of the city next to the film studios in Barrandov. It was far away from everything, but there were fields and woods to walk in. It would not have been bad for a young couple by themselves, but we moved there with my parents so as to avoid requisitioning too much space. Some of our furniture was sold, and the rest crammed into this new apartment. The business was moved to a new location in the center of Prague.

On August 20, 1940, we got married. Jewish marriages were no longer permitted in Prague's beautiful City Hall—only in a small district hall on the outskirts of the city. We were not allowed to ride in taxis anymore, and I refused to go on the tram with the enormous bouquet of white roses that Joe presented me. The problem was solved by asking one of our young apprentices to carry it for me in a shopping bag.

In consideration of the times, I had decided to get married in a simple black dress, but I had an unbelievably silly pale-blue hat that I carried in a paper bag and only put on for the photographer in the waiting room. The little district office was crowded with my staff and friends, and afterward we had a luncheon at Père Louis, a restaurant we had visited regularly during our courtship and whose owner circumvented the anti-Jewish laws simply by closing "for illness."

Our four-day honeymoon took place in Zlín, an ugly, industrial town and home to the Baťa works, simply because this was the only hotel in the country that still admitted Jewish guests. Even there we had to eat in our room because the dining room was off-limits. After those four days, our honeymoon and our privacy were over. We returned to my family's small apartment in Prague, where I was still considered "the child" and my husband was treated like an adopted sibling.

By then, I was the only wage earner in the family. Our former employee Marie had undergone a subtle change over the course of the year. Being the owner of a thriving business had given her a status she had previously only dreamed of. Incessant anti-Semitic propaganda by the occupying forces had given this simple girl an idea of the risks she was taking by continuing to employ my mother and me, and, perhaps, even a justification of our reversed roles. For the moment, the Germans were winning the war and there was not the slightest sign in the air that the status quo could not continue for our lifetimes.

After our move to Barrandov, Marie decided that one Rabinek was enough to keep the old clients coming to the salon. This put my parents out of work. My new husband had not held a regular job since the German occupation. It was a precarious situation. Our savings were disappearing at an alarming rate as we bought food and other necessities on the black market. Czechoslovakia, which had been an exporter of farm products and meat, was now on ration cards, because the occupiers siphoned everything off to the Reich. Jewish ration cards were stamped with a capital *J* and shopping hours restricted to two hours in the late afternoon when there was not much left in the stores.

The value of Czech currency dropped by the day. So did prices for jewelry and art objects, because of the oversupply. Foreign currency skyrocketed. Every morning I pedaled to work on my bicycle, a shoulder bag covering my yellow star, and scanned Marie's face to assess her mood. Would she fire me today? Tomorrow? Next week? When?

Then, six weeks after Joe and I were married, I found myself pregnant. Actually, my mother diagnosed it, claiming that I had a different expression on my face. A check with a doctor proved her correct. My father held forth about the irresponsibility of having children at a time like this and demanded that I have an immediate abortion. For once, I was in total agreement with him. I did not want a baby. I was twenty years old, saddled with responsibility for four people, wanting to amuse myself as much as possible within the constraints of our severely limited way of life. Besides, my husband was such a playmate that the idea of him becoming a father made me laugh.

Joe, of course, was delighted by the news and did not want to understand any arguments against the birth of his child. Mutti became very sentimental: having a grandchild had enormous appeal, but even she had misgivings about the timing. Abortions had always been illegal in Czechoslovakia, but the law was regularly circumvented. The problem now was that Jewish doctors no longer had offices, and Christian physicians were forbidden to see Jewish patients. Joe found a young Czech gynecologist through one of his army buddies to perform the operation, but it had to be done in his office on a Saturday and he could not give me much anesthetic. I had to be in and out as soon as possible. His wife assisted him.

The night before my abortion, Joe's mother died of a heart attack. In spite of that, Joe went with me to the gynecologist's office and pleaded until the last moment for me to change my mind. Afterward, I was bundled into a friend's car and driven home, where Mutti made an inordinate fuss, watching my temperature round the clock. Joe was quite shaken by the events, and I was too wrapped up in myself to realize the trauma he must have gone through. There had never been much love between my mother-in-law and myself. She had always disapproved of me because I was more interested in my business than in Joe's shirts or the kitchen. I could never forgive the stupidity that had led to my parents' ordeal at the hands of the Gestapo. For the sake of appearances, I had to go to the funeral two days later and looked so drawn and sick that everyone was surprised at how deeply I seemed to mourn her passing.

7

Life stabilized somewhat, and for a year, we lived a very quiet life, removed from the tensions and rumors of Prague's center. My parents took my puppy, Tommy, for long walks to the city limits; Jews were not permitted to walk beyond them anymore. My father and Joe played chess and kept the war maps up to date. The river was still free, and we went swimming often that summer. There was one café assigned to Jews, where a combo played and where we could dance on a Saturday afternoon. Somehow, we became accustomed to our strictly circumscribed existence. We spent New Year's Eve of 1940 with our Jewish neighbors, two young couples who were still living in their own house, drinking to a speedy end of the war.

Nocturnal visits like these were not very frequent and somewhat risky because diagonally across from our house lived a Sudeten German collaborator named Lachmann, who spent a large part of his time looking out his window and surveying the doings of the four Jewish families living on the street. Because of the curfew, we had to wait for darkness and then walk over in slippers so as not to attract his attention. This self-appointed guard haunted us day and night. He kept track of whether we observed the shopping hours allotted to Jews in our little grocery store. Our puppy was a particular thorn in his eye, and he dropped hints all over the neighborhood that Jews should not be allowed to keep dogs for their pleasure.

In October 1941, we heard about the first deportations of Jews. Only the wealthiest families were taken and sent to Lodz, in occupied Poland. Soon there was news that they were doing all right, and at first, this did not seem the most horrible of fates to us, aside from the inconvenience. To the Jews remaining in Prague, it did not seem too different from being relocated by Nazi orders to the former ghetto, where most Jews now lived one family to one room. We were still safe and forgotten out in the sticks of Barrandov.

But to be on the safe side, Jewish housewives began to bake cookies, hoard sugar and all kinds of fat—just in case. Everyone started dying sheets and pillowcases dark colors so as to save on soap in the uncertain future. We all acquired large duffel bags and knapsacks at black market prices, to be packed within twenty-four hours if necessary. Every time a family member left the house, he or she would carefully carry out a package containing some prized possession—a piece of china, a small rug, or a painting removed from its frame—and take it for safekeeping to a trusted Christian friend. Joe and I carried out our whole library, book by book.

It was a good way to keep busy and prevent us from brooding too much. Strangely enough, I was still working, smiling at our loyal customers, and listening to the German ones assure me repeatedly that they had absolutely no personal animosity toward me or my mother, never forgetting to send her their greetings. Our Czech clients were like rays of sunshine, offering whatever help they could give. Many an heirloom from our house found its way into theirs. They also—very forcefully—kept Marie aware of the fact that I was the reason why they kept coming to the salon. It was those clients and my friends from school and sports that helped me keep my faith in the human race.

Frustrated that I was supporting the entire household, Joe had gotten involved with a group of young men trading foreign currency on the black market to bring home some money. Initial success led to carelessness, and in February 1942, they all got arrested and sentenced to five months in prison, which was bad enough in itself, but made far worse by the assassination of Reichsprotektor Reinhard Heydrich.

In June, after this success of the Czech Resistance, the Nazis went berserk, terrorizing the population, combing the city for the culprits, arresting people by the hundreds, picking prisoners at random every day and gunning them down in the courtyards of jails.

Joe had been able from the start of his term to send me messages via a Czech guard, who proved so reliable that I had even received a four-foot-high white lilac bush for my twenty-second birthday at the end of February. Then, I had been able to visit Joe in prison once a week and bring him food and clean clothes. Now, he bombarded me with pleas to get him out. My father treated these desperate appeals with disdain; he called it "unmanly" to ask a woman for help in such a dangerous situation. In his view Joe only got what he deserved for the risks he had been taking on the black market.

To my constant amazement, my father still accepted German rules and regulations as valid law, if not exactly justice. But all of us were being conditioned to regard the hundreds of absurd decrees as a part of life. Not even the Jews were immune to the incessant barrage of the Nazi propaganda machine.

After the Nazis destroyed the entire town of Lidice in reprisal for the Heydrich assassination, it wasn't so easy to access someone who would take a bribe. I was unable to find anyone who would stick his neck out for Joe during that June of 1942. The constant arguments with my father made me even more tense, and for the first time in my life, I began to stand up to his very often unfair criticisms. Mutti had her hands full trying to maintain family harmony and often wound up as a lightning rod for both of our angers. To make matters even worse, Marie informed me that given the precarious situation, I could no longer set foot in the business. My pride was so hurt that I didn't even ask her for a small amount of money.

At a loss for what to do with the abundance of free time I now had, I began to clean house, waxing and polishing everything in sight. I also learned to cook a little, as much as our severely limited supplies allowed—mainly vegetables. I never again want to eat a carrot cake, or potato goulash, or any of the other concoctions of that time.

Once, having nothing to do, I attached a Star of David to my puppy Tommy's collar, telling him that he was a Jew too. Before we left for our walk, Mutti called after me to take that star off the dog. In the fields, I let him off leash, and he soon disappeared from sight, hunting rabbits. After whistling and calling for him for quite a while, I returned home alone. I wasn't really worried because he used to run around freely and always came back. When he didn't show up by nightfall, all three of us got concerned, but because of the curfew, we had to wait until morning to look for him. We fanned out in different directions. On our return, we found Mutti crying on our doorstep. She had heard that Lachmann had seen the dog and, supposedly mistaking him for a rabbit, shot him. It's callous to admit, but we mourned the dog more than my mother-in-law, and the loss only added to my sense of impending doom. I began to wish for something to happen—anything, just a change.

8

It came sooner than I expected. In the middle of July, Joe finished his sentence and was released from prison. Two weeks later, the dreaded narrow blue strip of paper was delivered to our door, calling him up for a transport to Terezín. This transport was for young men only. They were to build an extension track from the existing station in Bohušovice to Terezín, the old military garrison built by the Habsburg emperor Joseph II in the eighteenth century and named Theresienstadt for his mother, Empress Maria Theresa.

We were aware of the ongoing transports, and after Joe left, it was clear that our days at home were numbered. But then, oddly, the transports suddenly stopped. This was the reason why we had decided, at long last, that I should have my tonsils removed. I had been putting it off for years simply because I had been too scared.

Father walked downtown to the Jewish community offices where the transport slips were dispatched to find out if there were any transports planned for the next two or three weeks. Assured that there did not seem to be any, I entered the one and only Jewish hospital in Prague in the early morning. I was operated on at eight, under local anesthetic, but the doctor ran into some snags and this ostensible triviality lasted almost two hours. I was asleep when in the afternoon a friend of Joe's who was working there as a male nurse came to my bed with an unhappy face. After hesitating for a while, he finally told me that there had been a call-up during the day and that my parents and I were on the list for a transport.

He also explained that I was exempt because of my surgery. I thought it over, but there really was not much to consider. I felt that I belonged with my parents. I had wanted a change, and what on earth would I do all alone in Prague anyway? I remembered how often, during my growing-up years, I had wished to be free of my parents, but suddenly realized how close and dependent we were on each other. I also felt responsible for them, as if they somehow had become my wards over the last few years. The thought of letting them face whatever it was in Terezín alone was more unbearable than the pain in my throat. The next morning, I left the hospital against the advice of the doctor, and before my parents could visit me, I arrived home to help with the packing.

Two days later, we took the tram to the Industrial Palace. An exception was made for our last ride through our beautiful city. We rode along the river, past my childhood playgrounds; past the National Theater and the castle of Hradčany, where for me, despite the fluttering swastika, the ghost of T. G. Masaryk had never left; and the ancient Charles Bridge, where every saint was an old friend of mine. Never before had I realized how much I loved my city. We were all silent during this last passage through Prague. Isolated, yet bound together by our separate memories.

9

I must have fallen asleep, because I remember Mutti shaking me gently and saying that it was time to get up and on line to be counted, that we would march to the train.

At four a.m. we walked through the sleeping streets, five abreast, to the freight yards well out of sight of the rest of the population. Old and young alike were tagged with numbers, written on cards and attached to strings around our necks. Laden like mules with our belongings, we proceeded at a snail's pace, to the great annoyance of the SS escort that walked alongside the columns prodding us and shouting, *Schneller, Schneller, Saujuden, Bewegung.* Incredible confusion at the train. Suitcases had to be put on a separate car, only hand luggage could be kept, and no one was willing to let go of anything. Children were lost, found, and crying, yet in the end this entire human cargo was herded into the waiting train and the doors locked. After more shouting and more delay, the journey began. Terezín was only fifty miles away, but it took until noon to get there.

When the train stopped in Bohušovice, we saw a company of Czech gendarmes standing guard, about two or three dozen SS men guarding the gendarmes and/or us, and a large group of prisoners whose job it was to do the unloading and organizing. Many were friends or relatives of the deportees. One quickly told me to hold on to as much as possible because it was doubtful that we would ever see our larger pieces of luggage again. He also gave me a message that Joe was awaiting me in the ghetto.

The late summer sun was at its zenith, and we were all dressed for Siberia so as to bring along as much warm clothing as we could. Weighed down with backpacks and toting whatever we could possibly carry, we then set out on the longest four-mile hike of my life. Progress was painfully slow, with stragglers being herded over and over again into a semblance of an orderly column. The sun burned down mercilessly on the open road.

People began to stumble and fall, and were picked up by relatives or by the ghetto boys. It was absolute and total misery; nothing mattered but the next step. My post-tonsillectomy throat was a ball of fire, but I was choking with pity for my father, whose neck arteries were visibly throbbing, and my mother, who seemed to get smaller and smaller under her load. Never before or after this moment did I hate those Teutons more. The shouting had stopped and the procession moved in eerie silence. After what seemed an eternity, we reached the ghetto gates.

Terezín was a fortress built under Maria Theresa for a garrison of 3,500 men. During the Republic, an identical number of soldiers were stationed there for military duty, plus about 1,500 civilians, mostly small shopkeepers, innkeepers, and their families. In the summer of 1942, 35,000 Jews were interned there. We were led along the "Main Street" of the ghetto to an outer embankment, into stables with vaulted ceilings and dirty straw spread on the floor. This was to be our quarantine. Quarantine for what? As we walked, I looked for Joe but didn't catch even a glimpse of him. Disappointed and exhausted, I threw myself on the ground and refused to talk or even open my eyes.

Mutti, however, started to scout around for drinking water, tried to coax my father to eat a bite and to nudge me out of my stupor. Ever since the German occupation she had acquired courage and stamina in direct proportion to the adversities that befell us. For as long as I could remember, she had been a pretty fragile creature, given to both real and psychosomatic illnesses. Now she was feeling strong and well, and never even voiced a complaint. Slowly her words started to reach my dulled brain and make sense. Knowing Joe's resourcefulness, she guessed that he had already found a way to meet up with us, and what place would be more likely than the latrine, where everybody had to go?

She was right. When we made our way to that stinkhole, Joe was there, hiding behind a wooden partition. As far as he knew, our transport was in transit; after minor adjustments in its composition, it would leave in forty-eight hours for an unknown destination. But Joe begged us not to worry: we would not be on it since the work he was doing—building the railway spur from Bohušovice station to the ghetto—was considered essential, and families of the railroad workers were protected from further deportations. What he failed to mention, possibly in good faith, was that only his wife was considered immediate family—by no means his in-laws.

Joe also informed us that life in Terezín was quite bearable, if crowded. Once out of quarantine, we would be assigned to permanent quarters and surely adjust to our new environment. Not entirely reassured, we returned to our place in the stables, where we found my father sitting cross-legged on the floor in despair. While we were gone, rumors had been flying, and in no time, everyone learned that Terezín was only the first stop on a much longer trip. New pink call-up slips were distributed, and it was clear that the rumors had been true.

Very few people, like me, received the white slips that signified remaining in Terezín. I tried to assure my parents that there had been some mistake, and that Joe would find a way to fix it, but their optimism was gone. I believe that my father died at this moment, although in reality he lived on for a few more days.

This great gentleman, officer of the Imperial and Royal Austrian Army, this aesthete, was now sitting cross-legged on the floor in a mess of straw. Tears were streaming down his face as he tried to tell me everything that his pride and inhibitions had prevented him from saying for the previous twenty-two years. He told me how his daughter was the center of his universe, how much he loved her, and that he could not possibly go on living without her. Mutti and I were stunned by this totally uncontrollable flood of words. We had each, in our own way, believed that we knew him, but had never witnessed even a faintly similar outburst of feeling. The father I knew only kissed me when he went away on a long trip, and then only on my forehead.

In a burst of defiance, he told us that he would not wait for the Nazis to murder him and my mother. Patting his breast pocket with a strange expression in his face, he confided that he had the means to take care of both of them before things got too difficult: a vial of poison.

I should not have spoken, but I did. I confessed that after we had been arrested in Prague by the Gestapo, I had found the vial in his desk. Suspicious about its contents, I had taken it to a pharmacy to be analyzed and, after discovering what the pills were, had them replaced with saccharine. Then, for the last time, I watched my father fly into one of his familiar rages, shouting that a brat like me had no right to interfere in his affairs.

I felt like a worm. Mutti was as white as a sheet, and it dawned on me that she had known about father's secret escape hatch and now felt as helpless as he. The enormity of what I had done was suddenly clear. Instead of protecting him, I had deprived my father of the last possibility to decide his fate as a free man. I wanted to explain. I wanted to tell them that I had exchanged the pills only because I could not face the idea of being left alone without them. I wanted to tell them how much I loved them, but I could not utter a word.

I went to the Jewish functionaries to protest my exemption and begged them to let me leave with my parents on the transport. They replied that one could not bargain with the *Kommandantur* and, besides, was I perhaps out of my mind? Very little was said during the hours that seemed to drag and slip away at the same time. I hoped against the odds that Joe had been right and that by some miracle two white slips would materialize to save my parents. Another day passed with some shuffling in the composition of the transport and new people arriving to replace the ones who were to stay. With an uncanny certainty that it would be senseless to weigh themselves down with all the bundles scattered around us, Mutti dressed warmly and decided to take only a small bag with some food for the trip. I was to keep everything else with me in Terezín.

With these practicalities taken care of, she calmly told me, *Try to forget what your father said last night. I understand why you did what you did. I probably would also have done it three years ago. You are a grown woman now, and your place is with your husband. Your father and I have had our lives. We have had some wonderful years, and you have given us much joy and pride. Whatever comes now we have to face alone and together. You are very young and your only duty to us is to stay alive. Your life is before you. I know you will be courageous and strong and live to see these evil men punished. God bless you, my little girl.*

The call came to line up for the march back to Bohušovice.

Silently we kissed goodbye, and I walked with them as far as the door of the building when I simply refused to let go of them. I cried and begged to let me go along too, but heard a firm and quiet *No!* from Mutti. The ghetto boys grabbed me from two sides, trying to keep the scene from attracting the attention of the Germans in the yard, and my parents walked away from me, each holding one handle of their little food bag. They never looked back. An excruciating pain shot through my whole body, and I squatted on the floor. I could not stop weeping.

10

When the transport that took my parents left, the rest of us were led into the ghetto and assigned to different barracks. At first, I was quartered in the attic of a huge one called the Hamburger Kaserne, where we were allotted a mattress each. This was placed on top of my two suitcases, which had appeared by some miracle or more likely through the help of Joe's friends.

The drawback of this sleeping arrangement was that anyone over the age of ten wound up with either her head or her feet dragging on the floor. It would have been simpler to sleep directly on the floor, but the mattress provided a way of guarding one's possessions with one's body.

Later that day, the work administrators appeared. Terezín was self-governed, though closely supervised and controlled by the German *Kommandantur*. It had an appointed Jewish Council of Elders and its own hierarchy. Newcomers had to do the hardest and dirtiest jobs for the first one hundred days.

For my first one hundred days, I was assigned as a nurse's aide to a barrack overflowing with old, sick, and demented people. Reporting for work the next evening for the twelve-hour night shift, still weeping and in a state of shock, I found one amateur nurse in charge of a whole floor. She had been in Terezín for more than six months, had adjusted to her dismal surroundings, and had acquired the toughness necessary to keep one's sanity. Capable and extremely busy, she lacked any sympathy for the likes of me.

The barrack was dark but for a few naked bulbs in the long corridors. All the windows were shut and the blinds were drawn due to the blackout. There was no time for an explanation of my duties—just orders shouted on the run: bring water to this patient or take a bedpan to that one. There were about one hundred ghost-like people lying listlessly on their bunks or wandering around in search of food or drink. Two epidemics—dysentery and typhoid fever—were raging. The death rate was high, and the patients who were still alive looked like skeletons. Many had high fevers and were constantly ripping off their clothes and wandering around the corridors stark naked. Every time I looked into one of their faces, it seemed to change into my mother's or father's face. The stench was overpowering, and I didn't know where to run first in response to their cries.

Toward midnight, I became convinced that some were already dead and that their ghosts were trying to drag me down into their abyss. My superior found me vomiting in a corner, remarked sarcastically that this was exactly the sort of help she needed, then turned away in disgust. I knew that she had every right to be annoyed and wished I could sink into the ground and disappear. Somehow, I lived through that night and others like it, but the avalanche of events and emotions were more than I could handle, and I was unable to stop my endless, silent flood of tears.

After a few days in the attic I was assigned permanent sleeping space on the second floor of the Hamburger Kaserne. I came into a large barrack with three tiers of double bunks that held some seventy-two women. There was a Room Elder in command, and I was shown to my place on the middle level of a center bunk. A lovely young face with a halo of snow-white hair appeared smiling on the other side.

She introduced herself as Margot from Breslau, Germany, and said, *I'll help you get comfortable. Things are really not all that bad here. Just wait and see.* We put my stuff away behind the bunk head on a wooden plank, unpacked my blankets and green sheets, while Margot explained that she worked as a seamstress in the children's home and that her husband worked on the railroad siding with Joe. After only five weeks in the ghetto she had worked out a certain routine and seemed, to my amazement, quite happy.

Drawn to Margot's warmth and interest, I told her the miserable story of my last ten days. She did not offer any pious consolation. With what I was to learn was her characteristic tact, Margot just put her arms around me and hugged me tight. I knew then that we would become friends for life.

Evening came and, with it, my other roommates returning from work. My top-bunk neighbor was Mrs. T., one of the most glaring contradictions of the ghetto. The wife of a wealthy jeweler from

Prague, she was a pious convert to Catholicism who never missed her prayers, and seemed to regard herself as a latter-day saint, chosen by God to bear her internment as some sort of stigmata. On the bunk below me lived the sixteen-year-old granddaughter of the Chief Rabbi of Bohemia. Her mother was the Room Elder, and both were lovely, gentle human beings.

Below Margot's bunk was an enormously fat and funny spinster who held court. She came from Frankfurt, Germany, was a born clown, and entertained the whole room with her earthy sense of humor, mostly at her own expense. Above Margot resided Mrs. G., a customer of my mother's who talked incessantly about the furs, clothes, jewels, and other priceless possessions she had abandoned in her exquisite villa in Prague. She was a parvenue par excellence whose studiedly genteel way of speaking vanished when she fought with her oppressed and homely daughter.

After six, the men came to visit. They were allowed to see us until eight, and the room hummed with conversation and laughter. For the first time since my arrival, I was able to look at Joe without hatred when he arrived with Margot's handsome husband, Arthur. The last few days had been hard on my mate. He must have understood that I blamed him for the loss of my parents, even though he had probably saved my life. He tried to console me as well as he could. He pulled out a pack of cigarettes and offered me a few puffs in the hope that this might relax me and stop the flow from my tear ducts.

Smoking was strictly *verboten* in Terezín under penalty of deportation, yet everybody smoked. Cigarettes were the currency of the place. They were smuggled into the ghetto, and for Joe, it was fairly easy because he worked outside and came into daily contact with the Czech laborers working on the railway spur. He had already established regular contact with his Christian friends in Prague through one of them, and was running a busy illegal mail service for himself and his pals who had relatives or sweethearts on the outside.

The largest trade in tobacco was, of course, controlled by the Germans themselves, who sold cigarettes at exorbitant prices and kept these prices up by terror and raids. Everything could be traded for cigarettes, even the skimpy bread rations of some hopelessly addicted smokers. I was to join their ranks very soon.

As we talked to Margot and Arthur and exchanged information and experiences, I realized that Arthur enjoyed none of the advantages that working outside the ghetto entailed. He was a young lawyer from Berlin who had fled to Czechoslovakia, where he and Margot had met at the house of a relative. As Margot told me much later, it was love at first sight. They married and lived on in Prague when their efforts to emigrate came to nothing.

They had learned a smattering of Czech, came to love the city and its people, and had been eventually deported with a Czech transport to Terezín. In his work gang, Arthur was a foreign element, even though he was just as Jewish as the others. His slightly Prussian formality and ignorance of the vernacular put him at a definite disadvantage. Margot, who sewed for others or could charm the cook in the children's home into giving her a few extra portions of food, was better able to augment their rations than Arthur, who had the opportunity but not the savvy.

The young Czech Jews were the elite of the ghetto. There is no doubt that by virtue of their connections with the outside world, they had a much easier time than inmates from Austria, Germany, and, later on, Holland and Denmark. Even if we did not have outside work assignments, the Czech gendarmes who served as our immediate guards were, by and large, sympathetic and helpful to us in establishing communications with the outside world. Many of them had served in the army with our boys. True, they did accumulate a sizable amount of riches in the process, but this does not detract from the very real value of their help.

For Czech Jews, there was always the possibility of working in the kitchen or distribution system, or having a friend or relative working there, since the majority of these posts were manned by native Jews. The older people from other countries who had no family in the ghetto had no such advantage. They were forced to barter away, bit by bit, whatever of their possessions they had managed to salvage for food. There was, for example, a great demand for the plaid lap robes that the German Jews had brought with them in the belief that they were going to Bad Theresienstadt—a spa, the German authorities had led them to believe. This was an indirect bonanza for me. I earned quite a few chunks of salami and bread by fashioning these lap robes into skirts for the more affluent wives and girlfriends of our cooks and quartermasters.

11

The ghetto was, in fact, a microcosm of the society beyond its walls, in all its variety and with all its human traits—good or bad—reinforced. This socioeconomic division was definitely encouraged by the Germans, who endowed certain people with more or less power over the composition of transports, and access to the distribution of food and work. In general, the *Kommandantur* specified only the number of persons, their age, or their national origin in the case of transports. German interference in the day-to-day running of the camp was largely limited to surprise checks and demand for daily reports by the Council of Elders.

My husband had grasped the situation very quickly, adjusted, and made the best of it. Joe was certainly happier here than he had been during his last year in Prague. He felt needed by me and by his friends. The notion that he was able to outsmart the Nazis anytime he wanted gave his damaged ego a tremendous boost. For my twenty-third birthday, the first birthday that I celebrated in captivity—February 26, 1943—Joe produced with great pride a bottle of French perfume and a couple of pork chops that he had smuggled into the camp in hollow shoulder pads.

For me, the period of adjustment to Terezín took a little longer. But after several weeks, I ran into Mrs. W. in the street, and things began to change for the better. Mrs. W. was a former competitor of my mother's who had known me since childhood. After asking me about my parents' whereabouts, she wanted to know what kind of work I was doing in the ghetto.

When I recounted my inept attempts at nursing, she marched me into the Magdeburger Kaserne, where the administrative offices were located. There, she demanded my release from the compulsory hundred-day duty, so that I could work in the workshop she was running for the *Kommandantur*, which produced cheap cotton dresses for the Germans. Out of about one hundred workers there, only a handful were trained dressmakers, and production was limping badly. Later, when she was unable to meet the quota, she was dismissed as forelady and the operation changed into a repair shop for German uniforms. At that moment, though, her arguments carried some weight, partly because they were reasonable but mainly, I suspect, because she happened to be the second or third cousin of somebody in charge of ghetto productions.

This was the way some semblance of normalcy returned to my life. To perform ten hours of work I knew how to do was no hardship. A little rest with friends in the evening helped a good deal, and for the first time in months, I was able to sleep at night. My instinct for self-preservation took over and, with it, the realization that my fate was by no means unique. More important, my interest in other people revived, and I slowly came out of the monumental egotism of an only child.

My marriage had received a severe jolt, never having been on very solid foundations to begin with. Joe and I had never had enough opportunity to get to know each other deeply, and now we had no privacy at all. My feelings about his exploits were ambivalent. I did not like the risks he took, admired but did not share his elation about his successes, yet gladly partook of the advantages they brought. Uneasy about his daily escapades, I never came to a conclusion about why, exactly, he took so many chances, way beyond our immediate need. I envied Margot and Arthur, who were obviously very much in love with each other, and disliked myself for being unable to show my husband even minimal love and appreciation. Other young marriages fell by the wayside because of the insecurity of the future and the wish to squeeze as much pleasure out of life as possible.

The pressures of ghetto life and the constant coming and going of transports made people and relationships quite unpredictable. Old friends very often proved to be impossible to get along with in the suffocating new environment, while strangers became friends for life. A whole new standard of behavior evolved, much of it self-sacrificing and noble, but also frequently selfish and amoral. Religion began to fascinate me for a second time in my life. As a child I had been totally captivated by the mysticism of the Catholic ritual; now I was suspicious of Mrs. T. and other converts who were able to keep their faith intact in spite of the absurdity of the situation.

My friend (and Joe's first cousin) Vava was nominally a Catholic since birth. Her parents, like my own, were agnostics. She was now coming full circle back to Judaism under the influence of a Viennese rabbi who was a friend of hers. I did not quite relate to either Judaism or Catholicism. Out of a sense of isolation, I had gone to a midnight mass the first Christmas in camp that had been celebrated secretly in one of the many attics. Some fifty people of all ages had been present, going through the familiar motions. It was eerie. Not having the foundation of a true believer, I felt nothing: no consolation, no presence of God.

Later, I accompanied Vava to a Sabbath service in the oldest and most dismal barrack of Terezín. Here I found old men in prayer shawls, swaying and lost in a world I could not enter or even begin to comprehend. I left puzzled. Vava said that I was supposed to feel a kinship with these people, but I felt like a stranger and was absolutely unmoved. I wanted to do something more tangible to give some reason to our existence than to pray to a God who so obviously had forsaken us. I was, however, equally turned off by the very active but secret Zionist and Communist groups in Terezín.

A movement had sprung up at this time, where young couples like Joe and I, who were relatively better off than the rest of the prisoners, unofficially adopted children who were alone in Terezín because their parents were dead or imprisoned in different camps. The idea was to give them a small substitute for their families and also to improve their health by sharing the small surplus of food we had.

The official food rations were minimal. A typical daily allotment consisted of a three-inch piece of dark bread, two cups of black coffee—the resemblance to real coffee was purely accidental—a portion of pea or lentil soup (about a dozen dots swimming in the dark water), three or four potatoes boiled in their skin, and one ladle of tomato or mustard sauce or perhaps a piece of turnip. Meat was doled out sparsely and called goulash: this was brown gravy with a few cubes of horsemeat. Only meat stamped by the department of food supplies as "unfit for human consumption" was used. An extra bonus could be the occasional one-inch slice of salami, a third of a small can of liver spread, a one-inch square of margarine, or a tablespoon of prune butter. The children received somewhat better fare, mainly because it was cooked separately, but their diet was by no means conducive to their growth.

Joe and I went to the children's house to select a child to adopt. There was quite a choice available, and the lady in charge thought that in view of my own young age, we would all be best off with a three- to five-year-old. While we were discussing the matter, I noticed a dark-haired girl of about nine with enormous brown eyes standing alone in a corner, watching. Against the misgivings of the counselor, I insisted on adopting Gisa, who turned out to be twelve and did not say one word about our proposed arrangement, but consented to go for a walk to get acquainted with us. According to her file, Gisa's parents had been taken away at the time of the annexation of the Sudetenland and not been heard of again. She and her older brother were placed in an orphanage in Karlsbad and, after the occupation, transferred to another one in Prague. Four years later the whole institution was evacuated to Terezín.

Gisa's brother was already sixteen and had to work. He lived in the men's barracks and did not see her too often. Like a little mouse, she was suspicious of everything and everybody, and it took me weeks to coax a smile from her. In spite of obviously being hungry most of the time, she only nibbled at whatever we offered her and put part of it carefully in her pocket to eat later or maybe share with her brother—I never found out. When we gave her a piece of chocolate, we discovered that she had never seen or tasted chocolate before.

Gisa finally melted one day when I threw a few English words into our conversation with Joe. *You speak* English! she cried out. *Will you teach me?* From then on, we were friends. I taught her one hour a day, improvising as we went along. She soaked it up like a sponge and also happily started to eat more and fill out a little. I made over some of my clothes for her, because the outgrown things she was wearing made her look even tinier than she actually was. She became somewhat more communicative and even displayed a certain degree of vanity one day after she saw her reflection in a window on the street.

She talked about her parents, and as time went by, she told me more and more of what she remembered from the time when they were still with her. She never cried and always retained a certain very grown-up distance. She evidently accepted me as a friend, but there was no fantasy that I could possibly replace her mother.

12

During 1943, my own life seemed relatively stable even though transports were incessantly coming and going. Outgoing transports always created panic, and endless finagling over who was to go and who to stay. Sometimes it was only young people capable of work; other times, only the old and sick. The railroad spur from Bohušovice was still far from complete, and Joe and I did not worry too much. Rumors ran wild: this was to be the last transport, or the war was about to be over tomorrow, next week, at the latest in three months.

Small wonder that in this kind of atmosphere Margot and I decided to see a palm reader. We had heard about the old lady from Germany and visited her one evening in one of the barracks for the aged. We sat with her by the window. I studied her still-beautiful face while she held my hand between her wrinkled fingers. After a long pause she looked me in the face and said, *Child, you have a young and handsome husband, but I see you as a widow. He is engaged in something that will cost him his life. You will live and marry a man you have known since your childhood. You will leave Europe and go with him over the great ocean to raise a new family.*

I wanted to know what had happened to my parents, but she would not tell me and turned to Margot. She shook her head and said, *Too many widows, too many widows,* and after telling Margot some astonishing true events from her past, the palm reader assured her that she, too, would live but that her husband would not. We left a little unsettled and tried very hard to ridicule the whole episode, but it was difficult to forget her words.

In spite of all this, life could be pleasant, even amusing at times. There was chamber music, singing to the accompaniment of an accordion; opera; drama; and poetry readings produced under unbelievably difficult conditions. Scenery was created with stolen planks from the lumberyard, where many prisoners worked, and out of rags and empty potato sacks. Scores were copied by hand and music written down from memory and new works composed. Never again have I heard a more moving performance of the Verdi *Requiem.* Especially the "Libera Me" took on added significance when sung in Terezín by a brilliant young soprano from Berlin. Three weeks later she was deported "to the East."

The amount of talent assembled in this godforsaken place was utterly astonishing and impossible to keep shackled. Artists were painting, drawing, and writing on every scrap of paper they could lay hands on. And there were discussions, debates, and endless talking. Whenever an outgoing transport disrupted an art project, more artists appeared to take the place of the ones who had to go.

But the talent barrel was not bottomless, and by the end of the war only a pitiful remnant survived.

There were soccer games every Saturday afternoon, weather permitting. They were played in the courtyard of the Dresdner Kaserne, which had wide-open, loggia-like corridors all around. The perfect setting for a bullfight and almost as many people present. Everyone dressed in their best and cheered his team at the top of their lungs. For a few hours we were oblivious to the reality of the camp.

The older women, the mothers and grandmothers, were the most amazing inhabitants of our anthill. They had by far more energy and resourcefulness than their mates and managed, after a full day's work, to transform the few potatoes of our daily rations into tasty concoctions and their bunks into minuscule homes. Complaints were rarely heard, and their good manners prevailed even in unavoidable disputes, when they would hurl accusations or reproaches at each other, always addressing one another by the titles of their respective husbands. Their only indulgence was the fond recall of things left behind, and these former possessions seemed to grow as time went by until one would believe that there had been only rich Jews in our former life. I found this harmless, amusing, and seldom malicious.

After working for some time on damaged uniforms, I was combing my hair one day when I noticed little creatures crawling on the comb. For a moment I was too stunned to move, and then I burst into my dorm screaming that I had lice, *LICE*, and that I would never, never get rid of them and that Margot must have them too because we shared one bunk.

She was much less excitable than I and noted that I was not the first to be loused up. She "organized" (stole) a large can of kerosene from somewhere, and we doused our hair with kerosene for the next three days until we both developed eczema. The next problem was to get the stuff out of our hair with only cold water available, but we managed and turned our attention back to our regular nightly flea hunt. Our system was to light a candle with the blankets over our heads. A fire risk? Yes, but we developed an expertise in tracking down our tormentors.

Soon after this I came down with the mumps. Not just a normal case but, probably due to all the rinsing with cold water, a monumental one. I grew into the shape of an oversized pear, with only my forehead retaining its normal size, to the great amusement of my room and the doctor, who brought around his colleagues to show off this rarity of a patient. Needless to say, I did not find the situation funny at all, and when even Joe and Margot could not suppress their laughter at the sight of me, I got really furious. Children's diseases were rampant in the ghetto, and anyone who missed them as a child was sure to catch up now.

When I first arrived in Terezín, I had not been able to see my childhood best friend, Kitty, because she was quarantined with scarlet fever. This was a great disappointment for us both. Kitty and I had been inseparable since childhood: she was my second cousin and my alter ego since her birth two years after I was born. Living on the same block and both being only children, we had practically grown up together. Kitty had arrived in Terezín in December 1941 with one of the first transports, and we had missed each other badly during the eight months that we were separated. Her parents were in the ghetto as well. Her father was a House Elder and protected from further transports by virtue of being a prominent member of the community. She had come out of the hospital happy as a lark to see me, full of funny stories about doctors and nurses.

Kitty had a Terezín boyfriend by the name of Bubi, who became fast friends with Joe. The fact that she had a Christian fiancé back in Prague did not bother her too much for the moment. Things could always be explained later when the time came. Like many of the Czech old-timers, she was living in relative comfort with three other girls in a small room off the corridor in my barracks.

With characteristic generosity and a twinkle in her eye, she immediately offered Joe and me the use of her room for a few hours as a love nest. The four girls had worked out an elaborate schedule to accommodate their three love affairs and one marriage. In the evenings I used to visit them, and the entertainment there was always superb. Aside from the high spirits of this foursome, we very often enjoyed the visit of one of their beaus, a professional nightclub musician, who was a wizard in sneaking into the women's barrack after curfew. With his accordion the music and singing lasted often long into the night.

Kitty's boyfriend, Bubi, was in the ghetto police. This was a rather operetta-like outfit that was supposed to keep order, but very often helped along with all kinds of shenanigans to fool the gendarmes or the Nazis, at least the ones with a sense of humor.

The following year Bubi, Joe, and another ghetto watchman

named Honza built a *kumbal*. This was a roofless shed put up in several attics of the former residential houses in Terezín. It measured about nine feet by fifteen feet, and was made of "organized lumber" paid for with cigarettes and other contraband. Furnished with three cots and a few shelves, and decorated with our beautiful green sheets, the place had the look of a miniature weekend cottage and afforded a little bit of rare privacy, particularly since all the boys were working different shifts.

In any event there were never any quarrels about when it was desirable for two of the residents to disappear for a while. What was really nice about it was that we now had a corner of our own where we could see our friends on a Sunday afternoon—have a cup of real coffee without the prying glances of a dorm full of people, some conversation, and the illusion that everything was quite normal.

Of course it was just that—an illusion—because transports never stopped, friends were gone from one day to the other, and the death rate of the older generation soared. I will never forget the old-fashioned hearses drawn by people, moved up and down the streets alternately carrying corpses out of the ghetto and half-rotten potatoes in, and how their peculiar combination of odors hung in the air.

I lived under the administration of three Jewish Elders. The first was Jakob Edelstein, a Zionist of Polish origin, very capable and unafraid to stand his ground before the *Kommandantur*. He was replaced by Paul Eppstein from Berlin, who was by far less courageous, and had a tendency to favor his countrymen. He trembled before the Germans and often kowtowed beyond the call of necessity. The third was Benjamin Murmelstein, a Viennese rabbi.

These men and the Council of Elders had power and privilege, but their situation was not simple and they had no choice in the matter. What they *did* have was better and more food, better housing, the privilege of living with their wives, and the power to assign work and decide who left Terezín and when. So long as these men—and they were only human—were influenced only by their convictions as to who was worth saving, there could be no reasonable quarrel with their decisions. But when they were guided by considerations for friends and friends of friends and third and fourth cousins or in some cases by outright bribery, it became a radically different picture.

This system extended like a staircase down through the lower levels of ghetto administration and was part of a clever plan to set one prisoner against the other. The *Cripo*, or Jewish criminal plainclothes police, was based on spying and denouncing fellow inmates. It was not always successful but in too many instances played right into the hands of some power-drunk or sadistic person. Jews are no different from other people. The longer I lived in Terezín, the more I learned how difficult it was to preserve a value system, assuming that a person was mature enough to have one.

13

On December 15 and 18 of 1943, two transports with a total of 5,007 young people left Terezín. The reason, we were told, was that because of overcrowding in the ghetto, these people were needed to build a new one elsewhere. I am quite sure that the Council of Elders knew more about their destination than they let us know, but kept quiet, fearing for their own skins in the event of mass escapes or a possible uprising.

The events of November 11 were still fresh in everyone's memory. That day, the entire population of the ghetto—about forty-five thousand people—was marched out into a deserted field. We stood there all day in the drizzling rain, surrounded by Czech gendarmes with submachine guns, being counted and recounted by the SS. Shivering and frightened, many of us were convinced that we would never make it back to the ghetto alive. The census was inconclusive—there were people missing—and by midnight, we were marched back to our barracks, hungry and exhausted.

After this happened, Joe and I expected to leave with the December transports. The railway spur to Bohušovice was nearly complete, and Joe became very concerned about the elimination of the reason for his deferment from transports. To be on the safe side, he hit upon the brilliant idea that if I could possibly come down with scarlet fever, we would be covered on two fronts.

Our good friend Dr. V. gave me a strong shot of the bacteria, offering it first to Joe, who claimed to be immune because he had come down with the disease as a child. Then we waited for the symptoms to appear. Fortunately, I never got more than a headache and a slight temperature—no spots, not enough to be quarantined. No spots, no quarantine was the rule, and we were not called up after all.

Kitty was not that lucky. She had turned twenty-one the month before and was no longer entitled to be listed on the "protected" list with her parents. Her boyfriend, Bubi, and Joe's roommate, Honza, were deported at the same time, as were the majority of our friends. We all parted in a rather lighthearted way. Kitty even promised to keep the bunk next to her warm for me. Stupidly, we believed the story about a new ghetto.

A lull followed the departure of this group. Transports stopped going out. They only came in: now the Dutch and the Danes. But, in fact, great changes were taking place. The outer fortress, which had served as quarantine hall when I arrived, was not used for that purpose anymore, but was made into a gigantic warehouse for articles that had been confiscated over the past years. My uniform workshop was closed, and I was transferred to this warehouse, to sort and repair clothes so that the best could be shipped to the Reich.

Much stranger things were going on. The houses on the main street were being painted on the outside. Shops that had been converted into dorms were now being reconverted into stores, with display windows that displayed some of the best pieces we could find in the warehouse. More for display than for sale. A café was opened, with music, where one could visit for one hour with special coupons. Money was printed and a bank opened. An enormous circus tent that had been put up the year before to house mica production was hurriedly torn down and a music pavilion built on the town square. The ground was reseeded with grass; benches and even a playground were built.

In January, the Hamburger Kaserne that housed 3,500 women was completely evacuated. The barrack was converted into a processing station at the end of the now-finished railroad spur. In the ensuing confusion of reassigning spaces, I moved in with Joe, who was now alone in his *kumbal*.

On January 20, a passenger train filled with well-dressed people pulled in, and the reason for all the mysterious changes became clear. The newly arrived guests were Dutch Jews who were greeted personally by the Council of Elders with welcoming speeches. The SS *Kommandant* in person and his henchmen helped women and children from the cars, and the whole elaborate production was filmed for newsreels, later to be shown all over Europe as proof of how well Jews were traveling under the protection of the German Reich. Right after the welcome, these people were given postcards to write to their friends in Holland, to assure them of their well-being. Better was yet to come. The name Ghetto Terezín was changed to the Jewish Settlement Theresienstadt, and inmates did not have to salute the SS anymore, or stand at attention, or step off the sidewalk when passing them.

Failure to do those things had previously brought a lashing of ten strokes. The apartments of the prominent members of the Council of Elders were redecorated and furnished with Danish modern furniture. Obviously something more important than a newsreel was up.

14

Since the railroad spur was now finished, only a limited number of workers were retained for maintenance. After a mad scramble for these few remaining places, Joe managed to hold on, but his trips to Bohušovice now occurred at irregular intervals, when some work on the circular saw was needed. Contacts with his Christian counterparts became more complicated and visible.

One night during this time I had a dream. In it, I found myself in a place I had never seen before. It was like a forest of barbed wire where the ground had an unusual ocher color I had not seen anywhere in Central Europe. There were flashes of light shooting through a dark purple sky. I was all alone but had the feeling of thousands of eyes watching me. I awoke by my own screams, surprised to find myself in my bunk with Joe staring at me. Neither he nor Margot or any other of our friends had ever seen a place like this, and after much discussion, the nightmare remained a puzzle.

Then, one evening early in March, Joe told me that he was

worried about an incident that had happened that day. He was supposed to meet his contact in Bohušovice, but could not go because, at the last minute, another maintenance man was sent out. In order not to hold up communications, Joe had asked the man to take a note and money to his contact but, in case he missed him, not to bring it back into the ghetto. In that case, the man should leave the wad of paper in a pile of railroad ties stacked near the saw.

In the evening, Joe discovered to his horror that the two men had not only missed each other, but that the man had brought the little wad back and, trying to hide it overnight, had stuffed it into the hollow roll of a blackout shade. One of the few rats among the Czech gendarmes was standing across the dark street watching him do this and made a report to the *Kommandantur*. A few minutes later, the SS came into the dorm, went to the window, threatened the occupants of the whole room with reprisals, and took away their man. The note was signed only *Joe from the hut*, but it was very doubtful that this man would hold out for very long without giving Joe's full name.

There was nothing to do but to report for work the next morning as usual, but after a few hours, a friend of ours who worked at the gendarmerie as an orderly came to fetch me with the news that Joe was being arrested. A gendarme had already left to bring him to the *Kommandantur*. I would be able to see Joe—as if by coincidence—on his way through the ghetto, but the situation appeared bleak. I ran to the gate to meet them and saw Joe coming down the road, handcuffed to the gendarme. Suddenly, I remembered the palm reader and trembled with fear. Joe had aged ten years since the day before. All the color was drained from his face, and his first words to me were that everything was lost.

I tried to give him courage and mainly begged him not to involve his Christian friend, since they did not know his name. Joe replied that he was scared and that he did not believe he had the strength to withstand interrogation should he be tortured. Later, I discovered that this was exactly what happened and that, aside from his contact, he had dragged in one more person. A few days later he was sent to the "Small Fortress," the high-security prison near Terezín.

The tensions of the last years had finally taken their toll. I felt great pity for Joe but, at the same time, was angry at him. I also felt terribly guilty toward the wives of the other ten men who were now compromised because of their association with my husband.

Our friends rallied around me, trying to keep up my morale. My friend, Joe's cousin Vava, got busy trying to get me on the "protected" list of someone high on the Council of Elders. She achieved this in a very roundabout way without my personally doing a thing, or even meeting the gentleman in question. She was a good friend of the rabbi who was the head of the Council of Elders at the time. Through her good offices, I became part of his official household.

Unable to keep the *kumbal* to myself, I was assigned two new roommates. One was the girlfriend of a young pianist and composer, Gideon Klein. I was once again in a strange and restless mood, almost destructive of whatever security I had left, both wishing for and fearing some sort of change. For the moment, in view of the beautification program, there was little harassment, but incoming transports changed the national composition and made the ghetto population rise again.

My friends visited me every day. Particularly Dr. V. and F. O.— great pals and former clients of Joe's—checked to see whether I had enough to eat and to guard me against the wolves. It took me a while to discover that they were actually watching one another because, both having Christian fiancées in Prague, each suspected the other of having improper designs on me. Fooling around with the wife of a jailed friend was considered—even by ghetto standards— taboo. No one evidently credited me with enough judgment to look after myself.

Gideon Klein was staging and directing a production of *Carmen* at the time, with the blessing and even the help of the *Kommandant*, who made the use of their gym building available for the production. I went to a few rehearsals with his girlfriend, and these were experiences not easy to forget. Mounting an opera production with all the obstacles of ghetto life was nothing short of a miracle.

Sometime earlier, another interesting man had become part of our immediate circle. He was a well-known Czech writer, who was allotted a *kumbal* in our building and by special permission allowed to live with his companion of many years. Not only did he receive all his luggage, but also a whole bookcase of books. He gave me the run of them, and I started to read most of Dostoyevsky. The volume that made the deepest impression on me was *Notes from a Dead House*, a relatively short work about the prison camps of Siberia. I did not miss the analogies to our situation, and we had long discussions about who learned what from whom.

I had another protector at work. A Czech gendarme named Karel, brother of the gendarme who had to arrest Joe. Karel had also known Joe for a long time as a friend and helper. Karel now made it his business to look after me, namely to feed me whenever he was on duty. He used to come into my place of work, gruffly call me out, and take me to the guardroom, where he locked me in with a package of sandwiches and pickles his mother had prepared. Fifteen minutes later, he led me back with a loud admonition to work harder.

One day, he brought me a little crumpled note from Joe that said only that he was well and that he loved me. Karel told me that Joe was working on the truck that brought coal to the fortress and that if I was lucky I could see him someday because a little stretch of the road was visible from the window of the guardroom. I saw many trucks pass by, but they passed so quickly that I was never sure whether I had seen Joe or not. Just in case, I waved to all of them.

Spring brought persistent rumors about a visit by an International Red Cross commission. *Kommandant* Burger was replaced by the Austrian Rahm, who showed more understanding for the project of presenting to the commission a showpiece of humanitarian concern. The children in the orphanage were drilled to answer *Chocolate again, Uncle Rahm!* in case the *Kommandant* visited the children's home with the commission.

The success of this indoctrination was highly doubtful, and one infamous place of the ghetto certainly defied the sprucing-up operation completely. This was the mental ward. No amount of paint or white sheets could change the devastation in the faces of the inmates.

This made the Nazis quite uneasy, as well as the fact that the population had once again topped 40,000. To solve the problem, they planned three transports of 2,500 people each, leaving in intervals of two days, beginning May 15. Included were the orphanage and the mental ward, and a cross-section of the population with many young people who were considered potential troublemakers.

I was called up too. My remaining friends tried to pull every available string but soon discovered that my deportation had been ordered by name from the *Kommandantur*, as a reprisal against Joe's infraction of the ghetto rules. There were three others in the same situation: two wives of the other men involved in the affair and the four-year-old son of one of the couples.

Dr. Murmelstein tried until the last minute to save us, but with the third batch on May 18, we had to show up at the Hamburger Kaserne, all packed, tagged, and ready to go. We were hidden in a room facing out onto the waiting train while the Council of Elders delivered the requisitioned 2,500 people. We hoped that with the quota filled, the SS might mercifully forget us, and watched the loading of the train the whole day, one cattle car after another being filled, locked, and sealed. At five forty-five p.m. the last car was filled.

We held our breaths, hoping that the train would now move, when we heard a big commotion in the corridor and an unmistakable voice shouting. The door burst open.

Who are these people?

These are the special orders, Kommandant, replied Dr. Murmel-stein. *Only women and a child.*

What are you trying to do, put something over on me? Raus! Raus! Into the train, but fast! Saujuden.

They opened the last car and we were literally thrown in, our bundles after us. The door slammed shut and the train left with 2,504 people.

15

Inside it was dark, and it took quite a while to discern any figures. The car was so full that we could sit only with our legs pulled up to our bodies. It also happened to be the car containing the inmates of an old-age barrack, most of whom were sick and shocked out of their wits.

Our little group crouched near the door where we had landed, quietly sobbing. Terezín had been no paradise, but right now, it seemed so. I suppose I even felt worse than the rest, because I held myself indirectly responsible for their being on the transport. I felt bitterly sorry for all of us, but mostly for the little one huddled in his mother's arms.

These were my last actual tears, though I was to cry for the duration of the war. There was a barred window at each end of the car and two pails in a corner. One was meant to serve as a toilet; the other contained water. Both of them were too small for the eighty-odd people crammed together. After a few hours, we tried to bring a little order into the chaos around us.

At dawn the train stopped for a while. The door opened a foot and one pail was emptied on the tracks, while the guards refilled the other with water. As the trip continued, there were two more stops, but the stench, thirst, and moaning became almost unbearable. I thought of my parents. They had been in this same situation. But then I remembered someone from the *Transportleitung* telling me, at the time, that they had left on a passenger train, even occupying window seats. That relaxed me somewhat, and I resigned myself to whatever would come.

It was late the next night when we stopped at a platform with a big sign that read AUSCHWITZ. At this point, the name did not have any meaning for me. I only realized that we were in Poland because the other half of the sign read OŚWIĘCIM. Even before the doors opened, I heard a lot of bellowing in German and Polish. The cursing became louder when the cars were opened, and I saw on the ramp, aside from what seemed to be a whole detachment of SS men, a large number of strange creatures in striped blue-and-gray pajamas with shaved heads making almost as much noise as the Germans.

We were chased out of the car at breakneck speed, with only our clothes and the contents of our pockets. Our bundles left behind, we were pushed and jostled into a long column and made to march a dirt road. It was flanked on both sides by double walls of barbed wire, marked at intervals with little signs reading ACHTUNG HOCHS-PANNUNG ("Caution: High Voltage," in German). The whole spooky scene was illuminated by beacon-like light beams emanating from watchtowers every few hundred yards. There were dark structures visible behind the wires and dogs and SS men everywhere.

A few striped figures flitted back and forth in the dark, carefully keeping out of the way of the SS. About halfway through this trek, one of these creatures materialized next to me at one end of a stretcher with a covered corpse and said, *Nazdar!* ("Hi," in Czech). Startled, I recognized our friend Tommy, who had left Terezín in December. He looked old and hungry and explained hurriedly that everything of value would be taken from us, that Joe's old roommate Honza had sent him with the message to give him whatever I wanted to save and he would smuggle it into camp. I had very little: two wristwatches, a fountain pen, a toothbrush, a comb, some stockings. Pushing this under the cloth with the corpse, Tommy disappeared in the dark without being noticed.

We were brought to a large, stable-like barrack, separated from the men, and made to form single lines in front of tables where female Polish prisoners in striped uniforms were registering our data. The SS left and soon Honza himself came in and led me to the back of the room. He told me that the registration process would take hours, and I might as well sit down and eat something. He explained that we were in Birkenau, that it was part of the Auschwitz concentration camp. Here, in the so-called "Family Camp," Czech men and women were held in the same compound.

He told me that I was now in quarantine for processing. That meant registration, tattooing, work assignment, body search, and general intimidation. The rest of the prisoners were forbidden to have any contact with us for the duration; Honza was only able to be present because he happened to be the Block Elder—or *Capo*, as they were called here—of this barrack, which normally was the

81

children's house. It was the only place that received somewhat better food, and that was why he was able to feed me. He had already heard about Joe's arrest from the boys in the previous transport and had, in fact, been expecting me.

Honza now became my guardian angel. He had sent Tommy and offered to keep my watches for an emergency, in case I should get sick and need drugs. He considered the children's house one of the safest places in camp—which it was, for reasons I could never quite put my finger on. His deputy was the husband of a former apprentice of my mother's. He looked me over after joining us and remarked offhandedly that I would never be able to keep the riding boots I was wearing and offered to salvage them for me.

I missed a signal from Honza's eyes and agreed. His feet were small for a man, but the swap was made. My boots obviously pinched his feet while I slid around in his shoes, yet he was terribly happy about the deal and I really did not care at this point. Besides, he promised we would swap again when the heat was off.

During this first long night, I also learned to beware of the Polish prisoners, who hated the Jews just as much as the Nazis did and often more. All prisoners had to wear little colored triangles on their sleeves to denote their status, such as Jews, Political, or Criminal. Some of these categories overlapped: for example, there were Jews among those who were classified Political. Generally, they were Communists, Socialists, or adherents of a variety of opposition groups from all over Europe. Some of them had been imprisoned from five to eight years before coming to Auschwitz.

There was no doubt that the Poles were the most powerful of all, mainly because they had been in Auschwitz right from its inception in 1941. Due to their natural tendency to anti-Semitism, they had the ears of the Germans in many instances and made the most of it. Most of these people had been arrested individually for specific or preventive reasons.

The Criminal contingent was exactly what the word means: no different from criminals elsewhere, with many of them serving life sentences. By virtue of their long tenure, many were *Capos* and scribes in various other sections of the concentration camp and consequently had access to more information than only Birkenau. Typically, a good many became rather friendly with some SS men— maybe a case of kinship of souls? At the bottom of the scale were the Jews and gypsies. We were not considered political prisoners, although to my thinking, we were just that.

The lines at the tables were slowly thinning. My lesson was ended. Honza needed some sleep, and I got up to await my turn. The scribes were tired out, and less hostile and bossy than in the beginning. After giving my personal data, I quickly and painlessly acquired a tattoo on my left forearm. I was assigned to Block 12, with most of the old women who had fallen back to the end of the lines. This dismayed me a little but turned into a stroke of luck.

The *Capo* of Block 12 happened to be a friend from Terezín, where she had been a cook and I had made a few clothes for her. She now welcomed me with open arms and favored me from the start. She assigned me a choice upper bunk near a little window, slipped me a piece of bread or salami once in a while, and also made sure that I got my soup from the bottom of the barrel. Nina* was a leftover from the September 1943 transport, with a fairly solid position in camp, largely because she was exquisitely beautiful, with blue eyes and long blond hair, and because a criminal German *Capo* was deeply and sincerely in love with her. This way she was not only able to keep her mother with her and eat better, but our block also received less harassment than the others.

At dawn, a strange little man sporting an armband with the initials *CP* (Criminal Police) appeared and started pacing up and down the long brick horizontal chimney that ran down the length of the barrack. He was a Jew like the rest of us, but endowed with a highly exaggerated sense of his own importance: a perfect caricature of an SS man—except that he was not trying to be funny. He had become just like his masters.

He gave a very strict lecture on the dos and don'ts of the camp, threatening fire and brimstone. He made it perfectly clear that we were not allowed to keep *anything*. Coats longer than twenty inches? *Verboten*. Also extra stockings, jewelry, shoes, and, naturally, money. He warned that we would be searched and searched again and that noncompliance would carry severe penalties.

If I had not been so stunned and tired, I would have laughed at this extraordinary performance. As it was, I got busy as soon as he left. I took out of my pocket the little nail scissors I still had and began to cut to size my still-beautiful camel-hair coat. It was the

---

* Editor's note: Names that I am certain are pseudonyms are marked with asterisks.

last remnant of our spring collection of 1939, a copy of a Marcel Roche. It took hours to cut through the heavy material and longer to hem it, using the threads I pulled out of the seams.

Just as I finished, our *Cripo*-Clown returned with a few helpers and a search began. Coats piled up on the chimney. Rings, fountain pens, lipsticks, even buttons were collected in a bag. When they came up to me, I just shrugged.

You still have your wedding ring! the *Cripo* snarled. *Who do you think you are? Some sort of privileged character?*

In the heat of salvaging my coat, I had forgotten the ring. Now I slowly pulled it off and threw it in his bag.

16

Kitty came running into the barrack as soon as quarantine was lifted.

Why did you come here? You fool, don't you know that we're all going to be burned June twentieth? You should have run away after they locked up Joe. The only reason why we from December are still alive is that the bastards want a nice round number for the operation and there weren't enough of us left from March. Don't you know that to commemorate Masaryk's birthday, they sent 3,750 young people up the chimney? The March transport was brought in to replace them. Nobody leaves here alive. The limit is six months and no more. Why on earth did you have to come?

I sat there, convinced that she had gone raving mad. This could not possibly be my lifelong pal, the social butterfly with beautiful dark eyes that always smiled, even when she was serious. Now they could not hold still even for a moment. They shifted back and forth while she blurted out this totally irrational nonsense. Why hadn't Honza said one word about all this?

A very strange sensation took hold of me then. I stared down at my tattooed arm, and like a badly focused picture in a camera, it slowly detached itself and became two arms. But only one had a tattoo. I tried to focus back, but the movement continued until there were two of us: me and A-4116. I thought, *What is she doing here, poor devil? I know her. I'm sorry for her. I'll watch her. She looks just like me.*

Listen to me, said Kitty. *I can see by your face that you don't believe one word I said. Come out and I'll show you.*

A-4116 climbed down from her bunk and followed Kitty out into the camp. There, in the distance, Kitty showed her a group of chimneys spewing smoke into the sky, and for the first time since her arrival, she became conscious of a peculiar odor in the air, like burning hair or bones.

Still incredulous, A-4116 said, *But all this is quite impossible. Anyway, how do you know? This is a big camp and they might just be burning corpses of people who died a natural death. You know how Germans are about cleanliness. Besides, there're enough old and sick people around to keep a crematorium busy.*

Oh yeah? said Kitty. *Then how do you explain that 3,750 people disappeared overnight?*

They could have been deported somewhere else. This is 1944. There are international laws. They could never get away with murder on a scale like this. Have you forgotten that there is still a world out there that could do the same thing to German prisoners?

Shit, you are so naive. The world doesn't give a hoot what happens to us here—for all we know, they might not even believe it if they saw it. Just like you. What about your Capo, Nina. Why do you think she stayed alive—and with her mother at that? That boyfriend of hers went through all kinds of trouble to stash them both away on the ty-phus quarantine block because HE knew what was up and he also knew that the typhus block would not be taken. They are all here in your own block. Go ask her.

The two girls were walking up and down the camp road as they talked, stopping here and there to greet old friends. A-4116 noticed how much everybody seemed changed in the months since she had seen them in Terezín. They were all thinner, and their clothes and shoes made them look like extras out of *The Beggar's Opera*. Everybody seemed to be clutching a little bundle and be in a hurry to get somewhere. Since this was the only time of the day when men and women were allowed to see each other, the road was very crowded.

There were seven barracks on each side of the road, with the latrine in the center of the women's row. Birkenau formed a quadrangle surrounded by two rows of loaded high-voltage barbed wire. At one end was a large gate dominated by a large sign reading ARBEIT MACHT FREI ("Work Makes You Free"). Beyond the gate were the guardhouses of the SS. At the other end one could see a railway yard. On both sides, the same kind of gigantic cages stretched as far as the eye could see.

Appell sounded and everybody had to return to their barracks. This was a twice-daily routine and lasted from one to three hours, depending on how quickly the officer in charge could add. The inhabitants of every barrack had to stand outside in perfect rows of five and come to attention when the SS officer arrived. The *Capo* reported the number present, sick, or dead. The SS entered the barrack to check on the accuracy and recounted the assembled prisoners. A-4116 watched the proceedings with detached interest, amused at the frantic efforts of the *Capo* and her two helpers, a deputy and a scribe, to keep the rows straight and neat—a difficult task, since they were dealing with people not drilled in military discipline.

Her amusement faded when it was explained in whispers that if the rows were not perfect, blows would fall on the *Capo*'s head and the whole camp would be made to stand until order was established. The *Capo* across the road in the men's Block 13 was so zealous that he boxed and slapped his men into shape even before the officer arrived.

She recognized him. It was Richard, who had been part of her crowd in Terezín. What had happened to him? She knew he was a tough sort of guy who played center forward on the soccer team and was not very choosy about the expressions he used. But what he displayed now was out-of-control brutality. She wondered whether his attitude had also changed toward the girl he had a relationship with in Terezín, whom she knew quite well.

Appell over, it was chow time. Soup and a bread ration about three inches thick, to last for the next twenty-four hours. Some people would eat it in one sitting; others would carefully divide it up into three pieces, eat one, and hide the rest in a little bundle under their straw mattress. It was getting dark quickly now. The lights were turned out. The day was over.

A-4116 lay on her bunk, her eyes wide open, unable to fall asleep despite not having slept for the last sixty hours. Images were chasing each other as in a crazy film montage. Chimneys, raggedy people, Kitty's eyes, chimneys, Honza with his gentle smile, chimneys, Richard hitting and bellowing at some old man, barbed wire, German shepherds, chimneys, Nina, Mutti's face, Father—where were they?—until it all became a fiery ball spinning before her eyes. Faintly, she seemed to hear Mutti's voice: *Your only duty to us is to stay alive.*

I will, she said out loud. *I will.*

17

Unsurprisingly, A-4116 was assigned to the sewing shop. Judging by the uniforms that came in for repair, the war was not going too well for the Germans. In Terezín, there had been torn-off buttons and ripped linings; in Birkenau, there were gaping holes that had to be patched and dark stains that could only have been blood. Still, the uniforms had to be repaired for further use.

This was small consolation for an empty stomach. In the evening, she sometimes went for a walk with Kitty to see Honza at the children's block, where Gisa also lived. The children all worshipped him, instinctively sensing his inherent goodness. His mother worshipped him too, and this was a decidedly two-way affair, since his father had died when he was a young boy. Here, as in Terezín, they always walked arm in arm, and no girl ever got close to tying Honza down, although he was one of the most attractive and eligible bachelors around. He had actually come to Auschwitz as a volunteer when his mother had to go. He was one of the few people who had not been vulgarized by camp.

A-4116 asked him, *Why didn't you tell me about the chimneys the night I arrived?*

To what end? I knew you would find out soon enough, and besides, I'm firmly convinced we will survive. God knows I have no rational explanation for what I believe, but somehow, I know it won't be the same this time. There could be an uprising. Maybe we could burn down the whole place, but I can assure you that no one will go quietly to the gas chambers singing the national anthem like they did in March. We're too young to die without a fight, and something will be organized before that cursed deadline. Just keep your mouth shut and be careful. There are spies all around. Don't trust anyone, even people you've known for a long time. People have changed here.

Lost in thought, A-4116 walked out into the sunshine toward Kitty's block.

Well, look who's here. Nazdar. Two young men she used to dance with in her teens stood in front of her, grinning, one a former salesman in a fabric shop in Prague.

Still the well-dressed young lady, said Willy.

Yeah, and a grass widow in the bargain, Mirko pitched in.

How do you like our lovely village?

I bet that being as smart as you are, you managed not to let the Cripo rob you clean. What did you manage to bring in?

Not much, really, just a couple of watches, but I don't want to sell anything right now if that's what you're after.

If you keep that in your bunk, you won't have it very long, remarked Mirko. *They find everything in time.*

Don't you two worry about me. They're well put away, and you can bet your life that I won't tell YOU *where. See you.*

She continued on her way to Block 4, where Sylva,* one of the prettiest girls of Prague, was *Capo*. Always a spoiled brat and incredibly stupid, she took her function quite seriously and ran her block like the ruler of a good-sized duchy, regarding the inmates as her loyal subjects. Oddly enough, many of them seemed to go along with this fiction.

As her knight and lover she had Heini, a *Capo* in another part of Auschwitz who came to Birkenau regularly with deliveries of provisions. He was a criminal from Hamburg, serving a sentence of ninety-nine years for armed robbery. Aside from this disturbing aspect of his personality, he had a heart of gold and was a truly fine human being. He was well liked by the SS and was a frequent guest at their drinking sprees. Gifted with natural diplomatic skills, he had a way of drawing them out about their plans and intentions for Birkenau.

He was one of the best sources of information for the camp, not only in matters of immediate concern, but for news of the war. Fortunately, he was friendly with some male prisoners as well, because his tidings often got warped beyond recognition in Sylva's retelling. Kitty suggested that A-4116 see Sylva to arrange a transfer to Block 4, but after watching the scene for ten minutes, she tactfully declined and preferred to stay perched above the old ladies in Block 12 with Nina. This was going to be rather lonely, but better than becoming a lady-in-waiting at this ridiculous court.

One of the curiosities of Birkenau was the selection of its *Capos*. All of them were young. The SS ostensibly preferred to deal with pretty faces and good figures. So much for the women. The men were chosen mostly for their ability in playing soccer. The SS loved to watch it often, being too lazy or drunk to play it themselves. The *Cripos* were handpicked for their lack of scruples, after careful observation.

Another curiosity was the latrine. This was the meeting place of the camp, particularly in bad weather and during working hours. It was simply a ditch with four-by-four planks on each side, one for men, the other for women, with no partition. A fairly good sense of balance was required in order not to fall in. After a while, one learned to recognize friends by their naked rear ends. Toilet, or any other, paper was a memory. Opposite the planks were tin sinks with water faucets, and this comprised the entire sanitary facilities for the ten thousand prisoners. The water from the sinks drained into the ditch and so formed a very efficient arrangement.

Still wanting more information about the events of March, A-4116 went to see Nina one night.

How is it that you and a few others are still here from the December transport?

Didn't anybody tell you that Mother and I both had typhoid fever? Nina replied. *It's as simple as that. I don't want to talk about it. What else do you want to know?*

Why is there only one woman in Birkenau with her hair shaved off, while in the neighboring compounds all of them have shaved heads?

All the women in Auschwitz have shaved heads except the Capos

96

and the inhabitants of Birkenau. Now, with Sarah, the Capo of Block 2, it's a special story. Quite funny, if you can still laugh at it. You know how difficult it is to get together with a man in this place, even if you happen to be a Capo. So she and her husband decided that the kitchen would be a good place to use as a refuge for a little lovemaking after morning Appell. It was lovely for a while, but suddenly they were rudely interrupted by one of the SS men, who had unexpectedly decided on a spot check of the kitchen. Her husband was lame for weeks from the beating he received, and she had to have her hair shaved off.

You'll find out that the Germans are inventive when it comes to their personal entertainment. Take the kids. I mean the boys between twelve and fifteen. It's a disaster for them if they're pretty. All Hitler's race laws don't prevent the SS from keeping them around their barracks, feeding them all kinds of goodies, and giving them license to do as they please as far as the other prisoners are concerned. Just as long as they're blond and blue-eyed. Sometimes when they get tired of playing with them, they hang or shoot them for the fun of it, but mostly they send them back to the men's barracks, where they are impossible to manage. Sylva's brother, Eddie, is a "peeple"—that's what they call the boys. It's late. Are you hungry? Here, have a piece of salami, but don't let the others see it. Go to sleep. Go.

18

The next morning, before the main soup break, Eddie came into the workshop. Standing in front of A-4116, he announced, *Cripo Schlesinger wants you in his office. Step on it.*

Arriving, she found that striped clown sprawled behind a desk.

So you think you can get around me? Where are those Swiss watches? You do realize that it is illegal to hide valuables from the authorities. Or don't you?

Of course I know that, but I'm not hiding anything. If you don't believe me, why don't you send someone over to search my bunk or frisk me here?

You are a liar and you know it, but I'll teach you. First we'll shave off your head and maybe then you'll remember the truth.

While screaming these threats, his own bald head getting redder and redder, the door opened and in walked Willy and Mirko, her former dance partners, with a few pieces of jewelry they had found on an old woman in Nina's block, where they had been sent to search for A-4116's treasure. An argument ensued among the three as to how the loot would be divided, and realizing that for the moment she was forgotten, A-4116 slipped out the door and returned to her workshop, happily caressing her tresses. Hopefully, Schlesinger's head would cool off and he would leave her alone.

After this experience, A-4116 retreated into her own private world populated with people from the past, and nurtured wild fantasies of escape. This retreat naturally and very quickly earned her a reputation for arrogance and snobbishness. She spent the hours of the night before sleep working out meticulous plans for an escape. She would somehow have to find some insulated wire cutters, cut holes into the barbed wire, make her way to the railroad ramp, and hide in the underbelly of a cattle car until it left. If the Count of Monte Cristo could get out of Devil's Island, she would get out of here.

With daylight came the terrible awareness of the impossibility of these pipe dreams. Other nights, she spun out endless fantasies about a platonic love affair she had had at the age of seventeen that ended with the emigration of the young man. Now she imagined the wildest love scenes that had never taken place, feeling his arms around her, even smelling the scent of his pipe. Strangely enough, her husband never played a role in these sexual fantasies. She did miss Joe. He would have been good to have around, if only to keep away hooligans like Mirko and Willy.

She also found that she was becoming totally incapable of feeling pity or concern for the old ladies living with her and became very impatient with their sometimes naive questions. She was also always looking for ulterior motives when someone offered a favor or asked for one. The only people she still trusted were Kitty, Honza, Gisa, and Aunt Hella, a cousin of Mutti's whom she had discovered here in Block 2.

But even with them she kept a protective distance—for different reasons in each case. She went to see them occasionally, and left feeling lonelier than before. She was hungry most of the time, but did not go to see Honza too often for fear of being thought a beggar, knowing that he was one of the rare men in camp who did not demand, much less expect, any kind of payment. Flirting and necking had here evolved into outright prostitution for food. Far from being critical of many of her contemporaries, she just felt she hadn't sunk deep enough for that.

She had always loved Aunt Hella, but her likeness to Mutti was too much to bear for any length of time and she fled from her well-meant interest and concern. She knew very well that Gisa needed her more than ever, but suddenly could find nothing to talk about with the child. Gisa must have felt this too, as their walks together became fewer and fewer. Even Kitty was becoming a different person in her eyes, with her fear verging on paranoia. Kitty was in the midst of their old crowd from Prague, the girls she had rejected because of their kowtowing to Sylva but now sometimes longed to belong to.

May became June, and the camp atmosphere grew tenser and more hostile with every day. The SS were stepping up their favorite entertainment, which was to have anywhere from fifty to a few hundred prisoners report for calisthenics. They would order push-ups, knee bends, and running in place until at least half dropped from exhaustion. Each prisoner that fell added to their nefarious amusement, proving the theory of the inferiority of the Jewish race.

The signal that the camp was waiting for was the distribution of postcards to be sent to friends and relatives in Terezín. This had happened in March, when the condemned were made to write that they were well and working. The postcards were postdated March 25, while the people were actually disposed of on March 7. Because the March *Aktion* had taken place exactly six months after the arrival of the September transport, it followed by simple arithmetic that the people who had arrived in December would go in June. Both transports had come with the designation *Rückkehr Unerwünscht* (Return Undesired). Most of the May people tended to be more optimistic, simply because they had not lived through that particular catastrophe, and mass hysteria had not yet taken complete hold of them in the short weeks they had been in Auschwitz. The whole idea still sounded preposterous to them, in spite of all the evidence to the contrary.

Anxiety peaked when postcards were actually distributed on June 10, 1944. The prisoners had to write *Birkenau* and their name and birthdate as a return address. It was impossible to convey anything of consequence in the limited number of words permitted, and evidently even prearranged codes were misunderstood back in the ghetto. Even if the rumors of Auschwitz had reached them, the name Birkenau had no meaning or association for them. According to an agreement with her friends that she would write the exact opposite of what she meant, A-4116 wrote, *I am fine. Wish you were here.* Considering the later fate of Terezín's population, these messages did not accomplish anything at all.

The planning and plotting inside Birkenau went into high gear; rebellion and fury hung in the air. One young inmate, an excellent sportsman and youth leader, broke down and walked into the charged wires one week later, when sacks filled with replies arrived from Terezín. The camp was now ordered to write new cards dated June 2.

On June 18, Heini the burglar arrived with some startling information: the treatment of Jews was to undergo a drastic change. He claimed that the order had come directly from Berlin—from Göring himself. The new idea was not to kill Jews capable of work, but rather send them to places with acute labor shortages and let nature take its course.

Heini implored everyone to calm down; there would be a selection in the next few days in which people between fifteen and forty years of age would be chosen to be sent away to work camps. He warned that women with children would be excluded as well as the older and younger groups, but argued that this was better than a rebellion. That had no chance of success at all and would only annihilate the whole camp. He was understandably elated that his beloved Sylva would be saved, and had already made plans to escape and find and marry her if and when the Russian front would get close enough. She now had the problem of keeping her forty-four-year-old mother with her.

It all sounded too good to be true, but on June 20, 1944, the children's block was made ready for the first selection of men.

Dr. Mengele, the SS medical officer in charge, arrived and smilingly picked up a few small children to joke with. After this, the process of picking the strongest and healthiest men began. It took all afternoon, and when it was finished, the men selected were immediately marched out of the camp. Hours of anxious waiting followed. The pessimists still maintained that the whole thing was a ruse to get the able-bodied out of the way first because information about the planned rebellion had leaked out and reached the ears of the Germans.

Hours turned into days as the wives and mothers of the men took turns watching the visible railroad ramp to ascertain if their men were being put on a train. It appeared that the pessimists had been correct when on July 1 a large group of prisoners with bald heads and brand-new gray prison uniforms emerged on the ramp. A little girl posted as a lookout gave the signal and half of the female camp population raced dangerously close to the wire fences to see if these were really their men. The distance was too great to be able to recognize individual faces, but seeing the crowd, the men looking toward the camp started to wave and blow kisses. In tears the women watched the loading of the train and saw it leaving.

During the early afternoon of the same day, the procedure was repeated with the women. A thunderstorm was coming up, and it was getting darker and darker as some 2,500 women massed in the children's block. They crowded at one end in frightened silence, while at the other Dr. Mengele stood, arms crossed over his decorated chest, in shining black riding boots, with his aides and scribes.

Someone barked an order to strip to the skin and to put clothes over the left arm. A parade began in single file. At arrival in front of the doctor, each woman had to come to attention and answer several questions. Afterward, Mengele indicated with a slight movement of his thumb to move to the right or left side of the hall. Very soon, a pattern emerged: the group on the left was clearly intended for the chimneys, since it included all the weak, old-looking, spectacle-wearing, or scarred persons. The storm was now directly above us. The thunder and lightning made the scene—a few thousand naked women standing in front of twenty booted Germans in green uniforms—look like the fantasy of an insane surrealistic painter.

A-4116 watched the proceedings with her detached interest, making a mental note of the fact that even young and strong girls with appendectomy scars wound up on the wrong side; that by some strange coincidence everybody had become a dressmaker, factory or farm worker overnight; and that every last housewife had disappeared. When she reached the dashing doctor, he fired the questions at her.

Number?

A-4116.

Age?

Twenty-four.

Married?

Yes.

Children?

Yes.

Profession?

Electrician.

What? Electrician? Is that true?

Yes.

YOU know how to pull wires and such?

Yes.

To the right—and make a note of that, he ordered the scribe.

Happy, she joined Kitty, who had already made it there, and pulled on her clothes. The other girls crowded around, wanting to know what had caused the change of pace in the metronomic rhythm of the proceedings. A-4116 explained in whispers that the idea of declaring herself an electrician had come to her on the spur of the moment, when she was frantically thinking of something original to distract the eyes of the doctor from the appendectomy scar on her belly. It wasn't an outright lie, since her father was an electrical engineer and had always encouraged her to learn how to fix faulty wiring or an appliance at home.

In any event, she said, this would be forgotten tomorrow, and for now, it had served its purpose very well. Many others had lied during this long afternoon, especially about their age and occupation, more or less successfully. Only one denied that she had a child—a four-year-old boy who was born when she was only seventeen—and no one had the nerve to criticize her for that. She could not have helped him, even if she stayed with him.

That evening after the selection, leave-taking was hard for the lucky ones picked to go. A-4116 went first to see Aunt Hella, her last link to the older generation. She found her in a serene mood, with not a trace of fear of her assured death. They sat with their arms about each other, the young one tongue-tied, just soaking up the warmth of the motherly woman, while the older one echoed Mutti's parting words, encouraging her to stay strong and try her best to stay alive. Hella told her not to pity her, that this was the one thing she could not take, and told her of the beautiful life she had had and the many happy times with Mutti. It all sounded so strangely familiar.

On the way back she met Gisa, making her way to Block 12 with a pair of shoes A-4116 had given her in Terezín when she had outgrown hers. Gisa was barefoot. Together they entered the block and sat on the bunk holding hands while Gisa explained that she had brought the shoes because they were much better than the ones A-4116 had acquired after foolishly swapping her boots, which had never been returned. *I won't need them anymore*, she said. *Right?*

There was no answer for this child who understood the score only too well, even though the grown-ups had tried all along to keep the truth from her. Gisa was now thirteen, but physically not developed enough to pass for a fifteen-year-old and so not even eligible for the selection. A few girls her age had slipped through the net as well as a dozen or so young-looking women over forty, but "A concentration camp is no kindergarten" was the slogan of the rulers. The goodbyes were said, and the ones about to leave went to sleep with a heavier heart than the ones to be left behind. The thunder and lightning had stopped and all was quiet.

19

T he following morning before *Appell*, the chosen women were called out from their barracks by number and name. They were marched off at a brisk pace some two kilometers and arrived at a huge compound with the sign KONZENTRATION-SLAGER A I FRAUENLAGER.

This camp was much larger and more crowded than Birkenau. The barracks were built of stone. The roads were in better shape, although the base was the same ocher-colored loam, but here they were dotted with rough cobblestones. Instead of the male SS guards, SS women were very much in evidence. The prisoners here wore raggedy striped uniforms and generally looked much more decimated than the girls from Birkenau. The exception were the *Capos* and their deputies, who looked positively well fed and clean, with their long hair worn in ponytails caught with neat black bows. The same could be said about the young teenage runners, who were the exact counterpart of the *peeples* in Birkenau. It was almost impossible not to be reminded of a pet Pekinese or poodle when observing them.

Most of the rank and file had shaved heads or very short hair, just beginning to grow in. Walking was seemingly forbidden, since everybody was constantly running. Counted off by groups of five hundred, the newcomers were herded into low, Russian-style barracks with tiny windows. Inside, instead of bunks there were long shelves about five feet deep against the walls and another similar construction running through the center. There were no pallets, no blankets, and no straw. They were chased up into these cage-like contraptions with a flood of curses and shoves from the Polish *Capos* and strictly admonished to stay there or else.

The *Capos* seemed to be absolutely incapable of speaking in a normal tone, much less to be talked to or asked a question. Every shouted sentence was preceded by a curse. *You Czech whores who think that you are different!* Or, *Dirty Jew bitches, who deserve to drown in their own shit, we'll teach you what Auschwitz is all about! You haven't seen anything yet.* All this in Polish, which many understood but few spoke. All got the meaning anyway.

No sooner were they packed in than they were chased out to stand *Appell.* This time, a number of individuals were called out by their numbers and taken away for reasons no one understood until later. Twins were taken out for medical experiments Dr. Mengele was running in the camp hospital; also nurses and some others who were supposed to stay in A I for reasons they did not know.

Various SS women came and went, inspecting the rows standing at attention. Talking was forbidden. One of the SS caught a girl whispering to her neighbor and made her kneel on the stony ground, her arms lifted above her head, and then placed a heavy rock in each hand. Every time her arms relaxed a little, a guard or *Capo* would yell at her to stretch them out or else. This went on for hours. Finally when *Appell* was over, the girl had to be held up on both sides by her friends. Her knees would not carry her.

Next, a dozen stools were brought and their hair was cut. It came as a pleasant surprise that our hair was not shaven, but just cut short to the ears. That seemed like a good omen, considering that it's easier to shave a live body than a dead one. If they were destined for the gas, the reasoning went, all of it would have come off for the German arts and crafts shop. There was a good deal of scuttling and regrouping during the relatively less guarded period of the haircutting, with the effect that a few girls, including Kitty and A-4116, succeeded not only in saving their manes but also managed to form a cluster that vowed to stay together come what may. Even having seen the men leave, many still did not trust the accuracy of Heini's information.

After all these hours everybody had the desperate need to go to the latrine, and groups of ten were relayed there by *Capos*. The time spent there was strictly rationed, and whoever took too long in the view of the escort was poked in the buttocks with a pitchfork. This was accompanied by a flood of invective utilizing every filthy word contained in three languages. With the echo of the favorite curse *Cholera should take you!* they were chased back to their barracks to stand for another long *Appell*. At last they were given a mugful of black liquid called coffee and a slice of bread and locked inside the barrack.

With darkness, another kind of assault materialized in the form of the biggest bedbugs ever seen by anyone present. They were the size of fully grown cockroaches, and they attacked without mercy. The shelves were so overcrowded that sleep was only possible sandwiched like spoons between one's neighbors. When one turned, the whole row of some fifty people had to turn as well. A-4116 had always been irresistible to bugs of any kind, and was now so bitten up that she could not sleep at all. Disregarding the order not to leave the bunks, she slid down in the darkness to the stone floor, where she found a barrel covered by a blanket. She pulled it over herself and, feeling warm and comfortable, dozed off. The next morning, she slept so soundly that Kitty and a few others had to spend a considerable time bringing her back to consciousness. The barrel contained chlorine and the blanket was soaked full of its gases.

The next day, the group was taken under armed guard to a different section of Auschwitz where the other Birkenauers were already assembled in front of a building marked SAUNA. This immediately revived our anxieties since it was well known that the gas chambers were camouflaged by this title. There were flower beds all around, and to A-4116, the bright red of the begonias looked positively obscene against the dismal gray of the windowless building. Still outside, in full view of their escort of SS men, they were ordered to strip and throw their clothes and shoes onto two separate piles.

Hysteria flaring up here and there around them, the two cousins stood silently holding hands. Two by two, they were slowly let into a room where a big, fat SS woman stood in front of a dirty surgical table with stirrups, a white coat thrown over her uniform. Brutally she inspected every single one of our orifices without once changing her rubber glove. One of the girls, determined to save a souvenir from her lover, clutched a few buttons of his coat in her hand. Realizing that there was absolutely no place to hide them, she finally swallowed the keepsakes.

The next stop in the processing were the showers. Groups of one hundred were let in at a time. The orders were: one minute of water; one minute of soaping, with a piece of ersatz soap distributed to each foursome; one minute to rinse; and no noise. Hesitantly, the herd entered the shower room, prodded by guards and *Capos*, peering with unspeakable horror at the showerheads reputed to carry gas as well as water.

Sh'ma Israel Adonai Eloheinu was heard in a whisper. An eternity seemed to pass. Then a hissing sound from overhead: water! Boiling-hot water! A shout of relief went up, and the whole scene changed to a mad ballet in an effort to avoid the scalding streams. Coming out on the other side, each woman was given a pair of underpants and a gray prisoner shift and ordered to pick shoes from the pile outside.

This was practically impossible. How could anyone find her shoes in a mixed-up pile? The result was too ridiculous for words, but the fights that broke out when one person found her shoes on someone else's feet were not.

Another long *Appell* and the *Lagerkommandant* arrived for inspection. A-4116 stood in the first row when the lady slowly started her review. The command *Achtung!* was given, but A-4116, who had already recovered some of her natural sass, neglected to take her hands out of her pockets.

The *Kommandant* stopped in front of her. *Hands out of your pockets, Jew bitch!* A blow flat across the face with the back of her ringed hand came almost simultaneously. The prisoner's hands flew forward for her throat, but Kitty and another girl already held her elbows so tightly that she could not move. The group was ordered to march out of A I in the direction of the ramp.

After being provided with a piece of bread each, the group was loaded into rather clean cattle cars with fresh straw. To their delight and surprise, the doors remained open about a foot, and after some more delays and shouted commands, the train started to move. Slowly gathering speed, it took at least twenty minutes to get out of the Auschwitz complex. The administration buildings formed a little town in itself. Only in broad daylight did one get an idea of the immensity of this death factory. Countless square compounds separated by barbed-wire fences were dotted with watchtowers, and from the train, the inmates seemed like crawling ants.

Then, quite suddenly, the view changed. Moving in a western direction, the train passed through flowering meadows with bubbling brooks: lush, green, totally unbelievable. The sight of farmers working in the fields, grazing cattle, and ordinary people just going about their business brought us a sudden awareness that there was a life to be lived after all and that maybe soon one would be part of it again. It was the fourth of July. The sun was brilliant in the sky, the smoke of Auschwitz was receding in the distance, and someone started to sing:

> *The world is ours.*
> *There's room for every one*
> *and on the ruins of the ghetto we will laugh.*

It was a song from a prewar avant-garde revue that had been adapted for Terezín, and was a favorite among all Czech prisoners. Song followed song, and after running through the repertory of Czech pop and folk songs, we sang "Old Man River" and "Anchors Aweigh." The scene was reminiscent of a youth hostel trip. Empty stomachs were forgotten; the women laughed, teased, and tickled each other like an exuberant bunch of kids intoxicated with the sheer joy of living. Even the armed escorts riding in the cabin of each car could not suppress a smile.

20

The doors of the cars were locked when the train neared the more industrial regions of Germany. But not even this could dampen the girls' high spirits. A-4116 and Kitty were surrounded by girls from Prague, with a sprinkling from the provinces. They belonged to the same generation and had known each other long before the emergence of Adolf Hitler. Bound by their recent experiences, they swore to try to stay together and help each other.

A very strange scene awaited the travelers the next evening when the train slowed down and, finally, ground to a halt in Hamburg. It stopped in front of a dark row of buildings three stories high, with huge sliding doors on every floor.* Those doors and the windows were hung like vines with young men! Boys of every shape and size,

---

* Editor's note: This was Dessauer Ufer, a sub-camp of the Neuengamme concentration camp located inside the port of Hamburg, in operation from July 1944 until April 1945. It was the first sub-camp for women in Neuengamme.

wearing unfamiliar uniforms without insignia, were laughing and shouting all at the same time, obviously delighted with the arrival of a trainload of young women.

The ladies were puzzled, then smiled back and waved. Car after car was unloaded under the supervision of an extremely handsome and elegant SS *Hauptscharführer*, who was instantly christened Petrovich,* after a popular German movie star. The women were divided into two groups and sent up into what had been a warehouse for river barges with loading facilities on both sides. One side of the building faced the tracks, and the other side was directly on the water.

Inside the warehouse were several round openings like manholes, with thick ropes for pulleys, and rows of bunks arranged in blocks of six. On the track side was a low sink with many water faucets in the center, and a partitioned corner reserved for the *Capo*. The whole place was dark and cavernous and, even in the summer, very cold. The Czech group dashed to the opposite windows to stake out claims to a row of bunks. Some immediately climbed on a bench to look out.

The boys next door, having had the same idea, were already crowding their windows, and introductions did not take long. There were some initial language problems since they were all Italians— either deserters from Mussolini's army or captured partisans who had fought with Tito against the Fascists. Many of them spoke some French or broken German. On the Czech side, German, French, and rusty school Latin had to serve.

Meanwhile, another group of the new arrivals started a veritable water orgy at the other end of the hall. Naked, they sprayed each other from the faucets, holding fingers against the pressure, completely oblivious to the fact that for several minutes Petrovich had been standing in the doorway with a group of guards, watching the scene. One by one, as they became aware of the men's stares, the girls disappeared into the bunks, until only Sylva was standing on top of the sink like a marble nymph. Chuckling, Petrovich ordered her down and to the *Kommando* quarters two floors below. One can only guess at what happened there, but Sylva did not seem to be upset by the episode and certainly did not look maltreated on her return.

The boys next door had abandoned their positions the moment they discovered the presence of the guards, but returned in full force with the falling darkness. Unfortunately, there was only one window that was close enough to enable a conversation, with room for not more than three at a time, so turns had to be taken.

This immediately led to fights about whose turn and for how long. The group nearest to the window established a monopoly, doling out space and time as special favors. There had been a tall blond man in the door of the Italian house when they arrived who had focused his eyes on A-4116 from the moment the train had pulled in. They were now talking together, explaining their circumstances. His name was Bruno and he came from northern Italy. Unable to chat for any length of time, since turns had to be taken, he asked her to come back to the window later, mentioning something about having an idea.

After her return from Petrovich, Sylva had to get in on the fun and immediately struck up a mad love-affair-at-first-sight with a Roman named Flavio. They could hardly communicate, but just looked deeply into each other's eyes and sighed *Flavio* and *Sylva* over and over again—a situation that quickly became boring to everyone not immediately involved, particularly since all this took place twenty yards apart and at least forty feet above sea level.

When A-4116 returned to the window, there was Bruno with a little package tied to a long laundry rope, which he started to swing parallel to the building until she was able to catch it. The system worked beautifully, and the next hour was spent in this highly satisfying activity. At least fifty girls acquired "their" Italian that night. The package A-4116 received contained a comb, toothbrush, cigarettes, a pencil, a pair of socks, chocolate, paper, and a long letter that read something like this:

Dear Francesca,

When the train that brought you pulled up in front of our prison today, my heart went out to all of you. You looked so scared and lost and so young and pretty at the same time. It has been a long time since we saw some pretty girls. I spotted you even before the train stopped and could not tear myself away from the expression in your eyes. What have they done to you, and where did you come from? My name is Bruno, as you know by now, and I come from Treviso, not a very big city. I have eleven brothers and sisters and I miss them very much. When the war broke out I was drafted in the Army, but I never liked the Blackshirts and soon I fled across the water to Yugoslavia with a group of friends to join the partisans. One day we were captured by the Germans and sent here to work. The work is hard, but we are treated quite well and can write home and receive packages. My friends here think that you are all wonderful, and we will help you as much as we can. But you are special for me. I think I love you and I want to marry you when the war is over. You would like it in Italy. It is so beautiful there. We would have many little bambini, and I would make you very happy. Please don't answer me right away because this must be a surprise to you, but maybe soon you will love me too. I can take care of you and the bambini very well. I have a very good job with a furniture factory, and because I know French, I will surely work in the export section after the war. The Americanos have landed in France, and we will be free and happy soon. I am sending you a few things because I saw that you had nothing with you, but mostly paper, so that you can write me long letters telling me all about you. I have to finish because time is short and you have to sleep. I will wait in the window tomorrow night, mia cara piccola bambina. *I would like to kiss you, but you are too far but very near too.*

Your Bruno

The feeling of being recognized as a woman was warm and beautiful, especially since she felt anything but pretty at the moment. The toothbrush and chocolate were shared with Kitty—as well as the letter, of course.

The commotion eventually subsided, and no sooner had they fallen asleep than an alert sounded and, ten minutes later, all hell broke loose. The nightly bombardment of Hamburg had begun. This observer sat cross-legged on her bunk, Kitty's head buried in her lap, in an eerie state of elation. Every flare that burst in the sky and the subsequent crash of an exploding bomb made her feel more exhilarated. Below her, eighteen-year-old Marion was kneeling, reciting one Ave Maria after the other. Others had pulled their blankets over their heads to muffle the noise, but for A-4116 there could not be enough of it and she was sorry when the all clear sounded. This was a very strange reaction from someone who since childhood had been afraid of shooting and who used to hold her hands over her ears in the last act of *Tosca* because she could not bear to hear a shot. It just proved again that she had really left her old self.

The night was disturbed only one more time, when a rat ran over Gerti's* face, reducing her to hysterics. Rats were big and plentiful, being so near the waterfront, and hungry too, since there were now humans living where grain used to be stored. At five a.m. reveille sounded, and after putting on the flimsy, drab overalls issued the night before and sloshing down some black coffee, the girls lined up in front of the building. Broken up into groups of twenty with two guards to each section, they marched off singing a Sousa march toward another canal, where they boarded a steamer to take them to various places of work.

In contrast to Auschwitz, the guards were now older members of the Wehrmacht, unfit for front duty. Some of them, to be sure, were ambitious zealots taking their duty with deadly seriousness and could be very unpleasant. Most were much less vicious than the SS men they had learned to fear.

It was chilly on the boat that early in the morning, and A-4116 huddled against the chimney trying to get warm. One of the men running the old crate came up laughing at her hopeless attempts to light a cigarette in the strong breeze.

You are not a sailor, I see, he said, and taught her how to cup her hand and light the match and cigarette with one flick of his wrist.

He then wanted to know who they were and where they came from. When told that they were Jewish prisoners his friendliness froze and he vanished in a hurry.

From the water, one could see the devastation of this once-beautiful city. Whole city blocks were only piles of rubble. Smoke rose to the sky from burning oil tanks after the bombardment of the preceding night. The lovely rich suburb of Blankenese gleamed curiously untouched atop the palisades of the river. The boat docked at an oil refinery called Erdoel, and here the work detail debarked. The prisoners were given shovels as far as they were available and assigned to clear the rubble from the air attacks into huge piles. They were also instructed to report any unfamiliar object found to the guard, so that a Russian POW detail could be called to deal with it in case it was an unexploded shell.

The refinery was still working, even though many of the buildings and tanks were in ruins. There were slave laborers of every nationality of occupied Europe everywhere. The POWs were mainly French, but also Russians, who were in the most pitiful state, obviously starving and dressed in the torn rags that had once been their uniforms. They were too downtrodden to communicate with any-one, and their guards also treated them with exceptional cruelty.

The rest were civilian forced workers from all over. Communi-cation with the French was quickly established when the guards looked the other way, or in the latrines, where knots in the wood were conveniently pushed out to make conversation easier. This very soon led to a lengthy, rather good-natured tirade by a Bavar-ian guard who could not understand why it took us so long to tinkle: *What are you girls doing in there for such a long time? When I have to piss I run in like a young stag, take a leak, and out again. Well, what can one expect of women?*

The French POWs understood the situation right away, having the longest experience with the system, and helped as much as they were able. They were considerably better off than us because under the rules of the Geneva Convention, they were allowed to receive packages and money. They were also not afraid to take risks to help, whereas the civilian laborers trembled before anyone in a German uniform. The German workers completely ignored every-body, making it their business to look the other way when faced with a group of foreigners or prisoners.

The work was hard, and harder still for women who had never held a shovel in their hands before. It took days to learn the trick of swinging a full shovel up onto a truck, and some never learned. A-4116 rather enjoyed the work once she mastered the movement and was often accused by her coworkers of working too hard. But for her restless nature, that was better than to lean on her shovel and brood about the past or the uncertain future. Besides, one kept warmer that way.

The picking up and loading of broken bricks was not any easier. A chain was formed from pile to truck with the shards passed from hand to hand, and after an hour of this, everyone's fingertips were bleeding.

Relief came at noon when a truck from the "German People's Welfare" drove up with barrels of thick soup based mainly on turnips and potatoes. It tasted vile but was hot and filling, at least for a few hours. By comparison with Auschwitz, a vast improvement.

Kitty had acquired a French friend during the morning who soon slipped her a piece of bread and a little note with a promise of more to come when she met him the following day at the latrine. He was a Parisian by the name of Pierre, smiling and winking at her whenever he passed by. At six p.m., the whistle sounded and a very tired column shuffled back to the boat for the return trip, a good deal of the elation of the last few days gone.

On their return, there were long lines for a bowl of watery soup and a piece of bread, after which most of the girls collapsed exhausted on their bunks, cursing their sore feet and aching muscles. Bruno and his friends were already waiting at their windows, and the scene of the previous night repeated itself in a somewhat less rambunctious tone. This time he threw over a sweater after having watched A-4116 shiver at *Appell* in the morning.

She wrote him a letter thanking him for his gifts and his very touching proposal, but also told him that the idea of marriage was problematic, because as far as she knew she was already married. It was a calculated risk to tell the truth; it could easily have cut off Bruno's much-needed help, but the sincerity of his first letter left really no alternative. He took the news philosophically, resolved to treat her like a sister from now on, and a very strong friendship developed.

21

The bombardment of the first night repeated itself every other night with clocklike precision, with the difference that now, at the sound of the sirens, the women were chased out of their bunks and herded into the cellar, which served as an air-raid shelter. It slanted toward the water, and since the canal rose and fell with the tides, it was often half-submerged. It was cold there, and they sat shivering on the ground in total darkness with the rats scampering over their legs. Hearing only the sounds of explosions above, they were more uneasy than they had been upstairs at the thought of how to get out in case of a direct hit. The two cousins hated the cellar and, whenever possible, hid under their bunk.

The only advantage the cellar had was that it was connected by arched openings with the adjoining buildings below water level at high tide. This opened up interesting possibilities at ebb tide, which took several weeks to utilize. Meanwhile life fell into a routine. Hunger ever present, but alleviated with the help of the French and

Italians. Lack of sleep made everyone grouchy, and all remnants of courtesy and consideration fell by the wayside.

Envy of the foreign boyfriends on the part of those who had none accounted for a good deal of tension, and language became a gutter jargon. This led to a splitting up into groups of anywhere between two to six, which called themselves communes and looked out for their members. Violent arguments between these clusters were the order of the day. Curiously, very few people became ill— even common colds were rare. Whatever sick calls there were, were mostly minor accidents at work.

A month after their arrival, Petrovich was driving down the road on the opposite side of the canal and noticed the strange goings-on at the waterside of *his* storehouse. A-4116 was blithely hanging out the window when a powerful slap on her rear interrupted an interesting conversation with Bruno. Irritated, she turned around to see who the joker was and stared straight into Petrovich's cold eyes. Pulling her down, he was up on the stool in an instant, pulled out his revolver, and was shooting wildly in the direction of the Italians.

He could not do much harm because they all withdrew at high speed, but the event put an end to a marvelous mail service. Oddly enough, there were no other repercussions except for a stern lecture on the propriety of conduct for young ladies, with an admonition never to do it again. Why, the man had not totally lost his sense of humor after all.

Clearly, some other form of communication had to be found. Vera,* the *Capo* who did not go out to work with the rank and file, had an Italian boyfriend, who was the maintenance man for the whole complex of buildings and whom she had met when he came around to open some clogged drains. This Italian had succeeded in bribing the old German soldier who was often on day duty, and had become Vera's frequent visitor while the others were out at work. He now came to the aid of Bruno, Flavio, and the other boys and acted as letter carrier.

Sometime later, the old Kraut was put on night duty during the time of low tide, well before the usual alert. Taking advantage of such favorable conditions, the boys arranged for a meeting with their girls in the cellar at considerable cost and with painstaking planning. Only three had the guts to go along with that dangerous undertaking, and A-4116 made it a foursome after some initial reluctance. The night chosen was one when Petrovich was out on the town. After all the prisoners had gone to sleep, the German led the quartet quietly downstairs to the cellar. There, they had to promise to be back in one hour, because that was when the tide again began to rise. With a weak flashlight they picked their way through the knee-deep water into the next cellar, where the Italians were impatiently waiting.

Scattered and settled on higher ground in pairs, Bruno momentarily forgot his brotherly feelings and became very passionate. His partner did not exactly put up a stiff fight, but when it came to the moment of giving in completely, she froze rigid. All feelings drained away; she was suddenly only conscious of the dampness, the rats, and the utter ugliness of the situation.

With infinite tenderness, Bruno let go of her and, holding her in his arms, assured her of his understanding and love. When it was time to go, he kissed her hands and thanked her for coming. There were no hurt feelings, no reproaches about a missed opportunity, and their friendship became even stronger than before. Still, later she often regretted her lack of generosity. There must have been more of these meetings, but neither Bruno nor she made another effort to come together.

After discovering that there were identical openings leading out into the water, Bruno and Flavio hatched a plan whereby they, A-4116, and Sylva would swim to the opposite bank of the river, walk through Hamburg to the seaport, and convince a fisherman from neutral Sweden to take them out of the country.

The plan sounded possible but had several drawbacks. First, they had no contact with a Swede. He would have to be found on arrival, assuming that they could make it through Hamburg without attracting attention. Second, it would entail a separation from Kitty, and considering that the war was supposedly in its last stages, it did not seem worth it to risk drowning in the North Sea in case of a storm or a mine. After much discussion back and forth, the plan was rejected by all concerned.

Through Pierre, the cousins met another Frenchman, Marcel, who never brought them any food but passed whole bulletins of news through the holes in the latrine wall at Erdoel. He seemed to spend most of his nights glued to his self-built radio, listening to the BBC. He was a staunch Communist and argued that with the landing of the Americans in Normandy and the tide turning on the Russian front, it was only a matter of time before Germany would be ground up between two millstones.

The most important thing was to maneuver so that one would not be caught with the Germans. This was all very true, but did not change the day-to-day race for survival. The winter weather had started early, and the prisoners were freezing in their light overalls, their footwear in such a state that it became a full-time job to stuff their shoes with rags and paper in the attempt to keep dry feet. The older women started to show the effect of overwork, undernourishment, and lack of sleep. Sick calls multiplied, but more often they kept it secret for fear of being sent away.

Very few of them had help from the POWs, who were more attracted by the younger women. In desperation they took to scavenging in garbage piles and collecting cigarette butts, which they rerolled in whatever paper they could find and swapped for a piece of bread if they did not smoke it themselves. Not one of them was over fifty, but their endurance was eroding much faster than the stamina of the younger ones, who with the callousness of youth more or less disregarded their plight except when it came to their own mothers.

By the end of October 1944, rumor had it that they would be moved because the buildings were going to be reassigned for different use. Petrovich received orders to report to the front. The days of hinterland jobs for the SS were over. The Italians were to be given civilian status and integrated into the huge foreign labor force in the area.

Parting was sad. The boys provided their Czech friends with whatever they could spare and promised to stay in touch if they could ever discover where the girls were being taken. The result was tragicomic, for when they lined up to leave and Petrovich took a last review of his troops, they were all carrying bundles, although they had arrived four months earlier practically naked. Musing about this phenomenon, he stopped briefly in front of A-4116 and, pulling some cigarettes out of her breast pocket, asked, *Well, well now, where would these come from?*

I find them, Hauptscharführer.

You do? Where?

Every day in the same place, Hauptscharführer.

With that he shook his head, replaced them, and walked on. Loaded on trucks, the girls were taken to Neugraben, a suburb of Hamburg some fifteen miles away. Ten days later old Kraut told them that the storehouses on the canal had received a direct hit and had been leveled to the ground. The Italians had also been gone at the time.

22

Compared to all the previous places of detention, Neugraben was beautiful: a small camp with only four barracks set against a wooded area. But, alas, no visible neighbors except for the cluster of houses occupied by the new *Kommandant*.

He was an old man who looked like Captain Hook, but was actually a retired stationmaster hurriedly put into an SS uniform. His bark was worse than his bite, and he loved to give sermons at *Appell*, especially in the rain. Most of the old Wehrmacht guards had come along with us. Work was again clearing rubble and loading and unloading sand and bricks, but now the women were farmed out to different places each day and had to march anywhere from one to two hours each way.

They worked on the outskirts of Hamburg, sometimes in residential, middle-class neighborhoods, a circumstance that afforded more opportunity to "organize"—a euphemism for *steal*—all kinds of things in the half-destroyed houses on the way to and from their destinations. One could find all sorts of useless objects in the houses, seldom anything to eat. But one could dig for forgotten potatoes in the harvested fields one passed, or turnips. The guards were tired and did not pay too much attention when someone fell behind for a while.

One day one of the details passed an apple orchard on the way back to camp. There was some unpicked fruit still hanging on the trees, and in a second a few girls were up in them, throwing down apples to their comrades. By the time the group was brought back to camp, there had been a telephone complaint to the *Kommandantur* by the owner. This upset Captain Hook greatly, and outraged, he called an immediate *Appell*. Pent up with fury, he walked up and down the rows, unable to speak for a while, and then it came.

WHO has ever seen anything like THIS? JEW WENCHES on apple trees. Have you gone crazy? Hah, I will show you. YOU are going to swing LIKE SO from the trees. And then I'll shoot you personally. And then YOU'll be surprised and astonished.

The back rows were choking with laughter while the front row had to keep a straight face and the assembled guards broke out in uncontrollable fits of coughing.

From the German point of view the situation had seriously deteriorated, and some zealot sent in a report to the higher echelons. Only a few days later old Kraut told them that a dozen of the guards were being replaced by SS women and that Captain Hook would be exchanged for a new SS *Sturmbannführer*. The party was over.

The new *Kommandant* arrived a few days later with twelve SS women and made it immediately clear that he considered the state of the camp a stinky mess, and that reorganization would start forthwith. His name was Spiess.* He was a carpenter by trade, with a face like a squashed turnip and a mouth full of evil-smelling stumps, which caused a shower of spit to come out every time he spoke. He conducted his first *Appell* armed with his service revolver, plus a yard-length of rubber hose, which he swung around while introducing himself, warned that he would not hesitate to use it.

He had a passion for doing everything himself, or rather having the inmates do it. He was given to violent temper tantrums, during which foam would appear at his mouth like on a mad dog. The camp had a complicated system of bookkeeping, whereby it got paid for the labor performed by its inmates and, in turn, had to pay for food and other supplies. Hell-bent to streamline this obviously mismanaged outfit, Spiess's first act was to trim down the number of prisoners who stayed inside the camp for maintenance, and to scrupulously check the morning's sick calls to eliminate cheaters.

He retained Greta,* the top camp *Capo,* a former nightclub dancer from Berlin who had ended up here because she was married to a Czech Jew. She had ingratiated herself with Captain Hook by virtue of her *Berliner Schnauze* (Berlin attitude). Although pushing forty, she was just the type that was compatible with the overlords, and she succeeded in getting whoever she personally liked appointed as *Capos* and their deputies.

She was justified in one case. Her friend Mimi* was, at this juncture, five months pregnant, having conceived before she left Auschwitz. Mimi herself did not even know she was pregnant until the fifth month because almost all the prisoners had long since stopped menstruating, many of them after they entered the Industrial Palace in Prague. In itself, this was certainly no hardship. On the contrary. But it did not prevent conception, as many discovered too late. Greta now proposed that Mimi work for Spiess as a secretary, in order to keep her indoors during the cold winter months.

Unaware of the circumstances, he agreed, and quickly got used to her. Mimi was an excellent typist, so good that when Spiess eventually discovered her condition, he agreed to let her deliver the child in camp under the condition that it had to be disposed of the moment it was born. This was puzzling behavior from a man who was capable of beating inmates into unconsciousness for the slightest misdeeds. More so, in view of the very strict and explicit guidelines in regard to sick or pregnant prisoners: these had to be immediately dispatched to Bergen-Belsen. An SS medic visited the camp every two weeks for exactly that purpose, although it was ostensibly to check on the supplies for sick bay.

Not only did Spiess give Mimi an apple now and then, but he also locked her in a closet every time the medic came for inspection.

The second day after his takeover, while studying the papers gathering dust in his office, he discovered that there was an electrician among the inmates. A shout went out from block to block. *A-4116 to the Kommandantur! On the double!*

Expecting the worst, she was ushered into Spiess's office.

You are an electrician, he said, without looking up.

Yes, Sturmbannführer.

I am moving this office to the other end of the barrack, where the window looks out on the camp. I want this telephone moved there right away. The cable is here in the corner. Verstanden?

Jawohl.

He stalked out, leaving her without the faintest idea about how to do it. Gingerly she unscrewed the wall box and made a diagram of exactly how the wires were connected, using colored pencils from his desk. Then she removed the box, connected the new cable, isolated it, and drew it along the long corridor. She tacked it to the wall, praying to the patron saint of electricians to make the damned thing work. When she got to the other end of the barrack, she remounted the box, connected the telephone, and picked up the receiver in a cold sweat. A dial tone sounded just as Spiess returned to see how far the work had progressed.

From that moment on, Spiess developed the ridiculous idea that she could do almost anything. The next day, he decided to keep her on as an indoor worker, with the title of Camp Maintenance Woman—to the annoyance of Greta, who had to let go of one of her protégées.

Next, Spiess decided that the food delivered for the *Kommandantur* from a central supply kitchen was not tasty enough. With so many women around, it could be greatly improved, especially since it would be possible to help himself to more provisions by curtailing the camp allotment. The staff barracks had no kitchen— one would have to be installed, and he and A-4116 would convert a nearby dilapidated garage for just that purpose!

There was no electricity and therefore no light, also no stove and no chimney, but the latter was a minor detail he could not be bothered with now. First, the current had to be brought in from a high-voltage pole between the two buildings. He made complicated sketches with fuse boxes here and there, and produced some needed tools, but to A-4116 the whole project looked highly dangerous, since she was to do most of the work—albeit with Spiess's "expert" advice. What if by some mistake she burned the whole place down? Seeing no way out of the bind, she finally asked for some strong leather gloves so as not to electrocute herself.

On the first dry morning, Spiess arrived with a long ladder, and after taking off his own gloves and handing them over, he sent her up on the pole. Pulling together all her wits, she worked on that line the whole day, breaking the circuit twice by fuse boxes, and by evening, lo and behold there was actually light, although the cable swung dangerously in the wind.

The next day Spiess requisitioned a stove, pots, and pans, and commandeered the camp kitchen crew to cook for him and his staff under the supervision of a hefty SS woman named Erika.* In his view, the kitchen crew were just polishing their asses all day having to cook only coffee and one soup for some five hundred people.

After this, a grudging sort of respect for A-4116 came over Spiess, to the point that once, while sprawled behind his desk, feet on the table as she stood at attention receiving the day's orders, he growled, *At ease. Are you sure you are a Jewess?*

I wouldn't be here if I weren't, would I?

I've never heard of a goddamn filthy Jew working with his hands, yet you can. How so? Those parasites are only good for squeezing labor out of honest working men, or sitting around in cafés and plotting a Bolshevik revolution. Those rich Jew bankers even embroiled America into war with us. It's all in the Stürmer *every day. Well, say something! I'm not going to hit you.*

Sturmbannführer, I think you should not believe everything you read. Don't you know that there are millions of working Jews, some of them very poor? What about all the tailors, shoemakers, postmen, mechanics? And how do you figure that they can plot a Bolshevik revolution and be capitalists at the same time? Maybe things are not all black or white?

Nonsense. Fix that window here and then get to work. We haven't got all day.

Still shaking his head, he strode out of the room, carefully leaving one cigarette on the edge of the table. A-4116 shrugged her shoulders, trying to fathom Spiess, and got busy on his window.

There was plenty of work to do, particularly at the *Kommandantur*. The circuits were constantly overloaded by all the small appliances belonging to the SS women, and she spent hours in the low attic of their barrack, where all the wires were lying loose on the ceiling boards. Flat on her stomach, she fixed loose connections and short circuits. But she also killed a lot of time just daydreaming, or listening to the radio below, warm and dry and rather happy with her lot. According to the German newscasts, the Reich was victoriously pulling back on all fronts.

During November 1944, a shipment of coats from Bergen-Belsen finally arrived none too soon. The garments were old and had large yellow crosses painted with enamel on the backs. But the shoe situation continued to be a disaster. The girls walked in rags tied up with strings to work, and not even Spiess, with his warped sense of paternalistic concern for his prisoners, was capable of getting an allotment of even wooden sabots.

23

There were major problems with Kitty now. Somewhere in the rubble and filth, she had picked up a very itchy skin infection. She kept scratching and it developed into impetigo. Eventually, due to lack of vitamins and general malnutrition, she had full-blown furunculosis, covered with boils from head to foot. Some of them were so big they had to be lanced by the camp doctor, who, having been a young pediatrician before the war, did not have too much experience in surgery, and was handicapped by a dire shortage of bandages and disinfectants.

When Kitty developed boils in the glands of her armpits, she began to run a constant temperature that rose quite high. The doctor kept her inside for a few days at a time, but had to be careful. Spiess had the uncanny faculty of remembering faces at sick call and was liable to report anyone who did not seem to get well fast to the inspecting medic.

Kitty had been Room Elder of her dormitory; now, the other girls began to grumble about her cutting and touching their bread. This made her feel like a leper and sent her into an abyss of depression. It took some resourcefulness to get her out of these moods. A-4116 took to cleaning and dressing the endless abscesses and, to prove that she did not consider Kitty repulsive, started to sleep beside her under one blanket.

Greta took pity on her and talked Spiess into letting Kitty stay inside to clean the latrines. A-4116 tried in desperation to get a letter to Kitty's Christian fiancé in Prague. She was now officially permitted to walk the three hundred yards between camp and the *Kommandantur* without a guard and often encountered a German who wished her *Guten Tag*. This gave her the courage to stop one day, ask him to mail a letter to Prague, and bring back a reply in case there was one. She gave him ten of the two hundred marks that Bruno had given her, which she carried tied around her neck. He agreed and, in fact, came back some three weeks later with a small package of disinfectants, bandages, ointments, and a letter.

The letter did more for Kitty than the medicines (which were largely ineffective), for it proved to her that she was not forgotten. She carried it around with her, repeating its passages over and over, and for a while seemed to get better. Ivan's description of his never-ending love and yearning for her, as well as the news that his parents could not wait to have her back and were in fact redecorating a room of their house for her homecoming, was better therapy than what the camp doctor could provide.

The whole dorm shared the warmth and comfort of this loving message from home on the relatively quiet nights when power was often cut off by seven or eight p.m. Bombing alerts continued, but the bombs fell at a distance, and only the glow of the ensuing fires was visible. There was nothing to do in the cold and dark but to wrap up in the flimsy blankets and talk. They discussed the future, which seemed to be hidden in thick fog, and speculated about how many of them would be able to last to the end of the war. Not everyone was confident that things would automatically fall into place once the Nazis were beaten.

There was already widespread anxiety about just how they would cope with the demands of normal life: performing productive work, paying rent and gas bills, not to mention returning to mates who might not be the same men they had known. Many had acquired a slave mentality, living by their wits and ruses from day to day. An orderly or unregulated existence seemed utopian at this point.

The girls took long, imaginary walks through Prague, making it a game and awarding points to the ones who could best remember street names, stores, and many other details. The most popular and lush fantasy was of sitting in a hot bath.

A deep longing for Mutti overcame A-4116, and she started to write her letters in a notebook she had organized from Spiess's desk. Lying in the attic of the *Kommandantur*, supposedly work-ing, she wrote down all that had happened since Mutti was taken away. She kept the book hidden inside her pallet in the hope of . . . what? She didn't know.

The duties of the indoor crew included the unloading of camp provisions and weekly trips to the outside to bring in bread and other supplies. These were holidays for the four girls assigned. The guard sat in the warm cab with the driver; the crew were high up on the open back of the truck, rejoicing in the general destruction around them.

When they arrived at the bakery, the guard immediately disappeared into the office for coffee and pastries, and the loading was left to the girls under the supervision of the bakery owner. Being the accomplished thieves they were by now, it did not take long to discover that the woman was not counting the loaves put on the truck—only the wooden boards on which they were carried out. Once the twenty loaves on each were emptied into the truck, the boards were stacked against the wall.

It was a cinch to put not only the bread but also the board up into the truck at a moment when the woman was distracted. On the way through the bakery, A-4116 also discovered some bricks of yeast stored on a shelf. She thought, *Vitamin B for Kitty*, and one of the bricks rapidly vanished under her coat. When the truck set out on its return trip, the girls had only two problems: disposing of the long wooden board on a crowded road and bringing into camp five loaves of bread each, without attracting attention to their suddenly expanded size.

The first problem was solved by throwing the plank overboard on a bridge across a canal; the second, by eating one loaf of bread right away. A-4116 was stuffing down the still-warm bread at such high speed that it suddenly got stuck in her esophagus and would not budge either way. Her face got red as a turkey, to the extreme entertainment of her pals, who massaged her frantically until the wad finally moved downward. The loot was brought in without a hitch, although Eva* claimed that the guard at the gate had given her a long and suspicious look.

For a few days the four and their respective communes went to sleep without their ever-present hunger pangs. The yeast did wonders for Kitty. It took the bakery woman four whole weeks to discover that she was always short of bread on the days the Neugraben camp came, and even then she had no proof, but she informed Spiess that she now had a truck available for deliveries.

This was sad news mainly because contact with the outside had become a matter of chance. No POWs worked in the area, and the civilian workers were stingy and scared. This left only the possibility of scavenging in the ruins, at which some girls had become virtuosos. Contact with the Italians had been lost completely, but a handful of girls had some Free French laborers who came to see them on some Sundays. Dita was once caught holding hands with her suitor through the barbed wire and was severely beaten by Spiess with his rubber hose. At *Appell* he held up the event as an example on moral grounds: it was unseemly for young girls to have secret meetings with Frenchmen. Evidently he was confusing a concentration camp with a nunnery.

nother odd relationship came into being inside the camp, something quite usual and noticeable in A I in Auschwitz but not experienced as yet in the Czech group. A young SS woman called Bubi*, who was not only harmless but occasionally quite kind, became very friendly with Sylva. So friendly that she came often at night to visit, leaving at dawn. Sylva's roommates kept their mouths shut, and the subject was not widely discussed except for a few raised eyebrows among the more righteous. The fact was that neither Sylva nor her mother was very hungry from then on, and who was there to judge?

Out of the nightly rap sessions came the memories of the Liberated Theater in Prague and the highly improvised performances of its stars, Voskovec and Werich, who had been the idols of a whole generation of young people for their biting satirical revues and songs. Why not put together a show for Christmas? Some of the inmates had been professional singers, actresses, or writers, and there were lots of enthusiastic amateurs able and more than willing to get in on the fun.

Greta was won over and commissioned to secure permission from Spiess, as they wanted to use the mess hall for the project. Surprised, he consented under the condition that it had to be done in German, and that he and his staff had to see it first. A-4116 took on the technical side, and a committee was formed to write, stage, and direct various skits. A movable stage was built with tables and lights installed. Costumes were made from five hundred handkerchiefs that had just arrived as an allotment in place of shoes, and the SS women graciously offered some makeup supplies.

Annie,* who was a journalist on the staff of the *Prager Tagblatt* in Prague, wrote an original skit about an imprisoned princess (Kitty), her nurse (A-4116), and the white knight (Zdena*) who comes to her rescue and kills the Monster (to be played in the manner of a marionette moved from above on strings).

Another number was a scene from Schubert's *Dreimäderlhaus*, this mainly to satisfy the German taste for kitsch, starring the three camp beauties—Sylva, Eva, and Gerti—dressed in crinolines made of handkerchiefs. Greta did one of her nightclub routines, from twenty years before she became the respectable Mrs. Kohn, and A-4116 freely re-created the monologue play *The Human Voice* by Jean Cocteau that Vava had performed in Terezín. Poor Cocteau.

But the highlight of the production was Zdena, with a group of songs from operettas for the Germans and another one from the revues of V & W and other avant-garde anti-fascist composers. The whole production was an enormous labor of love with daylight hours for rehearsals in short supply and the problem of staging the entire show in two languages. They did not have the slightest intention of making the Czech version as tame as the German one.

Rehearsals were held on two Sundays and late into the nights by the light of one kerosene lamp. For once, everyone worked together without thoughts of selfish gain. The sewing shop stitched costumes without expecting a favor in return, and even Greta and A-4116 managed to be civil to each other.

On Christmas Day, 1944, everything was ready. The lights checked out, the curtain made of four blankets was in place, and the orchestra, consisting of a foursome blowing on combs covered with tissue paper, was ready. Spiess with his retinue marched in. They sat down in the first two rows of benches. The rest of the space was taken by the rank-and-file prisoners sitting at a respectable distance behind. The overture started and—out went all the lights. The power had been cut off.

With a rare show of good nature, Spiess sent out his men to bring all the kerosene lamps from the *Kommandantur*, and the show went on. The curtain opened on Zdena standing alone on the dimly lit stage, actually looking the part of the lonely soldier, standing watch with a piece of wood slung like a rifle over her shoulder, and singing the strangely appropriate lyrics from a German operetta in her husky bronze voice:

Have you above all forsaken me,
the one who yearns so much for love.

You who have angels in heaven with you,
send one down to keep company with me.

The orchestra watched the Germans as they blew on their combs. When Greta did her solo of a lascivious tango, Spiess sat there wetting his lips in total rapture, while the rest of the staff had expressions of absolute disbelief. The audience didn't know what was more entertaining: what was happening on the stage or in front of it. In any case, the evening was such a huge success that when it was over, Spiess ordered Greta and her crew to the *Kommandantur* and they came back with arms full of salami, bread, and pickles for the cast.

The next two evenings the lights stayed on, and the show went even better when the cast could really let loose in their native tongue. The attitude of the Germans changed subtly after this project, with Spiess dropping a remark to Mimi that he had not realized that the inmates were actually ladies, and quite pretty at that. Why, some of them could even be German women!

For a few days nothing but the show was discussed, and morale went up in spite of the foul weather and the countless daily miseries. On the afternoon of New Year's Eve, Spiess even had one of his one-way conversations with A-4116, during which he consoled her that the war would be over soon.

It won't be long now, and you will leave here. You see, our scientists have invented a new weapon. It is top secret, of course, but it is said to be a device that will cut England off from the continent.

But Sturmbannführer, what will England do? Swim to Canada?

Canada? Where's that? Anyway, once the war is over and won, you will all be resettled on a beautiful island called Madagascar. That's what the Führer said.

With this hilarious information A-4116 returned to camp to celebrate the night with her pals. She got stone drunk on nothing stronger than tap water, reinforced by another news bulletin from the Free French that was considerably more optimistic and by an unexpected event: most of the guards came to wish them a Happy New Year.

The year 1945 started with a letdown. The winter was grim, the sick line grew longer every morning, and there was the first death of pneumonia. Spiess insisted that the coffin had to be made in camp and provided a blueprint for a conically shaped chest for A-4116 to make. Her protestations that it was against Jewish law to be buried in anything but a simple box consisting of six rough planks were to no avail, and after watching her trying unsuccessfully to cut the boards according to his specifications, he pushed her away and made the coffin by himself.

Firewood was scarce and the supply limited to whatever the work details could organize among the ruins in town. Besides, the small iron stoves in the barracks did not give enough warmth even when wood was available. Everybody was constantly shivering and coughing. Many started to bring up blood. The water pipes and the latrine drain froze; the contents reached ground level and spilled over. After inspecting the stinky mess, Spiess produced a pair of hip-high rubber boots and a ten-foot iron pole and ordered A-4116 down into the muck to open the drain hole. She poked a few holes into the ice and the shit level fell, but the next morning the drain was frozen solid again.

Every other day, she went down into this stink-pit, until she smelled so foul that even from a distance, everyone who saw her coming made a large detour. Her roommates griped about having to sleep in the same room with her, but to no avail, since there was no other place to go. Kitty tried to make the others see the humor of the situation, but there was not much laughter left now. A few warmer days eventually solved the predicament.

One morning, around the end of the month, Mimi, doubled over with pain, supported by Greta, staggered through camp toward sick bay. A-4116 followed them and stood outside the door in case some help would be needed. But there was not a sound to be heard for many hours. Most of the indoor workers were unaware of the drama being enacted inside. Finally, in the late afternoon before the others returned, the thin wailing of a baby was heard.

A moment later it stopped, and about ten minutes afterward Greta and Dr. K. came out carrying a shoebox and walked toward the gate. After a short exchange with the guard, he accompanied them into the woods adjoining the camp, and sometime later all three returned empty-handed. A veil of silence descended over the event, and three days later Mimi was back at her typewriter in Spiess's office. Much later, Dr. K. said that it had been a healthy boy who could have lived.

At last a communication arrived to send a truck to another camp to receive the repeatedly requisitioned shoes. The delivery foursome arrived, and while their guard went into the office to sign the papers, they waited on a bench in the corridor of the administration building under the supervision of another soldier. He walked around with a decidedly lecherous look in his eyes until he planted himself, legs apart, right in front of them.

So you're the NEW ones.

New ones? What for?

Nu ja, for the brothel, of course.

Oh no, we are Jewesses and we came to get shoes issued for our camp in Neugraben.

As if bitten by a viper, the man turned his back, spat on the floor, and didn't look in their direction again. Loading some one hundred pairs of wooden sandals for five hundred inmates, the girls decided that there were certain advantages to being Jewish after all.

25

The war was going from bad to worse, and even the most patriotic Germans were beginning to have some doubts about the accuracy of newscasts, now telling them of the previously planned regrouping of their forces in order to achieve ultimate victory over the Allies. Spiess and his henchwomen were in a vile mood most of the time, and he went into an insane rage when he discovered another pregnant woman at *Appell*.

The fact that Vera, the *Capo* of Block 2, was expecting a child whose father was Benedetto,* had been known to most inmates for quite some time. Everyone hoped that Mimi's experience would repeat itself, that Greta's diplomatic skill in handling Spiess would keep Vera safe, and that maybe the war would end before the baby's arrival.

Illogically, this time Spiess flatly refused to leave bad enough alone, stood rigidly by the rules, and started proceedings to have Vera transferred to Bergen-Belsen. No separate pleadings by Greta, Mimi, or A-4116 could do anything to make him change his mind.

He only ranted and raged and accused them of trying to take advantage of his fatherly feelings for his prisoners.

A frantic search for Benedetto began, to inform him and get him to come and help Vera escape. Even a few of the guards helped in the effort to locate the Italians. He was actually found and arrived breathless on a Saturday night at the fence, only to discover that it was too late. Vera had been sent away the previous morning under the escort of the SS woman Erika, who was not a person who made deals.

Vera had been immensely popular on her block, with all of her women sharing the task of keeping her reasonably well fed during her pregnancy, accepting the coming baby as their common responsibility. Anyone replacing her was bound to have a hard time at best. The lot fell to A-4116, whom Spiess appointed in his proverbial stinginess since she was working inside the camp anyway. This way he had one more slave to send out.

The reception on Block 2 was predictably chilly when she took up her post. The first few days passed quietly. Then two SS women, accompanied by Greta, came on their regular inspection tour. In Room 2, Erika noticed that the corner of one of the ceiling planks was not flush with the rest and ordered A-4116 up on the bunk to push the plank higher to see what was above. Every inhabitant of this type of barracks knew about these low attics and the fact that they made ideal hiding places. It did not help to announce that there was nothing to be seen up there because now the bitch was up on the bunk herself and discovered a cache of provisions.

Erika ordered everything cleared out and piled on the table, to be taken on a wheelbarrow to the *Kommandantur*: a bag of potatoes, a few turnips, some flour and barley, and some half dozen glass jars with stewed fruit, plus other odds and ends that the inhabitants of the room had organized on their forays into the ruins—all now to be delivered to the Germans. A-4116 was fascinated by a jar of cherries, always her favorite. The temptation to keep them became stronger and stronger. She snatched them and managed to shove them under her bunk.

When the girls returned in the evening from work, they instantly discovered that their hideout had been looted. They descended in righteous fury upon their new *Capo*, whom they accused of having led the SS woman to the place on purpose in order to chalk up good marks with her. No protestations to the contrary helped, and Greta kept her mouth shut partly because she and A-4116 had never been great friends. Also because she resented the fact that Spiess had appointed A-4116, so to speak, over her head.

The commotion had almost died down when one of the girls from Room 2 burst into the block room with a new complaint and found A-4116 eating her cherries. This infuriated the whole block again, being proof of treason, and they embarked on a policy of passive resistance and total contempt. The truth of the matter was that A-4116 did not like what she had done either, but no one was willing to listen to an explanation, much less an apology, and although she felt guilty, she did not consider her action a capital crime.

Trouble started on Sunday when the inmates were supposed to clean up and wheel out the garbage under the supervision of their *Capos*. This Sunday they flatly refused. It had rained all Saturday, and they were sitting half-dressed on their bunks, drying their clothes by a meager fire. When A-4116 asked them to do something, they just told their *Capo* to go to hell. In itself this was not upsetting, since it made little difference whether she wheeled the garbage out six or seven days a week, but it bothered Spiess, whom she ran into on her way to the dump.

What are you doing with that garbage? That's not your job. You have one hundred and sixty prisoners to do this.

The girls came home soaking wet last night, and their clothes haven't dried. I don't mind doing this myself.

I'm not interested in all this Quatsch. What kind of a goddamned Capo are you if you can't make your people work? Demoted. Back to your old block and tomorrow out to work!

Glad to be relieved of an untenable situation, she returned to her old room, where conversation abruptly stopped when she entered. What smarted most was that not even Kitty would speak to her beyond a "How could you?" Hurt by the apparent unwillingness of anybody to listen to her side of the story, she crawled into her shell with only her notebook of letters to Mutti as a companion.

Not long afterward, Erika discovered the book during another of her inspections. Intercepted at the gate at her return from work, A-4116 was promptly whisked into Spiess's office for questioning. Since the letters were written in Czech, Mimi had to give a running translation, which she did in a very perfunctory manner, skipping the most derogatory passages.

You realize that what I'm holding in my hands is an illegal document and that it is my duty to report this and let you bear the consequences? Spiess said.

She only nodded.

Here, he said. *Burn it right now in this stove and scram.*

She opened the top of the stove, saw the flames devour her innermost feelings, and thought, *Maybe it will reach Mutti after all.*

After this incident and after Mimi's retelling of the contents of the notebook that she had read, the attitude of A-4116's roommates softened and, more importantly, Kitty became her old self again.

At the end of February 1945, the camp in Neugraben was reassigned for use by civilians who had been bombed out of their homes. The prisoners were suddenly moved to another place in an industrial section of Hamburg called Tiefstack. During the transfer on open trucks, they saw the immense extent of the destruction of the city. Rows upon rows of streets were level with the ground, with people living in the cellars of the ruins like rats, seemingly not much better off than the prisoners themselves. One look at the new camp was enough to convince anyone with eyes that this was the center of a perfect target for bombings.

The fenced-in group of four wooden barracks was framed in a web of railway tracks with two huge gas tanks and an electrical power station in its immediate vicinity. The air raids now came by day and night, with bombs exploding all around. By some miracle, the camp had not been hit yet. This was so incredible that one came to believe that the British and American pilots had exact maps designating even the smallest prisoner camp. Every night when the girls returned from work, they were astonished to find the place still intact, while everything around seemed on fire. Their admiration for the Allies' intelligence and precision knew no bounds.

26

On March 20, 1945, the sick bay, which now took up two-thirds of one barrack, was full—with almost a quarter of all the prisoners. A-4116 was lying on an upper bunk with a broken toe, due to an accident that had happened the day before: a curbstone had slipped out of her frozen hands and dropped on her foot. Next to her was Kitty, with one of her glandular fevers, when the alert sounded.

Watching from the window, they saw the guards scramble for their bunker, and only minutes later, the formations of the American bombers with their white condensation tails approached. It was really a beautiful sight in the cloudless sky, except that there seemed to be a very strong wind up there blowing their white tracks away very quickly. Just as the onlookers were beginning to worry about what this would do to the accuracy of pinpointing their targets, there was a familiar hiss and the explosion was upon them.

Thrown into the air, they landed facedown on a heap of broken bunks with the roof coming to rest on their backs. Realizing that this must have been a very close hit, they started to call the names of the other girls in the room through the noise of the continuing attack and the moans and cries of the ones trapped below. Some answered, some just whimpered, but many did not.

When the all clear sounded, rescue parties from the neighboring workplaces arrived. The roof was lifted, and incredibly, A-4116 crawled out on her own steam. The next thing she saw was Kitty, being lifted out of the rubble by her shoulders, looking like a rag-doll dredged in dust. One by one, the rest of the girls were brought out and laid on the ground. Twenty were dead, and the rest more or less seriously wounded. Zdena, the girl with the bronze voice, and Annie, the author of the whimsical fairy-tale skit—both dead. Dr. K. had a broken back and so many other injuries that she would never walk again. Only the coincidence that she had been on her rounds had saved her life.

The bomb had directly hit the treatment room at one end of the barrack. Only the girls in the top cots of their bunks had gotten away with relatively lesser injuries. The barrack was now a pile of broken lumber and glass. There was not one unbroken window in the other houses, and not one door would stay closed. There was indescribable chaos when the rest of the inmates came back from work, and had to take in the victims.

Spiess put all his men in a cordon around the compound to prevent escapes through the partly damaged fences. Even so, five or six girls managed to get away that night and survived the war hiding in the ruins of the city. Once again, A-4116 and Kitty debated the possibility of escape, but decided against it, since one was exhausted by fever and the other could not walk very well. Their coats with the yellow crosses were also a problem: without them, they would freeze. They were deep in German territory with not the slightest inkling about the direction of the front lines, and the dangers seemed to outweigh the advantages.

That night Spiess personally supervised the soup distribution. Outside it was raining and windy, and the draft constantly blew open all the doors. A-4116 was standing last in line when he shouted at her to close the door. She limped over and shut it, but two minutes later the wind had blown it open again.

Verflucht nochmal ("Damn it to hell"), I told you to shut that door, he bellowed.

Damn it, I did shut it! she yelled back.

At this, he grabbed one of the heavy earthen soup bowls and threw it at her. She ducked. The bowl crashed against the wall when she was already through the open door, and the shots from his revolver went out into the night. From now on, she kept out of his sight, stood in the last row at *Appell,* and made herself as inconspicuous as possible.

The next days were nightmares. When alerts sounded, the girls were herded into a barn that was still standing outside the compound and bolted inside, while the guards ran for cover in their bunker. A-4116 finally lost her aloofness and pleasure in air raids and was seized by abysmal terror every time the bombs started to fall. Standing packed like sardines in the barn, they were all trembling, crying, praying, or simply in a state of shock, unable to contain their bowels or bladders.

There were no more hits, but whenever they went outside, they could see that the whole city was a sea of flames. Even so, they were still sent to work every single day.

On April 5, they were suddenly lined up in the morning and loaded into freight cars to be evacuated. The train moved for an hour, then stopped in the middle of nowhere for two hours, moved again, stopped, went backward, moved again. For twenty-four hours. From time to time they were let out to urinate on the side of the tracks, covered by the soldiers with guns. Three times the train was attacked by low-flying planes. The guards scrambled for cover under the cars while the prisoners were locked inside.

During one of these stops Erna, who was a native of Hamburg, was persuaded—literally forced—by her companions to run away. She hesitated, being unfamiliar with the area, but mainly because she was loath to leave the herd. Finally, while the others created all kinds of little disturbances to distract the soldiers, she crawled away under the cars and disappeared into the night.

The following day the train reached Bergen-Belsen. There ensued a long hassle between Spiess and the *Lagerkommandant*, who refused to accept any more prisoners regardless of where the orders came from, while the train engineer refused to take them back. At last they were unloaded and brought inside the camp.

The ghoulish sight that greeted them topped anything they had seen to date.

In a quadrangle one mile long and some four hundred yards wide were forty thousand people who looked like corpses and thirteen thousand unburied real corpses. Those were strewn in heaps of about fifty to one hundred all over the place. Some sort of death dance seemed to be in progress, with one of the living dragging a dead one by the feet toward the mass graves—in slow motion, despite the shouts and kicks of the SS to hurry up. The ground in and out of the huts was crawling with lice. They formed a line—like ants—away from the corpses and toward the living.

There was no food. Water was scarce. Some people were eating dirty grass; most were just sitting or lying around, waiting to die. Some of the piled-up corpses still had a flicker of life in them. One of the newly arrived girls found her cousin with her eyelids still moving. With the help of friends, she pulled her out and incredibly brought her back to life. Asking around among the older inmates for Vera, they discovered that she had died of spotted typhus before her baby was born.

The few friends the girls did find called out to them; otherwise one could not recognize anybody. These were only skeletons covered with a gray, parchment-like skin, and eyes sunk deep in their sockets. Aside from wandering aimlessly in search of friends or relatives or for something edible, there was nothing to do but pick off each other's lice.

Still, the obligatory *Appell* was called twice a day with German thoroughness, a pointless undertaking since no one could possibly produce an accurate count anymore. People who were alive in the morning would be dead by noon. The sleeping quarters were largely empty huts, with most of the bunks having been used up for firewood. There were no pallets or blankets, and they were so overcrowded that the inhabitants had to sleep on the bare floor with their heads on somebody else's buttocks.

The typhus epidemic had started only two months before, when two cases were brought in from Hungary. There was no need for gas chambers now that people were dying at a rate of 250 to 300 per day. There was talk about cannibalism in the men's section, and considering that many corpses had a piece of their thighs chopped out, it was very probably true.

Once, there was a sudden distribution of bread rations, although the food distribution had come to a virtual standstill days before. The starved inmates sunk their teeth into the bread only to discover a strange grating sound while chewing: ground glass baked into the dough. Nobody knows how many people died of intestinal bleeding because many ate it regardless of the danger. It was not easy to think rationally anymore, being so hungry that objects and people began to double in front of one's eyes.

The SS was still putting on a show of strict discipline in their polished high boots with their whips swinging right and left, but one morning the camp woke up to discover that they had all gone, disappeared without a trace. Instead, Himmler's Hungarian SS had taken over their posts.

Naively, some of the prisoners believed that the Brownshirts would be more lenient than their predecessors, but these were absolute maniacs who shot from their rifles at anyone who came within ten yards of the barbed wire. The battlefront was coming closer all the time. One could hear the artillery all around the camp; it sounded as though they were being bypassed on all sides.

A strange new prisoner showed up in the Czech group that day. It was Sylva's friend Bubi, the SS woman from Neugraben, who arrived dressed in a brand-new striped prison shift and simply stayed, while nobody paid the slightest attention to her. On April 13 and 14, nobody left the huts anymore, because the Hungarians used their rifles the moment anyone showed her head out of the door—using it for target practice.

The door was open a crack when on the morning of April 15 one of the girls remarked in a toneless voice that there was a tank coming down the center road.

We're probably going to be machine-gunned now, someone replied.

There's a white star on the side of it, the hatch is open, and the soldiers are wearing black berets, the same girl insisted.

Go to hell with your fairy tales, somebody grumbled, but a few others, unable to resist their curiosity, crawled to the door to look. She was right. The tank was no mirage. Nor the star on its side, nor the long convoy of vehicles that followed it.

The British were finally here, the Union Jack fluttered in the wind, but the inmates were too far gone to take in the reality of it or feel joy. Hesitantly, still expecting to be shot at, they ventured out of the huts one by one. As the truth became clearer, they began to walk, crawl, and run to the fences to see their liberators close up. One after another, the armored vehicles came down the road, with the soldiers turning their pockets inside out and throwing the contents—chocolate bars, K rations, cigarettes, and other little things—over the fences and lifting their fingers in a V salutation. Many of them were crying. The things they threw immediately caused scores of bloody battles among the starved prisoners.

Somewhat later, Brigadier General Glyn Hughes made a walking tour of the camp, with his aides requesting everyone to keep calm and asking people with some knowledge of English to come forward and help with the food distribution and first aid. Tears were streaming down the general's cheeks, which he made no attempt to hide at the sight of the abysmal misery. People wanted to touch him and his men, to kiss their hands, but the soldiers had orders to keep a distance of ten feet, not being immune to typhus.

By afternoon, big lorries drove up to deliver food for distribution that the Britons had evidently found in the first German storehouse they took over. A two-pound can of meat from Czechoslovakia and a small can of condensed milk per person. Kitty dug in with her fingers and ate the contents of pork—40 percent of which was pure lard—in one sitting, washing it down with the undiluted condensed milk. A-4116 was sure she would die within hours from dysentery, since she herself was unable to force down even a mouthful.

The next day the British opened the no-man's-land between the two barbed-wire fences, making the entire compound accessible to men and women, and threw open the doors to the German storehouses. Here were several buildings with huge red crosses painted on their roofs, containing enough foodstuff and clothing to provide for an army, let alone the forty thousand inmates of Bergen-Belsen. With suicidal greed, every person still in an ambulatory state crowded into these storehouses, using the doors and windows alike. In a state of mass hysteria, people literally drowned, their heads inside barrels of pickles, mustard, prune butter, and the like, while others tried to get in over them.

A-4116 and Kitty watched the scene from the outside, feeling too weak to join the battle. But later, when they noticed their skeleton-like comrades emerging from another, less crowded store-house, dressed up in German uniforms and boots, they ventured inside. They helped themselves to two magnificent military fur-lined greatcoats, which reached all the way to the floor, and a tent.

Thus equipped, they occupied one of the deserted watchtowers in the no-man's-land in order to get away from the lice. It did not upset them that right in front of it was a heap of corpses that seemed to change facial expressions with the different light of day or night. Nor did it bother them that the little tower was open on all sides, just a sort of balcony ten feet off the ground and very cold and drafty. After putting up the tent against the wind, they wrapped themselves in their fur coats and slept like princesses in their castle.

27

The following days were very strange indeed. There was, of
course, no way of letting the camp population simply go
home while an enormous epidemic was going on. Our
situation was suddenly reversed: former prisoners strolled through
the camp watching SS men and women brought in to bury the
dead and do all other dirty work.

Within three days they looked exactly like the inmates. Under
the guard of British Tommies and groups of jeering prisoners, they
were now taunted and prodded to work *Schneller, faster, you bitch,
you bastard*. Bodily injury was not tolerated by the soldiers, but
otherwise they thoroughly enjoyed the exchange of roles between
the prisoners and their former tormentors.

Bubi's presence had been reported on the first day of the liberation. She had been arrested and was now working with the other
SS women. One of the youngest survivors of the Czech group, a
little guttersnipe who had grown up in camp, took a particularly
vicarious pleasure in watching, and once conveyed to the British

guard through a highly effective pantomime that she wanted the boots one of the SS women was wearing. It took a while for him to comprehend what she wanted, but then he gave a big grin and walked over to the woman and ordered. *Du Frau. Boots off. Stiefel,* someone shouted. *Shtee-fell, off,* he repeated, pointing with his bayonet. She finally understood and the little one walked away to the applause of the surrounding bystanders.

There were some feeble suggestions that Sylva could maybe put in a good word for Bubi, since she had really been harmless and, in Sylva's case, definitely helpful in keeping her mother above water, but Sylva was too busy flirting with the Tommies at a ten-foot distance to be bothered.

British organization of the rescue operations was a model of efficiency, and within a few days, people were not only regularly fed but an evacuation to quarantine facilities in Celle began. This was a gigantic logistical problem, because every person had to be deloused, and his clothing burned and replaced with clean garments. Thanks to DDT, nobody's hair had to be shaven. The sick had priority and were the first to leave.

One week after liberation, A-4116 and Kitty were in the first group of volunteers chosen to help with the registration and repatriation. They left Belsen on a small pickup truck with a British lieutenant and his driver and five other English-speaking freed prisoners. When they arrived on the parade square of the garrison in Celle and were helped from the truck, A-4116 fell straight into the officer's arms.

This is a very sick girl was the last thing she heard, and the next thing she knew was being in bed in a hospital ward, being asked over and over again her name and country of origin, and being unable to remember. A little doctor, herself a former prisoner recovering from typhus, examined her and said, *Sorry, girl, but you got it.*

After that, she drifted in and out of consciousness. She mustered a fierce effort to drag herself to the pail in the corner whenever she had to use the john, aware that whenever she opened her eyes, one of her companions was being carried out feetfirst, covered by a sheet. And those were always the ones who had been unable to hold their bowels and bladders the day before.

Most of the patients were delirious at one time or other, and once, one of them got out of her bed, staggered over to A-4116, and, mistaking her for an SS woman, tried to strangle her. Day after day, during the few lucid moments when the fever dropped, A-4116 tried to remember who she was and where she was but, tired out by the effort, drifted again away into another world.

After more than two weeks of twilight, she awakened in a state of absolute panic. Sitting straight up in bed, she screamed for someone to open a window, claiming that she was choking to death. Gasping for air, she was sure of hearing gunshots all around, and terrified that the Germans were returning, she insisted on getting up and running away. Two nurses and an injection finally quieted her down, and she sank into deep sleep.

28

When I woke up later the same day, the sun was shining through the windows and the room seemed different than it had been before. The girl who had tried to strangle me was smiling with clear eyes and explained in her accented German that now I would be all right, that the crisis was over. My temperature had dropped almost back to normal, and I learned that the gunshots I had heard were real: they had been fired in celebration of the armistice. It was May 8, 1945.

Very weak, but with a clear mind, I marveled at the white sheets and the cleanliness of the room I found myself in. I was the only Czech there. The other patients were all Hungarian. The doctor and nurses were mostly Polish, freed prisoners who were all immune to typhus because they had survived it earlier in Belsen. Ironically, with this mixture of nationalities, the only common language was German.

The British ran and supervised the hospitals, but did not come into direct contact with the patients. Their presence, though, was very much in evidence, and every day a cart pushed by a Tommy would appear with some delightful surprise. Cigarettes, which I could not smoke yet but kept under my pillow just to look at the picture on the package of Player's; a cake of Ivory soap; and one of my greatest pleasures: pajamas printed all over with little flowers, made in Canada. There were also other goodies like candy, chocolate, and cookies—none of which I could digest as yet. Between naps, I tried to unravel the puzzle of why Kitty had not come to visit me, fearing that she, too, had come down with typhus and maybe died. In a state of total lethargy, I pushed away thoughts of my parents and Joe, resolving to think about it later.

Every day someone came in writing down data and names of next of kin for almost everyone except myself. They seemed to include all nationalities but no Czechs. I grew very impatient because I could not understand the reason, and complained bitterly to the doctor until at last a registrar arrived one morning to whom I voiced my indignation. When I told her my name, she gave out a cry of surprise, telling me that poor Kitty had spent the last weeks poring over lists and lists of hospital inmates, trying without success to find my name. Now she was visiting one hospital barrack after another in the hope of discovering my whereabouts.

The explanation was very simple. I had been brought into the ward without identification, and put into the first empty bed available. This happened to be in a room full of Hungarians. It was assumed that I was one of them. I was, consequently, recorded only by my number, A-4116, on the Hungarian lists, which Kitty evidently didn't look at.

Now she arrived, making her entrance like an apparition from another world: her honey-blond hair in a shiny pageboy, wearing lipstick and mascara, and dressed in a pretty print dress with white sandals. All her abscesses had healed and she smiled from ear to ear, speaking in Czech.

Francinko, I thought I had lost you, and I really couldn't go home without you. I'm getting you out of here—you'll only die in this joint. I've already started to negotiate with your doctor. I have a car outside with my British factotum, and I'm not leaving you out of my sight for one more minute.

I was flabbergasted by her appearance. The doctor, who had joined us in the meantime, voiced her alarm at Kitty's idea, considering me much too weak for transportation. She warned that my diet needed to be supervised and that a relapse was almost always fatal.

Kitty would have none of it. She argued that she was perfectly capable of taking care of me, and after signing an affidavit that she assumed complete responsibility, it was agreed that she could pick me up the following day. Kitty arrived with an armful of clothes and told me to get out of my pajamas and get dressed. I flatly refused to let go of my prized sole possession that had come all the way from Canada. A little tiff ensued, but she won again.

With a warning from the doctor to take it easy and treat me with care and to feed me only small amounts of food at a time, we left in a jeep driven by a sergeant, who introduced himself as Sunshine. After a short, wild ride, during which Sunshine had to grab me at every curve to prevent my falling out, we arrived at a modern brick army barrack, where Kitty had her own room with two large, comfortable beds overlooking the garrison square.

I was put to bed, this time in a polka-dotted nightgown. Kitty left the radio on for me and told me to be a good girl, and that she would return soon. Two hours later, she found me semiconscious on the bathroom floor. Mindful of the doctor's orders, Kitty had removed everything edible to what she believed was beyond my reach, but soon after she left me alone, I started exploring my new quarters and discovered two large bowls on top of the wardrobe. With great effort I climbed a chair and ate the goulash with sauerkraut in no time at all. The result was predictable.

After this mishap, Kitty always arranged for me to have a baby-sitter whenever she had work to do. She recruited anyone from a fellow former prisoner up to the rank of captain in the British Army for the job. She was working as a liaison with the Repatriation Division and had a wide circle of friends. At teatime, she invariably brought along at least two or three officers, and under their combined tender loving care I began slowly to feel better.

One of them was a doctor, who suggested a rotating system of therapeutic junkets into the countryside "out of the camp atmosphere" once the quarantine was lifted. The atmosphere in the camp was anything but oppressive compared to what we had been used to, but it was a lovely thought. Our saviors showed infinite kindness, concern, and tact—never overt pity. Even though I was extremely hard of hearing and my hair was falling out in huge bunches as an aftereffect of my illness, they made me feel young, female, and attractive again.

Although Kitty and I never discussed it in so many words, we both felt a definite reluctance to go back home and face the balance sheet of the last years. At first, the quarantine was a good-enough reason for not being able to go; later, I was too weak to travel. But May became June, and though many busloads of survivors were being sent home, we made no motions to repatriate ourselves. Our friend Eva had left for Prague with the first bus and had come back with not-quite-unexpected dismal news. All our parents were dead. Joe was missing. Eva's husband was dead, and Kitty's fiancé, Ivan, had married another girl in February. Not ready to face the situation at home, Eva had come back to us and her job with repatriation.

Under these circumstances there seemed to be even less hurry to leave, especially since—at twenty-three and twenty-five—Kitty and I were having a rather good time working, playing, going to Red Cross officers' dances, and enjoying being the center of attention. The more I thought of Joe, the less I wanted to go back to him. I was seeing a lot of a young British captain who was one of my volunteer drivers and who had started to give me driving lessons.

Jason was tall and dark-haired, with the typical pink complexion of an Englishman, uninterested in small talk and a master of understatement. It took me a while to discover that what I initially took for dullness was really extreme reserve. Scratch the surface and one found the intelligence and compassion of a somewhat shy man. While out on a driving lesson, I once became frightened by a lorry entering the road and crashed into a tree. We were not seriously hurt, but still needed some attention because Jason was bleeding from a cut on his forehead and I had a gash on my knee.

The soldiers from the lorry, worried about being the indirect cause of an accident with an officer, took us to the nearest hospital—a German hospital. It suddenly occurred to me that we were surrounded only by German personnel. While I was sure that they would not harm Jason for fear of reprisals, I panicked at the idea of having a German doctor touch me. Clutching Jason's hand, I insisted that nobody could come near me unless he was present.

On our way back to Celle, Jason took my hand and said, *You will have to learn not to be afraid. These people can't hurt you anymore.* Maybe so, but just to bear me out, a few days later when we returned from a walk in the heather, we found all four tires of the jeep slashed.

29

After I told Jason about the news that Eva had brought from Prague, our relationship became rather close, although there were certain subjects we never discussed. The recent past was carefully avoided, so much that when we went to see a movie—*Song of Russia*, as I recall—and it was preceded by a newsreel showing the liberation of Bergen-Belsen, I watched in total detachment, incredulous about what I was seeing. One of the shots showed two girls standing in a former watchtower next to a pile of corpses, waving to the camera.

My God, that's you and Kitty! exclaimed Jason, with very uncharacteristic excitement.

Oh, no, I said, *it couldn't be.* But I was shaken.

Kitty, who had lived on the fixed idea that she would get married right after the war since she had received her one and only letter from her fiancé, Ivan, now drowned her sorrow in rounds of parties and an involvement with our friend Major Dr. Jack, whom we knew to be a married man. Romances were blossoming all over, and quite a few of our girls married Englishmen without ever returning home.

Others stayed on for different reasons. The Polish Jews did not want to return to their homeland and were waiting to establish contact with whomever was left of their families in order to emigrate to Palestine or America. The Red Cross was the meeting place of the camp, and maintained a huge bulletin board of announcements and messages from all over the world.

Among the Czechs, the people from small towns who spoke little German and had been the most assimilated of all Czech Jews were most eager to return, but many who had been brought up in German schools were unsure of the reception that awaited them. In part, this was because Czechoslovakia had started a vigorous campaign of expulsion of all German elements in the population—with the exception of the Jews, to be sure, but German-speaking Jews were by no means certain that they would be welcomed back. Even our group, which was entirely Czech, was in many cases confused and worried about just what our welcome would be like.

True enough, the representative of the Czechoslovak government, Captain Sejnoha, and the drivers of the buses who came to Celle to bring us home were urging us to come and worked tirelessly at the colossal job of getting the flock together. But in our eyes, these were idealists, who perhaps, just perhaps, were not totally representative of the general population. The mere fact that they were driving dilapidated buses, running on little woodblocks, for thousands of miles all around the Russian zone—because the Russians refused to give them transit permits—proved that they were the ones who had always been our friends. Alienated as we were and schooled in the effectiveness of six years of German propaganda, many of us were unable to grasp their outstretched hand.

For the moment, the status quo seemed perfectly acceptable even though we were still living in a military compound. We were fed, there was no rent to pay, most of our modest wishes were taken care of, and entertainment was thrown in as a bonus.

When he left Prague in 1941, Joe and I had agreed on a place to meet or send mail at the end of the war. I now wrote him a long letter in care of our friends, letting him know that I was alive, but also explaining that I had changed very much and that I did not want to return to him. Without putting the blame on either one of us, I tried to make clear that we had rushed into marriage under highly unusual circumstances and that I suspected that I was not exactly made for wedlock. I asked him not to come to Celle to try to make me change my mind, that I needed to think things through, and that in many ways I felt as if my life was just beginning and that I needed my freedom.

It was not Jason who made me write that letter, because our relationship—though close—also had a definite remoteness about it, filling a need in both of us at a given time in our lives. I did not know too much about his life in England, out of uniform, and did not ask—probably because I was not ready or able to fall in love with anybody. He, in turn, accepted me for what I was, including my long silences, and simply made himself available whenever I wanted his company.

In addition to our male friends, Kitty and I also had a protectress in the form of Colonel M.,* the South African lady who headed the Red Cross and who, for no apparent reason, had taken a great liking to the two of us. She even approved of our constant companionship with the two officers, although she was known in other cases not to be all that tolerant. She chaperoned the dances and preferred to use her matchmaking talents in favor of her own Women's Royal Army Corps. Maybe it was our facility in English that made us different in her eyes. She constantly gave us presents, took me to the dentist when I had an infected tooth, and generally mothered us.

I was much better now. My hair was growing back in little tufts, and with the parties came a renewed interest in clothes. I decided, to Kitty's delight, to make some of the beautiful Canadian beige and blue blankets into skirts and Eisenhower jackets, and was handicapped only by the fact that we did not own a sewing machine.

When we brought this problem up with Colonel M., she sent Sunshine to drive us into the country to requisition one somewhere, which he did with pleasure. We picked a nice-looking house at random in a pleasant residential area and rang the bell. A woman opened the door, and in that moment, I could see the exact same fear in her eyes that I felt when a German uniform showed up at my front door years before. When she discovered that Sunshine only wanted her sewing machine, she was so obviously relieved that she offered us thread and other supplies with it. Sunshine gave her a receipt and I went to work.

Then came the day toward the end of July when our friends

came in full force to have a heart-to-heart talk with us and a few other girls. They had rather solemn faces and had brought Colonel M. along for moral support. They told us that they were going to be replaced by new occupation forces, and that they wished for our sakes and their own peace of mind for us to return home. They suspected that the attitude of soldiers who had not been part of the liberation of Bergen-Belsen would be quite different toward us and that it would be difficult for them to comprehend the difference between a liberated Jewish prisoner and a German *Fräulein*.

This was quite true, as I had already discovered a few nights earlier when I had been dancing with a newly arrived major from Scotland. While doing the swing, he in his kilt and I dressed in US Navy pants, he remarked that he found it somewhat bizarre to have one's telephone number tattooed on one's arm. Angered by his stupidity, I had left him standing on the dance floor wondering what had made me behave in such a rude way. Colonel M. had winced and now added her voice to the convincing sincerity of the others.

They were right, of course. It was high time for us to go home. The parting was bittersweet, singly and collectively. During the following days, our liberators showered us with a trousseau of blankets, cases of soap, canned food, cigarettes, even German money. When Kitty and I were packed, we had between us thirteen pieces of luggage, plus a radio. Too much to take on the bus, and as we did not trust anybody with our possessions, we decided that Kitty would take the old sightseeing bus that was shuttling between Prague and Celle, while I would follow on a truck with the baggage in the company of three young male prisoners and the driver Pepik.

30

It was the first week in August of 1945 when these two conveyances started off toward home. The truck was an antique, and by nightfall, we had lost sight of the bus. None of the men spoke English, and our vehicle got stuck every fifty or sixty miles with clockwork precision. It was trouble enough to find the necessary fuel, but after we passed into the American zone, the mechanical problems became staggering. The American GIs could not understand why anybody in his right mind would drive a piece of junk like this and offered helpful advice—we should leave it in a ditch instead of trying to repair it.

It took all my powers of persuasion to explain that we were political prisoners going home to Czechoslovakia, which had been an occupied country for the past six years, and that most vehicles in Europe were in similar shape. Since I assumed the US Army was not willing to make us a present of one of their own trucks, would they please try and help us make ours roadworthy for the trip to

Prague? Most of the time they rose to the challenge through their mechanical skills, and treated it as they would a jigsaw puzzle.

Compared to the British, I found the American GIs amusingly naive, curious, and direct. They had no inhibitions whatsoever when it came to questions about the tattoo on my arm and propositions that could be warded off by a simple *no*. Except one, who gave advice to his buddies left and right about how to fix a disintegrating part and who turned out to be a taxi driver from New York. Intrigued by a lone English-speaking girl in the company of what must have looked to him like four hobos, he asked, *Why?* Noting that the repair job would take a few hours, he offered me his bed and affections, including some hot chocolate and Spam. My reply that I was not interested and that I was no German *Fräulein* made no impression on him, but he went on his way.

We could only drive during daylight, not trusting our vehicle (now christened Rocinante, after Don Quixote's horse) at nighttime, when it was nearly impossible to find help. We were unable to do more than some 150 miles per day at best. This left us (or rather myself) with the problem of a place to sleep. The boys never wanted to leave Rocinante unattended, and slept on top of the baggage. Every night, some attentive American noncom materialized, and offered to commandeer lodgings for me.

This sometimes led to comic situations, because I was afraid of all Germans and, if there were any around, also requested a bodyguard. South of Kassel, which we had passed through one afternoon, we had to stop, and the American sergeant on duty in the area went into the first private house to ask for a bed for me. After a lot of hemming and hawing that they had nothing suitable for a guest, it was agreed to make room for me on the living room sofa.

Sergeant Bob left after assuring me that he would be around and that I should just yell out of the window in case of need. Distrustful of my reluctant hosts, I settled fully dressed on the sofa. An hour later, the grandfather of the household, an old man reminding me of Spiess, walked in to ask whether I was comfortable. He rambled on to assure me that nobody in the German population had known what was going on in the concentration camps.

Dripping with phony pity, he started patting my tattooed arm as my panic grew with every second. Finally, I jumped up and ran to the window, screaming, *Bob, Bob! HELP!* He was inside the house in an instant, chased the old lecher away, and took me to another house on the same street, where a young woman lived with her small child. She put me next to her, in her missing husband's bed, assuring Bob that I would be well taken care of. There was something about her that made me suspect that this was not the first time she had met Bob and that, maybe, I was taking up his usual place.

On our journey through postwar Germany that summer of 1945, the vast destruction of the "thousand-year Reich" was manifest. Like Hamburg and Bremen, the large coastal ports, inland cities like Kassel and Schweinfurt were almost entirely in ruins. The members of the German population I came into contact with were, in my judgment, just as repulsive in their new servility to their conquerors as they had been in their former righteous and blind obedience to their *Führer*.

In Bad Hersfeld, we had to wait several hours for repairs. I met the commanding officer, Major Klein, a Jew from Philadelphia whose family had originally come from Czechoslovakia. Over a breakfast of powdered eggs, bacon, and Nescafé he asked me a thousand questions in his agonizing search to find a trace of his relatives. He did everything in his power to make our Rocinante capable of finishing the second half of our trip—something of a miracle since, by now, our fenders were held up by ropes and our brakes practically nonexistent. Luckily, Rocinante did not do more than thirty miles per hour, and on downgrades Pepik used to brake her by shifting into low gear. We eventually reached the Czech border near Tachov. Here we left the American zone and I met my first Russian.

While Pepik went into the guardhouse to check our travel papers, a little squat soldier with a bazooka and a red star on his cap ogled me curiously. Unable to communicate in any other language, he pointed his finger to my mouth and asked in Russian, *Ty Kurva?* (Are you a whore?) Even we understood this, and the boys on top of the truck burst out laughing. Pepik, who had returned, now informed our friend and liberator that most girls in Europe wore lipstick and that it was not necessarily a sign of loose morals.

We went on to Plzeň, where I hoped Kitty would be waiting, since she had a half sister married to a Christian doctor living in that city. But we discovered that the bus had discharged the people from this region, waited for us for two days, and left that morning for Prague, its driver believing that we must have crossed the border at another place. We unloaded the baggage marked for Plzeň and decided to push on to Prague no matter how long it would take, even though it was already dark.

From the moment we crossed the border, I had been overwhelmed by my love for the Bohemian countryside as by an avalanche, and my excitement mounted with every mile. At three a.m., on an up-grade some ten miles out of Prague, Rocinante sputtered, coughed, and refused to budge. At the end of his endurance, Pepik let out a juicy, familiar *Do prdele!* (an untranslatable Czech curse akin to *Oh shit!*) and threw himself across the cab-seat, announcing that he was going to sleep. I begged, cajoled, and offered to push Rocinante to no avail. He was already loudly snoring.

Frustrated, I walked up a few hundred yards to the top of the hill, from where I could see the aura of light over Prague while being stuck with a broken truck and a snoring driver. It just did not seem fair.

As it was getting a little lighter, Pepik woke up. After a look at my unhappy face, he opened the hood and poked around in the motor. In desperation, he gave the whole thing a violent kick, and surprisingly, the engine started. We drove into the city at five a.m., bypassing the ostensible triviality of the required quarantine and registration station, directly to the house of a former school chum of Kitty's, where we had planned our rendezvous. The whole street woke up from the noise we made as she, Jirka, his mother, and his grandmother ran down to welcome us. I was home almost exactly three years after I had left.

31

B ut was it really *home*? Here I was with three lovely people I had met ten minutes before, who fussed over food as if they had to make up for all the undernourishment we had suffered for three years in one meal, in a tiny three-room apartment that they were ready and happy to share with us.

After breakfast and a few telephone calls, we left for downtown. Like well-trained dogs, we walked back to the last car of the tram and stood on the rear platform although there were plenty of empty seats inside, not realizing that all the offensive signage about Jews had disappeared. I was to meet Max, a family friend who was married to a Christian, and at whose home Joe and I had agreed before the war to meet or leave messages.

The city was glorious in the sunshine, with relatively little damage. Since it hadn't been bombed, it looked the same as it had looked for hundreds of years—yet to me, not quite so. Stores had different names, and all these people in civilian clothes struck me as an unusual sight. I felt out of place in my cheap little cotton dress and bare legs among the still-chic, though rather dated, elegance of the late-morning crowd in Wenceslas Square.

Max looked somewhat ill at ease in his meticulously tailored prewar suit, not sure of what to say or do. First, he handed me the unopened letter I had written to Joe. My husband was dead, he said. It had never occurred to me that Joe might not survive, and a wave of shame and regret engulfed me for having written that letter. After awkwardly passing me a thousand crowns to tide me over the first few days, he invited me for dinner and, with some excuse, left.

After that, I went to the Jewish community center to find out about the process of becoming a full-fledged citizen again and about the possibility of obtaining an apartment. I did not own a single document—all my papers had been handed in three years before. I filled out endless forms, and was given a list of addresses where I might get copies of my papers. I was informed that there was a tremendous housing shortage, that single people had no right to an apartment of their own, and that families and married couples had preference. I looked through the lists of the dead and missing and the places to which they had been deported, and left so depressed that I would have taken the first bus back to Germany if that would have solved anything.

I then dropped in at my former place of business. Marie welcomed me with the same embarrassed expression as Max, immediately pointing out that nothing of mine was on the premises anymore. She had put everything in storage toward the end of the war, in the event of any accusation from the Czech authorities that she could have enriched herself with Jewish property. She also hastened to make clear to me that none of our old customers were coming to her and her husband, who was a tailor, anymore. They had refurnished the place at their own expense, and with the lease in her new name: it was all theirs.

I got the message loud and clear and left to visit Max and his family. There I was served dinner on my own tablecloth. We drank out of my mother's glasses without the slightest indication on their part that this could possibly seem strange to me. I was too embarrassed for them to comment, but did ask during our conversation what had happened to Joe's clothes that I had left with them. I didn't have much to wear for the winter and could alter some of his suits for myself.

They were telling me about the terribly hard times they had all been through and the fact that a lot of our stuff had been bartered for food when the older boy, now eighteen, came into the door dressed in Joe's suit. Alena blushed and I quickly reassured her that it did not matter, that I understood, and that the suit looked better on Jarousek than it would on me anyway. But I did *not* understand. Not then and even less when the same scene in different variations repeated itself over and over in the next few weeks.

There were, of course, many others who had an entirely different reaction to my return, but it was difficult to shake off the initial bitterness. I went to a small town to visit a former customer of ours, with whom my mother had left a certain amount of money and her diamond earrings. My mother had made this client's wedding dress, and now she, her mother, and her husband welcomed me like a long-lost child. They gave me triple the sum that was due to me, maintaining that money had lost that much of its value, and they did not want to let me leave. Having no children of their own, they even came up with the idea of legally adopting me. I appreciated their good intentions, but found it impossible after a few days to accept the idea of living in a small town with relative strangers.

There were others who invited me to their houses and fussed over me, trying to arrange my life and always a little uneasy about inadvertently hurting my feelings. I came to hate the clichés that I was being drowned in.

How you people could survive is a miracle!

Nobody before the war had ever referred to me as *you people.*

I also heard, *You have no idea how much starvation we had to suffer here. Everything was on coupons!*

And, *A pretty, clever girl like you will get married again in no time, and all your problems will be over.*

These phrases and dozens more like them infuriated me, and I found I could relax only in the company of my surviving friends from Terezín. Some of them who had returned early after liberation were living in apartments confiscated from the Germans. Others were again living in their old homes, especially if they had owned the building, although very often without a stick of furniture. With these friends, at least, I did not feel apologetic for my existence. They tried to cheer me up, assuring me that I would adjust, that things had a way of falling into place—and, by the way, why on earth had I taken so long to come back? All things considered, we were alive, and what else did I want?

That was obviously true, but for the first time in six years, I felt drained of all my energy, confused, tired, and hopelessly alone. Now it was Kitty who pushed me to do this or that, to collect my possessions, to go out, to do something—that is, when she found the time in her growing social life.

She had come up with a place to stay for the two of us with the family of her former boss, who had a large, underutilized apartment on the Old Town Square facing the monument of Jan Hus. They offered us a room under the assumption that Kitty would eventually marry the forty-five-year-old bachelor who had been in love with her ever since she started working for his firm as a teenager. He had been waiting for her to grow up for years. He had even been imprisoned for two years, after being caught leaving the ghetto after one of his clandestine visits to Kitty and her parents in Terezín. For the time being at least, we had a roof over our head.

Unlike Kitty, I was incapable of responding to the kindness and concern of people, yet desperately lost without their company. The bureaucracy was driving me crazy. It took weeks to get copies of my documents. I was offered a job as a multilingual assistant with an export firm, attractive because it would entail immediate travel. When I applied for a passport, it proved necessary, in addition to my other papers, to provide proof of my registration as a Czech national in the census of 1930. After a wait of two weeks, I received a slip of paper in the mail, with the information that my father had entered *German* as his and my nationality. Disgusted, I tore up the official notification, which prevented or held up the issuance of a passport, regardless of the fact that I was a Czech citizen, born in the Czechoslovak Republic, and had been ten years old at the time of the census. I later substituted proof of my schooling in French schools, which were considered the equivalent of a Czech education, but by then the job had been filled by someone else.

I had no motivation to look for another job and no desire to reopen my old business. Having no financial worries, with a little money, a government pension, and few expenses, I just drifted along. Walking the streets for hours, I imagined my parents on every familiar corner. The only place that could lift me out of this melancholy state was Smetana Hall, the home of the Czech Philharmonic. Music was the only language that had not acquired a double meaning for me.

Meanwhile I went out with a number of different men, hating to have to sit at home and stare into an empty room. I got involved in some quite impossible situations. I was seeing entirely too much of a married man, a former friend of Joe's whose mother had been in Terezín while he, married to a Christian girl and the father of two technically Aryan children, had survived comfortably in Prague. He had become obsessed with the notion that his dead mother had wanted him to marry me, because she had once said— years before, when I was introduced to her as Joe's fiancée—that I was the kind of girl he should have married. I was completely indifferent to his intentions, but also to the feelings of his wife, who tried to commit suicide when she discovered where and with whom her husband spent most of his time. Evidently, her mother-in-law's pronouncement had been a bone of contention in many a marital argument, the implication being that he should have married a Jewish girl.

Finally my old friend and visitor from Terezín Dr. V. put an end to this nonsense, of which he was highly critical, by announcing that I was his mistress, which was quite untrue at the time. There was also a Slovak partisan with long hair and a dashing mustache à la Stalin, who titillated my bent for the mysteries of the underground but who turned out to be more stupid than heroic. And there were a few old flames I had carried a torch for when I was sixteen and had considered very interesting.

After a few dates, these idols usually proved to have clay feet, but mostly, their minds seemed to operate on an entirely different level from mine. They belonged to different political parties and everybody wanted me to join theirs. All I wanted to join was the human race.

Under President Beneš, who had returned to Prague from exile, we had a coalition government, including a fairly strong Communist Party. Its ranks were swelled by many of the returned prisoners, who had nothing to lose except their freedom, once more a fact that many did not seem to realize. After the betrayal at Munich, there was a feeling among many of my generation that only Communism could avert a recurrence of fascism. I spent whole nights listening to these arguments, particularly among artists.

My own opinion had not crystallized, yet I argued that the Communists would only substitute the bourgeoisie for the Jews in another totalitarian system. I stayed clear of any commitment, never having been a joiner. Our entire social situation was still quite abnormal, with inflation rampant, the continuing housing shortage, and the generally low work morale. I, for one, was so conditioned to being ordered what to do that I was incapable of any initiative. The prospect of having to go to some official place to obtain a document made me tremble with fear of and contempt for whoever was in charge. *Authority* had become a dirty word. My characteristic self-discipline had fallen by the wayside around my time in Bergen-Belsen; I found neither money nor possessions worth working for.

Back in Celle, at the suggestion of Colonel M., I had given the Red Cross a list of names of my relatives who had fled in the early days of the persecutions, though I didn't know where they had found refuge. These lists were posted at embassies and consulates in most cities of the western world. It was in this way that my cousin Peter Sachsel discovered that I was alive.

When his first letter arrived, I felt a happy shock. Peter was special. We were both born in 1920 and had been playmates up to the age of five, when he moved with his parents to Bratislava. But we visited often, and Peter's father, Emil Sachsel, my mother's favorite brother and my favorite uncle, was an even more frequent visitor when he came to Prague on business. The last time I had seen Uncle Emil was in 1939, before I got married. He had noted how happy he was that Peter was in Lyon. Peter had left to study in France before the German invasion. Unable to return and not foolish enough to try, Peter had made his way via Cuba to the United States in the hope that his parents and little brother would follow.

By the fall of 1945, when I saw Peter's return address in the United States, I had given up all hope of ever hearing or seeing anybody from my family again. As I read his letter, I could well imagine his joy when a friend informed him that the Czechoslovak Consulate was looking for him, mixed with the disappointment that he must have felt when he discovered that it was only I who was seeking him instead of his parents or brother.

The Sachsels—Peter's parents and younger brother—had been deported from Bratislava, and had vanished in the death machines of Eastern Europe without a trace. During our correspondence, it became painfully clear to me that Peter could not face coming back to Czechoslovakia, if only to claim his property, although I desperately wanted to see him. Like me, he apparently was trying to put the recent catastrophic past in a locked box and start anew. This plan was, of course, easier to resolve upon than to carry through, since the memories and questions of why one had been spared in the general slaughter stubbornly refused to go away.

32

With fall came the bad weather and the devaluation of the Czech currency. The first curtailed my aimless wanderings through the city; the second reduced my cash reserves to one-tenth of their value. Our savings accounts were frozen, although some money could be released in emergencies for returning prisoners. I still had my pension, but this put me on a tight budget.

Partly for this reason, but mostly to kill the time I couldn't walk the streets anymore, I took a job. It offered no challenge, bored me to death, but paid quite well, mainly because my new boss was flattered to have the previous owner of a rather well-known firm as his employee. During that time, I ran into our former customers, who, after first inquiring about the fate of my mother, asked me how soon I planned to reopen my own business. They had not bought any new clothes since I left, and thought it a shame that I was working for somebody else. I, in turn, shied away from the red tape involved in any restitution, the return of licenses, and the responsibility for employees.

Eventually, I did go see the erstwhile contents of the salon at their place of storage: a half-open shed. The Louis XIV furniture was mildewed and fell apart at the slightest touch. There was, naturally, not one inch of fabric left, nor any other supplies, these having been used up by Marie. Only the machine heads were still usable because they had been heavily oiled.

Starting over again just seemed like too much of an effort. Still, one of our old clients who had also been a good friend of my mother's kept at me with dogged tenacity, arguing that Mutti would not like my loafing and indecision at all. She countered all my protestations by offering me a studio adjoining her place of business.

Claiming that she had the political leverage through the Communist Party to get the restitution of my license moving, I let her go ahead, assuming correctly that, even so, it would take months before anything concrete would materialize. My lack of enthusiasm must have been exasperating to her, but she put me in contact with a gentleman who sat on the commission dealing with the return of Jewish businesses. He declared himself willing to help—in return for my dead husband's ski boots—even though I did not belong to the Communist Party. Every commission had four members, each representing a political party of the government coalition, and worked in this "I'll do you a favor and you do me a favor" way.

When nothing happened for several weeks, my man informed me confidentially that there was a tremendous backlog of applications and that the tendency was "not to hurry with the restitution of Jewish businesses." I never discovered whether this was only the Communist viewpoint or characterized the entire commission. However, it was clear that the German occupation had left a legacy of anti-Semitism, albeit of a much subtler and hidden kind. This was also apparent in the Union of Liberated Political Prisoners, where a very fine line was drawn between repatriated Jews and Christians.

This, though, did not seem to affect the general population, as attested by the hundreds of new mixed marriages, aside from marriages of returned widows and widowers. However, many of these people decided very soon that life without their families brought too many bitter memories, and that the official emphasis on our liberation—by the Russians—did not bode well for the future. These people started emigration proceedings, preferring to raise their children in countries in less vulnerable geographic positions.

I did not succumb to either the marriage or the emigration fever. In the first case, I had made a firm resolve never to marry again after what I considered the fiasco of the first time. And I felt an incapability or perhaps a fear of getting deeply attached to any other human being. In the case of emigration, no matter how I assessed my immediate situation, whatever roots I had were in Prague. I still believed in the basic decency of the nation, particularly with Beneš as president and the extravagantly loved and admired foreign minister, Jan Masaryk, representing the Czechoslovak Republic in the United Nations.

These two symbols of the prewar state were "building bridges to the West," and many of us were convinced that they would be successful, that the political situation would stabilize, and that the strength of the Communists would deflate. Colonel M., who had remained in touch with me by mail, floated the idea of my settling in South Africa in one of her letters. She noted that I did not seem happy in my native country, but I thought that what I heard about hers was too much like anti-Semitism. I pushed the suggestion aside.

Increasingly I began to feel like fair game for every man I encountered, a situation that I perhaps unconsciously encouraged out of my need for human warmth. It seemed like I was expected to pay for every dinner or theater invitation with a night in somebody's bed—and, moreover, feel flattered in the process. To counteract this state of affairs, I went out and bought a puppy, a wirehaired fox terrier similar to my murdered Tommy. I took it with me everywhere, even to work, where it dotted the establishment all over with little puddles, to the dismay of the customers but tolerated by my boss, who in any event only put in an appearance once a week to collect the receipts. My own therapy worked only too well. I became overly attached to this soft little creature and afraid that, somehow, it would come to harm if I kept it. On the spur of a moment, I gave it to my boss's children as a present.

One day I had a call from an old friend from Terezín, acting as an intermediary for our friendly gendarme Karel, who was too shy to dial my number himself, requesting a meeting. I arrived at the restaurant we had agreed upon and was looking for a policeman in uniform, when a slight blond man in a navy suit with a pearl in his tie got up to greet me. We sat down, followed by some awkward moments of surprise at our changed appearances and positions.

In answer to his questions, I gave him a sketchy account of my adventures. Somewhat later and hesitantly, he came out with his motive for asking for this rendezvous. He had heard that my husband was dead, and that made him think that, well, maybe we could go out together and that, maybe, if it worked, he blushed, we could one day get married. He was dead serious, and in good Bohemian country tradition, he hastened to assure me that I would be well taken care of. He had left the gendarmerie and bought himself a farm so large that he had to use hired help to work it.

There was no need for Karel to tell me that he was well-off; I had already noticed the large diamond ring on his finger. *Jewish property* flashed through my mind, but I kept quiet. Karel had, after all, helped a great many people and had been more than kind to me. His proposition, though, struck me as totally incongruous, even though I knew a former denizen of Terezín had married "her" gendarme right after the war and was already expecting a baby. Not wanting to hurt Karel's feelings, I told him how surprised and honored I was by his proposal but that I had decided never to get married again.

When he objected to such an obviously rash resolution at the age of twenty-five, I told him that the whole subject was academic anyway because, legally, I was not free. This was true. It would take six months to issue an official death certificate for my husband after I found an eyewitness to his death, and longer if there was no proof. Karel's parting words to me were, *I'll wait; meanwhile we can still be friends.*

I had found out from Karel that Honza had returned, and was

now in a state hospital suffering from tuberculosis. Considering that Honza was only in his early thirties, I was glad to hear that he was alive and let a few weeks pass before I went to see him. When I finally did, I was shocked to find him in the terminal stages of the disease, with no hope for recovery. He managed a feeble smile when I took his skeletal hand, and could barely talk through a racking cough that seemed to bring up all the blood left in his emaciated body. Why, why did this brilliant and good man, who would have had so much to contribute to humanity, have to die now when it was all over? Why was destiny so capricious, always destroying the best among us? Tormented by these thoughts, I slipped into uncontrollable crying spells like the ones I had not been able to shake after my parents left Terezín.

As if on cue, I found Margot sitting in the waiting room of a doctor we had both gone to see with various complaints. Weeping, we fell into each other's arms, almost instantly recalling the prophecy of the old woman in the ghetto. Margot had completed her years of captivity in Mauthausen, in Austria, where she had been found near death by a Czech colonel, himself a prisoner for close to six years. Although she was a citizen of Germany, she wanted to return to Prague, where she hoped to find Arthur. Colonel S. offered to use his influence to obtain temporary permission to do so. When Margot arrived in Prague, she discovered that she was a widow. Arthur had died in one of the death marches in the last weeks of the war.

Margot moved in with friends and determined never to return to Germany. She had initiated emigration proceedings for the US, where a brother of her dead husband's lived in Cincinnati. She had a long waiting period ahead because of the complicated American quota system, made more difficult by the temporary nature of her Czechoslovak residency permit. Monthly renewal was mandatory and annoying. When we met, she was having a liaison with Colonel S. that had evolved out of gratitude for his help in getting her back into Czechoslovakia. He was a Jew and, by a strange coincidence, was the one able to tell me the details of my husband Joe's odyssey.

When Joe was brought to the Small Fortress near Terezín, he was put into a cellblock with jailed officers of the Czech army. When these prisoners were later moved to Auschwitz, he was sent with them, losing by some oversight of the jailers his designation as a Jew. This was not even discovered in Auschwitz, largely because his mother had refused to have Joe circumcised but also because his name did not sound Jewish. The prisoners in his group considered him and Colonel S. as two of their own and never gave the Germans the slightest hint that they had Jews among them. This way Joe escaped being a candidate for the ovens.

As the eastern front neared, these prisoners—regarded by the Nazis as hostages—were evacuated to Mauthausen, where conditions were similar to Bergen-Belsen. I was told that Joe wrenched out the gold caps of his teeth to sell them for bread because his legs were swollen to triple their size with hunger edema. By the middle of March there was a call for volunteers for the salt mines in Ebensee, with the promise of higher food rations. Against the age-old maxim of the military to never volunteer for anything, Joe swallowed the phony bait and went.

He died inside the mines around the time that I had been liberated in Belsen. It seemed as if he had always dared and courted death at the same time. With him, his entire family was wiped out, as if they never existed. I had known for quite some time that my husband was dead, but the details now put the stamp of finality on it. Until then, I had, irrationally, always expected that he would walk through the door one day with a big grin and a wild story of some improbable adventure.

It was different with my parents. No matter how many people I talked to and how many questions I asked, I could not find one surviving person from their transport. Their destination was listed in the official documents as Riga, but that could mean any number of smaller camps in that area. Contrary to all common sense, I simply could not believe deep down that they were gone forever. I knew it, yet would not convince myself of this reality.

Kitty and I still lived together in the same apartment, but were growing apart more and more as the need for the physical protection of one another diminished. Except for a few common friends, our circles were rather incompatible. I leaned more toward the company of artists and intellectuals, whereas Kitty preferred the moneyed, pleasure-loving crowd that tried to recoup their prewar way of life as fast as possible.

Kitty refused to speak to her former fiancé, Ivan—even on the phone—so the task of collecting her belongings from him fell to me. When I went to see him, I could not suppress a sarcastic question: why had Ivan written such a glowing love letter, a letter that would have done honor to a great poet, in December and then married another girl in February? It seemed to me that with the information available in Prague, he must have known that the war was drawing to an end and that he could have at least waited until Kitty's return.

To this, he could only say with visible embarrassment that it was none of my business, but that he had thought that Kitty was so incurably ill that it would have been madness to think that she could ever become the mother of his children. This conviction must have been very strong, because the clothes he now returned to Kitty had already been altered to his wife's size without the bother of even having them dry-cleaned.

In November 1945, after three months living in the apartment of Kitty's boss and his family, their pressure to set a wedding date began to grow. An argument ensued, during which Kitty declared that she had never been officially engaged to her boss and that, in any event, she had no intention of getting married—now or in the near future, to him or anybody else.

After this we had to move in somewhat of a hurry.

Kitty went to stay with a distant relative of her father's, who had a studio apartment, with room only for one. I was stranded for a few weeks accepting hospitality here and there, some afternoons not knowing where I'd spend the night, when good old Dr. V. offered me his place for a few months while he was substituting for an ailing colleague in a provincial town. The apartment had been his own before the war, and he had succeeded in getting it back, but the furniture was gone and it contained nothing except a few suitcases used as coffee tables and a folding cot. Grateful to have a roof over my head, I bought a couch and moved in.

Actually, Dr. V.'s filling in for a colleague was more of a flight from Prague than a necessity. I had first met him in Terezín as a client of Joe's mail service. He had been engaged to a Christian girl, his former operating room nurse. He was, at the time, an almost legendary figure in the ghetto for his steadfast fidelity to his fiancée, and had to endure many a ribbing for this medieval devotion. As his confidante I had listened to unending songs of praise about the character of this golden lady. Moreover, Dr. V. was an assimilationist who carried the idea to the extreme. He claimed that the only salvation for the Jews lay in their disappearance into the general population, citing the marriage of his favorite aunt to a well-known Czech painter. He also thought that Jewish women were too possessive of their men.

No sooner had he returned to Prague than it was brought to his attention by the hospital grapevine that his beloved had been living for three years with an SS officer. This German man had been an administrator of the hospital and, in fact, had been arrested at her apartment. At first, Dr. V. dismissed the information as malicious gossip, but finally confronted Jarmila with these allegations. Her side of the story was that she had been forced into the relationship with the German under threat of imprisonment or worse.

Deeply hurt and unsure of the truth, he retreated into work and his empty apartment, while continuing to see Jarmila on and off. This was the state I found him in when I returned to Prague. I listened to his agonized searching for a workable solution and realized that he was in love with his own concept of Jarmila, which had no basis in the real person. In the end, Dr. V. decided to let intelligence and magnanimity win over his wounded feelings and give her another chance. As it happened, the mind was willing but his body revolted: ergo, the escape to the provinces.

The apartment was a mixed blessing, as his absence deprived me of my favorite escort to concerts. I had become very fond of Dr. V., mainly because—like most alumni of the camps aged closer to forty than twenty—he had had a firmly established set of values in place at the time of our incarceration; he had barely been vulgarized or corrupted by the experience. This was certainly connected with one's stage of life at the time. My own faith in people was greatly shaken, and I had become somewhat of a cynic.

In the music of Gustav Mahler, I discovered a sort of mirror image to my own state of mind, vacillating between violent spurts of energy, hope for the future, and deep despair. I wanted very much to be the independent, self-sufficient, free woman. Yet I kept casting around for a fatherlike figure to keep me from foolish escapades, often not trusting my own judgment. The masculine side of my nature, always present and encouraged by my father, had become much stronger during the years of captivity, when I had played the role of protector for Kitty and lived and worked like a soldier in the field or worse. It showed itself in my gestures; even my voice had become much deeper than before.

For the first time in years I was now living entirely alone in the sometimes ghostly quiet of my new quarters. At times I enjoyed my solitude, but it also invited incessant rethinking of the past. Somewhere along the way, I had acquired the notion of a certain complicity in the murder of my parents that I found myself incapable to reason away. I had kept my promise to survive through sheer luck and willpower, but this was not enough to allay my self-reproach of not having done more to save them. Yet I did not know at all what I could have done.

Christmas drew near, and my pride made me refuse several invitations, considering them like bones thrown to a hungry dog. Snow had fallen and I eyed my skis and boots—among my few possessions that had been returned to me—standing in a corner. I toyed with the idea of escaping to the mountains from the city filled with memories.

On New Year's Eve, I spent a few hours in the place I felt most comforted when depressed: a hot bathtub. A little mouse emerged from a hole in the wall and slowly made her way toward me on the rim of the tub. Lost and undecided which way to go, she seemed a symbol of my own existence. We stared at each other for quite a while, and then she decided to return to her hole. Suddenly I felt this as the last unbearable loss and fled the apartment, intending to go to a party after all. But instead, I started to walk through the passageways of the old city toward the river and down to the lower embankment, which used to be a sort of lovers' lane in spring and summer, and where I had my first kiss some nine years before.

I arrived at a recess in the river wall with a step to the water and a large iron ring for tying up boats. Suddenly I had a vivid memory of being five years old and on my way home from a gym class with Mademoiselle. That day, for the first time in my life, I had seen a drowned man fished out of the river and tied to that boat ring. He must have been in the water a long time, because he was all green and slimy, and reeked of dead fish and decay. I had pushed my way through the legs of the curious onlookers to the front and had stared at the figure for quite a while before my governess realized that this was not the most suitable sight for a little girl.

In a nightmare the following night, I had confused the drowned man with the Waterman, a legendary figure in Czech folklore who lures innocent girls into the depths of the water. I had often been threatened by the maids that he would come get me if I misbehaved. Twenty years later now, that image was alive again. He was calling my name and telling me how dark and soft the water was. I stood there transfixed, staring at my beloved river with its slowly moving ice floes, remembering how often I had skated not far from where I now stood, and how I had loved to go swimming in summer on the opposite side. The water looked cold yet peaceful, with the reflection of the streetlights dancing on it like little stars.

I felt a hand on my shoulder. A white-haired policeman said, *Miss, this is not a good place for a midnight walk alone. It's too cold for that. Tell me where you live; I'll walk you home.* As if awakening from a dream, I let myself be led away and dropped exhausted into my bed.

The next morning was New Year's Day, 1946. I woke up with a clear head, packed a bag, took my skis, and caught the first train to the mountains, arriving in the late afternoon. The following day I took the gondola up to the summit, worrying a little about how good a skier I would be after a break of six years.

On top, the mountains were decked out in their most festive finery. The sky was cloudless and the pine trees were heavily sugared with new snow. There was not a soul around to take away the sudden intimacy between myself and the universe. Awed, I looked at the miraculous beauty surrounding me, as if especially created for my welcome. If there was a God, I felt His presence here, as well as gratitude for being alive. I buckled on my skis, and whistling the last movement of my favorite Brahms symphony, I schussed down the hill.

Franci and her mother, Josefa Rabinek, August 1922

Franci (*left*), age three
and a half in 1923 in Prague,
with her cousin Peter

Franci and her
architecture
student boyfriend,
Leo Oppenheimer,
in Prague, May
1937

Last photo of
Josefa Rabinek,
Franci's mother,
1940

Emil Rabinek, 1930s

Marianne Golz, Franci's
cellmate in Pankrác prison,
in June of 1939

Franci and Joe
Solar wedding
photo, 1940

Joe Solar with
dog Tommy

Gisa, 1939

Franci (*left*) and Kitty with a
British soldier in Celle, 1945

Red Cross Colonel Margaret Emmeline Montgomery (*seated*)
with other British personnel in Celle, summer 1945

Franci (*left*) and Kitty after liberation in Celle, summer 1945

Franci and Kurt Epstein wedding photo, December 21, 1946, Prague City Hall

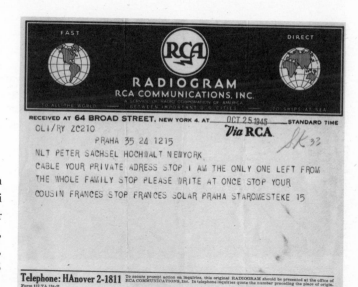

Cablegram
from Franci
to her
cousin Peter,
October 25,
1945

Franci's exit
document, 1948

Margot Körbel in Israel, 1951

Franci, dress designer in New York City, 1955

AFTERWORD

In the spring of 1946, Franci Solar set about assembling the documents, premises, and staff with which to open her new salon. She wrote to her cousin Peter, now in the American army, to send her fabrics, and the latest *Vogue* and *Harper's Bazaar*. She was planning to rest up at a spa in Slovakia in August before opening in the fall. Then, in July, she wrote him that she was getting married.

It all happened very quickly, actually all in one week . . .
His name is Kurt Epstein . . . He's forty-two years old, a
head taller than I am and very good looking (he's a well-
known athlete, a swimmer, and related to the Petschek
family). I've known him since I was twelve, when he was
our trainer at the swim club and I hated him with all my
heart because he was so obnoxious to us teenagers that I
always thought of him as an awful, arrogant person. And
all of a sudden Mr. Epstein wasn't obnoxious at all.

Kurt Epstein had been one of the one thousand Jewish men deported to Terezín in December 1941. Terezín had been his military garrison when he was a reserve lieutenant in the Czechoslovak Army, and Kurt was soon appointed one of the camp's eight quartermasters. Unlike Joe Solar, he was the antithesis of a black marketer; he worked to ensure that the food he distributed actually arrived in the mouths of the prisoners it was intended to feed. His parents were deported to Auschwitz in the same transport as Franci, but they had been murdered there. Like Franci, Kurt had been selected by Dr. Mengele for a forced labor camp, and he was the sole survivor of his family.

He's a wonderful person who holds rather old-fashioned views of women, Franci wrote to Peter in September, *which is good because he behaves with a certain honorableness that younger men don't have. He also loves me—which does not blind him to my faults. It's in every way the opposite of my first marriage, where my husband idolized me and let me do all kinds of stupid things. In the end I only hated him for his weakness and lost my last bit of respect for him. It looks like Kurt won't make this mistake and will keep a certain authority. It helps that he's sixteen years older than me. You know, my girlfriends are the happiest about all this. I was always such an "enfant terrible" and everyone who knows me is glad that finally there's someone who won't let me dance around his head.*

As far as finances go, Kurt makes enough money but I want to have my own business. I don't feel good when all I have to think about is a household. Also one never knows what will happen and it would be madness to abandon my clientele. I would be terribly unhappy at home and Kurt knows that I have too much energy for my life's achievement to be dusting.

Kitty begged Franci to marry Kurt, even though he was not her usual type. Other friends thought she was making a mistake. He was a provincial, who fell asleep at concerts and, despite all his prowess as a swimmer, didn't ski. Franci's best friend, Helena, later told me that she thought Kurt would be a good husband but didn't believe Franci was in love with him. He spoke nothing but Czech, and had no street smarts.

They married on December 21, 1946, in Prague's City Hall and, after taking out a mortgage on the Epstein home in Roudnice nad Labem, bought an apartment in Wenceslas Square. Franci opened her salon at 20 Old Town Square. She wrote to Peter that she now employed seven seamstresses, was planning a trip to Paris to see the collections, and that Kurt was earning a good salary working for a fellow survivor's company. He was also coaching the national water polo team, and was a member of the National Olympic Committee. And . . . she was expecting a baby.

Dear Uncle, Franci wrote on January 9, 1948, I've become a totally besotted mother . . . Helen will have a nurse but she isn't here yet, so for the moment I'm doing everything myself. For the time being, the baby doesn't need much and no one can breastfeed her for me anyway. I need the day to have at least thirty-six hours. But I definitely like this role of mother and have already decided (with the father, of course) that we'll have more . . . I still like to go to the theater or go dancing but the fact is that when I go, I worry whether my little girl isn't crying at home. It's a good thing I'm breastfeeding since the scarcity of milk is catastrophic.

January was Czechoslovakia's last month as a democratic state. The scarcity of milk was due to a drought, exacerbated by Soviet policies, that had put Czech agriculture in crisis. The coalition government was also in crisis. The Communist Party organized mass demonstrations, and a Soviet envoy arrived in Prague. On February 25, President Edvard Beneš appointed a new Communist government.

There is no letter to Peter documenting my parents' decision to emigrate. The family story is that Kurt surveyed the armed militia marching in the streets, called them "Nazis in different-color uniforms," and vowed that he would not make the mistake of remaining in his country twice. Franci argued that she was not going anywhere. She had just turned twenty-eight. She had just re-created her salon. She had a three-month-old baby. For the first and only time in their marriage, my father slapped her.

Furious, Franci stalked out into the cold. Then she returned. Any doubts she had about emigrating were dispelled on March 10, when the body of Jan Masaryk, the hope of the democrats, was found in the courtyard below his office in the Czechoslovak Foreign Ministry.

Thousands of Czechs fled immediately. Fortunately, Kurt Epstein had applied for an American visa in 1945, when he returned from the camps. In March 1948, during a trip to France with the national water polo team, Kurt telegraphed his cousin, Franzi Petschek, in New York. She had married into the banking family that had evacuated their family members and employees on a special train in 1938. The Epsteins had been invited to leave Czechoslovakia on that train but had decided to remain.

My parents flew out of Prague on July 21, 1948, with two suitcases and me in a canvas bag. Franci wore all the clothing she could. Along with diapers, she packed the Epstein and Rabinek family photographs and three porcelain figurines that had belonged to her mother.

Whenever I asked about her arrival in New York, Franci replied that it had been over a hundred degrees, the flight had taken twenty-six hours, and of the ten dollars they had each been allowed to take out of the country, the New York Port Authority had taken eight. The Petscheks settled them in the Hotel Colonial, across from the planetarium on Manhattan's Upper West Side. She never mentioned any feelings.

Franci's friend Helena Slavíčková had predicted that Kurt Epstein's sports reputation would not travel if they emigrated, and that Franci would wind up supporting the family. She was right: Kurt Epstein spoke no English. He could not find a job. The Petscheks did not believe in hiring relatives. There was no demand for water polo coaches in Manhattan and few swimming pools.

Franci turned for help to her Prague obstetrician, Dr. Karel Steinbach, who had also emigrated and was now the hub of Manhattan's

Czech community. Within two weeks, Dr. Steinbach sent her a fashion client: Czech soprano Jarmila Novotná, who was singing at the Metropolitan Opera and needed a dressmaker. It was illegal to work in the Hotel Colonial, so Franci found a cheap basement apartment, bought a sewing machine, and once again started sewing.

My parents had a very difficult first decade in the United States. Although Franci often pointed out that her Manhattan Czech social circle was far more interesting than the one she had had in Prague, she had serious medical problems. For most of the 1950s, she was the breadwinner, cook, household manager, mother, and wife. In 1951, she had a difficult birth with my brother Tommy. The family's financial situation was precarious: my parents juggled the monthly rent and salon creditors, trying to maintain a middle-class style of life. After nearly starving to death in the camps, my parents insisted on eating meat every day. Franci also insisted on attending concerts and the theater. In 1956, she had a nervous breakdown, serious enough to warrant extended, intensive psychoanalytic treatment. Her cousin Peter, who was now earning a good living as a chemist, helped pay for it.

Kurt slowly learned English and took intermittent menial jobs. He was a devoted father, but hopeless in the kitchen or around the house. Like Franci's father, Emil Rabinek, he helped his wife by doing the bookkeeping for her business. Eventually, he was able to join the International Ladies' Garment Workers' Union and worked in a factory as a cutter in Manhattan's garment center. In 1960, the Epsteins' third child, David, was born.

During the 1950s and 1960s, Franci exchanged letters with her sister survivors—Kitty in Prague, Margot in Jerusalem, and others in Israel, North America, and Australia. Occasionally, I would meet one of them in our living room. Then, in 1964, after a protracted and painful legal effort, Franci received reparations money from the German government and used part of it to visit the two women with whom she had been in the war: Kitty and Margot.

Since 1948, Kitty had been living in a tiny apartment in the center of Prague with her husband and son. A social butterfly even in the gray Communist world, Kitty modeled herself on Hollywood starlets, and dyed her hair blond. She, too, was the sole survivor of her family. She married Kurt Egerer, a fellow survivor with whom she had a son. She worked as a multilingual secretary, using her German, French, and English, first for an export firm and then for the Chief Rabbi of Prague. After her husband died, she lived with her Czech Protestant boyfriend, who shared her joy of life. She spoke very little about the war, she told me when I visited Prague, but the scars she carried were not only from the boils she had developed in Hamburg.

Margot, who was living with my parents in Wenceslas Square when I was born, had difficulties of another kind. She had been liberated at Mauthausen and returned to Prague with a Czech colonel who had been imprisoned there. But as a former citizen of Germany, she was not welcome in a Czechoslovakia that expelled its Germans. She emigrated to the newly established State of Israel in 1949, where she met a Berlin-born survivor named Bier. The two lived, improbably, in an old Arab house on the premises of the French convent in Jerusalem's Ein Karem. Bier was the nuns' handyman and chauffeur to the director of the Israel Museum. Margot worked in a dress shop for a few years and never had children, but served as my surrogate mother while I was a university student in Jerusalem. During that time, she told me a great deal about her relationship with my mother during the war.

The sisterhood of Czech Jewish survivors remained in close touch. They exchanged news about their current lives as well as war stories—who had done what to whom and what that meant after the war. They discussed the televised hearings of the Eichmann trial in 1961. They talked about every war movie they saw, including *Night and Fog* (1956), *Judgment at Nuremberg* (1961), *The Pawnbroker* (1964), and *The Shop on Main Street* (1965). And they also discussed books.

Franci was probably the best-read among her friends. She had attended French, German, and English schools in Prague and was familiar with the classics in all three languages. She also loved the Russian writers. Every Sunday, she read the *New York Times Book Review* and ordered whatever interested her from the New York Public Library. She loved the novels of Vladimir Nabokov and, of the survivor authors, most admired the work of Primo Levi.

I don't know if she read Olga Lengyel, Gisella Perl, and Vladka Meed, women survivors who published their books in the late 1940s, but I do remember her buying Czech survivor Zdena Berger's autobiographical novel *Tell Me Another Morning* in 1961. Then, in 1964, the *Times Book Review* reviewed a translation of Ilse Aichinger's novel *Herod's Children*, based on her experiences as a half-Jew in Vienna during the war. Recognizing the characters, Franci discovered that her cousin Ilse had become a famous Austrian author. She wrote to her and reconnected with the Viennese branch of the Rabineks—now scattered throughout the world—who assumed Franci had been murdered in the war. Over the next decade she told and retold her wartime experiences to them.

I don't know when Franci began thinking about writing her own book. Perhaps she never stopped thinking about the notebook of letters to her mother that she had written in Neugraben and had been forced to burn page by page. In the mid-1950s, she retold many of her camp experiences, first to an antagonistic German doctor assessing her wartime injuries for the purpose of monetary reparations, and then to a sympathetic American Jewish psychoanalyst. In February 1974, she retold her story—in chronological sequence— for the William E. Wiener Oral History of American Holocaust Survivors, a then-unique project that audiotaped two hundred testimonies. She was just short of her fifty-fourth birthday.

That validation of her experience may have been the impetus for Franci to finalize her memoir. She titled it *Roundtrip*, a sardonic reference to the route she had taken through the Second World War from Prague to Terezín to Auschwitz to Hamburg to Bergen-Belsen to Celle and back to Prague. In a now-dated preface that she titled "Explanation," Franci wrote:

> Why do I feel compelled to add my voice to the great chorus of statistics, learned reports, psychological studies as well as more or less successful treatments in fiction and drama already written? There is no one answer, but perhaps

my first and foremost concern is with my children and their generation, who seem to me almost as troubled as I was at their age. They are prone to deep exasperation about the status quo, and to flight into drugs. My daughter, of course, asked me questions from the time she became aware of the tattoo on my arm, and has never stopped, a fact perhaps brought about by the natural identification of a girl with her mother. My sons never showed much interest, getting almost visibly uneasy or bored when the subject came up in conversation.

Since children tend to be strangers to the inner life of their parents and their motivations and reactions, and having no fortune to bequest, I can only try to give them an honest and true picture of their mother in her youth and of my way of dealing with the perplexities of existence. It might give them some understanding of the diversity and often puzzling behavior of the human animal, in addition to the dreadful corrupting force of power in the hands of a few individuals, who usurped it with the help of an indifferent, intimidated, and dissatisfied population.

The deciding factor was a trip to Colorado where I was visiting friends whose ancestors had settled the West. I found myself in the company of a group of young people far removed from the experience of anyone with my background. Having studied twentieth-century history in college and disturbed by the staggering facts of World War II, they plied me with questions about how it had felt from the inside. Uninhibited by the delicacy of their elders, they convinced me that here was a generation who really wanted to know what had happened to me, so that they could perhaps relate it to their own experience. Like my own children, these young people were desperately trying to find their own raison d'être in a world still full of injustice, violence, and oppression. They were engaged in various forms of political protest, draft evasion, or escape from reality. The thought occurred to me that if my own contemporaries, particularly in Germany, had voiced their doubts and opinions more intelligently and forcefully, we could have possibly been spared the terror and mass annihilation of the Hitler era.

In 1973 and 1974, when I think Franci was finalizing her memoir, Germany was still two countries divided by the Berlin Wall. President Richard Nixon was struggling to stay in office in the aftermath of Senate hearings into the Watergate scandal. The civil rights movement, the war in Vietnam, and the women's movement had deeply polarized America. In Israel, the 1973 Yom Kippur War had once again raised the issue of Jewish (and Margot's) survival. Franci and her customers talked about all these subjects during fittings. Some of them were themselves refugees with similar backgrounds. Some were Americans with little connection to Europe or Jews.

As had been the case in Prague, Franci was her customers' confidante and they were hers. All knew she had survived the Second World War in the concentration camps. Some preferred not to discuss it, but none could avoid seeing the Auschwitz tattoo on her forearm. Her favorite client, Marya Mannes, a prominent journalist who had put Franci in one of her books, may have encouraged Franci to write down her story. Another client, literary agent Cyrilly Abels, sent it to publishers in 1975. It was rejected by every one.

In the mid-1970s, many American Jews—and I would bet some of the editors Cyrilly pitched—wanted to distance themselves from concentration camp victims. Holocaust studies courses at universities and Holocaust centers were still in their infancy. Not until 1978 would the term *Holocaust* become publicized through the internationally popular television miniseries. Although the U.S. Holocaust Memorial Museum later became the most visited museum in Washington, it would not open until 1993. And although second-wave feminism was growing in the United States and Jewish women were among its leaders, the movement had not yet made much of a dent in the Jewish community.

In its attitude, language, and content, *Franci's War* was far ahead of its time. With the exception of Anne Frank's posthumous diary, Holocaust literature in the United States was dominated by male writers, particularly Elie Wiesel—then the prototype and spokesman for the thousands of victims who were coming to be called "survivors." Few male memoirists in the Jewish community wrote much about women's lives during the Holocaust. It was a non-Jew, William Styron, who published *Sophie's Choice* in 1979—and that novel was about a Polish non-Jewish survivor. In Israel, largely due to the sensationalist novels of Yehiel Dinur (who wrote under the pseudonym Ka-Tzetnik, the Hebrew abbreviation for "concentration camp prisoner"), Holocaust survivors were viewed as damaged goods. Czech-Israeli author Dita Kraus, who accompanied Franci on most of her wartime route, told me that even the great Israeli statesman David Ben-Gurion allegedly said, "Every man who survived was a *Capo*, and every woman a prostitute."

Franci focused almost entirely on the experiences of women in her text. In addition, she viewed her wartime experience through the lens of a highly assimilated Prague Jew and proud Czechoslovak citizen. Neither she nor her parents were religious. She did not speak Yiddish. Moreover, Franci wrote candidly and dispassionately about sexuality and love, including homosexuality and sexual barter. She knew how potentially damaging and even dangerous that was in the early 1970s, because she disguised the names of those women whose sexual choices she describes.

Not many writers are able to separate rejection of their work from rejection of themselves, and Franci was no exception. The rejections of her text wounded her and confirmed her suspicion that no one was interested in her experience. She gave the manuscript to me, to use as I saw fit. After all, she said, I was the professional writer in the family.

The last thing I wanted in 1975 was my mother's book. I had lived with it all my life. It was her story, not mine. I wanted to get away from, not into, it. Even though I was then in my late twenties, I had neither been able to rebel against my parents nor truly leave home. I was in the process of writing my own book, *Children of the Holocaust*, in an effort to separate what was mine from what was hers. My book, about the intergenerational transmission of history, trauma, and resilience, was published in 1979, and it was emotionally complicated for us. We never discussed it explicitly, but I felt that while Franci was proud of her journalist daughter's first book and enjoyed participating in its promotion, she felt that her own experience had been overlooked. She began to speak about her war experiences at local venues, but she did not pursue the publication of her memoir and neither did I.

In the spring of 1989, Franci experienced a brain aneurysm, went into a coma, and died without being able to speak to any of her children again. Over the next seven years, as my own form of mourning, I researched her and her maternal ancestors' lives for a book that became *Where She Came From: A Daughter's Search for Her Mother's History*. In it, I traced three generations of dressmakers in Central Europe and drew on *Roundtrip* as a source for the section about the Second World War. After I finished that book, in 1997, I filed away the memoir with my other research materials and focused on my own work.

Over the years, I had often been asked to help write or translate other survivor memoirs, and sometimes, when I was particularly interested in the subject matter, I agreed. Together with the author, I retranslated Heda Margolius Kovály's memoir *Under a Cruel Star: A Life in Prague, 1941–1968* from the Czech, and it became an important college text. I translated part of Vlastá Schönová's Terezín memoir *To Be an Actress*, and worked with Paul Ornstein on *Looking Back: Memoir of a Psychoanalyst*. I also wrote introductions to the work of two Canadian survivors. I was sent so many manuscripts about the Holocaust to read and review that I had to refuse almost all of them in order to do my own writing.

During the last twenty years, however, I have tried to keep up with the work of feminist-influenced scholars researching the experiences of women in the Second World War.

Then, in 2017, a friend alerted me to the existence of a videotaped testimony my mother had made in 1985 for the Fortunoff Archive at Yale University that neither my brothers nor I knew existed. In October of 2017 my family obtained a copy and watched it for the first time. That same month, the *New York Times* and the *New Yorker* both broke stories of Harvey Weinstein's sexual abuse of employees and associates and the international #MeToo movement hit the headlines.

After watching Franci's videotaped testimony and sharing it with friends, I reread my mother's text, and recognized it as an important primary source. Several of the people Franci describes have become famous or infamous since the 1970s; some can be found on Wikipedia. They include not only Josef Mengele, but Franci's well-informed Pankrác cellmate, Marianne Golz; Jewish prisoner Lotte Winter (Franci's Sylva); and Nazi guard Anneliese Kohlmann (Franci's Bubi). Spiess, the Nazi who forced her to burn her journal, was tried by the British for war crimes; his real name was Wilhelm-Friedrich Kliem.

I discussed the idea of publishing Franci's memoir with my two brothers. We agreed that she had wanted her book to be published, and would want us to get it published for the seventy-fifth anniversary of her liberation from the camps. We agreed that I should do minimal editing and offer it to publishers in Europe, Israel, the United Kingdom, and the United States. Franci would be pleased to know that it was bought first by Ikar, a large Slovak publisher, and Mladá Fronta, a large Czech publishing house.

Nothing in my mother's book—including the heterosexual and homosexual relationships and acts of sexual barter—came as a surprise to me. I had heard the stories, met many of the people, and knew some of them—Kitty, Margot, and Peter—very well. Unlike many Holocaust survivors, Franci was never reticent about her experiences—if anything, I believe she told me too much too soon. My brother Tommy refused to learn Czech or listen to the survivors who conversed in our living room. I chose to listen but adapted Franci's psychological defense of dissociation for myself. I heard the words but refused to understand what they meant.

It was not until I myself had spent almost a decade in psychotherapy and wrote my own memoir, *The Long Half-Lives of Love and Trauma*, that I felt able to address *Franci's War*. I grew up in awe of my brilliant, candid, and pragmatic mother: awed by what she had lived through and impressed by the lessons she drew from it. A dropout from two elite high schools in Prague (a German gymnasium and a French lycée), Franci often referred to the camps as her "university," where she had received a unique education in human behavior.

In her "Explanation," Franci wrote:

An American doctor once asked me, after discussing the irreparable damage to my nervous system, whether I hated the Germans.

I do not, mainly because I feel that hate is a sentiment I can ill afford, since it ultimately leads to the hatred of one's self. I certainly cannot hold the people born after 1930 accountable for what their parents did to me and my family, but every German older than that makes me decidedly uncomfortable, as if the blood of my dead companions were still on his hands.

I do resent greatly the publications of books by former Nazis and the buildups these receive.

I do resent the meager rehabilitation payments the present regime makes to its victims, determined by courts where the accused has become the judge, and hampered by bureaucratic red tape which leaves thousands of cases unresolved years after the war, as if waiting for the victims to die before a settlement of their claims is made. While the considerable restitution payments to the state of Israel show a certain goodwill and wish to make amends, the sum total of German reparations can never even partially make up for the devastating material and psychological damage done to their victims. Try as I may, I cannot find any reason to admire the nobility or basic justice of the German dealing with this problem.

My feelings toward them are best characterized as indifference mixed with pity for my German contemporaries and their elders. Just how does a father of a German son or daughter answer their questions? Can he sit down and give an honest account of his actions during the Nazi era without feeling his ears burn? Where were the voices of the intelligentsia, the great artists and humanitarians of the golden period in Germany's cultural past? How is it that one is hard put to find a German who will admit ever having been a member of the SS or Nazi Party? Could the infernal plans of the leaders really have been carried out without the cooperation or at least tacit approval of the vast majority of the population?

The trial of Adolf Eichmann, like the Nuremberg judgments before, left me without any sense of satisfaction or revenge but only with the bitter aftertaste of futility. Necessary as they may have been.

I could not care less about what happens to this divided country or its separated families in the East and West, and refuse to join in the shedding of crocodile tears over their fate.

I do consider it a supreme irony of history that West Germany is today so much better off economically than England, who held the fort for so many years alone, and that Germany is courted from all sides as an ally against the Communist Bloc.

All this, though, does not add up to hate—more to a curiosity whether there, in fact, exists a new Germany. Could this new Germany withstand another mass hysteria to "Follow the *Führer*" if another madman arose in another disastrous economic depression, with a need for a scapegoat?

My greatest concern is the possibility that due to human nature, it could happen again in a different form, under different circumstances, anywhere in the world.

EDITORIAL NOTE

Editing *Franci's War* posed several challenges. My brothers and I assume Franci must have written at least parts of her memoir by hand, before 1974, but we found no manuscript pages among her papers after she died in 1989. Her memoir was typed on an English-language typewriter, on the thin onionskin paper that she used for airmail correspondence. Her will makes no mention of the memoir or her wishes regarding it.

The typescript is corrected in Franci's handwriting or crossed out with typed *X*s. Nevertheless, there are grammatical errors, missing words, typos, misspellings (Osveczin instead of Oświęcim, *Sturmbandführer* instead of *Sturmbannführer*), run-on sentences, and very long paragraphs. The narrative is not divided into chapters, and punctuation is inconsistent. I made corrections and broke the narrative into chapters. Page 2 of Franci's typescript is missing. I used the gap to move the Rabinek family history ahead several pages.

Franci presented some key quotes, conversations, and letters within quotation marks, left others unpunctuated, and chose to translate the entire text of a love letter she received (in Italian)!

Had a publisher accepted and worked with her on the text in the 1970s, Franci would have had the opportunity to look over the text, correct errors, and discuss her narrative decisions as well as her sardonic title: *Roundtrip*. But her unexpected death of a brain aneurysm at the age of sixty-nine in 1989 made all of that, as well as the decision to publish in 2020, impossible.

While my brothers and I are certain that she would have wanted her memoir to be published, we are less certain about other matters, starting with the author's name. Our mother wrote the book as Frances Epstein but we feel that in 2020, she would have preferred to be Franci Rabinek Epstein, especially since the *Stolpersteine* (memorial stumbling stones) laid for her and her parents in the center of Prague bear that name.

Because there were multiple corrections required to update her original preface, I decided to quote from it in the afterword rather than to insert my own voice into her narrative. I (and the copy editor) did minimal line editing.

It was relatively easy to check and correct dates. Names, however, presented a challenge. Franci used the real names of her cousins Kitty, Vava, and Peter but created pseudonyms for other people—I assume that she did so to protect the privacy of her sister prisoners and their families. I marked all pseudonyms I recognized with an asterisk and left it to scholars to identify them. Franci also used the pseudonym "Buchwald" for the forced labor camp of Neugraben, one of eighty-five sub-camps of Neuengamme. In reality, there was no forced labor camp named "Buchwald," and it is unclear why she used that name.

In another perplexing reference, Franci names "Ilse Koch" as the female commander at Auschwitz who inspected her group of Czech Jewish women inmates before they were sent to Neuengamme. I think that my mother was aware that Ilse Koch (known as the "Bitch of Buchenwald") was not the woman she encountered in Auschwitz. Franci may have been using the name "Ilse Koch" figuratively, or she may have confused her with Irma Grese, another sadistic Nazi female commander who was in Auschwitz. I eliminated the name.

Forty-five years after Franci wrote her memoir, largely due to the internet, I was able to check many facts that were unavailable to her at the time.

In March 1993, Gunter Buck, then a thirty-seven-year-old teacher in Hamburg, contacted me. Buck was researching a former forced labor camp in his neighborhood when an Israeli interviewee told him that Franci had been a prisoner there and that her daughter had written about her. I gave Buck permission to quote from my book, *Children of the Holocaust*, and he provided me with many details of my mother's time in Hamburg for the sequel, *Where She Came From: A Daughter's Search for Her Mother's History*. He identified "Spiess" (the German word for "Sarge") as Wilhelm-Friedrich Kliem. Born in 1896, Kliem was a master carpenter conscripted into the Wehrmacht, an SS guard at Auschwitz, then the commander of Neugraben. He was tried for war crimes in 1946 by a British war crimes tribunal in Hamburg and sentenced to fifteen years in prison.

University of Warwick Professor Anna Hájková, a scholar of queer Holocaust history, women, and sexuality, has definitively identified "Bubi" (1921–1977), the female SS camp guard at Neuengamme, as Anneliese Kohlmann and the prisoner my mother named Sylva as Lotte Winter. She also put me in touch with Alyn Beßmann, archivist at the Neuengamme Concentration Camp Memorial, who sent me a copy of Franci's registration card in Neugraben. Given this documentation, I replaced "Buchwald" with Neugraben in the text.

In 2018, Ronnie Golz, who read about Franci's time in Pankrác prison with Marianne Golz in 1939 in *Where She Came From*, sent me photographs and his website for Marianne (1895–1943). She was his father's first wife.

In preparing *Franci's War* for publication, I queried the Facebook group Jewish Genealogy Portal and was sent documentation of Franci's Aunt Hella (Helena Sachsel, 1883–1944); her Terezín adoptee Gisa (Gisela Kauffman, 1932–1944); and her Red Cross protector Colonel M. (Margaret Emmeline Montgomery, 1901–1993), who was a sister-in-law of Field Marshall Bernard Montgomery and is warmly remembered in the recollections of at least three other Holocaust survivors.

Finally, my brothers and I are very fortunate to possess original prewar family photographs. Many descendants of Holocaust survivors have none. Our mother's and grandmother's customers of Salon Weigert in Prague are responsible for their survival during the Nazi occupation of Czechoslovakia. After the Velvet Revolution of November 1989 (which Franci did not live to see), I was able to obtain additional photographs and documents from the

Jewish Museum, the Museum of Decorative Arts in Prague, and the Terezín Memorial. Because Franci and Kitty worked as interpreters for the British Army in 1945, Franci was given several photographs taken by the British that summer. Her cousin Peter Scott saved her telegram of 1945 and all her postwar letters and returned them to me in 2015.

Helen Epstein
Lexington, Massachusetts

ACKNOWLEDGMENTS

Many friends, family members, and colleagues helped bring *Franci's War* to publication. I'm especially grateful for the early and enthusiastic encouragement of scholars Dr. Michael Berenbaum, Dr. Atina Grossmann, and Dr. Betsy Anthony in the US; Dr. Zoë Waxman and Dr. Anna Hájková in the UK; Dr. Kateřina Čapková and Dr. Arno Pařik in the Czech Republic; and Gunter Buck and Alyn Beßmann at the Neuengamme Memorial in Hamburg.

Elisabeth Benjamin, Jean Hearst, Susan Kahn, Irena Klepfisz, Susan Hecker Ray, Rochelle Rubinstein, Sandy Fong-Ging, Joelle and Leon Gunther, Ilse Browner, and Tom Manoff provided valuable early support. Franci's sister survivor Dita Kraus, who accompanied Franci from Terezín to Celle and has written her own memoir, was kind enough to read and fact-check Franci's.

For help in documentation, I thank my brothers Tom and David Epstein; our cousin Karel Ehrlich; and the resourceful members of Facebook group Jewish Genealogy Portal, especially Kaye Prince

Hollenberg and Doron Leitner, who identified Franci's Terezín "adoptee" Gisa Kauffman.

I thank my imaginative and indefatigable agents, Kristin Olson in Prague, who brought *Franci's War* to the attention of Czech and Slovak publishers, and Carolyn Savarese in Boston, who brought it to Penguin in the US and to Michael Joseph in the UK.

My husband, Patrick Mehr, adored his mother-in-law, and was involved in every step of bringing her memoir to publication. He never once doubted its value. My writing partner, Helen Fremont, was also essential every step of the way.

Lastly, I thank the warm and professional team at Penguin, who made the publishing process a pleasure: Kathryn Court, Victoria Savanh, Bennett Petrone, Bel Banta, Kate Hudkins, and the many others whom I did not meet but who contributed to the creation of this book.

Readers who would like to see and hear Franci may access her videotaped Holocaust survivor testimony at the Fortunoff Archive at Yale University.

TIMELINE

October 28, 1918	Establishment of First Czechoslovak Republic following the collapse of the Austro-Hungarian Empire.
November 11, 1918	Armistice signed to end First World War.
February 26, 1920	Franci born to Josefa and Emil Rabinek in Prague.
January 30, 1933	Adolf Hitler is appointed chancellor of Germany; first German concentration camps established in March.
March 12, 1938	Germany annexes Austria in what is called the "Anschluss."
September 30, 1938	The Munich Agreement enables Hitler's annexation of the Sudetenland (parts of Czechoslovakia with a predominantly ethnic German population).
March 15, 1939	Hitler enters Prague and annexes the rest of Bohemia and Moravia; appoints Konstantin von Neurath as Reichsprotektor. He quickly abolishes Czech political parties and trade unions, and institutes the Nuremberg racial laws for Jews.

June 1939   The Rabineks are arrested by the Gestapo and are interned for two weeks in Pankrác prison.

September 1, 1939   Germany invades Poland; Second World War begins.

April–June 1940   Germany invades Denmark, Holland, Belgium, and France.

August 1940   Franci Rabinek marries Joe Solar.

June 1941   Germany invades the Soviet Union.

September 1941   All Czech Jews ordered to wear a yellow star.

September 1941   Hitler replaces Konstantin von Neurath with Reinhard Heydrich as Reichsprotektor.

October 16, 1941   First deportation of Czech Jews to Lodz.

November 24, 1941   First deportation of Czech male Jews, who transform military garrison of Terezín into a concentration camp.

May 27, 1942   Operation Anthropoid: Czech and Slovak Resistance fighters assassinate Heydrich.

June 10, 1942   Hitler orders reprisals for Heydrich assassination. The villages of Lidice and Ležáky are targeted and 1,300 Czechs, including 200 women, are murdered.

August 1942   Joe Solar is deported to Terezín and works on the new rail line connecting the camp to Bohušovice station.

September 1942   The Rabineks are deported to Terezín; Franci remains there, but her parents are sent to Maly Trostinets, now Belarus, where they are shot to death.

September 6, 1943   5,007 Jews are deported from Terezín to Auschwitz II-Birkenau. All are tattooed and registered into the Czech Family Camp.

December 1943   Kitty is deported to the Czech Family Camp at Auschwitz-Birkenau.

March 1944   Joe Solar is arrested and imprisoned in the Small Fortress, the prison of the Prague Gestapo in Terezín.

March 8–9, 1944   3,700 prisoners of the Czech Family Camp gassed to death in Auschwitz.

May 1944   Franci Solar deported to Auschwitz-Birkenau as part of large transport to lessen crowding at Terezín before visit by the International Red Cross.

July 14–16, 1944   Franci, Kitty, and their group of 500 mostly Czech women deported from Auschwitz to Dessauer Ufer in Hamburg.

July 20, 1944   Attempted coup against Hitler fails.

September 1944   Franci's group moved to Neugraben, where Franci works as an electrician.

January 27, 1945   Auschwitz liberated by the Russian Army.

February 3, 1945   Massive US air attack on Berlin.

TIMELINE

February 1945	Franci's group moved from Neugraben to Tiefstack.
February 13–15, 1945	Allies bomb Dresden; Hamburg was subject to extensive strategic bombing by the Allies from 1943 to 1945.
April 5, 1945	Franci's group moved to Bergen-Belsen.
April 15, 1945	British Army liberates Bergen-Belsen; Franci and Kitty are moved to Celle one week later.
April 30, 1945	Adolf Hitler commits suicide during Battle of Berlin.
May 4, 1945	General George S. Patton's army enters Czechoslovakia; Patton and British prime minister, Winston Churchill, advocate Allied liberation of Prague, but Allied supreme commander in Europe, General Dwight D. Eisenhower, accepts Stalin's demand that the Red Army liberate the city.
May 5–6, 1945	Prague Uprising by Czech Resistance; German Luftwaffe bombs Prague.
May 8, 1945	Victory in Europe Day (V-E Day): Allies formally accept Germany's unconditional surrender.
August 1945	Franci and Kitty leave Celle to return to Prague.

NOTES ON THE
CONCENTRATION CAMPS

Terezín (in Czech) or **Theresienstadt** (in German) was a former military garrison town sixty kilometers northwest of Prague that the Nazis turned into a unique combination of assembly point, transit camp, and ghetto in November 1941. Some 148,000 Jews were transported to Terezín, most from Bohemia, Moravia, and Germany, but also from Austria, the Netherlands, Slovakia, Hungary, and Denmark. The majority were immediately or eventually deported to extermination camps. More than 33,000 people died of illness and/or malnutrition in Terezín. Among its prisoners were some of the most prominent Central European Jewish artists, performers, philosophers, rabbis, writers, and educators. Terezín was controlled by the SS, guarded by Czech gendarmes, and administered by Jews coerced into executing Nazi policy. Touted in Nazi propaganda as a "model ghetto," it had a vibrant cultural life and schooled its children. On June 23, 1944, after a deceptive beautification effort by the Nazis, an International Red Cross team was invited to inspect the camp and fell for the ruse. Their report helped discredit accurate accounts of Terezín and other Nazi concentration camps. Terezín was liberated by the Soviet Army in May 1945.

The Czech Family (or Theresienstadt) Camp, also known as BIIb, was a sub-camp of **Auschwitz-Birkenau**. On September 6, 1943, 5,007 Jews from Terezín were transported to **Auschwitz-Birkenau**, tattooed, registered, put behind electrified barbed wire, but not shaved. They were allowed to keep their clothes and their children, who were housed in a children's barrack. Their papers were marked "special treatment" and "six months." The mortality rate was no lower here than in the rest of Auschwitz, but as in Terezín, the children received somewhat better food and were taught by teachers. After six months, those who had arrived in September 1943 and were still alive were murdered. As they went into the gas chamber, they sang the Czechoslovak national anthem, "Kde Domov Můj" ("Where Is My Home"); the Jewish national anthem, "Hatikvah"; and "The Internationale."

In December 1943 and May 1944 (Franci's transport), freight cars from Terezín brought 12,500 more prisoners to **Auschwitz-Birkenau**. At the beginning of July 1944, some (including Franci's group) were selected to work in forced labor camps. The remaining (nearly 7,000) prisoners were gassed to death. The killings of the Czech Family Camp inmates in March and July of 1944 constitute the largest mass murder of Czechoslovak citizens during the Second World War. Of the 17,500 prisoners sent to the Czech Family Camp, only 1,294 survived. Kitty and Franci were two of them.

Dessauer Ufer was part of the Neuengamme network of Nazi concentration camps in northern Germany that consisted of a main camp and more than eighty-five satellite camps. Tens of thousands of people from across occupied Europe were imprisoned there, including French, Italian, and Russian POWs and slave laborers, and Jews. At least 42,900 people died inside the Neuengamme camps, on the death marches when the camps were evacuated, during bombings, or after they were transported to other concentration camps.

In mid-July 1944, a transport of 1,500 mostly Czech Jewish women left Auschwitz-Birkenau, including Franci. Five hundred of them were sent to Dessauer Ufer, near Hamburg's oil refineries, to clear the rubble caused by Allied bombings. In September 1944, those five hundred were moved to Neugraben. In February 1945, they were moved to Tiefstack. In the first week of April 1945, they were moved to Bergen-Belsen.

Bergen-Belsen was a concentration camp located in northern Germany, established in 1940 to house prisoners of war. It came to include Jews, political prisoners, Roma "asocials," criminals, Jehovah's Witnesses, and homosexuals. Late in the war, it became a dumping ground for thousands of Jews driven from other camps on death marches. Approximately 50,000 people died in Bergen-Belsen, including Anne and Margot Frank. Poor sanitary conditions and lack of food and water led to starvation and an outbreak of disease. Franci contracted typhus, but there were also outbreaks of tuberculosis, typhoid fever, and dysentery. The British Army liberated the camp on April 15, 1945. More than 13,000 former prisoners died after liberation. Franci and Kitty recuperated in the town of Celle, eleven miles away, where the British Army set up a hospital. Because of rampant disease, they later evacuated and then burned down the camp.

MADHUR
JAFFREY'S
FLAVOURS

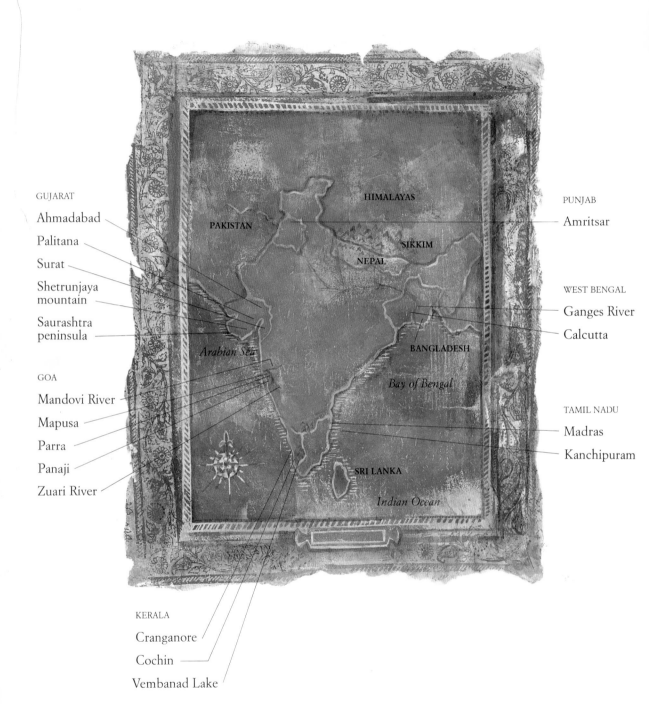

GUJARAT
Ahmadabad
Palitana
Surat
Shetrunjaya mountain
Saurashtra peninsula

GOA
Mandovi River
Mapusa
Parra
Panaji
Zuari River

KERALA
Cranganore
Cochin
Vembanad Lake

PUNJAB
Amritsar

WEST BENGAL
Ganges River
Calcutta

TAMIL NADU
Madras
Kanchipuram

HIMALAYAS
PAKISTAN
SIKKIM
NEPAL
Arabian Sea
BANGLADESH
Bay of Bengal
SRI LANKA
Indian Ocean

Madhur Jaffrey's Flavours of India

~

BBC BOOKS

This book is published to accompany the television series entitled *Flavours of India* which was first broadcast in 1995
Published by BBC Books,
an imprint of BBC Worldwide Publishing,
BBC Worldwide Ltd, Woodlands, 80 Wood Lane
London W12 0TT

First Published 1995
Reprinted, Hardback 1995 and Paperback 1995 (three times)

© Madhur Jaffrey 1995

ISBN 0 563 37074 2 (hardback)
       0 563 37077 7 (paperback)

Designed by Barbara Mercer
Map by Linda Baker Smith
Recipe photographs by James Murphy
Styling by Jane MacLeish
Home Economist Allyson Birch

Set in Simoncini Garamond by Ace Filmsetting Ltd, Frome
Printed and bound in Great Britain by Butler & Tanner Ltd, Frome
Colour separation by Radstock Reproductions Ltd, Midsomer Norton
Jacket printed by Clays Ltd, St Ives plc

Metric, Imperial and, where relevant, American cup measurements are given in the recipes. Always follow one set of measurements only.

Page 2: A temple boat in Kerala.

Pages 6–7: A Hindu wedding ceremony in Calcutta, West Bengal.

CONTENTS

INTRODUCTION   6

KERALA   10
GUJARAT   50
GOA   90
WEST BENGAL   134
TAMIL NADU   174
PUNJAB   214

SPECIAL INGREDIENTS   259
EQUIPMENT   281
TECHNIQUES   285
MAIL ORDER SUPPLIERS   291
INDEX   293
ACKNOWLEDGEMENTS   319

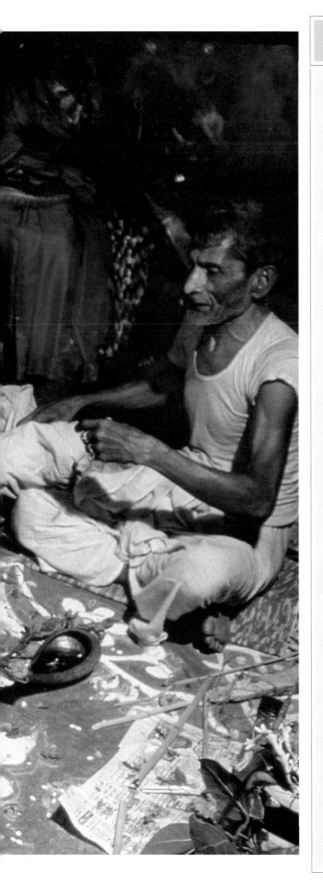

INTRODUCTION

INDIA NEVER FAILS TO surprise me. That is the least I expect of it.

This vast sub-continent, with its diverse tongues and faiths and its complex culture, is an amalgam of haphazardly arranged states that are really mini-nations. Over the last 5000 years these mini-nations, each with its own blend of historical and geographical circumstances, have evolved at their own speed, with their own influences that have come from the inside or from the outside, by land and sea.

Not even India's inhabitants know everything about their nation. Even they find gems of art, nature and culinary creativity where they are least expected. While they may know, in general, what their country holds there are millions of specifics that they may only discover with time, if they are lucky. Perhaps it is those who know India best who realize how much it is that they do not know. Like a clever, seductive paramour, India reveals itself slowly.

Perhaps all this is my way of answering a question that you may well ask me, 'Why another Indian cookbook? What is there left to be said?'

A great deal, is the short answer. Every time I return to India I find new and wondrous foods. During a filming trip to Assam, near India's eastern frontier, I once found myself eating with a member of the Khasi tribe who also happened to be my designated hairdresser. She offered me two relishes – a chutney made with a fermented soy bean paste, green chillies, garlic and lime juice and a bamboo-shoot pickle – both of which I had never eaten before and could not have even imagined. I immediately jotted them down in my notebook. East Asian and South Asian, compressed into one. That was over 20 years ago. Those recipes sleep in a notebook, waiting for me to find the precise spot for them.

There are other recipes that have never even made it to notebooks because I could not locate their true sources. About 10 years ago – or was it more? – when I was preparing for a trip to Kerala on India's south-western coast, I received a detailed letter from a Keralite friend who lives in England, Norma Moss, telling me all the different foods that I should be on the look-out for in her home state. She casually mentioned a 'boatman's curry' that I should try and find. It was something that was made and sold by the boatmen who ply Kerala's Venice-like network of inland waterways. Norma added that she had eaten this curry on childhood voyages and that it probably did not even exist any more.

On every trip to Kerala since then I have asked about this 'boatman's curry' to no avail. I, too, was convinced that the evolution to more modern, fast-moving water-buses had taken care of that particular dish. Not so. I found it this year on a rice boat in the middle of Lake Vembanad! You will find the recipe on page 30.

I always knew that the state of Gujarat had dozens of noodles – 'pastas' would perhaps be a more accurate title – made out of wheat and chick pea flour. Most of these, I thought, were fried and eaten in a dry, crisp form as snacks or made into milky, vermicelli desserts. I did not learn until this year that 'pastas' here may be dropped into exquisite, savoury sauces and eaten as main courses.

In all the Indian cookbooks that I have written, I have never had a recipe for the very typical, sweet and sour, cauliflower-turnip-radish pickle that is made annually in most Punjabi homes and stored in large crocks. It is never served in a restaurant. This mustardy pickle is made at home and served at home. When I was at school in Delhi and we all brought home-made lunches in tiffin-carriers, a Sikh friend from the Punjab often let us share her simple delights – thick flaky breads (*parathas*) stuffed with potatoes or grated white radish and these pickles. They were incomparable. Well, you will find the breads and the pickle in this book.

While you will find here some new variations of dishes that you already know and some easier versions of recipes in my other books, most of the dishes are new discoveries. I have had great pleasure in finding them and I hope you will have great pleasure cooking and eating them. I have looked in some depth at six of India's states – Kerala, Gujarat, Goa, West Bengal, Tamil Nadu and Punjab. In the future, I hope to look at six more and then six more . . . It is a lifelong task. India has so much.

THIS BOOK IS DEDICATED TO
THOSE WHO ARE MY DEAREST

Sanford
Zia
Meera, Craig and Rohan
Sakina, Frank and 'Grainy'-in-the-womb

KERALA

MILLIONS OF BLACK, FLUTTERING forms swirl in ever-changing patterns, silhouetted against the glowing red of the setting sun. Disturbed sometimes by the sultry breezes that come off Vembanad Lake and sometimes by passing boats, these Siberian ducks will nonetheless settle down for the night on the gentle waters. They are in Kerala for the winter as any mortal in his right mind would also want to be.

Kerala, nestling along India's southwestern coast and rising skywards from the Arabian Sea to the mountainous western Ghats, is a warm, fertile heaven on earth, a sprawling Venice leavened with the lushest of tropical greenery, its land and waters proffering an endless array of delicious edibles from the 'king' of spices – black pepper – to king (jumbo) prawns, the size of small lobsters.

Arching palms and paddy fields line a vast network of inland waterways that include lagoons, canals, rivers and bays. Known generally as the 'backwaters', these have, over the centuries, not just yielded foods but have acted as Kerala's roads. Houses are built along them as are schools. Boats – long, slim canoes, or palm-covered 'rice boats' used for transporting goods, or plain old 'water buses' bursting with passengers – are often the only mode of getting from here to there.

I arrive in a canoe that has been blackened with age and water and land in front of a wrought-iron gate. Behind the gate is an old, white house. It has three wings, all supported by sloping tiled roofs, very Chinese in the way they curl up at the ends. The Chinese have traded on this coast since antiquity and left behind a rich legacy in pickling jars, cleavers and wok-like cooking vessels, to say nothing of architectural styles and fishing nets.

Two wings of the house, fronted with pillars, are right on the water. One is for the enjoyment of the men in the family, landed Syrian Christians who, as a community, claim to have been converted by St Thomas himself in the first century. The other is for the storage of coconuts from the family's many trees. They take their coconuts seriously here. The name of the state, Kerala, means 'the land of coconuts'. The coconut is bankable not only for its oil and its coir but also for its daily use in every single kitchen. A breakfast chutney requires it; so does the prawn (shrimp) *thoran*, prawns (shrimp) steamed with a coconut chilli-paste, that is devoured at lunch; the tapioca *bonda*, a fritter nibbled at tea-time; and the country-style duck curry eaten at dinner. One local culinary authority, a Hindu and a strict vegetarian, has already told me with some firmness that for her *avial* (poached vegetables in a curry-leaf-flavoured coconut-yoghurt sauce), only coconuts from old-fashioned trees would do. None of the new hybrids for her.

Previous page: Chinese fishing nets line the harbour-side at Cochin, Kerala.

The main wing of the Syrian Christian household is set back a little. There is a courtyard in front, dotted with pots of flowering bougainvillaea, then a narrow pillared veranda with beautifully carved eaves. Behind the low, central door – solid carved wood studded with brass details – is the granary. It is here that freshly harvested rice gathered from the family's fields is stored and it is here that it awaits a respectable rise in prices before it is released into the market. In the olden days, a guard slept in this room, sometimes right on top of the rice, to ensure its safety.

Rice is Kerala's premier grain, eaten at every single meal. Generally it is short-grained 'boiled' (converted) rice, par-boiled, and then partially milled so that it is reddish in hue and exceedingly nutritious.

Some Kerala delicacies have already been prepared in the kitchen. As the youngsters jabber on about how they all learned to swim in the canal that fronts the house, using banana trunks as floats and often taking flying leaps straight from the house into the water, or how they loved hiding in the dark cellar where banquet-sized *uralis* (wide but shallow cooking vessels used for *payasams,* grain puddings) are stored, the older women have laid out a welcoming feast.

There is *stew*, a festive dish of lamb, potatoes and carrots simmered gently in coconut milk. It is almost always eaten to break the Lenten fast at Easter. Because it is so good and so soothing, it is also eaten at other times, whenever there is the slightest hint of a celebration. To sop up the cardamom and clove-flavoured juices of the *stew*, there is a stack of creamy-white *appams* – soft, slightly cupped rice pancakes, plump and spongy in the centre (the more specific name would be *kalappams* as there is a whole family of them). There is a freshly prepared rice vermicelli – *idi appam*, made by putting a rice dough through a special press and then steaming it – a dryish meat, stir-fried with tiny coconut chips (*erachi olathu*) and a delicious black *halva* made with wheat gluten and jaggery.

Also gracing the table are cylinders of coarsely pounded rice and coconut (*pootu*) that have been steamed together in hollowed-out bamboos (these days aluminium tubing is frequently used). They are either eaten at breakfast with bananas and milk or as the starch with dishes such as the *meen vevichathu* set before us: in a bowl, sardines float in a fiery red chilli and shallot sauce, soured to perfection with the judicious use of *kodampoli*, a local dried fruit of the mangosteen family.

I would happily fly to this coastal state just for its fish. A woman once said to me, 'People are so lazy here. They just have to open their mouths and food falls in.' There certainly seems to be an over-abundance of very fresh fish and seafood. At some beaches, such as the one near Fort Cochin where the Portuguese, Dutch and eventually the British once held sway, strollers can buy freshly caught creatures of all sizes and shapes – white salmon (*rawas*), large tiger prawns (shrimp), white and red snapper, mullet, crabs, baby sharks and pomfrets – from a fishmonger's shack and then take them to a neighbouring shack to be cooked. You want a quick sauté? A blackened frying-pan comes out, in goes some oil, some garlic and shallots. Meanwhile, some urchin has peeled the prawns (shrimp) and rubbed them with salt, turmeric and ground red chillies. These get thrown into the pan. A few good tosses and the contents of the pan are emptied into a saucer. A tinny spoon is stuck in. Go sit on a rock by the water and enjoy.

You want your fish fried? A more prosperous shack has a sign FAST FOOD . . . FISH FRIED BY ORDER. You could take your snapper there, if you wish. Meanwhile, in homes all across the state, squid rings are being dropped into a gingery coconut sauce, sardines are being poached with shallots, ginger and green chillies, whole pomfret are being stuffed with a paste of coconut, green chilli and fresh green coriander and then baked, crabs are being stir-fried with curry leaves and mustard seeds, and oysters are being made into fritters.

Fish are caught everywhere. Little boys begin catching them just outside their homes with crude fishing rods. Some of these youngsters will graduate to run prawn (shrimp) farms one day. The demand for more and more prawns (shrimp) by Japan as well as the West has encouraged some of the most imaginative farming. During the monsoon season, when there is plenty of fresh water falling from the heavens, precious fields are used to grow rice. Once winter comes and the only water available is from the brackish inland waterways, the fields are flooded with it nonetheless and used to farm prawns (shrimp)!

Some of these same little boys will grow up to manipulate the Chinese fishing nets that dot much of the coastline. Looking like monstrous, primeval, moving sculptures, the nets consist mainly of five solid teak poles that arch upwards to a height of at least 30 metres (100 feet). These hold and move the net. As the contraptions are lowered and raised with ropes, these lumbering giant spiders, dating from the time of Kublai Khan, scoop up all the fish that are finning by. The nets are considered so valuable that brides' families even offer them as dowries.

Some of the children might end up owning the trawlers that drag the floor of the Arabian Sea, bringing in everything from kingfish to mackerels. Some might even grow up to be *karimeen* fishermen.

The *karimeen* fishermen are unique. They work in groups of four to catch one of the most prized of fish. Flat, with black and gold stripes over a white-spotted body, the *karimeen* likes only fresh water. Vembanad Lake, a dammed lagoon, is a favoured habitat.

Two of the fishermen, their skins burnished to a glowing black, tie a rope to their skimpy loincloths and dive in from their boat. The rope, with bunting-like strips of white plastic attached to it, will be pulled along the water in a wide U-shape. Its purpose is to disturb and scare the fish. The *karimeen* will look for cover in the silty bottom. A third fisherman, with steady eyes and steady hands, will dive in, find the *karimeen* in the silt, grab it with a bare hand, swim up with it and, taking careful aim, toss it into the boat.

The fishermen will do this for 5–6 hours, by which time sun and water will have taken their toll. All the black canoes that dot the lake will head to a port where the fish will be auctioned off.

Munambam Harbour, opposite Cranganore where St Thomas is supposed to have landed in AD 52 and where a wide backwater empties into the Arabian Sea, is one such port. Boats of all sizes that left home in the middle of the night begin to return in the afternoon. By the time the sun is low, casting a golden sheen on the water, the boats are five or six deep all along the harbour. As soon as the first catch hits land, the auction begins.

An auctioneer moves to the fish and yells the opening bid. Buyers yell out the price they are willing to pay. Though the need to shout seems unnecessary, the decibel level of the entire transaction, by tradition, remains high, maintaining the quality of a rough, country quarrel. The

A fish market at Trirandrum, Kerala.

winner walks off with the baskets of gleaming prawns (shrimp) or squid or red snapper. Some of the fish, which have been earmarked for foreign markets, will go immediately for processing.

The prawns (shrimp) may end up in the prawn (shrimp) 'factory' in Chavadi where truckloads seem to arrive every hour. There is no mechanization of any sort and 160 women work in long rows, squatting on flat boards that barely keep them off the wet floor. Tables were tried to enable the women to stand. The experiment failed. The women found standing uncomfortable. They preferred to squat.

Each of the mostly unmarried women, in sarong-like *pawadas* and with hair sleek with coconut oil, has seven or eight gleaming, stainless steel bowls on the floor in front of her. In their hands, the women wield sharp, single-edged blades. Their job, tedious as it may be, is to peel the prawns (shrimp) and sort them into sizes. They work with jet speed, some doing a prawn (shrimp) per second. Since they will be paid by each pre-weighed bowlful, speed means money. Skins go flying into one bowl, the peeled prawn (shrimp) into the others. As soon as a bowl – any bowl – is filled, it is taken away by one of the few males on the premises. From here the prawns (shrimp) will be taken to another factory for freezing and shipment to destinations as far away as Japan and the United States.

Most of the fish will be eaten right here in Kerala. E. X. Anthony is an attendant at the sixteenth-century St Francis' Church in Cochin where Vasco da Gama was once buried and where long matting, hand-pulled fans still run along the length of the building. Shielding himself from the heat outside, he sits on a bench in a cool corridor, his tiffin-carrier open in front of him. He is having lunch. With his white, par-boiled rice, there is '*meen* (fish) curry'. Did he make it himself? 'Oh, yes,' he says, shaking his head happily. 'I ground up some coconut, red chillies, cinnamon, turmeric, coriander, garlic and shallots. Then I added some water and cooked this sauce for 30 minutes. Then I slipped in some small fish and cooked them for a few minutes. Finally I heated some oil, put into it some mustard seeds, sliced shallots and green chillies and threw the oil and spices into the pot with the fish.'

Damodaran is a boatman with even less ready cash then E. X. Anthony. He can afford no oil at all. Yet his boatman's curry (for which I have been searching, having heard of it from an old Keralite friend) is exquisite. A boat is more precious than a life to Damodaran and his family. He will accept the death of a family member more readily than the loss of his boat which provides food for them all and will do so for generations – especially *his* boat. Damodaran is the proud owner of a rice boat. These strong, sturdy vehicles, solid wood with a curving roof of waterproof matting, used for transporting rice and other goods, now cost upwards of £20 000 ($30 000), a fortune in Kerala. Expensive hotels display them as pretty curiosities.

I am invited inside the rice boat – a working boat – for a meal, which Damodaran prepares himself, as he does every single day of his life. I take off my shoes and climb in. The patina of the thick, dark teak wood which can take much buffeting by wind and water, would be the envy of any antique dealer. It glows with use. A plank is removed near the prow. Lo and behold, a kitchen appears. At least a stove does. On either side, neatly tucked into the hollows of bamboos so that they disappear, literally, in the woodwork, are all the spices as well as the shallots and ginger needed for cooking.

Damodaran produces a grinding-stone and grinds with swift efficiency, adding sprinklings of water as he does so. Coconut, coriander, chillies, turmeric are all turned into a ball of paste. This goes into an earthen pot with some water and boils away. Now in go some lightly crushed shallots, some crushed ginger, green chillies, *kodampoli* (the sour tamarind), curry leaves and salt. Lastly, *karimeen* pieces are slipped in and allowed to poach. This is eaten with the local, red par-boiled rice. I cannot say if it was the boat itself or the absolute freshness of the fish or Damodaran's cooking or the watery scene replete with swaying palms on the banks and the boat slowly cutting its way through a thick carpeting of pinkish-purple water hyacinths, but fish has rarely tasted as good.

The swaying palms on the banks give every home the coconuts it needs in its daily cooking. Except in very big cities, of which Kerala does not have too many, coconuts rarely need to be bought. Vegetarian Brahmins may use them to make *olan*, in which small cubes of vegetables (ripe cucumber, gourds, pumpkins) are poached and then mixed with par-boiled split peas and coconut milk, or to create a whole world of fudges, *halvas* and puddings. Coconut oil is the chief cooking medium and any talk of it being a saturated oil only brings derisive laughs at ever-changing Western fads, with hands pointing to healthy grandmothers and grandfathers who have eaten it all their lives.

Snacks are fried in it. A trip to Willingdon Island in Cochin takes me to a small shop, MALABAR CHIPS. Some of the finest chips, crisps really, are made here. Not potato chips but banana chips, jackfruit chips and tapioca chips. Suresh, a young man with film star looks, slices three green plantains at a time on a mean-looking mandolin. These will be fried in an enormous wok of coconut oil, cooled and then bagged in plastic to be munched on boat rides, in cinemas and while watching athletic Kathakali performers as they leap and grimace, telling the stories of Hindu religious epics in long evenings of song and dance.

Today, the state of Kerala exports frogs' legs to France, squid to Japan, prawns (shrimp) to the United States and labour to the Gulf. But none of these have made the kind of mark in world commerce, politics or history that its spices have.

This is the natural home of black pepper, which many call the 'king of spices' and of cardamom, a fairly logical 'queen'. The teeming moist soil and the generous sun also encourage rhizomes like ginger and turmeric to spread their fingers, allowing the Western world to indulge in gingerbreads and ginger cakes and, using curcumin (the colouring matter) from high quality turmeric, to give millions of chickens in the United States and hundreds of pounds of cheeses in the United Kingdom a decidedly yellow hue.

It was the quest for these spices that brought the ships of the earliest Phoenicians, of King Solomon, of early Syrians, Egyptians, Greeks, Romans, Arabs and Chinese to the shores of India. Their interest was trade. They came and went easily. It was only in the late fifteenth century, after Pope Alexander VI had divided the 'undiscovered' world between Spain and Portugal, that bloody wars began with the Portuguese, Dutch, French and British all fighting for a slice of this rich, spice-bearing coast. The British won and set up

a factory and spice depot in 1683 in Tellicherry, a name still associated with good quality Malabar pepper, each berry of which is justly renowned for its aroma, weight and size.

Today, an independent India produces about a third of the world's pepper with much of it coming from Kerala. Most families with small kitchen gardens let the vines clamber casually up their pillars and porches, even up their garden trees, but those who grow it professionally – and many conglomerates are in the business now – make the vines climb up specially spiky tree trunks so that they get a good grip and bear fruitfully. All the harvesting is done by hand. Once the green peppercorns are dried, they turn black. They are then graded and are ready for the auctions at the Pepper Exchange in Cochin and for the Futures market. They are also ready for all the *steak au poivres* we wish to eat and ready to fill pepper-grinders in millions of homes across the world. For the people of Kerala, the green ones may be pickled but what about the black peppercorns? How about roasting them and grinding them to flavour a *meen pappas*, fish poached in a sweet, sour, creamy coconut sauce?

Selvaraj's Stew

LAMB STEW

CHRISTIAN KERALITES EAT THIS at Easter and Christmas and all other festive occasions. It is particularly welcome at Easter after the Lenten Fast. It is almost always eaten with Savoury Rice Breads (page 39), though plain rice would also be very good. It is a stew. To all intents and purposes it looks like Irish stew, but the sauce is enriched with coconut milk and there are cardamom pods and cinnamon for aroma and green chillies for heat.

❧

4 tablespoons vegetable oil
3 cardamom pods
2.5 cm/1 inch cinnamon
   stick
3–4 cloves
About 30 fresh curry leaves,
   if available
2.5 cm/1 inch piece of fresh
   ginger, shredded

1 medium-large red onion
   (100 g/4 oz), finely sliced
450 g/1 lb boneless lamb
   from the shoulder, cut into
   2.5 cm/1 inch pieces, with
   the fat removed
2 medium-sized potatoes
   (225 g/8 oz), cut into
   2.5 cm/1 inch dice

2 carrots, peeled and cut
   into 2.5 cm/1 inch chunks
1¼–1½ teaspoons salt or to
   taste
2 fresh hot green chillies
300 ml/10 fl oz/1¼ cups
   coconut milk from a well-
   stirred can or thick fresh
   milk (page 266)

❧

Heat the oil in a large, wide, preferably non-stick pan or wok over medium-high heat. When hot, put in the cardamom pods, cinnamon and cloves and half the curry leaves. Stir once or twice. Add the ginger and onion. Stir and fry for 4–5 minutes until the onion is soft.

Turn the heat up to high. Add the meat. Stir and fry for 8–10 minutes until the meat is just beginning to brown. Add the potatoes, carrots, salt and 1.2 litres/2 pints/5 cups water. Cover and bring to the boil.

Turn the heat to low and simmer for 1 hour. Add the chillies and remaining curry leaves. Gently simmer over medium-low heat for 10–15 minutes or until the meat is very tender and the sauce has the consistency of a puréed soup. (I sometimes need to mash 1 or 2 potato pieces against the side of the pan to achieve this.)

Just before serving, add the coconut milk, stir, and bring to a simmer.

SERVES 4

Mr A. R. Sunil's Erachi Olathu
'DRY' LAMB ENCRUSTED WITH SPICES

OF ALL THE MEAT dishes in Kerala, this remains one of my favourites. It may be that I developed a weakness for it because I first had it in the home of a close Syrian Christian friend, with a stack of *appams* as an accompaniment. The meat is first stewed with a mixture of fennel – which makes the dish unusually good – and spices. It is then stirred until all the sauce has dried up and the spices cling to it in a most delicious way.

The coconut chips are optional – they may be added for an extra Kerala taste, but you may leave them out if you cannot get fresh coconut.

❧

FOR THE SPICE POWDER:
1 tablespoon vegetable oil
2.5 cm/1 inch cinnamon stick
10–15 cloves
3 tablespoons coriander seeds
4–6 dried hot red chillies
1 tablespoon black peppercorns
½ teaspoon cumin seeds
1½ teaspoons fennel seeds
6 cardamom pods

YOU ALSO NEED:
5 tablespoons vegetable oil
120 g/4½ oz/1 cup plus 1½ tablespoons fresh coconut (page 265), first cut into thin slices and then into 1 cm/½ inch chips
¼ teaspoon ground turmeric
1 teaspoon salt
2 teaspoons brown mustard seeds
40 fresh curry leaves, if available

10–12 shallots (150 g/5 oz), finely sliced
2.5 cm/1 inch piece of fresh ginger, peeled and finely sliced
3 garlic cloves, peeled and finely chopped
1 kg/2¼ lb boneless lamb from the shoulder, cut into 2.5 cm/1 inch dice
2 tablespoons white wine vinegar

❧

To make the spice powder: Heat the 1 tablespoon oil in a large frying-pan or wok. When hot, put in all the spices. Stir until the chillies darken. Put the spices into a clean coffee grinder and grind to a fine powder. Set aside.

Heat 1 tablespoon of the remaining oil in a large frying-pan or wok over medium heat.

When hot, add the coconut chips, turmeric and ½ teaspoon of the salt. Stir and fry for 3–4 minutes or until the coconut is toasted. Set aside.

In a clean, large frying-pan heat 3 tablespoons of the oil over medium-high heat. When hot, add 1 teaspoon of the mustard seeds. Stir until the seeds pop, a matter of a few seconds. Now add about 20 of the curry leaves, 6–8 of the shallots, the ginger and garlic. Stir and fry for 3–4 minutes until the shallots become lightly browned. Add the meat and the spice powder. Stir to coat the meat well, then add the vinegar, toasted coconut chips, ½ teaspoon of the salt and 750 ml/ 1¼ pints/3 cups water. Bring to the boil, then turn the heat down and cover. Simmer for about 50 minutes to 1 hour or until the meat is almost tender. Remove the lid and continue to cook for another 10–15 minutes until the sauce

becomes very thick and clings to the meat, increasing the heat if necessary.

Meanwhile, heat the remaining 1 tablespoon oil in a small pan over medium heat. When hot, add the remaining mustard seeds. When the mustard seeds pop, add the remaining shallots and about 20 curry leaves. Stir and fry until the shallots become golden-brown. Add the contents of pan to the meat. Mix well and remove from the heat.

S E R V E S   4

Overleaf: Lamb Stew (page 19) with Savoury Rice Breads (page 39).

Mr A. R. Sunil's Taharava Kootan

DUCK CURRY, COUNTRY STYLE

DUCKS CAN BE SEEN in every paddy field and backwater. It is not surprising that they make their way into curries and roasts. Serve with plain rice.

❧

FOR THE SPICE POWDER:
1½ tablespoons ground
   coriander
2 teaspoons cayenne pepper
¼ teaspoon ground turmeric
¼ teaspoon freshly ground
   black pepper
5 cm/2 inch cinnamon stick
6 cloves
4 cardamom pods

YOU ALSO NEED:
4 tablespoons vegetable oil

1 small red onion
   (50 g/2 oz), finely sliced
2.5 cm/1 inch piece of fresh
   ginger, peeled and cut into
   long, thin slices
18 garlic cloves, peeled and
   finely chopped
6 fresh hot green chillies,
   split at one end
One 1 kg/2¼ lb duck,
   skinned and cut into
   7.5 cm/2 inch cubes
1½ tablespoons white wine
   vinegar

1½–1¾ teaspoons salt
300 ml/10 ml oz/1¼ cups
   coconut milk, well stirred
   from a can or thick fresh
   milk (page 266)
1 large potato (200 g/7 oz),
   cut into 5 cm/2 inch pieces
1 teaspoon *ghee*
1 teaspoon brown mustard
   seeds
3–4 shallots (50 g/2 oz),
   finely sliced
About 30 fresh curry leaves,
   if available

❧

Put the coriander, cayenne, turmeric, black pepper, cinnamon, cloves and cardamom pods for the spice powder into a clean coffee grinder. Grind to a fine powder. Set aside.

Heat 3 tablespoons of the oil in a large, wide pan or wok over medium heat. When hot, put in the onion. Stir and fry the onion for 3–4 minutes or until soft. Add the ginger, garlic and chillies. Stir and fry for another 2–3 minutes. Add the duck, spice powder, vinegar and salt. Stir once then add 100 ml/ 3½ fl oz/½ cup of the coconut milk and 300 ml/10 fl oz/1¼ cups water. Bring to the boil. Cover, turn the heat to low and simmer

gently for 1½ hours or until the duck is almost tender. Add the potatoes and cook for 20 minutes. Add the remaining coconut milk. Stir and gently simmer for 5–6 minutes.

Meanwhile heat the remaining oil and the *ghee* in a small pan over medium-high heat. When hot, add the mustard seeds. As soon as they pop, a matter of seconds, put in the shallots and the curry leaves. Stir and cook for a few minutes. When the shallots have browned slightly, empty the contents of the pan into the pan with the duck. Stir to mix.

SERVES 4–6

Mr Balasundaram's Nadan Kori Kootan

COUNTRY CHICKEN CURRY

THIS COUNTRY-STYLE DISH MAY be made with all manner of wild fowl or with ordinary chicken. It is best served with plain rice and any vegetables and salads of your choice.

If you wish to substitute unsweetened, desiccated coconut for fresh coconut use 75 g/3 oz/1 scant cup. Barely cover with warm water and leave for 1 hour, then proceed with the recipe.

❧

FOR THE GINGER AND GARLIC PASTE:
1 cm/½ inch piece of fresh ginger, peeled and coarsely chopped
6 garlic cloves, peeled and roughly chopped

FOR THE SPICE POWDER:
12 dried hot red chillies
1 tablespoon cumin seeds

1 tablespoon black peppercorns
3 cloves
2.5 cm/1 inch cinnamon stick
2 cardamom pods
½ teaspoon salt
150 g/5 oz/1¼ cups freshly grated coconut (page 265)

YOU ALSO NEED:
5 tablespoons vegetable oil

1 medium-large red onion (100 g/4 oz), finely sliced
½ teaspoon ground turmeric
1¼ teaspoons salt
One 750 g/1½ lb chicken, skinned and cut into 5 cm/2 inch pieces
3 medium-sized tomatoes, finely diced
6–7 shallots (75 g/3 oz), peeled and finely sliced

❧

Put the ginger and garlic for the paste into the container of an electric blender. Add 3 tablespoons water. Blend to a smooth paste. Remove from the blender and set aside.

Put the chillies, cumin seeds, peppercorns, cloves, cinnamon, cardamom pods and salt for the spice powder into a clean coffee grinder. Grind to a fine powder. Put the spice powder into the blender. Add 100 ml/3½ fl oz/½ cup water and the coconut. Blend to a smooth paste. Set aside.

Heat 4 tablespoons of the oil in a wok or large, wide, preferably non-stick pan over medium heat. When hot, add the onion. Stir and fry for 4–5 minutes until golden. Add the garlic and ginger paste. Stir once, and then add the turmeric and salt. Stir once or twice and add the chicken. Stir and fry for 10–15 minutes over medium heat until the chicken is lightly browned.

Add the tomatoes to the chicken. Stir and cook for 2 minutes. Add the spice paste and fry again for 3 minutes. Now add 600 ml/ 1 pint /2½ cups water, turn the heat down and continue to simmer gently for about 10–15 minutes or until the sauce becomes thick and the chicken is tender.

Meanwhile, heat the remaining oil in a small frying-pan over medium heat. When hot, add the shallots. Stir and fry for 3–4 minutes until brown and crisp. Remove with a slotted spoon, spread on kitchen paper (paper towels) and set aside. When the chicken is cooked, sprinkle with the fried shallots and stir them in.

SERVES 4

Mr A. R. Sunil's Fish Moilly
FISH STEW

THIS SIMPLE AND DELICIOUS dish may be made with kingfish steaks, cod steaks or chunky pieces of halibut or haddock fillets. In Kerala, this sauced dish is always served with rice but you may serve it with boiled potatoes and a salad.

About 1¼ teaspoons salt
½ teaspoon ground turmeric
450 g/1 lb fish steaks or fillets, cut into 5 cm/2 inch cubes (see above)
4 tablespoons coconut oil or any other vegetable oil

1 medium-large red onion (100 g/4 oz), finely sliced
6 fresh hot green chillies, finely sliced
2.5 cm/1 inch piece of fresh ginger, peeled and finely shredded

About 30 fresh curry leaves, if available
200 ml/7 fl oz/1 cup coconut milk, well stirred from a can or thick fresh milk (page 266)
2 tablespoons lime juice

Mix ¼ teaspoon of the salt and ¼ teaspoon of the turmeric together. Rub over the fish. Set aside.

Heat the oil in a large, wide, preferably non-stick pan or wok over medium heat. When hot, add the onion, chillies and ginger. Stir once or twice. Add the curry leaves. Stir and fry for 3–4 minutes until the onion is soft. Add ¼ teaspoon turmeric powder and 150 ml/5 fl oz/¾ cup water. Mix well. When the mixture boils, add the fish. Spoon the sauce over the fish. Add ¾ teaspoons salt. Turn the heat down. Cover and simmer for 4–5 minutes, spooning the sauce over the fish and shaking the pan gently to prevent sticking. Add the coconut milk. Shake the pan and check the salt, adding a little more if needed. Cover and simmer for a further 3–4 minutes, shaking the pan now and then. Add the lime juice. Shake the pan gently and remove from the heat.

SERVES 4

Shoba Ramji's Meen Pollichathu
FISH BAKED IN FOIL

WHOLE FISH ARE GENERALLY 'baked' in a wok lined with a banana leaf. Since we in the West seldom have access to a banana leaf, I have wrapped the fish in foil and baked it in an oven. You may use whole fish such as red snapper, turbot, grey mullet, kingfish – as I have done here – or, for greater convenience, steaks from swordfish, salmon or cod. The timing will, of course, vary depending on the size and thickness of the fish.

If you use more than one fish, or pieces of fish, it would be a good idea to wrap them separately before putting them in the oven. Although this dish is normally served with rice, you may eat it with boiled potatoes and sautéd vegetables.

❦

FOR THE SPICE PASTE:
2 teaspoons coconut oil or any other vegetable oil
4–6 75 g/3 oz shallots, peeled and roughly chopped
4 garlic cloves, peeled and roughly chopped
1 cm/½ inch piece of fresh ginger, peeled and finely sliced
15–20 fresh curry leaves, if available

4 teaspoons cayenne pepper
½ teaspoon salt
1 tablespoon vinegar
1 teaspoon black peppercorns

YOU ALSO NEED:
3 tablespoons coconut oil or any other vegetable oil, plus extra for greasing
1 medium-large red onion (100 g/4 oz), finely chopped

4–6 fresh hot green chillies
1 medium-sized tomato, finely diced
1 tablespoon sesame seeds
½ teaspoon salt
Two 750 g/1½ lb kingfish, cleaned and gutted
2 tablespoons coarsely chopped, fresh green coriander

❦

Pre-heat the oven to 200°C/400°F/Gas 6.

Heat the 2 teaspoons oil for the spice paste in a small pan over medium-low heat. When hot, add the shallots, garlic, ginger and the curry leaves. Stir and fry for 2–3 minutes until the shallots begin to soften. Add the cayenne pepper and salt. Stir once or twice. Put in the container of an electric blender with the vinegar and 2 tablespoons water. Blend.

Put the peppercorns in a small, heated pan. Stir and roast over medium-high heat for 2 minutes. Crush in a mortar and add to the

Duck Curry, Country Style (page 23) with Vegetable Rice (page 38).

shallot mixture. Put to one side. This is the spice paste.

Heat the 3 tablespoons oil in a wide pan or wok over medium-high heat. When hot, add the onion. Fry for 3–4 minutes until soft. Add the chillies. Fry for 3–4 minutes until they begin to soften. Add the tomato, sesame seeds and salt. Stir and fry for 4–5 minutes until the tomato is soft. Put to one side.

Make 3–4 shallow, slightly diagonal slits on either side of each of the fish. This will allow the flavour to infuse. Smear the fish with the spice paste.

Grease 2 pieces of foil, each roughly 30 cm × 30 cm/12 inch × 12 inch in size and big enough to wrap a whole fish in. Sprinkle the centre of the foil, where the fish is to sit, with the coriander. Divide half of the fried onion mixture between the pieces of foil, sprinkling it over the coriander. Place the fish on top. Put the remaining onion mixture over the fish. Wrap the fish lightly in the foil. Bake in the oven for 20–25 minutes until just cooked through. Uncover gently. Lift the fish out with a long fish spatula and place on a serving dish. Pour the extra juices over them and serve.

If you are at all worried about breaking the fish, you can loosen their undersides with a spatula and slide them on to a serving plate or else serve them directly from the foil.

S E R V E S   4

Shoba Ramji's Meen Patichatu
MARINATED AND STEWED SARDINES

SARDINES ARE A COMMON fish here, loved by people of all means. As one travels along the backwaters, it is not uncommon to see villagers on the banks cooking sardines in fiery red sauces.

In this particular recipe the sardines are smeared with a coconut paste and left to simmer with curry leaves. They are best served with plain rice. Sardines that are used here range from 13 cm/5 inches to 20 cm/8 inches in length. They are generally cooked whole, but if they are the larger size they are frequently cut in half first. You may, if you prefer, use kingfish, swordfish or halibut steaks, remembering to cook them in a single layer.

If you wish to substitute unsweetened, desiccated coconut for fresh coconut use 25 g/1 oz/5 tablespoons. Barely cover with warm water for 1 hour. Squeeze dry then proceed with the recipe.

FOR THE SPICE PASTE:
7 fresh hot green chillies, roughly chopped
1 cm/½ inch piece of fresh ginger, peeled and roughly chopped
1 small red onion (50 g/2 oz), roughly chopped
3 garlic cloves

50 g/2 oz/½ cup freshly grated coconut (page 265)
5–10 fresh curry leaves, if available
1 teaspoon salt

YOU ALSO NEED:
4 fresh, whole sardines, about 325 g/12 oz each, cleaned and gutted (net weight about 250 g/9 oz each)

3 tablespoons vegetable oil
4–5 dried hot red chillies
20 fresh curry leaves, if available
2½ tablespoons tamarind paste (page 278), diluted with 2 tablespoons water

Place all the ingredients for the spice paste in the container of an electric blender. Add 120 ml/4 fl oz ½ cup water and blend until smooth. You may need to push the paste down with a spatula from time to time.

Take the sardines and smear each of them well with the spice paste. Set aside.

Heat the oil over medium-high heat in a pan, preferably non-stick, that is large and wide enough to cook all the sardines at once in a single layer. When hot, add the red chillies and the curry leaves if using. Stir once then lay the sardines in the pan. Cook for 2–3 minutes on either side over low heat. Shake the pan gently now and then, spooning the sauce over the sardines. Add the tamarind paste. Shake the pan to mix. Cover and cook for another 15–20 minutes, shaking the pan occasionally.

The sauce should be quite thick and should coat the sardines.

S E R V E S   4

Mr Damodaran's Vallamkarnanda Meen Kootan
BOATMAN'S CURRY

THIS RECIPE WAS TAKEN from boatmen plying the inland waterways near Kumarakom. They make their living fishing and carrying goods – such as rice – and people. This is a dish they cook on their rice boats for themselves and any passengers. The fish used here was the very popular flat, freshwater *karimeen* (page 14) but steaks from any firm-fleshed fish such as kingfish, cod, swordfish or salmon may be used. The *karimeen* are cleaned and then cut, crossways, into 2 or 3 pieces, head and all. Steaks will need to be cubed.

This is one of the few times that I have reduced the amount of chillies. The boatman's curry was utterly delicious but incendiary! It may be worth noting that no oil is used in the cooking.

If you wish to substitute unsweetened, desiccated coconut for fresh coconut use 75 g/3 oz/1 scant cup. Barely cover with warm water and leave for 1 hour, then proceed with the recipe.

❧

FOR THE SPICE PASTE:
4–6 dried hot red chillies, soaked in hot water for 15 minutes
1 teaspoon cayenne pepper
1 tablespoon paprika
3 tablespoons ground coriander

1 teaspoon ground turmeric
150 g/5 oz/1¼ cups freshly grated coconut (page 265)

YOU ALSO NEED:
2½ tablespoons tamarind paste (page 278)
3–4 fresh hot green chillies, split into halves

2.5 cm/1 inch piece of fresh ginger, peeled and lightly crushed
4–5 shallots (75 g/3 oz), peeled and lightly crushed
1½ teaspoons salt
750 g/1½ lb fish steaks, about 1 cm/½ inch thick

❧

Put all the ingredients for the spice paste into the container of an electric blender. Add 100 ml/3½ fl oz/½ cup water. Blend to make a smooth paste.

Put the spice paste into a medium-sized, heavy-bottomed pan. Add 100 ml/3½ fl oz water. Stir. The paste should have a similar consistency to that of a puréed soup.

Heat the spice paste over medium-low heat. Bring to a gentle simmer. Add the tamarind paste, green chillies, ginger, shallots and salt. Stir and simmer for 2–3 minutes. Slip in the fish. Stir once and cover. Simmer gently for 10–15 minutes until the fish is just cooked.

S E R V E S   4

Mr A. R. Sunil's Kannava Varitiyathu
SQUID WITH COCONUT

SQUID AND CUTTLEFISH OF every conceivable size are common to these shores and are eaten all along the coastline, although not further inland for some reason. Today, a lot of the squid is exported to Japan for a very good price. Here is one of the many ways in which it can be cooked. Serve it with plain rice. This dish is quite hot but deliciously so. If you wish to lessen the heat, just cut down on the cayenne pepper. If you wish to substitute unsweetened, desiccated coconut for fresh coconut use 25 g/1 oz/5 tablespoons. Barely cover with warm water and leave for 1 hour, then proceed with the recipe.

❧

50 g/2 oz/½ cup freshly grated coconut (page 265)

5 tablespoons coconut oil or any other vegetable oil

1 medium-large red onion (100 g/4 oz), finely chopped

1 cm/½ inch piece of fresh ginger, peeled and finely chopped

About 40 fresh curry leaves, if available

1 teaspoon ground turmeric

1 tablespoon cayenne pepper

1 tablespoon ground coriander

450 g/1 lb cleaned squid (page 285), sliced into 1 cm/½ inch wide rings

1 teaspoon salt

2 shallots (25 g/1 oz), peeled and finely chopped

❧

Put the grated coconut into the container of an electric blender. Add 100 ml/3½ fl oz/½ cup water and blend to a smooth paste. Set aside.

Heat 4 tablespoons of the oil in a large, wide, preferably non-stick pan or wok over medium-high heat. When hot, add the onion, ginger and about 20 curry leaves. Stir and fry for 3–4 minutes until the onion is soft. Add the cayenne pepper, turmeric and coriander. Stir and fry for 2–3 minutes. Add the squid and salt. Stir and fry for another 2–3 minutes. Now add the coconut paste. Turn the heat up and stir and fry for 5–7 minutes or until the squid is just cooked.

Heat the remaining oil in a small pan over medium heat. When hot, add the shallots and remaining curry leaves. Stir and fry until the shallots are golden.

Add the shallot and curry leaf mixture to the squid. Mix well and cook for another 2 minutes. The sauce should coat the squid. Remove from the heat and serve.

SERVES 4–6

Mr Balasundaram's Avial

⊘ MIXED VEGETABLES WITH COCONUT

SOUTH INDIA HAS DOZENS of dishes in which lightly boiled or steamed vegetables are 'dressed' with a sauce made out of freshly grated coconut. Each sauce is different from the next. This one has yoghurt and cumin in it.

There is a story about the creation of *avial*. A sixteenth-century king ordered his kitchen to provide a feast for his subjects that would last 30 days. For 29 days the food stocks held up. On the 30th day, the chef realized that all the oil – except for a few drops – had gone and that only bits and pieces of different vegetables were left in the larder. This is the dish that he came up with.

If you wish to substitute unsweetened, desiccated coconut for the fresh coconut use 100 g/4 oz/1¼ cups. Barely cover with warm water and leave for 1 hour, then proceed with the recipe.

❧

100 g/4 oz okra, cut into 2.5 cm/1 inch pieces

1 medium-sized carrot (100 g/4 oz), cut into 2.5 cm × 5 mm/ 1 inch × ¼ inch pieces

1 medium-sized potato (100 g/4 oz), peeled and cut into 2.5 cm × 5 mm/ 1 inch × ¼ inch pieces

100 g/4 oz green beans, cut into 2.5 cm/1 inch pieces

100 g/4 oz green, cooking plantains, peeled with a knife and cut into 1 cm/½ inch thick rounds

200 g/7 oz/1¾ cups freshly grated coconut (page 265)

5–6 fresh hot green chillies, coarsely sliced

1 teaspoon ground cumin

150 ml/5 fl oz/⅔ cup natural (plain) yoghurt

1½ teaspoons salt

40–50 fresh curry leaves, if available

1 teaspoon coconut oil (optional)

❧

Put the okra, carrot, potato, green beans and plantains in a large pan. Cover with 300 ml/ 10 fl oz/1¼ cups water. Bring to the boil over high heat. Turn the heat to medium and simmer for 10–12 minutes until the vegetables are tender. Drain and put to one side.

Meanwhile, put the coconut, chillies, cumin and 100 ml/3½ fl oz/½ cup water in an electric blender. Blend to a smooth paste.

In a large, wide pan or wok, very gently mix the vegetables, coconut paste, yoghurt, salt and the curry leaves. Set over low heat. Remove the pan from the heat before the *avial* comes to the boil.

Add the coconut oil if you wish and stir gently to mix.

SERVES 4

Shoba Ramji's Thenkapal Varadhiniya

⊘ AUBERGINES (EGGPLANTS) IN COCONUT MILK

THESE AUBERGINES (EGGPLANTS) ARE perfect with rice and breads.

❧

FOR THE SPICE PASTE:
½ teaspoon ground
  coriander
1 teaspoon black
  peppercorns
¼ teaspoon cumin seeds
¼ teaspoon ground turmeric
¼ teaspoon fennel seeds
2.5 cm/1 inch cinnamon
  stick
2 cloves

YOU ALSO NEED:
1 medium-sized (200 g/7 oz)

aubergine (eggplant), cut
  into 2.5 cm/1 inch pieces
½ teaspoon ground turmeric
½ teaspoon cayenne pepper
¾–1 teaspoon salt
6 tablespoons vegetable oil
1 small red onion (50 g/
  2 oz), peeled and finely
  sliced
2.5 cm/1 inch piece of fresh
  ginger, peeled and finely
  chopped
1 garlic clove, peeled and
  crushed

8–10 fresh curry leaves, if
  available
2–3 fresh hot green chillies,
  finely sliced
1 tablespoon white wine
  vinegar
100 ml/3½ fl oz/½ cup
  coconut milk, well stirred
  from a can or thick fresh
  milk (page 266)
Extra fresh hot green
  chillies, slit down the
  middle, to garnish
  (optional)

❧

Grind the ingredients for the spice paste in a clean coffee grinder. Empty into a small bowl. Add 2 tablespoons water. Mix to a fine paste. Set aside.

Put the aubergine (eggplant) in a medium-sized bowl with the turmeric, cayenne pepper and ¼ teaspoon of the salt. Mix well.

Heat 3 tablespoons of the oil in a large, wide, preferably non-stick pan over medium heat. When hot, add the aubergine (eggplant). Stir and fry for 6–8 minutes until tender and golden. Remove with a slotted spoon and lay on kitchen paper to remove excess oil.

Heat the remaining oil in a clean pan. Add the onion. Stir and fry over medium heat for 3–4 minutes until soft. Turn the heat to low. Add the ginger, garlic, curry leaves and chillies. Stir for 30 seconds. Add the vinegar and salt to taste. Stir once. Add the spice paste. Stir and fry for 2–3 minutes. Add the coconut milk and 150 ml/5 fl oz/⅔ cup water. Stir and fry gently for 3–4 minutes. Add the aubergine (eggplant). Stir and cook for 2–3 minutes.

The aubergine (eggplant) will absorb some sauce. The remainder will thicken to coat the back of a spoon. Garnish with the slit chillies.

SERVES 4

Mrs Bavani's Olan

CUCUMBER COOKED WITH LENTILS

A SIMPLE DISH OF the vegetarian Nair community. It is as nutritious as it is good.
It is generally eaten with plain rice and a selection of other vegetables, pulses
(legumes), pickles, chutneys and yoghurt dishes.

---

50 g/2 oz/⅓ cup red lentils
300 ml/10 fl oz/1¼ cups
  coconut milk, well stirred,
  from a can or thick fresh
  milk (page 266)

450 g/1 lb cucumber, cut
  crossways into
  2.5 cm/1 inch pieces
4 fresh hot green chillies, cut
  in half lengthways

1 teaspoon salt
8–10 fresh curry leaves, if
  available
1 tablespoon coconut oil or
  any other vegetable oil

Wash the lentils in several changes of water, until the water runs clear. Then soak them in enough hot water to cover by 4 cm/1½ inches for 3–4 hours. Drain.

Put 100 ml/3½ fl oz/½ cup of the coconut milk and 400 ml/14 fl oz/1¾ cups water in a medium-sized pan. Add the lentils. Bring to the boil. Turn the heat down, cover and simmer for 10–15 minutes. Add the cucumber, chillies and salt. Cook over low heat for 3–5 minutes or until the cucumber is tender.

Meanwhile, heat the coconut oil in a small pan over medium-high heat. When hot, add the curry leaves. Stir once or twice and then empty the contents of the small pan, oil and leaves, into the pan with the lentils and cucumber. Add the remaining coconut milk to the cucumber and lentil mixture. Stir and cook on a higher heat for 3–4 minutes until the sauce is medium-thick.

S E R V E S   4

Marinated and Stewed Sardines (page 28).

Mrs Bhavani's Manga Kalan
ⓥ MANGO CURRY

MANGO CURRIES ARE A Kerala treat. This one may be served with all Indian meals. I serve it in individual bowls, to be eaten with a teaspoon.
If you wish to use unsweetened, desiccated coconut instead of fresh coconut use 150 g/5 oz/1½ cups. Barely cover with warm water and leave for 1 hour, then proceed with the recipe.

∾

- 3 medium-sized ripe mangoes, peeled, pit removed and flesh cut into 1 cm/½ inch pieces
- 1 teaspoon ground turmeric
- 1 teaspoon cayenne pepper
- 1–1½ teaspoons salt
- 50 g/2 oz jaggery or brown sugar, if needed

- 300 g/11 oz/2¾ cups freshly grated coconut (page 265)
- 3–4 fresh hot green chillies, coarsely chopped
- ½ tablespoon cumin seeds
- 300 ml/10 fl oz/1¼ cups natural (plain) yoghurt, lightly beaten

- 2 tablespoons coconut oil or any other vegetable oil
- ¼ teaspoon brown mustard seeds
- 3–4 dried hot red chillies, broken into halves
- ¼ teaspoon fenugreek seeds
- 10–12 fresh curry leaves, if available

∾

Put the mangoes in a medium-sized pan. Add 250 ml/8 fl oz/1 cup water. Cover and stew for 8–10 minutes over medium-low heat. Stir occasionally. Add the turmeric, cayenne pepper and salt. Stir well. (If the mangoes are not sweet enough, add the jaggery or brown sugar to make the dish sweeter.)

Meanwhile, put the coconut, green chillies and cumin seeds into the container of an electric blender. Add 250 ml/8 fl oz/1 cup water and blend to a fine paste.

When the mangoes are cooked, mash them to a pulp. Add the coconut paste. Mix. Cover and simmer over medium heat, stirring occasionally, until the mixture becomes thick.

This should take about 10–15 minutes. Add the yoghurt and heat, stirring, until just warmed through. Do not let the mixture come to the boil. Remove from the heat and put to one side. Check for salt.

Heat the oil in a small pan over medium-high heat. When hot, add the mustard seeds. When the mustard seeds begin to pop, a matter of a few seconds, add the chillies, fenugreek seeds and the curry leaves. Stir and fry for a few seconds until the chillies darken. Quickly add the contents of the small pan to the mangoes. Stir to mix.

SERVES 4–6

Mrs K. M. Matthew's Spinach Thoran
⦿ SPINACH WITH COCONUT

THORANS ARE GENERALLY COOKED in woks. Vegetables, or prawns (shrimp) for that matter, are lightly sautéd or poached and then pushed to the edges of the wok. A mixture of fresh coconut and spices is placed in the centre and covered over with the main ingredient. The wok is covered and the dish is allowed to cook gently. The results are light and delicious. Serve with any Indian meal. In this recipe rice is used as a spice, adding an unusual nutty flavour.

If you wish to substitute unsweetened, desiccated coconut for fresh coconut use 65 g/2 oz/10 tablespoons. Barely cover with warm water and leave for 1 hour, then proceed with the recipe.

❧

2 garlic cloves, peeled

1 small red onion or
2–3 large shallots
(50 g/2 oz), peeled and
chopped

¼ teaspoon cayenne pepper

120 g/4½ oz/1 cup plus
1 tablespoon freshly grated
coconut (page 265)

1 teaspoon salt

450 g/1 lb spinach, washed
and shredded

1 fresh hot green chilli,
finely chopped, and 1 fresh
hot green chilli, split in half

1 tablespoon coconut oil or
any other vegetable oil

½ teaspoon brown mustard
seeds

1 teaspoon rice

2 shallots (25 g/1 oz), finely
sliced

About 15 fresh curry leaves,
if available

❧

Put the garlic, onion, cayenne pepper, coconut and salt into the container of an electric blender. Add 6 tablespoons water and blend to a smooth paste. Set aside.

Put the spinach in a wok or large, wide, preferably non-stick frying-pan over low heat. Sprinkle 3–4 tablespoons water over the top and cover. When steam begins to creep out at the sides and the spinach has wilted, remove the lid. Make a well in the pile of spinach and spoon in the coconut paste and chopped chilli. Cover with the spinach and replace the lid.

Again wait until steam appears, then remove the lid.

Meanwhile, heat the oil in a small pan over medium-high heat. When hot, add the mustard seeds and rice. As soon as the mustard seeds begin to pop and the rice expands, a matter of seconds, add the shallots. Stir and fry until the shallots start to turn golden. Add the split chilli and the curry leaves. Stir and fry for a second. Pour over the cooked spinach. Stir to mix.

SERVES 4

Mr A. R. Sunil's Neyychoru
VEGETABLE RICE

A VEGETABLE PILAF ENRICHED with chicken stock, this may be served with all Indian meals.

〜

Basmati rice measured to the 450 ml/15 fl oz/2 cup level in a measuring jug
2.5 cm/1 inch mace blade
3 cardamom pods
3 cloves
2.5 cm/1 inch cinnamon stick
1 teaspoon black peppercorns
2 fresh hot green chillies, coarsely chopped

3 garlic cloves, peeled and coarsely chopped
1 cm/½ inch piece of fresh ginger, peeled and coarsely chopped
4 tablespoons *ghee* or vegetable oil
1 bay leaf
1 carrot, cut in half lengthways and finely sliced

1 medium-large red onion (100 g/4 oz), finely sliced
600 ml/1 pint/2⅔ cups chicken stock
3 tablespoons coconut milk, well stirred from a can or thick fresh milk (page 266)
1 teaspoon salt
5 raw cashew nuts, split into halves
1 teaspoon sultanas (golden raisins)

〜

Wash the rice in several changes of water, until the water runs clean. Drain. Cover with water. Soak for 30 minutes. Drain and set aside.

Put the mace, cardamom pods, cloves, cinnamon and peppercorns into a clean coffee grinder and grind to a fine powder. Set aside.

Put the chillies, garlic, ginger and 3 tablespoons water into the container of an electric blender and blend to a fine paste. Set aside.

Heat 3 tablespoons of the *ghee* or oil in a large, wide, preferably non-stick pan over medium-high heat. When hot, add the bay leaf, carrot and half the onion. Stir and fry for 2–3 minutes. Add the chilli-garlic-ginger paste. Stir and fry for a minute. Add the drained rice and the ground spices. Stir gently and fry for

1–2 minutes. Add the stock, coconut milk and salt. Stir and bring to the boil. Cover tightly, turn the heat to very low and cook 25 minutes or until the rice is tender and the stock absorbed.

Meanwhile, in a small pan heat the remaining *ghee* over medium-high heat. When hot, add the remaining onion. Stir and fry until the onion is brown and beginning to turn crisp. Add the cashew nuts. Stir and fry for a minute or until the cashews turn golden. Add the sultanas (golden raisins). Stir once or twice. Remove from the heat. Spread over the rice when serving or else mix with it.

S E R V E S   4 – 5

From the home of Uma and Zac J. Zacharias: Appam
⊘ SAVOURY RICE BREADS

PANCAKE-LIKE BREADS MADE OUT of a fermented rice batter, *appams* are soft and spongy discs, perfect to eat with meats, fish dishes and at breakfast with butter and honey. They are very much a part of the traditional Syrian Christian Easter meal when the Lenten fast is broken with a meat stew (see Lamb Stew, page 19). They are made in a deep, wok-like vessel and are, as a result, fat and puffy in the centre, where there is more batter, and flat, lacy and crispy brown at the edges, where there is less.

You may also cook *appams* in an ordinary, 20 cm/8 inch non-stick frying-pan. You will not get the traditional shape this way but you will get a flat, spongy pancake that will still taste wonderful. Once you pour the batter into the centre of the frying-pan, you will need to tilt it quickly in all directions in order to make the batter spread to about 20 cm/8 inches in diameter. Then cover the pan and cook until the batter is set and the pancake has crisp, brownish edges.

If you wish you may use 475 ml/16 fl oz/2 cups milk, heated gently until lukewarm, instead of the coconut milk and water mixture.

---

4 teaspoons flaked rice
  (cream of rice)
Rice flour (also called
  ground rice) measured to
  the 475 ml/16 fl oz/2 cup
  level in a measuring jug
2 teaspoons dry yeast

2 teaspoons sugar
½ teaspoon salt
350 ml/12 fl oz/1½ cups
  lukewarm milk
400 ml/14 fl oz can coconut
  milk, its contents well
  stirred and mixed with

50 ml/2 fl oz/4 tablespoons
  water then heated gently
  until lukewarm
3–4 tablespoons vegetable
  oil

Combine the flaked rice (cream of rice) and 120 ml/4 fl oz/½ cup water in a small pan. Bring to a simmer. Cook over medium-low heat, stirring constantly, for about 10 minutes until you have a thick paste. Allow to cool.

Meanwhile, in a bowl combine the rice flour, yeast, sugar, salt and the 350 ml/12 fl oz lukewarm milk. Stir well until you have a

smooth, thick but not stiff paste. Add the cooled flaked rice paste to the rice flour paste. Mix it in. Cover with cling film (plastic wrap) and leave in a warm place to ferment for 5 hours.

Add the coconut milk mixture (or the 475 ml/16 fl oz/2 cups lukewarm milk) to this fermented paste. Mix gently. The batter should now be of a pouring consistency. Cover with cling film (plastic wrap) again and set aside in a warm place for another hour.

Get everything ready to make the *appams*. Set up your wok or a non-stick frying-pan, keeping its lid nearby. Have near you the oil in a small cup with a pastry brush, a 25 cm/ 10 inch dish with a cover to hold the *appam*, the batter, a ladle or small cup that will hold about 85 ml/3 fl oz/6 tablespoons of the batter and a spatula, curved if possible.

Turn the heat under the wok to medium-low. When really hot, brush its inside surface lightly with some of the oil to prevent the *appam* from sticking. Stir the batter. Pour about 85 ml/3 fl oz/6 tablespoons of the mixture into the centre of the wok. Pick up the wok by its 2 handles (if it has one handle, wear an oven mitt and put your second hand where the second handle would be). Swish the batter around by quickly moving your arms in a circular motion, spreading the mixture until it is approximately 20 cm/8 inches in diameter. Cover and cook for 2–4 minutes or until the edges are crisp and golden and the centre is resilient and cooked through. Remove the *appam* carefully with the spatula. If not eating immediately, put the *appam* in a deep dish and cover it while making the rest. Make all the *appams* as you did the first, rubbing a little oil on the bottom of the pan whenever necessary and stirring the batter each time.

MAKES 10–12 APPAMS

Shoba Ramji's Erachi Uruga
MEAT PICKLE

FRIENDS AND RELATIVES OF mine have, over the years, brought jars of meat pickle back to me whenever they visited Kerala. I am so grateful finally to have my own recipe and not have to rely on the kindness of others. This Syrian Christian speciality is easy to prepare and enlivens the simplest of everyday meals with its meaty fieriness. Like most pickles, it will keep for several months in the refrigerator.

Although pork is ideal, you may substitute lamb for this pickle.

❧

FOR THE MARINADE:
2 teaspoons black
  peppercorns
2 dried hot red chillies
8–9 cloves
2.5 cm/1 inch cinnamon
  stick
¼ teaspoon fenugreek seeds
¼ teaspoon cumin seeds
½ teaspoon salt

1 tablespoon white wine
  vinegar

YOU ALSO NEED:
750 g/1½ lb lean pork from
  the shoulder, cut into
  1 cm/½ inch pieces
3 tablespoons vegetable oil
½ teaspoon brown mustard
  seeds

4 garlic cloves, peeled and
  finely chopped
1 cm/½ inch piece of fresh
  ginger, peeled and finely
  chopped
¾–1 teaspoon salt
¼–½ teaspoon cayenne
  pepper
¼ teaspoon ground turmeric
¼ teaspoon ground cumin

❧

Put the peppercorns, chillies, cloves, cinnamon, fenugreek seeds, cumin seeds, and salt for the marinade into a clean coffee grinder. Grind to a fine powder. Put the powder in a bowl and add the vinegar and 3 tablespoons water. Mix to a fine paste.

Rub the paste over the meat. Leave to marinate for 2–3 hours.

Heat the oil in a wide, preferably non-stick pan or wok over medium-high heat. When hot, add the mustard seeds. As soon as they start to pop, a matter of seconds, add the garlic and ginger. Stir and fry over medium heat for 2–3 minutes. Add the marinated pork and stir and fry for 8–10 minutes until browned. Add salt to taste and the cayenne pepper, turmeric and cumin. Stir and fry for 2–3 minutes. Turn the heat to low and continue cooking and stirring for a further 2–3 minutes to reduce the sauce until it is thick and nearly dry.

Cool and store in a clean, air-tight jar.

300 ML / 10 FL OZ /
1 ¼ CUPS

Mr A. R. Sunil's Kaya Varathathu
⊘ PLANTAIN CHIPS

PLANTAIN CHIPS, MADE FROM green cooking plantains, have always been sold all over the south. (Today, they are sold all over the north as well.) The best way to make them is to slice them directly into the hot oil using a mandolin or other slicing gadget.

❧

2 green cooking plantains
½ teaspoon ground turmeric
¼ teaspoon asafetida
1¼ teaspoons salt

Oil for deep-frying
1 fresh hot green chilli,
 finely chopped

15–20 fresh curry leaves, if
 available

❧

Peel the plantains with a knife, making sure that all the skin has been removed.

Combine the turmeric, asafetida, salt and 2 tablespoons water in a small cup.

Heat the oil over medium heat in a wok or frying-pan. The oil is suitably hot if a cube of bread sizzles nicely and turns golden-brown. Slice the plantains directly into the hot oil. The chips must be thin and round. Make just enough to have one, slightly overlapping layer. Quickly dip your fingers into the turmeric solution and sprinkle whatever liquid your fingers pick up over the chips. Stir and fry for 1–2 minutes, turning the chips half-way through this cooking time. Throw in a good pinch of chopped chilli and 2–3 curry leaves. Fry for another few seconds and remove with a slotted spoon. The chips should remain yellow in colour. Drain on kitchen paper (paper towels). Make all the chips this way.

Leave to cool and store in an air-tight jar. They should last a good week.

SERVES 4

Spinach with Coconut (page 37) and, from left, Cucumber Cooked with Lentils (page 34), Ginger Chutney (page 44) and Plantain Chips (above).

Shoba Ramji's Ingli Poli
Ⓥ GINGER CHUTNEY

CHUTNEYS AND PICKLES ARE eaten all over India. The main ingredients and combinations of seasonings vary according to the culinary idiosyncrasies of each state. Ginger is grown in Kerala. It is even exported in vast quantities. It is therefore not surprising that Keralites use it in a chutney. The use of mustard seeds, fenugreek seeds, curry leaves, coconut oil and freshly grated coconut makes it very recognizably Keralan. It is served at marriages and traditional banquets here. We can serve it at any time. It does have an exquisite flavour. If you wish to substitute unsweetened, desiccated coconut for fresh coconut use ½ tablespoon. Barely cover with warm water and leave for 1 hour, then proceed with the recipe.

❧

FOR THE SPICE PASTE:
1 teaspoon coriander seeds
¼ teaspoon cumin seeds
¼ teaspoon ground turmeric

YOU ALSO NEED:
3 teaspoons coconut oil or any other vegetable oil
1 tablespoon freshly grated coconut (page 265)
¼ teaspoon brown mustard seeds

¼ teaspoon fenugreek seeds
4 dried hot red chillies
10–15 fresh curry leaves, if available
1 small red onion (25 g/ 1 oz), finely chopped
1–2 fresh hot green chillies, finely chopped

5 cm/2 inch piece of fresh ginger, peeled and cut into very fine slices and then into fine julienne strips
100 ml/3½ fl oz/½ cup tamarind paste (page 278), diluted in 100 ml/3½ fl oz/ ½ cup water
1 teaspoon salt
2 teaspoons jaggery or brown sugar

❧

Put the coriander seeds, cumin seeds and turmeric for the spice paste into a clean coffee grinder. Grind to a fine powder. Put in a small bowl and mix with 1 tablespoon water to make a paste. Set aside.

Heat 1 teaspoon of the oil in a small pan over medium-high heat. When hot, add the coconut. Turn the heat to low and stir and fry

for 3–4 minutes until golden. Set aside.

Heat the remaining oil in a medium-sized, heavy-bottomed pan over medium-low heat. When hot, add the mustard seeds. As soon as they pop, a matter of seconds, put in the fenugreek seeds, red chillies and the curry leaves. Stir and fry for 1–2 minutes. Add the onion, green chillies and ginger. Stir and fry for 4–5 minutes until the onion is soft and beginning to brown. Add the spice paste. Stir and fry for 2–3 minutes until the mixture becomes dry. Add the tamarind paste, salt and jaggery. Stir and cook for 10–12 minutes until the mixture is thick. Remove from the heat. Add the coconut and mix.

Cool and use, or store in a clean, air-tight container or jar.

This chutney will keep for many months in the refrigerator.

1 5 0   M L / 5   F L O Z /
⅔   C U P

Shoba Ramji's Kaitha Chaka Pachadi
ⓥ SPICY PINEAPPLE-YOGHURT

PINEAPPLE WAS INTRODUCED TO Kerala by the Portuguese as early as the end of the fifteenth century. At first Keralites viewed it with suspicion, calling it 'the jackfruit of the donkey'. It has now been incorporated in their cuisine and is very much part of the daily diet.

This is a South Indian *raita*. It is quite spicy and has a slight sweet-sour flavour. Serve it with all Indian meals or eat it as a light lunch. In Kerala, it is often served as a salad to accompany spicy fish dishes. Rice is generally served on the side. You may use the same quantity of canned, sweetened pineapple if you prefer You will not need to stew it in sugar, in that case.

If you wish to substitute unsweetened, desiccated coconut for fresh coconut use 1½ tablespoons. Barely cover with warm water and leave for 1 hour, then proceed with the recipe.

300 g/11 oz/2 cups fresh
   pineapple, cut into 2.5 cm/
   1 inch chunks
2 tablespoons sugar
3 tablespoons freshly grated
   coconut (page 265)
½ teaspoon ground cumin

250 ml/8 fl oz/1 cup natural
   (plain) yoghurt, lightly
   beaten with a fork
3 fresh hot green chillies,
   finely chopped
½ tablespoon salt

1 tablespoon coconut oil or
   any other vegetable oil
½ teaspoon brown mustard
   seeds
3 dried hot red chillies
8–10 fresh curry leaves, if
   available

Put the pineapple in a small, preferably non-stick pan. Add the sugar and 100 ml/3½ fl oz/½ cup water and bring to a simmer. Stir and stew over low heat for 10–12 minutes until the water has been absorbed.

Meanwhile, put the coconut and cumin into the container of an electric blender. Add 1 tablespoon water (or more, if needed) and blend to a smooth paste.

Add the coconut paste to the cooked pineapple. Stir and stew over low heat for 2–3 minutes. Remove from the heat and allow to cool.

Put the yoghurt into a bowl. Add the green chillies and salt. Mix. Add the pineapple mixture. Stir to blend.

Heat the oil in a small, clean pan over medium-high heat. When hot, add the mustard seeds. As soon as the mustard seeds begin to pop, a matter of seconds, put in the red chillies and the curry leaves. Stir and fry over low heat for a few more seconds or until the chillies darken. Remove from the heat and mix with the pineapple yoghurt.

SERVES 4

Mr A. R. Sunil's Pazham Roast

ⓥ PLANTAIN ROAST

EVEN THOUGH THIS IS called a 'roast' the green plantains here are peeled, stuffed with a gorgeous mixture of coconut, raisins and cardamom, dipped in a batter and then deep-fried. They are a dessert and uncommonly good.
If you wish to substitute unsweetened, desiccated coconut for fresh coconut use 40 g/1½ oz/7 tablespoons. Barely cover with warm water and leave for 1 hour, then proceed with the recipe.

❧

FOR THE BATTER:
A good pinch of saffron threads
1½ tablespoons rice flour (also called ground rice)
50 g/2 oz/scant ½ cup plain (all-purpose white) flour
¼ teaspoon sugar
¼ teaspoon ground cardamom

¼ teaspoon salt
1 tablespoon beaten egg

YOU ALSO NEED:
65 g/2½ oz/⅔ cup freshly grated coconut (page 265)
5 raw cashew nuts, finely chopped
1 tablespoon raisins
¼ teaspoon ground cumin

½ teaspoon ground cardamom
1½ tablespoons sugar
4 green cooking plantains, peeled with a knife
Oil for deep-frying
2 teaspoons honey (optional)

❧

To make the batter: Soak the saffron in ½ teaspoon hot water for 10 minutes. Put the rice flour, flour, sugar, ¼ teaspoon cardamom and salt in a small bowl. Mix well. Add 200 ml/7 fl oz/¾ cup water, the egg and the saffron. Beat to a smooth, frothy batter. Set aside.

In a separate bowl, mix the coconut, cashew nuts, raisins, cumin, ½ teaspoon cardamom and sugar. Set aside.

To prepare the plantains: Make 2 parallel incisions along the length of the plantains about 1 cm/½ inch apart. Remove the plantain flesh from between the cuts to make a groove,

being careful not to break the plantain. Fill the groove with the coconut mixture.

Heat the oil for deep-frying in a large frying-pan or wok over medium heat. The oil is hot enough when a cube of bread sizzles nicely and turns golden-brown.

Dip the plantains in the batter and slip into the hot oil. Deep-fry the plantains for 4–5 minutes until crisp and golden. Serve immediately, either whole or sliced, and drizzled with honey if you wish.

SERVES 4

From the home of Uma and Zac J. Zacharias: Payasam

ⓥ MOONG DAL PUDDING

LIKE THE *KHEER* OF northern India, *payasam* is the grain or pulse pudding of the south. As Kerala is the land of coconuts, it is not surprising that both coconut milk and small fried coconut slivers are used in it as well. Fried cashews may be substituted for the coconut slivers. If you like, you may use both.

〜

Moong dal **measured to the 250 ml/8 fl oz/1 cup level in a measuring jug**
Dark muscovado sugar (dark brown sugar) or Indian jaggery measured to the 250 ml/8 fl oz/1 cup level in a measuring jug

600 ml/1 pint/2½ cups coconut milk, well stirred from a can or thick fresh milk (page 266)
½ teaspoon ground ginger
½ teaspoon ground nutmeg
½ teaspoon ground cumin

½ teaspoon ground cardamom or the seeds from 5 pods, well crushed
2 tablespoons *ghee* or unsalted butter
2 tablespoons fresh coconut, cut into fine 1 cm/½ inch slivers or 2 tablespoons desiccated coconut

〜

Set a heavy, preferably cast-iron frying-pan or wok over medium-high heat. When hot, put in the *moong dal*. Stir and roast it until it turns reddish, about 5 minutes. Wash the *dal* in several changes of water. Drain. Empty the *dal* into a heavy, medium-sized pan. Add 750 ml/ 1¼ pints/3 cups water and bring to the boil. Turn the heat to low, cover partially and let the *dal* cook for 40–50 minutes or until tender.

Meanwhile, combine the sugar or jaggery with 120 ml/4 fl oz/½ cup water in a small pan. Heat, stirring, over medium heat until the sugar has dissolved and you have a syrup. Add this syrup to the *dal*. Also add 475 ml/16 fl oz/ 2 cups of the coconut milk, stirring it well

before you pour it in. Stir and bring to a simmer. Cook over low heat, stirring frequently, until you have a thick, porridge-like consistency. This might take 20–30 minutes.

Add the remaining coconut milk as well as the ginger, nutmeg, cumin and cardamom. Stir the spices in. Cook, stirring, for another 5 minutes.

Heat the *ghee* or butter in a small frying-pan over medium heat. When hot, put in the coconut slivers or desiccated coconut. Stir and fry until lightly browned. Scatter over the *payasam* before serving.

S E R V E S   8

GUJARAT

I CAN SAY THIS unequivocally. If there is an *haute cuisine* for vegetarians – ancient, traditional foods with astounding flavours and textures, all based on sound nutritional principles – it can be found in the Indian state of Gujarat: delicate, silken 'pasta' rolls made out of a cooked chick pea flour batter (*khandvi*); a savoury, baked 'cake' made with a mixed batter of pulses (legumes) and vegetables (*handva*); fried chick pea flour noodles with a tomato-garlic sauce (*sev tamate*); and steamed diamonds of crushed peanuts with a rich ginger and chilli sauce – these are just some of the fine foods found here.

Part of this state which runs along India's upper west coast is desert and part is semi-desert, making water so valuable that medieval kings in the region, once they discovered an underground spring, would house it protectively in an elaborately carved structure known as a stepwell. Instead of rising upwards towards the sky as most Indian palaces do, the stepwell, a mini-palace, went downwards, whirlpool fashion, storey by storey, burrowing its way elegantly into the earth to the very source of the cool, precious liquid.

In a land where camels ply the caked earth (did I have any recipes for camel's milk, I was asked many times) and hedges are formed by closely planted cactus, most of this valuable water has, traditionally, been used to grow staples – grains and pulses (legumes). It is with these staples, and a smattering of fresh vegetables or fruit and nutritious seasonings such as sesame seeds and peanuts, that most vegetarian Gujaratis make their delicacies.

Let me describe to you a few meals eaten at the homes of Gujarati friends in Ahmadabad.

When I had gone to bed the night before at the house of a friend in Ahmadabad (Gujarat's most populous city and now adjacent to Ghandhi Nagar, the newly built capital), I had found fresh jasmines in a basket lined with a dampened cloth, placed strategically next to my pillow. Even on that steaming, hot summer's day, I was lulled to a cool and aromatic sleep, well in keeping with the Gujarati way of life which believes in taking care of the whole human being, body and soul. I woke up, bathed, and swung for a while on the carved wooden seat suspended in my room with ornate brass chains (all Gujarati homes seem to have such swings – to cool the body and calm the mind).

Breakfast was light and came to my room on a tray, my early rising hosts mindful that I had travelled a long distance – some chick pea flour pancakes (*pudlas*), which are rather like the chick pea flour 'pizzas' of southern France only much more delicate, well-drained yoghurt that had been flavoured with spring onions (scallions), fresh green coriander and peanut chutney,

some green chilli and lime pickle (*marchanu athanu*) and *khakra*, a very thin, crisp wheat bread rather like the breads eaten by Scandinavians but much more wafer-like.

Then, after a morning of sightseeing at the Calico Museum of Textiles, easily one of the best in the world (Indian fabrics, both ancient and modern, are to my mind quite incomparable) and the collection of Indian miniature paintings housed in a private Le Corbusier-designed museum, I returned to my hosts for lunch.

The dining-room had been planned to have a small, indoor pond at one end. (It was not exactly the stepwell of a medieval king but I was in the home of a modern noble, a textile magnate, who could get his architects to hint subtly at the symbols of past power as they installed cooling, decorative elements.) The table was set nearby.

As soon as we sat down, waiters came in bearing silver *thalis*, each with its array of small silver bowls (*katoris*) arranged neatly near the rim. The freshest of seasonal mango purée was in there to be eaten with thin, dainty, fluffy, white split pea diamonds (*idada dhokla*). Made with a batter of ground rice and *urad dal*, which is left overnight to ferment and then steamed with coarsely crushed black pepper, this dish belongs to a whole family of *dhoklas* found only in the state of Gujarat. My host, dipping a piece of the soft white sponge into the orange-gold liquid said, 'Many of us like to eat just this for lunch, all summer long – at least as long as the mangoes last.

Previous page: Women at a wedding in Gujarat.

Sometimes we eat mango purée with little *pooris* (deep-fried, puffy breads), sometimes we put it in our *kadhi* (a chick pea flour and yoghurt soup) – it provides the little sweetening we crave – and sometimes we put it into our thickened yoghurt dessert (*shrikhand*). Mangoes do wonders for the eyes. You eat them throughout the summer and their goodness will last you all year.'

Of course, there was much more on the *thali* than just the mango purée and *dhoklas*. There were little potatoes cooked with tomatoes (*batata nu shak*), young cabbage stir-fried with peas (*kobi vatana nu shak*), *moong dal* cooked rather like rice so that each grain was separate, spinach steamed with ginger, a 'salad' of bananas and yoghurt flavoured with crushed mustard seeds, delicate millet breads smothered with *ghee*, and, for dessert, some fresh litchis and a sweet coconut roll (*coco pista pasand*) which, shaped like a sponge roll, had sweetened coconut on the outside and chopped pistachios on the inside. The entire meal was vegetarian, but I was hardly conscious of this as I ate.

Another friend, belonging to the Sarabhai family that owns the Calico Museum – as well as textile and pharmaceutical industries – once offered me the most delightful of poolside lunches. In a bowl was an artfully created rice salad – soft, freshly cooked rice and yoghurt blended together with fresh green coriander and then given a *tarka* (or *baghar*, a seasoning in oil) of

cumin seeds, mustard seeds and fresh curry leaves. The top of the salad had been carefully dotted with fresh, pinky-red pomegranate seeds which were firmly moored but still exposed. Also stuck into the salad by their tips were a few green chillies that had been rubbed with yoghurt and salt, dried in the parched Gujarati air and then quickly fried to a crisp just before use. Adding texture and fire, they were to be nibbled at as we ate. Served with this was a large shallow bowl filled with *khandvi*, the silken 'pasta' rolls described earlier, and simple glasses of fresh watermelon juice. Nothing else was needed.

The art of making *khandvi* – which I have to admit I have not yet perfected (hence no recipe in this book but maybe in the next one) – combines the technique of making choux pastry in its first stages – it is a cooked, batter-like dough – with the rarer art of spreading the very hot dough out by hand until it is paper thin. I watched the Sarabhai cook, the maharaj, as he is respectfully called, do this. For my comfort, he cooked outdoors, under the generous shade of large trees.

'It is best to use fresh chick pea flour,' the cook began as he sifted some of this into a pan. Small chick peas (*chanas*), grown on Sarabhai land, had been ground into flour at their own mill. Double the volume of liquid, a mixture of yoghurt and water, was mixed in with the flour as well as some turmeric, salt, asafetida and lime juice. The pan was put on the fire and then stirred and stirred until the batter thickened enough to come away from the sides.

Now came the hard part. Dipping his hands into boiling hot batter, the maharaj removed just enough to spread very thinly on the back of a *thali*. He had to do this with great speed as more *thalis* waited to be covered and the batter had to remain hot or it would not spread. 'Your hands should get red when you finish,' the maharaj informed me.

The batter set almost instantly into a thin film. Now it needed to be rolled up tightly. This, too, was difficult as the *thalis* were a good 30 cm/15 inches in diameter and the thin 'crêpe' formed on the *thalis* was exceedingly delicate. The roll was then cut into 2.5 cm/1 inch segments and placed in a single layer in a shallow bowl. The next step was to heat some oil, throw into it some mustard seeds, some fresh curry leaves, some asafetida, a touch of red chilli powder and ground turmeric, and a few drops of water and pour this over the *khandvi*. Finally, some fresh green coriander and freshly grated coconut were sprinkled over the top and these flimsy silken masterpieces were ready to be devoured. 'I make these at least two to three times a week,' the cook said proudly. Clearly, much practice was needed to prepare them with his consummate skill.

As we sat eating our lunch in a leafy arbour (another Le Corbusier house, designed to have no front door), a shady oasis in a dried-up city, this host talked about the importance of dried beans in balancing the good and bad cholesterol in our bodies and of how the family of pulses (legumes) – dried beans and split peas – were such an under-rated source of protein in the Western world but so highly valued here and used on a daily basis, sometimes several times in the same meal. In fact, all his beans, as with most land-owning families, are grown on his own farms, harvested, then rubbed with castor oil (to keep bugs away) and stored for the year in large barrels that are kept near the kitchen. Drawing upon the pastas that already exist here, he is even experimenting with the production of dried, all-pulse (all-legume) pastas for the West. Gujaratis are nothing if not a forward-looking people, envied all over India for their great business acumen. He will probably succeed.

To confirm how grains and beans have been traditionally integrated into the daily lives of Gujaratis, I had only to visit the home of Surendra Patel. A designer, restaurant owner and dreamer, he found a mango grove in a village on the outskirts of Ahmadabad some years ago and built his house smack in the centre of it. Using mud as mortar, cow dung and clay as plaster for the walls, traditionally carved wood – some antique, some new – for window frames, shutters, lintels and doors, and regionally crafted quilts for cushions and divan

Cloth being dried in Ahmadabad, Gujarat.

covers, just as neighbouring villagers do, he came up with a modern yet ancient dwelling, fronted with formal, criss-crossing tanks replete with fountains, and backed with a freshwater pool. It is here that he lives and entertains.

It was here that he offered us an all-home-made, typically Gujarati breakfast of rice *papar* (poppadom), *cheewra* (a spicy, granola-like *mélange* of nuts, puffed rice, roasted split peas, dried fruit and chick pea flour noodles) and *leeli chai* (green tea) made with lemon grass and mint. The first and last are impossible to find outside Gujarati homes. The second, though now sold by Indian grocers the world over and a cousin to the so-called 'Bombay Mix', is still best when made at home using 'grand-mother's recipe'.

Smita Patel, Surendra's wife, explained that the deliciously crunchy, sesame-seed-encrusted *papar* were made by boiling green chillies, salt, bicarbonate of soda (baking soda) and ajwain, cumin and sesame seeds in water, adding rice flour to this water, stirring and cooking, then kneading all this into a dough, rolling out fine discs and drying them in the sun. Whenever anyone wished to eat them (friends were always dropping in), the poppadom were quickly roasted over charcoal and served to guests lolling on the quilt-covered divans on the veranda. White, crisp, crunchy and en-crusted with sesame seeds, these home-made poppadom were not only ex-quisitely delicious, but unlike anything I

had eaten in other parts of India. They were complemented, perfectly, by the milky lemon grass tea topped with fresh mint, which was served to us in generously sized, hand-crafted bowls.

India's vegetarianism comes mainly from some of the Hindu sects and castes scattered across the land, but it also comes from Jains who may be fewer in number but are fervent in their faith. Many of these Jains are Gujaratis.

Jainism developed about the same time or earlier than Buddhism, starting around the eighth century BC and becoming quite formalized by the sixth century BC. Like Buddhism, it grew as a protest movement against some of the excesses of the Vedic faith (which later became Hinduism), in-cluding the custom of animal sacrifices. The Jains believe in kindness to all life, from insects up. To this end, the strictest believers wear masks over their noses and mouths so as not to accidentally inhale or swallow the humblest of creatures. Not only do they refrain from eating meat but some will not eat root vegetables as pulling out a root kills a whole plant. They even have hospitals for injured birds.

Traditionally, there has been enormous wealth in the Jain community. Today, a disproportionate number of India's suc-cessful millionaire industrialists are devout Jains, who, like those of earlier centuries, have crowned their successful lives with the building of temples.

Pilgrimages to places such as the

temples atop Shetrunjaya mountain at Palitana are undertaken by the faithful at least once in their lifetimes, sometimes once a year. Journeys can start from quite a distance. But first, there is food to be packed. *Farsan* is easy to carry. This is the name for savoury snack foods, often made out of chick pea flour as well as other grains, nuts and pulses (legumes), sometimes pastry-like and sometimes not, often crisp, but sometimes not, that are eaten at breakfast and tea-time, and all other times in between. They may be made at home but can be bought from special shops that prepare large selections several times a day.

There is much hustle and bustle in these shops as families stroll in and out. Large chunks of yellow *khaman dhokla*, looking like wet Greek sponges, are piled high on one tray, dotted with mustard seeds and sprinkled over with fresh coconut; squiggly chick pea flour noodles (*sev*) of all sizes are arranged in neat hillocks on other trays; *khasta kachoris*, deep-fried, flaky, stuffed breads, may be bought with a choice of a sour mint chutney or a sweet one made with dates and tamarind. In the front of the shop, to lure customers with their cooking aromas, are the chefs manning their woks, churning out all manner of lasagna-like flat chick pea flour 'pastas': there is *papri* (crinkled ribbons made by pushing dough through a many-slitted griddle) and *fafra* (long, flat ribbons made by dragging the dough by the heel of a practised hand).

With the *farsan* all tied up in a cloth bundle, the pilgrims can begin their journey by car, by camel cart or even by scooter. The Gujarati women, quite traditional in their saris, oiled hair and red *tika* in the middle of their foreheads, will nonetheless think nothing of donning a baseball cap and speeding along, curving their way in and out of traffic, on scooters. Sometimes a whole family, man, woman and child, will travel on a single scooter.

Along the road, the travellers will surely come across an encampment of Rabaris from Kachchh (north-eastern Gujarat). These are the local gypsies, goatherders and shepherds on their never-ending search for water and pasture. Loaded with silver jewellery – even little infants have seven earrings down the lobes of each ear – they are easily recognizable. The men, in short white shirts that are flared and pleated from the armpits down, spend most of their time with their animals. The women, tattooed prettily on their hands, cheeks and chins, embroider and cook. And what embroidery. Exquisite mirror work that is sold in trendy European boutiques for thousands of rupees more than these poor itinerants were ever paid for it, simple quilts and blankets that are in the chic collections of international designers and backless blouses that can be seen on rich young nymphs in Bombay and Calcutta. The Rabaris' cooking, because of severe financial constraints, is much more basic. One woman, squatting on the caked earth, is making a patty out of a lightly salted millet dough. The dough looks very much like the earth. She adjusts the long scarf that falls back from her head, makes sure that her toddler daughter is within view and then flattens the patty with her hands into a thick, flat bread. No rolling pins seem to be required here. The bread is slapped on to a curved, earthen *tava* which has been heating over twigs from the thorny, desert *keekar* tree, the only fuel at hand. On good days, this bread (*bajri no rotlo*) is eaten with *doongri nu shaak*, a simple onion curry made with chilli powder and turmeric. On most days, however, what accompanies it is a raw onion, peeled and smashed with a fist (raw onion gives protection from the heat, they believe) and an incendiary chutney made with garlic, salt and plenty of red chillies (*lasun chutney*).

The travelling Jain pilgrims on their way to Palitana frown upon onions and garlic (which are not only live bulbs but are said to arouse base passions), but they may pick up some dried red chillies if they happen to be passing the village of Shertha. Fields upon fields have been producing chillies here for the last 200 years. Mountains of them, red and brilliant and all freshly dried, ooze their pungency into the air as vendors at roadside stalls grind and crush them. The soil, it is said, gives the chillies such a bright colour that it acts as an enticing natural dye in the food. The air, it is believed, is quite perfect for drying the chillies to a crisp.

If it is summer and they are passing through Ahmadabad, the pilgrims may stop and pick up egg-free ice-creams. Perhaps cardamom-saffron or saffron-pistachio. Perhaps the baby would like mango-grape?

If, on the other hand, it is late winter and the pilgrims are going through the countryside near Surat, the port where the British gained their first toehold in India in 1612, they may decide to feast on *paunk*. In a harvest ritual which must go back to antiquity, fresh grains of wheat or millet are roasted and then combined with balls of young jaggery made from the thickened juice of newly harvested sugar cane, to produce a snack that is best devoured with tall glasses of salted buttermilk.

If they are passing the village of Vartal, where little babes swing from cloth hammocks, they may pick up some flat, wholewheat noodles drying in coils on outdoor cots. Anthropologists today believe that noodles probably originated not in China or Italy but wherever there was wheat. This, they feel, points mainly to the Tigris-Euphrates valley in the Middle East and to the Indus valley now mostly in Pakistan but extending into northern Gujarat as well.

As towns dating back to the second millennium BC have been discovered here (with evidence of both wheat and sugar cane), it is likely that the wheat noodles in

Men at a wedding in Gujarat.

Vartal are completely indigenous, going back perhaps 4000 years.

The village preparation is very simple. Wheat dough is rolled out very thin and cut into 3 mm/⅛ inch thick strips. These are wrapped into small coils and dried in the sun. At the harvest festival of *Holi*, the coils are thrown into boiling water, drained and then eaten with melted *ghee* and sugar. The use of noodles is widespread in Gujarat. Apart from the chick pea flour *farsan* and the *khandvi* mentioned earlier, there is also that superb creation *dal dhokli*, in which 2.5 cm/1 inch wide strips made from a fresh wholewheat dough are dropped into a spicy split pea soup. This is very much a noodle-eating state.

As the pilgrims near Saurashtra, the land turns increasingly brown and barren. River beds meander aimlessly. There is not a drop of water in them. The flat earth is broken up with single hillocks that arise eerily from the ground without support from sisterly ranges. Finally, Palitana appears at dawn. It lies at the foot of Shetrunjaya, another vertical rise that seems to come without warning. On top of it perches a rising crescendo of 863 temples built over 900 years.

The sky glows red but a pale pink moon, egg shaped and obstinate, refuses to leave. Mindful of the day's heat, dawn seems the only rational time to attempt this climb. There are over 4000 steps and only those in the best of shape can manage them without resorting to the flimsy palanquins that are available for hire. There are a few water stops but very little shade.

The climb is arduous and takes two slow hours (young Jain nuns, it must be said, heads shaven and staff in hand, go leaping up the steps like young gazelles). But there are rewards for those who stagger to the top. Seated under a tree at the entrance are several women crying 'Eat yoghurt. Eat yoghurt'. This is some of the best yoghurt you can ever hope to find. Made out of rich buffalo's milk and set in shallow terracotta bowls, it is served with a light sprinkling of coarse salt or sugar and, of course, a liberal dash of divinity.

It would be highly improper to limit Gujarati food to that of vegetarians alone. As Islam spread from the Middle East in the eighth and ninth centuries, India was among the first places it came to. Gujarat, on India's north-west coast, was easily accessible by sea. Indeed, Arabs had traded their horses and pearls here for spices and textiles since antiquity.

Among the early converts to Islam in the eleventh century was the community of Bohris. Mohammad Kassim and his brothers are Bohris. They live in the heart of Ahmadabad, in the old walled city founded by the Muslim ruler Sultan Ahmed Shah in 1411. For the last seven generations, their family has made a good living selling china, glass and crockery. Today, they sell all those same items and have also become the biggest dealers in antique chandeliers and hanging lamps.

Narrow lanes, blocked now and then by goats and drying, block-printed fabrics lead to their front door. This opens into an enormous room whose ceiling is completely covered with row upon row of hanging lamps – blue, green, pink, ochre and, of course, the trendiest clear ones with delicate etchings. The family's trade is also their passion.

Two Gujarati swings with seats large enough for three or four people are also suspended from the ceiling. The women, their heads covered with scarves, swing and talk about the children and family recipes.

Lunch is served on a common metal plate (a *thal*) large enough to seat eight people around it. It is set upon a stool. Diners sit on the floor. All food is placed in the centre for the family to share. *Laganya sheek* is made with spicy minced lamb that is packed into a baking tin, covered with a layer of beaten egg and then with sliced tomatoes. It is cut into squares and served as the kebab course. To follow, there is an unusually delicious chicken cooked with a pesto-like green chutney containing fresh green coriander, mint, green chillies, garlic, ginger and coconut (*chutney ni murghi*). Liver, too, may be cooked this way, I am informed. There is a scrumptious lamb smothered in a most unusual sauce containing ground cashews, roasted peanuts, roasted chick peas and watermelon seeds (*kari*). It is to be eaten with a special black pepper pilaf. And there is the absolutely mouthwatering *khichra*. For this, meat, wheat and split peas are all cooked with spices and ground up into a porridge-like paste. This is spread out on a plate. Next you dribble a little garlic-flavoured *ghee* over the top. Then you sprinkle some crisply browned onion slivers, some chopped up green chillies, some fresh green coriander, lemon juice and *garam masala* over the top. Then you dig in. I could just live on that!

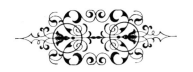

Mrs Kumud Kansara's Sev
CRISPY CHICK PEA FLOUR NOODLES

GUJARAT HAS MANY VARIETIES of pasta although they are not called by that name. *Sev* are crisp, fried noodles prepared from chick pea flour. To make them, a special press, a *sev*-maker, is used. Most serious Indian grocers sell them. If you cannot find one, use a potato-ricer instead.

Sev are generally eaten as a snack, at breakfast and at tea-time. They can also be turned into an appetizer or main course by clever additions of seasonings or sauces. See the next recipe and page 80 for these magical variations. They may be made several days ahead of time.

---

450 g/1 lb/3 cups plus 3 tablespoons chick pea flour, sifted

½ teaspoon ground asafetida

¼ teaspoon ground turmeric

2 teaspoons cayenne pepper

2½ teaspoons salt

120 ml/4 fl oz/½ cup peanut oil or any other vegetable oil, plus oil for greasing and deep-frying

---

Put the flour, asafetida, turmeric, cayenne pepper and salt into a large bowl. Stir to mix.

Put the 120 ml/4 fl oz/½ cup oil into a small bowl or jug with 250 ml/8 fl oz/1 cup water. Mix well with a spoon or whisk so that the oil and water combine. Add the water and oil to the flour mixture. Mix and knead, using your hands, to form a soft, sticky dough. Set aside to rest for 15 minutes.

Meanwhile, heat the oil for deep-frying in a large frying-pan or wok over medium heat. Fit a *sev*-machine with the disc that has the smallest holes or use a potato-ricer. Lightly oil the inside of the gadget you are using.

With lightly oiled hands, make a tangerine-sized ball out of the dough and put it into the *sev*-making gadget. When the oil is hot, hold the *sev*-maker or potato-ricer over it. Moving the machine in a circular motion over the oil, push out the noodles so that they fall in a continuous stream and cover the surface in a single layer. Let this layer fry for 15 seconds and then turn it over. Fry for a further 15 seconds until the noodles are crisp but not browned. Remove with a slotted spoon. Drain on kitchen paper (paper towels). Make all the *sev* this way, spreading each batch out on fresh kitchen paper (paper towels) to drain. Once the noodles have cooled, break them up slightly and store in a tightly lidded jar or tin. They will keep for several weeks.

WILL SERVE
10–15 AT A PARTY

Mrs Kumud Kansara's Sev Masala

CRISPY CHICK PEA FLOUR NOODLES WITH ONIONS AND CHILLIES

THIS IS BEST SERVED with drinks, hard or soft. Stick teaspoons into the bowl of noodles so that people can pick up spoonfuls as they want them. The mixture should be put together at the last minute or the noodles will get soggy.

100 g/4 oz Crispy Chick Pea
  Flour Noodles (opposite)
1 small red onion
  (50 g/2 oz), finely chopped

4–5 fresh hot green chillies,
  finely chopped
2–3 tablespoons finely
  chopped, fresh green
  coriander

2 tablespoons lime juice
A little salt (optional)

Put the noodles into a bowl. Break them with your hands so that they are in approximately 2.5 cm/1 inch pieces.

Add the onion, chillies, coriander, lime juice and salt, if desired. Toss with the noodles to mix. Serve.

SERVES 4

Nishrin Attarwala's Kari
LAMB IN A CASHEW NUT SAUCE

THE BOHRIS OF GUJARAT, a Muslim community, cook some of the best meat dishes on the west coast of India. This is one of their specialities. It is served with Black Pepper Rice (page 84), which helps to absorb the absolutely wonderful sauce. It is really the sauce that makes the dish. Rich with a ground mixture of nuts – cashews, the hazelnut-like *charoli* nut (sold by Indian grocers) and roasted peanuts – seeds such as watermelon seeds and spices such as star anise and cloves, it is both uncommon and good. If you cannot get any of the more unusual nuts or seeds, just increase the cashews or peanuts by a similar amount. This dish may also be made with chicken, which should be skinned and cut into 5 cm/2 inch pieces. Each of the two cooking stages would be 12-15 minutes.

FOR THE NUT, SEED AND SPICE MIXTURE:

2 tablespoons raw cashew nuts, split or broken
2 tablespoons *charoli* (*chironji*)
1½ tablespoons roasted peanuts
1½ tablespoons roasted chick peas, or roasted *chana dal* (page 260)
1½ tablespoons peeled watermelon seeds
1 teaspoon cumin seeds
7–8 cloves
1 teaspoon black peppercorns
1 teaspoon ground coriander
2.5 cm/1 inch cinnamon stick, broken
6–7 dried hot red chillies
2 star anise
¼ teaspoon ground turmeric

FOR THE FIRST COOKING STAGE YOU NEED:

4 tablespoons vegetable oil
2 medium-large red onions (225 g/8 oz), finely sliced
2.5 cm/1 inch piece of fresh ginger, finely chopped
5–6 garlic cloves, peeled and finely chopped
4 fresh hot green chillies, finely chopped
450 g/1 lb boned lamb from the shoulder, cut into 4 cm/1½ inch cubes
½ teaspoon salt

FOR THE SECOND COOKING STAGE YOU NEED:

3 tablespoons vegetable oil
1 teaspoon cumin seeds
20–30 fresh curry leaves, if available

2.5 cm/1 inch cinnamon stick
2–3 cloves
½ teaspoon black peppercorns
2–3 garlic cloves, peeled and chopped
2 large ripe tomatoes, puréed in an electric blender
400 ml/14 fl oz/1¾ cups coconut milk (page 266), from a well-stirred can, thinned with 300 ml/ 10 fl oz/1¼ cups water
½ teaspoon salt
3 tablespoons lemon juice
3 tablespoons finely chopped, fresh green coriander

Put the ingredients for the nut, seed and spice mixture into a clean coffee grinder. Grind to a fine powder. Empty into a bowl. Add 5–6 tablespoons water to make a thick paste. Set aside.

For the first cooking stage: Heat the 4 tablespoons oil in a large, wide, preferably non-stick pan or wok over medium-high heat. When hot, add the onions. Stir and fry for 3–4 minutes or until they turn brown at the edges. Add the ginger, garlic and chillies. Stir and fry for a minute. Put in the lamb and ½ teaspoon salt. Stir and fry for 2–3 minutes. Add the spice paste and 450 ml/15 fl oz/2 cups water. Bring to the boil. Cover, turn the heat to low and cook for 55 minutes.

For the second cooking stage: Heat the 3 tablespoons oil in a clean, wide pan or wok over medium-high heat. When hot, add the cumin seeds, curry leaves, cinnamon, cloves and peppercorns. Stir for 10 seconds. Add the garlic. Stir and fry until the garlic starts to brown. Now add the lamb and the sauce from the first pan, along with the tomato purée, stirred coconut milk, salt and lemon juice. Stir to mix.

Cook over medium-high heat for about 10–15 minutes until the lamb is tender and the sauce has become thick.

Sprinkle with the fresh coriander to garnish.

SERVES 3 – 4

Nishrin Attarwala's Chutney Ni Murghi

CHICKEN COOKED IN GREEN CHUTNEY

THIS CHICKEN MAY BE eaten with any Indian bread (you may even eat it with pitta bread) or with rice. A salad of tomatoes, onion rings and cucumbers may be served on the side.

If you wish to substitute unsweetened, desiccated coconut for fresh coconut use 50 g/2 oz/⅔ cup. Just cover with warm water and leave for 1 hour, then proceed with the recipe.

~

FOR THE GREEN CHUTNEY:

100g/4oz/2½ cups fresh green coriander, finely chopped

50 g/2 oz fresh mint leaves

12–15 fresh hot green chillies, roughly chopped

8–10 garlic cloves, peeled and finely chopped

5 cm/2 inch piece of fresh ginger, peeled and finely chopped

100 g/4 oz/1 cup freshly grated coconut (page 265)

YOU ALSO NEED:

6 tablespoons vegetable oil

2 medium-sized red onions (180 g/6 oz), finely chopped

1 teaspoon finely grated ginger

1 teaspoon crushed, peeled garlic

450 g/1 lb skinned chicken pieces, cut into 5 cm/2 inch pieces

¾–1 teaspoon salt

3–4 tablespoons lemon juice

~

Put all the ingredients for the green chutney into an electric blender. Add 8 tablespoons water and blend to a paste. Set aside.

Heat 3 tablespoons of the oil in a large, wide, preferably non-stick pan or wok over high heat. When hot, add the onions. Stir and fry for 3–4 minutes until they begin to brown. Add the grated ginger and garlic. Stir once. Put in the chicken pieces and ½ teaspoon of the salt. Stir and fry for 2–3 minutes. Add 120 ml/4 fl oz/½ cup water and bring to the boil. Cover and simmer for 15 minutes.

Heat the remaining 3 tablespoons oil in a separate, large frying-pan or wok over high heat. When hot, add the chutney. Stir and cook for 6–8 minutes until the oil separates from the chutney. Add the chicken pieces, their juices and ¼–½ teaspoon salt. Stir and cook over medium heat for 12–15 minutes or until the sauce has reduced to just coat the chicken and the chicken is tender. Add the lemon juice and toss to mix.

S E R V E S 4

Mrs Kumud Kansara's Kobi Vatana Nu Shak
ⓥ GINGERY CABBAGE AND PEAS

IF YOU CAN GET fresh peas, boil them first until just tender, drain them and then refresh them in cold water before using them in this recipe. Frozen peas should be defrosted thoroughly in warm water and then used.
You may serve this dish with any Indian meal.

❧

- **3 tablespoons peanut oil or any other vegetable oil**
- **½ teaspoon cumin seeds**
- **¼ teaspoon ground asafetida**
- **6–7 fresh hot green chillies, finely chopped**

- **7.5 cm/3 inch piece of fresh ginger, peeled and finely grated**
- **½ teaspoon ground turmeric**
- **450 g/1 lb green cabbage, finely shredded**
- **½ teaspoon salt or to taste**
- **½ teaspoon lemon juice**

- **1 tablespoon unsweetened, desiccated coconut**
- **½ tablespoon ground coriander**
- **1 tablespoon chopped, fresh green coriander**
- **100 g/4 oz/1 cup shelled, cooked green peas**

❧

Heat the oil in a large, wide, preferably non-stick pan or wok over medium heat. When hot, add the cumin seeds and, a second later, the asafetida. Stir once and put in the chillies, ginger and turmeric. Stir and fry for 30 seconds. Add the cabbage and salt. Stir. Cover and cook for 4–5 minutes or until the cabbage is just beginning to soften. Add the lemon juice, coconut, ground coriander, fresh coriander and peas. Stir and fry for 2 minutes. Remove from the heat and serve. The cabbage should still be slightly crunchy.

SERVES 2 – 4

Kumud Kansara's Gajar Marcha No Sambharo

CARROTS STIR-FRIED WITH GREEN CHILLIES

GUJARATIS EAT MANY VEGETABLES that are very lightly stir-fried. Rather like Chinese vegetables, they are expected to remain crunchy even after they are cooked. These carrots go well with all Indian meals. You may also serve them with a roast chicken or with plain sausages.

---

3 tablespoons peanut or any other vegetable oil

½ teaspoon brown mustard seeds

¼ teaspoon ground asafetida

550 g/1¼ lb carrots, peeled and very coarsely grated

6 fresh hot green chillies, slit in half and cut into long slivers

½ teaspoon salt

¼ teaspoon ground turmeric

½ teaspoon ground coriander

½ teaspoon lime juice

Heat the oil in a large, wide, preferably non-stick pan or wok over medium heat. When hot, add the mustard seeds. As soon as they pop, a matter of seconds, add the asafetida. Stir to mix. Add the carrots, chillies, salt, turmeric, coriander and lime juice. Stir and fry for 2–3 minutes. Remove from the heat. The carrots should remain slightly crunchy.

S E R V E S   4 – 6

Mrs Kumud Kansara's Batata Nu Shak

ⓥ SPICY POTATOES WITH TOMATOES

THESE POTATOES ARE HOT – and quite delicious. They are best served with Indian breads but may also be served with store-bought pitta bread. They can be a part of any Indian meal.

〰

4 tablespoons peanut or any other vegetable oil

½ teaspoon brown mustard seeds

½ teaspoon cumin seeds

2 dried hot red chillies

2 bay leaves

¼ teaspoon ground asafetida

10 fresh curry leaves, if available

4 small-medium potatoes (450 g/1 lb), peeled or unpeeled, cut into 1 cm/½ inch pieces

1½ teaspoons cayenne pepper

½ teaspoon ground turmeric

2 teaspoons salt

2 fresh hot green chillies, finely chopped

2.5 cm/1 inch piece of fresh ginger, peeled and finely grated

2 tablespoons finely chopped, fresh green coriander

2 medium-sized tomatoes, chopped into 2.5 cm/1 inch dice

1½ tablespoons unsweetened, desiccated coconut

½ tablespoon ground coriander

1 tablespoon jaggery, chopped up, or 2 teaspoons brown sugar

¾ tablespoon thick tamarind paste (page 278)

〰

Heat the oil in a large, wide, preferably non-stick pan or wok over medium-high heat. When hot, put in the mustard seeds. As soon as they pop, a matter of seconds, add the cumin seeds, red chillies, bay leaves and asafetida. Stir for 4–5 seconds and add the curry leaves. Stir once and add the potatoes, cayenne pepper, turmeric, salt, green chillies and ginger. Stir to mix. Add 150 ml/5 fl oz/⅓ cup water. Cover and simmer for 10 minutes over low heat. Now add the fresh coriander, tomatoes, coconut, ground coriander, jaggery or brown sugar and 350 ml/12 fl oz/1½ cups water. Stir to mix, then cover again and leave to simmer for a further 10 minutes. Add the tamarind paste. Simmer for a further 2–3 minutes.

Remove from the heat.

SERVES 4 – 6

Mrs Kumud Kansara's Mugh Ni Dal
℗ 'DRY' SPLIT PEAS

THE GRAINS OF *MOONG DAL* cook quite separately here and look, to all intents and purposes, like rice. Gujaratis like to eat them with Sweet and Sour Chick Pea Flour Soup (page 79) and plain rice. You may serve this with any Indian meal.

❧

Moong dal **measured to the 250 ml/8 fl oz/1 cup level in a measuring jug**
5 tablespoons peanut oil or any other vegetable oil

½ teaspoon cumin seeds
¼ teaspoon ground asafetida

4 fresh hot green chillies, finely chopped
¾ teaspoon salt
¼ teaspoon ground turmeric

❧

Wash the *moong dal* in several changes of water until the water runs clear. Drain. Soak in lukewarm warm water to cover by 2.5 cm/ 1 inch for 3 hours. Drain.

Heat the oil in a heavy, medium-sized pan over medium-high heat. When hot, add the cumin seeds. Let them sizzle for 10 seconds. Add the asafetida. Stir once. Quickly add the *moong dal*, chillies, salt, turmeric and 120 ml/4 fl oz/½ cup water. Stir to mix and bring to the boil.

Cover very tightly, turn the heat to very, very low and cook for 15 minutes or until the water has been absorbed.

S E R V E S   4

Lamb in a Cashew Nut Sauce (page 64) with Black Pepper Rice (page 84) and Carrots Stir-fried with Green Chillies (page 68).

The Rajmata of Jasdan's Mugphali Nu Shak

⟨V⟩STEAMED PEANUT DIAMONDS IN A GARLIC-ONION SAUCE

I GOT THIS RECIPE several years ago from the mother of the Darbar Sahib of Jasdan, a formerly royal kingdom in Saurashtra. The main ingredient here is a kind of home-made pasta cut into diamonds and then steamed. Perfect for vegetarians, it is made out of a nutritious mixture of chick pea flour and roasted peanuts. The sauce, flavoured with onions, garlic and mustard seeds, is as rich as many of the sauces for meat dishes.

∾

FOR THE STEAMED
PEANUT DIAMONDS:
100 g/5 oz/1 cup roasted, shelled peanuts
150 g/5 oz/1 cup chick pea flour
2 fresh hot green chillies, finely chopped
1 cm/½ inch piece of fresh ginger, peeled and finely grated
¼ teaspoon ground turmeric
½ tablespoon cayenne pepper
½ tablespoon ground cumin
1 tablespoon chopped, fresh green coriander

½ teaspoon salt
1½ tablespoons peanut oil or any other vegetable oil

TO MAKE THE SPICE
PASTE:
2 small red onions (about 50 g/2 oz), roughly chopped
5 garlic cloves, peeled and roughly chopped
¼ teaspoon ground turmeric
2 teaspoons ground coriander
1 teaspoon ground cumin
1 teaspoon cayenne pepper

YOU ALSO NEED:
3 tablespoons peanut oil or any other vegetable oil
½ teaspoon brown mustard seeds
½ teaspoon cumin seeds
½ teaspoon fenugreek seeds
3 dried hot red chillies
2 small red onions (about 50 g/2 oz), finely chopped
5 garlic cloves, finely chopped
4 tablespoons natural (plain) yoghurt, lightly beaten
1 medium-sized tomato, finely chopped
¼–½ teaspoon salt

∾

Make the steamed peanut diamonds: Put the peanuts into a clean coffee grinder. Grind to a fine powder. Put the ground peanuts and remaining dry ingredients into a bowl. Mix well. Add 100 ml/3½ fl oz/about ½ cup water

and ½ tablespoon of the oil. Mix to make a moist, coarse paste.

Lightly grease a 30 cm/12 inch *thali* (see page 283) or shallow cake tin with the remaining tablespoon oil. Put the peanut mixture into the *thali* and spread out evenly until you reach the edges. Press down firmly. The thickness of the pasta should ideally be a little less than 5 mm/¼ inch.

Get your steaming equipment ready. Heat a large, wide pan or wok with 7.5/10 cm/ 3–4 inches water in the bottom. Set the *thali* or cake tin with the peanut mixture over the water, resting it on a trivet or a bowl so that it stays above the water. Cover the pan or wok tightly with a lid and steam for 25 minutes. The steamed pasta should be firm and moist. Allow it to cool and then cut it into 2.5 cm/ 1 inch diamonds.

Put the spice paste ingredients into the container of an electric blender. Add 4 table-spoons water. Blend to a paste. Set aside.

Heat the 3 tablespoons oil in a large, wide, preferably non-stick pan or wok over medium-high heat. When hot, add the mustard seeds, cumin seeds, fenugreek seeds and chillies. As soon as the mustard seeds pop, a matter of seconds, add the onions and garlic. Stir and fry for 3–4 minutes until the onions darken. Reduce the heat to low. Gradually add the yoghurt, a tablespoon at a time, stirring it into the sauce each time. Add the tomato and salt. Stir to mix. Add 400 ml/14 fl oz/1¾ cups water and bring to a simmer. Simmer gently for 10 minutes, stirring frequently. Add the steamed peanut diamonds. Cover and simmer for a further 10 minutes.

SERVES 4

Mrs Kumud Kansara's Khaman Dhokla

SPONGY, SPICY, SAVOURY DIAMONDS

BELONGING TO THE GENERAL family of *dhoklas*, this is known locally as just plain *khaman*. *Dhoklas* are spongy, savoury cakes which can be cut into squares or diamonds. Wonderfully sweet, sour and slightly hot, all at the same time, they may be served as part of a meal or eaten as a snack with tea.

All *dhoklas* need to be steamed. (For more on steaming, see page 287.) It is important that you check your steaming apparatus before you start. A large wok, with a cover, is the ideal steaming utensil. The ideal steaming tray is an Indian *thali* (see page 283), about 30 cm/12 inches in diameter, with sides that are about 3 cm/1½ inches high. The steaming time varies according to the size of the steaming tray and the thickness of the batter. If you are using a large wok for your steaming and your steaming tray is the *thali* suggested above, your steaming time will be about 30 minutes. However, if your steaming gadget is smaller and you can only fit in a 20 cm/8 inch tray with 2.5 cm/1 inch high sides, the steaming would take about 15 minutes and you will have to steam in two batches. The way to test if a *dhokla* is done is to insert a toothpick into it as you would for a cake. If it comes out clean and the *dhokla* feels spongy and resistant, then it is ready.

If you are cooking a *dhokla* in two batches, divide all the ingredients in half. It is best to have two steaming trays. Make one batch and put it to steam. Then make your second batch from scratch, beating in the water and the bicarbonate of soda (baking soda) just before you are ready to steam. It is important that the batter be frothing and bubbling as you are putting it in to steam.

To start with, measure out all your dry ingredients, as you would for a cake, and grease your steaming trays. Get the water boiling in your steaming utensil and have extra boiling water ready in case you need it to refill the utensil.

❧

FOR THE BATTER:
1 tablespoon peanut oil or any other vegetable oil
250 g/9 oz/1¾ cups chick pea flour, sifted
75 g/3 oz/¼ cup plus 1 tablespoon sugar

2 teaspoons salt
½ teaspoon citric acid (sold by Indian grocers and chemists)
1 teaspoon bicarbonate of soda (baking soda)

YOU ALSO NEED:
4 tablespoons peanut oil or any other vegetable oil
½ teaspoon brown mustard seeds
¼ teaspoon ground asafetida

6 fresh hot green chillies,
 roughly chopped
1 tablespoon sugar
¼ teaspoon citric acid

½ teaspoon salt
2 tablespoons finely
 chopped, fresh green
 coriander

1 tablespoon fresh or
 desiccated coconut

Get everything ready for steaming (see left). Pour approximately 7.5 cm/3 inches of water into the wok. You should be able to fit the *thali* or tray near the top of the wok. You may need to rest it on a small dish so that it is secure rather than wedged in. It should sit above the water level. Bring the water in the wok to the boil. Grease the tray or trays with the 1 tablespoon oil.

If you are steaming the batter in one batch, put the chick pea flour, sugar, salt and citric acid into a mixing bowl. Slowly add 350 ml/12 fl oz/1½ cups water as you beat the mixture to a thick, smooth batter. The colour should become lighter and the mixture double in volume. Add the bicarbonate of soda (baking soda). Gently beat for a further 1–2 minutes. The mixture should bubble. Quickly pour the batter into the baking tray, place the tray in the wok, cover the wok and steam for 30 minutes or until a toothpick inserted into the cake comes out clean and the cake has a light, fluffy, sponge-like texture.

Cut into 2.5 cm/1 inch squares or diamonds.

(If the *dhokla* is to be cooked in 2 separate batches, divide the flour mixture into 2 equal lots. Add only half the water to each lot and beat it in just before steaming it. Follow general directions.)

Meanwhile, heat the 4 tablespoons oil in a small pan over medium-high heat. When hot, add the mustard seeds. As soon as they pop, a matter of seconds, remove the pan from the heat. Add the asafetida, chillies and 200 ml/7 fl oz/¾ cup plus 1 tablespoon water. Return the pan to medium-high heat. Add the sugar, citric acid and salt. Bring to the boil. Boil for 2 minutes or until you have a light syrup. Remove from the heat.

Pour the syrup evenly over the cooked *dhokla*. Sprinkle the fresh coriander and desiccated coconut over the top.

M A K E S   2 0 – 3 0
D I A M O N D S

Mrs Kumud Kansara's Handva

⊙ SAVOURY GRAIN CAKE WITH MUSTARD AND SESAME SEEDS

A SAVOURY, ALL-VEGETARIAN CAKE, encrusted with sesame seeds. Serve as a snack, with drinks or at tea-time.

❦

FOR THE BATTER:

Long-grain rice measured to the 475 ml/16 fl oz/2 cup level in a measuring jug

Chana dal (page 260) measured to the 175 ml/6 fl oz/¾ cup level in a measuring jug

Toovar dal (page 261) measured to the 175 ml/6 fl oz/¾ cup level in a measuring jug

200 ml/7 fl oz/¾ cup plus 2 tablespoons natural (plain) yoghurt

1 teaspoon baking powder

A little peanut or any other vegetable oil for greasing cake tin plus

150 ml/5 fl oz/⅔ cup

1 teaspoon brown mustard seeds

1 teaspoon sesame seeds

¼ teaspoon ground asafetida

8–10 fresh curry leaves, if available

7.5 cm/3 inch piece of fresh ginger, finely grated

4–5 fresh hot green chillies, finely chopped

1 tablespoon cayenne pepper

¼ teaspoon ground turmeric

2¼ teaspoons salt

3 tablespoons sugar

1 teaspoon citric acid

2–3 tablespoons finely chopped, fresh green coriander

2 medium-sized carrots (200 g/7 oz), peeled, cut into 5 mm/¼ inch dice, boiled for 5 minutes and drained

200 g/7 oz/1¾ cups shelled green peas, boiled briefly until just tender and drained (frozen peas may be used)

FOR THE FINAL SEASONING:

4 tablespoons peanut oil or any other vegetable oil

1½ teaspoons brown mustard seeds

1½ teaspoons sesame seeds

¼ teaspoon cayenne pepper

¼ teaspoon ground asafetida

❦

Wash the rice, *chana dal* and *toovar dal* in several changes of water until the water runs clear. Drain. Soak the rice and *dals* in water to cover by 5 cm/2 inches for 3 hours. Drain.

Put the drained rice and *dals* into the container of an electric blender. Add 600 ml/ 1 pint/2½ cups water. Blend to a smooth paste. You may need to do this in stages, pushing the mixture down with a spatula from time to time.

Put the rice and *dal* paste into a large bowl. Add the yoghurt. Stir to mix. Leave for 1 hour.

Add the baking powder and mix it in.

Pre-heat the oven to 200°C/400°F/Gas 6. Lightly oil a large 30 cm/12 inch square or round cake tin with 7.5 cm/3 inch high sides.

Heat the 150 ml/5 fl oz/⅔ cup oil in a large, wide, preferably non-stick pan or wok over medium-high heat. When hot, add the 1 teaspoon mustard seeds and 1 teaspoon sesame seeds. As soon as the mustard seeds pop, a matter of seconds, put in the ¼ teaspoon asafetida. Stir once and put in the curry leaves, ginger and chillies. Stir and fry for 2 minutes. Add the 1 tablespoon cayenne pepper, turmeric, the ground rice and *dals*, salt, sugar, citric acid, coriander and 150 ml/5 fl oz/⅔ cup water. Bring to the boil, stirring frequently. Reduce the heat to medium. Simmer gently and stir for 10 minutes. Add the carrots and peas and continue to stir and cook for another 5 minutes or until you have a thick mixture. Pour the batter into the oiled cake tin. Press down firmly.

Heat the 4 tablespoons oil for the final seasoning in a small pan or wok over medium heat. When hot, add the 1½ teaspoons mustard seeds and the 1½ teaspoons sesame seeds. As soon as they pop, a matter of seconds, add the ¼ teaspoon cayenne pepper and ¼ teaspoon asafetida. Stir once. Remove from the heat and pour over the rice and *dal*.

Put the cake tin into the pre-heated oven. Bake for 1¼ – 1½ hours or until the cake is cooked. Check after 1 hour and make sure it does not darken too much. Turn the oven down to 190°C/375°F/Gas 5 if it does. Leave for 10 minutes and cut into 5 cm/2 inch squares.

SERVES 10 AS A SNACK

Mrs Kumud Kansara's Kadhi
ⓥ SWEET AND SOUR CHICK PEA FLOUR SOUP

THIS IS NOT A soup in the sense that you can drink it as a first course. It is soupy, however, and is usually eaten with rice. As an unusual variation, you may put in 3 tablespoons of fresh mango pulp instead of the sugar.

❧

FOR THE SOUP BASE:
500 ml/17 fl oz/2 cups plus 1 tablespoon natural (plain) yoghurt, the sourer the better
2 tablespoons chick pea flour
2.5 cm/1 inch piece of fresh ginger, peeled and finely grated

4 fresh hot green chillies, finely chopped
1 tablespoon chopped, fresh green coriander leaves

YOU ALSO NEED:
1 tablespoon *ghee* or vegetable oil
½ teaspoon cumin seeds

¼ teaspoon ground asafetida
2.5 cm/1 inch cinnamon stick, broken into 2–3 pieces
5–6 cloves
2 bay leaves
1–1½ tablespoons sugar
¾–1 teaspoon salt

❧

Make the soup base: Put the yoghurt and chick pea flour into the container of an electric blender. Add 750 ml/1¼ pints/3 cups water. Blend thoroughly. Add the ginger, chillies and coriander. Blend to mix. Set aside.

Heat the *ghee* or oil in a large pan over medium-high heat. When hot, add the cumin seeds. As soon as they begin to change colour, a matter of seconds, add the asafetida, cinna-mon, cloves and bay leaves. Stir and fry for a few seconds or until the bay leaves darken in colour. Quickly add the soup base, sugar and salt. Stir and bring to the boil.

Reduce the heat to very low and leave to simmer gently for 15 minutes. Remove from the heat.

SERVES 4

Spongy, Spicy, Savoury Diamonds (page 74) and, left to right, Green Chilli and Lime Pickle (page 86) and Green Coriander and Peanut Chutney (page 86).

Mrs Kumud Kansara's Sev Tamate
ⓥ NOODLES WITH TOMATO

IN THIS DRY STATE, where vegetables do not grow with ease, a bag of crisp noodles can quickly be changed into a main dish with the addition of a sauce. Here the sauce is made with tomatoes spiced with ginger, garlic and green chillies. This is a very popular dish at all the vegetarian truck stops that line the state's highways. It is amazingly delicious as well. Although it is best made with home-made noodles, you may use the store-bought variety sold by Indian grocers. Look for medium-thick or thin *sev*.

2½ tablespoons peanut oil or any other vegetable oil

½ teaspoon cumin seeds

5–6 garlic cloves, finely chopped

1 fresh hot green chilli, finely chopped

2.5 cm/1 inch piece of fresh ginger, peeled, very finely sliced and then very finely chopped

¼ teaspoon ground asafetida

¼ teaspoon ground turmeric

½ teaspoon cayenne pepper

2 medium-sized ripe tomatoes, coarsely chopped

3 tablespoons finely chopped, fresh green coriander

¾ teaspoon salt

100 g/4 oz plain Crispy Chick Pea Flour Noodles (*sev*) page 62

Heat the oil in a wok or large, wide, preferably non-stick pan over medium-high heat. When hot, add the cumin seeds. Let them sizzle for 10 seconds. Add the garlic, chilli and ginger. Stir and fry for 2–3 minutes or until the garlic begins to turn light brown. Add the asafetida, turmeric and cayenne pepper. Stir once quickly and put in the tomatoes as well as 375 ml/13 fl oz/1⅔ cups water. Bring to a gentle boil and cook for 2–3 minutes over medium-low heat, stirring frequently. Add the coriander and salt. Simmer for 2–3 minutes or until the tomatoes are tender. Add the noodles. Stir to mix. Cook for 30 seconds to heat the noodles through and just barely soften them. Serve immediately.

SERVES 4

Mrs Kumud Kansara's Pudla
ⓥ CHICK PEA FLOUR PANCAKES

THIS NUTRITIOUS CHICK PEA flour pancake may be served with all Indian meals just as a bread might be. It can also be eaten at breakfast or as a snack with chutneys, pickles and other relishes.

❧

150 g/5 oz/1¼ cups chick
  pea flour, sifted
½ teaspoon salt
½ teaspoon cayenne pepper
½ teaspoon *ajwain* seeds
  (page 259)

1 small red onion
  (25 g/1 oz), very finely
  chopped
5 cm/2 inch piece of fresh
  ginger, peeled and very
  finely chopped
4 fresh hot green chillies,
  very finely chopped

5 garlic cloves, peeled and
  very finely chopped
2 tablespoons very finely
  chopped, fresh green
  coriander
About 3 tablespoons
  vegetable oil

❧

Put the chick pea flour into a large mixing bowl. Slowly add 250 ml/8 fl oz/1 cup water mixing with a wooden spoon to make a smooth batter. Add the salt, cayenne, *ajwain* seeds, onion, ginger, chillies, garlic and coriander. Stir to mix. Set aside for 15 minutes.

Smear a large, wide, non-stick frying-pan with 1 teaspoon of the oil and set over lowish heat. When very hot, stir the batter and pour about 70 ml/2 ¾ fl oz/⅓ cup on to the centre of the pan. Quickly tilt the pan in all directions as you would for a crêpe, spreading the batter to make an 18–19 cm/7–7½ inch pancake.

Cover and cook for 3 minutes or until the pancake is reddish-brown at the bottom. Dribble another teaspoon of oil around the edges of the *pudla*. Turn the *pudla* over and cook, uncovered, for a further minute or until golden. Remove from the heat and keep covered between 2 plates. Repeat with the remaining batter. Always remember to stir the batter before you use it.

(Left-over batter may be covered, refrigerated and re-used).

MAKES 5 PANCAKES

Mrs Kumud Kansara's Thepla

⊘ FLAT BREADS STUFFED WITH CABBAGE

THESE ARE SIMPLE, FLAT, wholewheat breads stuffed with cabbage. Serve with almost any Indian meal, especially a vegetarian one. You could also eat them by themselves with pickles and chutneys or any yoghurt relish.

∾

75 g/3 oz white or green cabbage, finely shredded

1¼ teaspoons salt

240 g/8½ oz/2 cups *chapati* flour or ½ and ½ sifted wholemeal flour and plain (all-purpose white) flour, plus extra for dusting

¼ teaspoon ground black pepper

½ teaspoon ground coriander

⅓ teaspoon ground turmeric

⅛ teaspoon ground asafetida

½ teaspoon white sesame seeds

1–3 fresh hot green chillies, finely chopped

2.5 cm/1 inch piece of fresh ginger, peeled and very finely chopped

2 tablespoons peanut oil or any other vegetable oil, plus extra for frying

∾

Put the cabbage in a small bowl. Add ½ teaspoon of the salt. Put aside for 30 minutes so that some water is drawn out from the cabbage. Squeeze out the water and pat dry.

Meanwhile, sift the flour into a large mixing bowl. Add the black pepper, coriander, turmeric, asafetida, sesame seeds, chillies, ginger and remaining salt. Mix well. Add the cabbage, oil and 150 ml/5 fl oz/⅔ cup water. Mix to make a medium to soft dough. Knead for 10 minutes. Cover with a damp cloth and rest for about 10 minutes.

Divide the mixture into 9 equal balls. On a lightly floured surface, roll each ball into a 15 cm/6 inch round. Heat a large, wide, cast-iron frying-pan or *tava* over medium heat. When very hot, slap on a rolled-out *thepla*. Leave for 10 seconds. Dribble a teaspoon of oil around the *thepla* so that it runs under the edges. Turn the *thepla* over. Cook for 10 seconds. Turn the *thepla* over and dribble another teaspoon of oil around the edges. Now cook, turning every 10 seconds, until the *thepla* is golden on both sides and has a few brownish spots. Remove to a plate. Cover with another plate. Cook the remaining *theplas* in the same way.

M A K E S   9   B R E A D S

Noodles with Tomato (page 80).

Nishrin Attarwala's Chaval

ⓥ BLACK PEPPER RICE

THIS LIGHTLY SPICED RICE is traditionally eaten with the Bohri dish Lamb in a Cashew Nut Sauce (page 64), though it may be served with any Indian meal.

Basmati rice measured to the 450 ml/15 fl oz/2 cup level in a measuring jug

2 tablespoons vegetable oil
2 bay leaves
1 teaspoon cumin seeds

½ teaspoon black peppercorns
1 teaspoon salt

Wash the rice in several changes of water until the water runs clear. Drain. Soak the rice in water to cover by 2.5 cm/1 inch for 30 minutes. Drain.

Heat the oil in a large, heavy-bottomed pan over medium-high heat. When hot, put in the bay leaves, cumin seeds and peppercorns. Stir and fry for 10 seconds. Add the rice and salt. Stir gently to mix. Add 600 ml/1 pint/2⅔ cups water and bring to the boil. Cover tightly, reduce the heat to very low and cook for 25 minutes.

SERVES 4

Mrs Kumud Kansara's Kela Nu Raitu

ⓥ YOGHURT WITH BANANA AND MUSTARD

A SIMPLE SWEET, SOUR and pungent yoghurt relish, this dish gets its bite from hulled and split mustard seeds. If you cannot get them, dissolve ½ teaspoon ordinary yellow mustard powder in a teaspoon of hot water, mix well and add that to the yoghurt. Serve as a salad with lunch or dinner or all by itself as a snack. It is best if the banana is sliced into the yoghurt just before serving.

500 ml/17 fl oz/2 cups plus 2 tablespoons natural (plain) yoghurt, lightly beaten

1 tablespoon sugar
1 teaspoon salt
1 teaspoon hulled and split mustard seeds (page 273),

plus a pinch more for garnishing
4 large, ripe bananas, thinly sliced into rounds

Put the yoghurt, sugar, salt and mustard seeds into a mixing bowl. Mix well.

Fold in the sliced bananas just before serving. (As a final touch garnish the relish with a light sprinkling of split mustard seeds if you like.)

S E R V E S   4 – 8

Mrs Kumud Kansara's Lasun Chutney

⊙ GARLIC CHILLI CHUTNEY

SOMEWHAT LIKE A FRENCH *rouille*, this is an enlivening seasoning made of red chillies, garlic and salt. It is traditionally pounded in a mortar or ground on a stone but it may also be made in an electric blender. Travellers going on long journeys in Saurashtra form a ball out of it which they rub with oil. This way it lasts for up to a month.

Before eating, a little bit of lime can be squeezed over the small portion on your plate. Serve it with any Indian meal. Lovers of garlic and chillies will just adore it. For greater convenience I have used cayenne pepper instead of chillies.

1 head garlic (100 g/4 oz), peeled
½ teaspoon salt
2½ tablespoons cayenne pepper

1 teaspoon ground coriander
½ teaspoon ground cumin

2½ tablespoons peanut or any other vegetable oil
¼ teaspoon ground asafetida

Put the garlic into the container of an electric blender. Blend to a smooth paste, adding a sprinkling of water, if necessary, to help the blending. Add the salt, cayenne pepper, coriander and cumin. Blend to mix. Alternatively, pound the garlic and salt first with a pestle and mortar, then add the cayenne pepper, coriander and cumin. Pound to make a fine paste.

Meanwhile, heat the oil in a small pan over low heat. When hot, add the asafetida. Stir for 2–3 seconds. Add the garlic paste. Stir once or twice to mix. Remove from the heat.

Cool. Put into a clean, air-tight jar. This chutney will keep refrigerated for 3–4 months.

1 5 0   M L   /   5   F L   O Z /
⅔   C U P

Niranjana Row Kavi's Leeli Chutney

⊘ GREEN CORIANDER AND PEANUT CHUTNEY

THIS NUTTY GREEN CHUTNEY may be served with all Indian meals.

3 tablespoons roasted, salted, shelled peanuts
120 g/4½ oz/2¾ cups fresh green coriander, finely chopped

6–7 fresh hot green chillies, finely chopped
5 mm/¼ inch piece of fresh ginger, peeled and finely chopped

½ teaspoon salt
¼ teaspoon sugar
1 tablespoon lime juice

Put the peanuts into a clean coffee grinder. Grind to a coarse powder.

Put the coriander, chillies, ginger, salt, sugar and lime juice into the container of an electric blender. Add 50 ml/2 fl oz/4 tablespoons water. Blend to a fine paste.

Put the peanuts and coriander mixture into a bowl. Mix well.

The chutney will keep for at least 2 days if covered in the refrigerator.

SERVES 4–6

Samina Hakimji's Marchanu Athanu

⊘ GREEN CHILLI AND LIME PICKLE

IN GUJARAT, PICKLES ARE eaten with snack foods and with all meals. The chillies are pale green, mild in their heat and somewhat squat. You may use any green chillies such as cayenne as long as they are not the very small, fiery ones.

1½ tablespoons salt
½ teaspoon ground turmeric
½ teaspoon ground cumin
250 g/9 oz fresh hot green chillies (16–24 depending on size), wiped with a damp cloth and dried off

2 limes (100 g/4 oz), each lime cut into 12 pieces
3 tablespoons mustard oil
100 g/4 oz/1 cup plus

1 tablespoon hulled and split mustard seeds (page 273)
1½ teaspoons white wine vinegar

Coconut Pistachio Sweetmeat (page 88).

Mix the salt, turmeric and cumin.

Make a shallow slit along the length of each chilli. Fill each chilli with a little of the salt, turmeric and cumin mixture. Put the chillies into an air-tight container or jar. Add the limes and shake well to mix. Seal the container and leave unrefrigerated for 2 days.

After 2 days, heat the oil in a small pan over medium heat. When hot, remove from the heat and leave to cool. Add the mustard seeds. Beat well. Add the vinegar and beat to mix well.

Discard any water or liquid in the jar of chillies. Empty the drained chillies into the pan of oil, vinegar and mustard seeds. Mix well then put the mixture back into the jar. Leave to mature for at least a week, shaking the jar now and then. This pickle will keep unrefrigerated in an air-tight jar for many months. It improves upon maturing.

600 ML / 1 PINT / 2 ½ CUPS

Mrs Kumud Kansara's Coco Pista Pasand
ⓥ COCONUT PISTACHIO SWEETMEAT

HERE IS AN INDIAN version of a sponge roll: the outside is sweetened coconut and the inside is pistachios.

FOR THE PISTACHIO FILLING:

2 tablespoons shelled, unsalted pistachios
1 tablespoon icing sugar (confectioner's sugar)
1 teaspoon white poppy seeds

½ tablespoon milk

FOR THE COCONUT CASING:

120 g/4½ oz/⅔ cup sugar
5 cardamom pods, crushed in a mortar or ground in a clean coffee grinder

120 g/4½ oz/scant 1½ cups unsweetened, desiccated coconut
4 tablespoons canned condensed milk

To make the filling: Put the pistachios into the container of a clean coffee grinder. Grind to a coarse powder. Put the ground pistachios, sugar, poppy seeds and milk into a bowl. Mix to a paste. Put aside.

To make the coconut casing: Put the sugar

into a small, heavy-bottomed pan. Add 4 tablespoons water. Stir and bring to a simmer. Cook over medium-high heat for 2–3 minutes until the syrup forms a single thread when a little is dropped from a spoon into a cup of cold water. Remove from the heat. Add the coconut and cardamom. Mix well. Add the condensed milk. Stir to mix.

Lay a 23 cm/9 inch piece of cling film (plastic wrap) on your work surface. While the coconut paste is still warm, roll it into a thick, 23 cm/9 inch sausage. Put the coconut sausage horizontally on to the centre of the piece of cling film (plastic wrap) and flatten it to form a rectangle about 9 cm/3½ inches wide.

Roll the pistachio paste into a separate sausage of the same length. Put the rolled pistachio sausage on the coconut rectangle, slightly below the centre, a little closer to your end. With the aid of the cling film (plastic wrap), fold the coconut paste over the pistachio paste. Press down on the cling film (plastic wrap) to firm up the roll. Now continue rolling, being careful to keep the cling film (plastic wrap) on the outside of the roll, until you have a slim 'Swiss roll' (jelly roll). Press down evenly on the cling film (plastic wrap) to get a neat roll. Let the roll cool and harden a bit. Remove the cling film (plastic wrap) and cut crossways into 1 cm/½ inch thick slices.

MAKES
8–10 SWEETS

Mrs Kumud Kansara's Shrikhand
ⓥ MANGO YOGHURT

COOLING YOGHURT IS EATEN throughout the year in different forms. Here it is transformed into a dessert. *Shrikhand* is generally served with the meal, though I actually prefer to serve it at the end.

❧

2.25 litres/4 pints/2½ quarts rich, natural (plain) yoghurt **350 g/12 oz/1¾ cups sugar** **300 ml/10 fl oz/1¼ cups mango pulp**

❧

Put a sieve over a small bowl. Line the sieve with a double layer of thin muslin or cheesecloth, large enough to tie into a bundle later. Empty the yoghurt into the sieve. Let the water drain into the bowl. You will not need it. Tie the corners of the muslin or cheesecloth tightly with string. Put a 2 kg/4½ lb weight on top to extract the remaining water. Leave for 2 hours.

You should end up with roughly 600 ml/ 1 pint/2½ cups drained yoghurt.

Put the yoghurt into a mixing bowl. Add the sugar. Beat for 4–5 minutes till smooth and thick. Add the mango pulp. Mix well. Serve chilled.

SERVES 4

GOA

SOPHIE GONSALVES' HANDSOME, COLONIAL Goan home with its tiled roof sits on a sloping hillside of brick-red earth in the pretty township of Parra. There is a dappled arbour of passion fruit on one side. The sweet-and-sour pulp of this yellow, golf-ball-shaped fruit will be used as part of the dressing for the fresh fruit salad served on Christmas Day. A dog snoozes in the arbour's shade.

Behind the arbour, beside a well, is the kitchen garden which produces everything from curry leaves, cinnamon, black pepper, mangoes, coconuts and guavas to jackfruit and bananas. (Sophie carries a cluster of bananas into the dining-room, saying 'You must try these – they are so sweet'.) Stretching on the hillside at the back is a grove of cashew nut trees.

The cashews are a major local crop along with rice. There are rice fields everywhere. Even the local, whitewashed church, where a midnight Mass will be held on Christmas Eve, seems to sit in the midst of a rice field.

Sophie's cashews have just been harvested and are being roasted over wood fires in her semi-outdoor kitchen so that their hard, bitter and toxic outer shells can be cracked and removed. The nuts inside, now licked lightly by wood smoke, will be stored inside old cans in old cupboards and will taste somewhat like chestnuts. They will be served to the large family that will gather at Christmas-time.

They will also be put into the many cakes and pastries – such as fudge-like *dodol*, cooked over a wood fire in great copper urns lined with steel and stirred endlessly with wooden paddles, and half-moon-shaped *neureos* (stuffed pastries) – made with local ingredients like coconuts and date palm sugar, that will be offered to visitors between Christmas Eve and the Feast of the Epiphany when the entire Catholic township of Parra will be lit, like the sky above, with three-dimensional stars.

Some members of Sophie's family – a daughter and granddaughter – are coming from as far away as England. Tropical Goa is an idyllic spot for them to come to. A small stretch of land, only 96 kilometres long and 64 wide and belonging to what is named the Union Territory of Goa, Daman and Diu, it lies 400 kilometres south of Bombay, right on the shores of the warm Arabian Sea. There are 130 kilometres of welcoming sandy beaches here, broken up with meandering rivers and creeks and a populace imbued with *'susegad'*, a laid-back feeling of general mellowness, a 'why-do-anything-now-when-it-can-be-done-later' attitude. Although Goa is in India, it hovers, at least in spirit, quite outside it. This may well be because for 451 years it has had a history and a dominant culture quite apart from that of the rest of the nation.

All the time India was under Mogul or British rule, Goa was a Portuguese stronghold, the nerve centre of Portugal's eastern empire. It is, perhaps, this southern European, very Latin, influence that accounts for the difference in the general attitude of the people and in the foods they eat.

In the late fifteenth century Goa, while largely Hindu, was in prosperous Muslim hands with excellent dock facilities for international ships. Dhows stood at the ready to take pilgrims to Mecca or to trade Arabian horses and pearls for rubies, emeralds, black pepper, cinnamon and other precious goods.

It was these very riches – indeed the riches of all of India – that inspired the greed and envy of the Europeans and caused them to come in droves to conquer and then to convert.

In the early 1500s, King Emanuel of Portugal dispatched Afonso de Albuquerque to conquer India. By 1510, he may not have conquered the nation but he had gained a solid foothold in Goa, making it, by mid-century, the capital of Portugal's eastern possessions. Once the land had been taken, souls were the next objective. Missionaries followed, the most famous of whom was St Francis Xavier whose body found a permanent resting-place in the Basilica of Bom Jesus in what was then the fortified capital, the city of Goa (now mostly in ruins and called Old Goa). This port city of Goa, up the Mandovi River, traded in everything from Chinese silks to asafetida and was so prosperous that it was nicknamed *'Goa Dourada'* or Golden Goa. It was said that those who had seen Goa need not see Lisbon. The Portuguese were transported about the city in palanquins by liveried servants. Their women bedecked themselves in brocade and cloth-of-gold gowns and insisted on wearing 15 centimetre/6 inch cork heels on which they could barely walk. Tavernas, local bars, sprang up in every neighbourhood. It was a good life.

The city flourished through the sixteenth century but then the good life of the conquerors began to fall apart. Trade was threatened by the envious Dutch, plagues hit and langour prevailed. The capital was eventually moved downriver to Panaji. In 1961, an independent India ended the four and a half centuries of Portuguese rule by marching in and planting its own flag.

With such a mixed Hindu, Muslim and Latin-Catholic heritage what happened to Goa's culinary traditions? With the strong influences of the fish-and-rice-eating Konkan farmers and fishermen, of the vegetarian Maharashtrians, of the pilaf-eating Muslims and of the olive oil, beef, seafood and pork-eating Portuguese, what happened to the food?

The Portuguese were mainly interested in controlling the coastline. That is where they settled. It was here that the people, along with acquiring Catholicism and Portuguese names, picked up a Latin way of life complete with afternoon siestas, lace mantillas and *fados* sung to the accompaniment of guitars and violins. The foods, important enough to create the saying 'You cannot think until you have eaten', became a glorious *mélange* of all the local traditions. If olive oil was unavailable, peanut or sesame oil would do. As a substitute for olives, there were pickled green mangoes. Instead of salt cod, there was salted shark! Coconut milk was often substituted for cow's milk in desserts, palm sugar replaced plain sugar and the cheaper rice flour sometimes replaced wheat flour. Portuguese dishes were gradually 'Indianized' and the local coastal dishes began picking up Portuguese accents.

Take Goa's most famous export, the *vindaloo*. On almost every restaurant menu in the West this has become synonymous with 'the hottest curry'. It was once quite different. The correct spelling, *vindalho*, gives away the main seasonings of the original dish which was once a kind of Portuguese pork stew seasoned with garlic (*alhos*) and wine (*vinho*) vinegar. There were probably some black peppercorns in it as well, especially at the tables of affluent families. The vinegar acted as a preservative, allowing the stew to be eaten over several days.

The Portuguese successfully decimated much of the ruling Muslim population in their early years. Pigs, which Muslims would have resisted, were allowed to roam freely and became the meat of choice for not just the Portuguese colonialists but the converted Hindus and the growing numbers of mixed race Catholic Goans. The original *vindalho* soon had added to it ginger, cumin, cloves, cardamom and an enormous number of dried red chillies which, rather like the red pepper used to make paprika, had more colour than bite. The chillies came from the New World with the conquerors. Goa took to them in a way Portugal never did.

Today, the *vindaloo* is treated as a festive dish (pork, like all red meats, is more expensive than some of the everyday fish) and is often made in earthen vessels several days in advance. The vinegar still preserves it though, with their tropical climate, Goans without refrigerators do take the precaution of bringing it to a boil once a day and refrain from touching it with soiled spoons. It is served either with the local 'red' rice, a short-grained, partially-milled, protein-rich variety, or with what is considered superior: a pilaf.

The pilaf, or *pillau* as they say here, is a possible throwback to Muslim times, or borrowed from Muslim India. It is made with Basmati rice, flavoured with whole spices such as cardamom and cooked in stock. *Pillaus* here may be made with the abundant prawns (shrimp), with local sausages or only with stock. The more Portuguese risotto (*arroz refogado*), on the other hand, is now made like Indian pilaf with Basmati rice, though it can contain very un-Indian pilaf ingredients such as sausage or duck!

A *vindaloo* is just one of the pork dishes served on these balmy shores. If you hear the exuberant strains of a brass band coming from under a canopy of palms, a wedding is in progress and an *assado de leitoa*, a roast suckling pig, is being readied. It is cleaned and washed, then stuffed with a mixture of mashed potatoes, the chopped-up heart and liver, green chillies, curry leaves and parsley. (The stuffings vary but this is a popular one.)

The piglet is then sewn up and brushed with a mixture of turmeric water and oil as it roasts. This somewhat Eastern roast is served in proper European style, sitting on a large silver tray with an apple ensconced in its mouth!

Ask any blue-collar Goan what he is going to eat at Christmas and he is likely to reply, 'Sorpatel with sannas'. *Sorpatel* is another pork stew, traditionally made out of the shoulder, neck, kidneys, liver, tail and ears of the pig, though today people such as Sophie Gonsalves tend to do without the tail and ears!

Sophie likes to cook her *sorpatel* and *sannas* in the outdoor kitchen over wood. 'It tastes much better this way,' she says with conviction as she huffs and puffs at the fire, poking at it knowledgeably at appropriate intervals. First she cuts her meat into small cubes and boils it. Then she grinds her spices – red chillies, cumin seeds,

A woman in traditional dress in Goa.

turmeric, cloves, peppercorns and cinnamon – in vinegar. After some onions, garlic, ginger and green chillies have been sautéd, in goes this spice paste and finally the meat. All simmers gently on the wood fire, stirred every now and then by Sophie's capable hands, until flavours meld and the meat is red, hot and sour. And what are the *sannas* that the *sorpatel* is eaten with? They are springy, crumpet-shaped steamed breads made in moulds with a batter of ground 'red' rice, ground coconut, salt, a little sugar and toddy.

Toddy is the sap collected from a palm before dawn. As the day progresses, it begins to bubble and ferment. All along this coast it is used as yeast.

Vinegary spice pastes, common to much of coastal Goan Catholic cooking, also go into the making of *chouricos*, the local sausages. Tart and spicy, they are made into curries to eat with rice, cooked along with red beans to make a glorious *feijoada*, and, best of all, eaten plain on the beach, sandwiched, along with a thin slice of onion, inside one of the local breads, the *pao*, which is a rectangular bun of white flour, or the *kunechi poee*, a butterfly-shaped, pitta-like, flatter bread that is quite heavenly, both in taste and its chewy texture. The best sausages are sold in select places. 'Try the blue-painted stall near the bridge over the Zuari River,' you might be told, or 'Go to such and such a shop in Mapusa market'. Here the shopkeeper will count the links, wrap them in newspaper and hand them to

you. The hungry can have a sandwich made and gobble it up on the spot.

If you wish to see the sausages prepared from scratch, you may visit a special house in the town of Mapusa. A country road winds around a lush hill. The house sits just below the road. You enter through a gate and see nothing but an exquisite tropical garden and dozens of songbirds in cages. Just when you think that you might have entered the wrong compound, you see a sign, TASTY GOAN PORK SAUSAGES BY JOAO INACID DE SOUZA. At the back, in a series of sheds with wall signs that say 'Do Not Spit' and 'No Smoking', there is nothing but pork meat. Pork being cut; pork marinating in its very red spice mixture (vinegar, red chillies, cumin, pepper, cloves, garlic, turmeric, cinnamon, ginger and *feni*, the liquor distilled from either the cashew fruit or the palm); pork being pushed by machines into parchment-like casings; and sausages drying on palm-leaf mats in the sun, guarded by ferocious dogs including a Doberman. You wonder if the dogs are perhaps guarding not the sausages but the sausage recipe – the owner, who knows he is on to a good thing, will not part with it.

Besides pork dishes, Goan Catholics make a delightful beef pot roast (*bife assado*). Beef is pricked and then left to marinate in a mixture of chillies, ginger, garlic, cumin, cinnamon, pepper, vinegar, salt and turmeric. Onions are fried and the meat and marinade put into the pot along with a little water and, later, some potatoes. Nothing more is needed for a meal other than some *pao* and a simple Goan salad which tends to consist of shredded lettuce, tomatoes and cucumber dressed with just lime juice, a touch of *feni* vinegar and salt. To precede it, there might be some *caldo verde*, a mild, almost purely Portuguese soup made with potatoes, onions, dill and a touch of imported olive oil if there is any to be had.

Another example of East–West cuisine with origins dating back several hundred years is the *xacuti*. It is as popular here as the *vindaloo*. Spelled with an exotic 'x' (and pronounced 'sha-koo-tee') this is generally made with chicken although rabbits and the herons that stand on long legs in the paddy fields may also be snatched and thrown into the pot. Goan catering students, now studying their own culinary history with avid interest, seem to feel that the dish originated in northern Goa. It was a vegetarian (*shak* means 'vegetable', *kooti* means 'cut small') dish of small-cut vegetables or greens cooked with the same spice mixture that is used today for chicken pieces: roasted shredded coconut combined with a long list of spices that must be roasted first and then ground on a heavy grinding-stone, giving the dish a unique flavour – spices such as chillies, coriander seeds, fennel seeds, peppercorns, cardamom, cloves, cinnamon, mace, poppy seeds and, surprisingly, star anise. Perhaps the use of star anise, common to Chinese cooking, should not be so surprising. China began trading with India's west coast well

before the start of the Christian era. In fact, the antiques that grace the grand homes of wealthy Goans are either of Portuguese or Chinese ancestry. The exceedingly spicy *xacutis* were considered almost medicinal and offered to farmers returning from long wet days in the paddy fields during the monsoon planting season. The spices helped flush out their coughs and colds.

Pork, beef and poultry are all very well but the basic, daily diet of most people consists of vegetables, dried beans and the local 'red' rice plus fish for the non-vegetarians. Breakfast could be a bowl of congee or rice gruel. It could also be *pao* and *chanyacho ros* (dried peas cooked with mustard seeds, curry leaves and roasted coconut). Lunch and dinner, on the other hand, would most likely be rice, and perhaps a vegetable such as *tamari bhaji* – a dish of red spinach from the fields, flavoured with onions, green chillies, freshly grated coconut and, for souring, the dried fruit called *kokum*. The beans could be *osanay samaray* (red beans cooked with coconut and sour mango seeds). There might be *sookhi bhaji* (potatoes cooked with mustard and cumin seeds) or *bibo upkari* (cashews cooked with cumin, mustard and chillies) as well as *bharli vaangi,* small aubergines (eggplants) stuffed with a paste of sesame seeds, peanuts, palm sugar and onions.

Fish is what coastal Goans thrive on. Pomfret, mackerel, kingfish, sardines and squid from the sea, prawns (shrimp), crabs and lobsters from the coastal waters and river estuaries. The fish could be cooked in one of many ways. The cheapest might be a handful of tiny dried prawns (shrimp) cooked with a paste of coconut, chillies, coriander, cumin, turmeric, garlic, ginger and dried green mango slices. This makes a flavourful, slightly sweet, slightly sour and very hot sauce to put over rice. An aristocratic, Portuguese-speaking family might eat *carangrejo recheado* (crabs stuffed with onions, garlic, tomatoes and green chillies then dusted with breadcrumbs and baked) or *quisado de peixe* (fish and potatoes on a bed of onions and tomatoes). The flat fish, pomfret, might have deep slits cut on both sides of its backbone, the slits stuffed with a special spice paste called the 'Rechad' masala and the whole fish is then fried in a frying-pan.

The *rechad* spice paste, ground on stone, sits in jars in almost every home. Because the red chillies, cinnamon, cardamom, cloves, peppercorns, onion, garlic and ginger that make up the paste are ground in vinegar, it lasts for months.

The same spice mixture is used to cook squid (*ambot tik*). Fresh, juicy prawns (shrimp) may be curried (*samar codi*) with coconut milk. Tourists who are regulars in Goa order this as soon as they land. They hasten to one of the thatched, beach restaurants, order a cool cashew *feni* to drink, let the soft breeze waft through their hair and wait for their order of prawn (shrimp) curry and rice. Prawns (shrimp) can be cooked with green chillies and poppy seeds (*caldin*),

they may be made into soup (*sopa de camarao*), made into a pie where the 'crust' is made of rice (*apa de camarao*) or made into a preserve (*balchao*). They can be cooked with okra and pumpkin too. The more oily fish, such as mackerel and sardines, are often cooked with *teflam*, which is none other than Sichuan pepper. It is reputed to 'cut' the oiliness. The spice is so well liked that one island, Divar, devotes a whole day to its celebration. Flags of all the villages are hoisted and young men load bamboo 'guns' with the peppercorns to shoot at the girls of their choice!

There is a billboard on the way to Panaji from Goa's airport that says, '8 Layer Bibinca. Don't Leave Goa Without It'. It is advice to be heeded. The *bebinca* is a 'cake' of layered pancakes that uses coconut milk in the batter. The traditional recipe once began, 'Take forty egg yolks' and ended 'preparation time: 10 hours', a nightmare not only for those who tremble at the word 'cholesterol' but for most ordinary, faint-hearted chefs. Such recipes were developed by once-cloistered nuns in places such as the Convent of Santa Monica where there were many quiet moments. Today's recipes are easier on the working family. Just ten egg yolks are required and only 2 hours of time. It is a smaller cake. As only thin wedges are eaten (many people are tempted to eat several thin wedges), not too much damage is done. *Bebinca* is not made every day. It is a festive cake for Christmas, so the minor damage is sea-

A fishing scene in one of Goa's many harbours.

sonal. The cake is so good, it is worth it.

Other desserts worth carrying out from Goa are the coconut cake (*batica*), the coconut-stuffed pancakes (*alebele*) and *culculs*, tiny cookies that are pressed against a comb and allowed to roll into the shape of cowrie shells. This way you will be carrying away tasty memories of sunny, balmy Goa, its swaying palms and its warm sea.

Jude Sequeira's
BEEF OR LAMB CHILLI-FRY

THE GOANS HAVE BORROWED most recently from the Chinese and this is now
a new local delicacy, found in most of the thatched shacks along the beaches.

---

340 g/12 oz tender beefsteak
  or boned lamb from the leg
  or shoulder
2 medium-sized onions
  (175 g/6 oz), peeled and
  finely chopped
5 garlic cloves, peeled and
  coarsely chopped

2 cm/1 inch piece of fresh
  ginger, peeled and coarsely
  chopped
½ teaspoon cayenne pepper
½ teaspoon ground turmeric
1 teaspoon ground
  coriander

1 teaspoon ground cumin
¾ teaspoon salt or to taste
5 tablespoons vegetable oil
3–4 fresh hot green chillies,
  seeded and cut into long
  strips

Cut the beef into thin strips as you would for
Chinese food. Put half of the onion, the garlic
and ginger into the container of an electric
blender with 2–3 tablespoons water. Blend.
Add the cayenne pepper, turmeric, coriander
and cumin. Blend to a paste. Rub the beef with
2 teaspoons of this paste and ¼ teaspoon of
the salt.

Set aside for 10 minutes.

Heat 2 tablespoons of the oil in a wok or
large, preferably non-stick frying-pan over high
heat. When hot, put in the remaining onion.
Stir and fry until lightly browned. Put in the
beef and stir and fry over very high heat until
the meat begins to lose its raw look. Remove
the beef and onion.

Wipe out the wok or frying-pan and put in
the remaining 3 tablespoons oil. Set over
medium-high heat. When hot, put in the
chillies and stir and fry them for a minute until
lightly browned. Put in the spice paste and stir
and fry for about 5–6 minutes until it is lightly
browned. Now put in the beef and onion,
½ teaspoon salt and 6 tablespoons water. Stir
over high heat for 1–2 minutes. Taste to check
the salt and add more if necessary.

S E R V E S   4

Jude Sequeira's Beef Xecxec
BEEF WITH MUSHROOMS

A GOAN FIVE-SPICE MIX, very similar to the north Indian *garam masala*, is used
to give aroma to this hot and sour Goan dish. It is normally served with local 'red'
rice but you may serve it with any rice, even a pilaf.

FOR THE GOAN FIVE-
SPICE MIX:
10 cardamom pods
½ teaspoon cloves
**1 teaspoon broken-up pieces
of cinnamon stick**
1½ teaspoons cumin seeds
**1 teaspoon black
peppercorns**

YOU ALSO NEED:
**675 g/1½ lb lean stewing
beef, cut into 5 cm/2 inch
cubes**

1 teaspoon salt or to taste
**2 tablespoons lime or lemon
juice**
**5 cm/2 inch piece of fresh
ginger, peeled and coarsely
chopped**
**6 garlic cloves, peeled and
coarsely chopped**
**3 fresh hot green chillies,
coarsely chopped**
1 teaspoon ground turmeric
3 tablespoons vegetable oil

**1 large onion
(175 g/6 oz), peeled
and finely sliced into
half-rings**
**2 medium-sized
tomatoes, chopped**
**225 g/8 oz/4 cups
mushrooms, sliced**
**2 tablespoons
tamarind paste (page
278)**

Put all the ingredients for the Goan five-spice
mix in a clean coffee grinder and grind. (Any
left-overs you have may be stored in a tightly
lidded jar.)

Mix the beef with the salt and lime or lemon
juice and marinate for 1 hour.

Meanwhile, put the ginger, garlic and
chillies into the container of an electric
blender. Add 3 tablespoons water and blend to
a paste. Add 2 tablespoons of the Goan five-
spice mix and the turmeric. Process briefly to
mix. Take half of this spice paste and add it to

the meat. Rub in well and set the meat aside
for another hour.

Heat the oil in a large frying-pan over
medium-high heat. When hot, add the onion.
Stir and fry until the onion is medium-brown.
Add the tomatoes. Fry for a further
2–3 minutes. Add the remaining spice paste.
Continue to fry for 3–4 minutes, then add the
marinated meat. Stir and fry to seal the meat.
Then add 600 ml/1 pint/2½ cups water. Bring
to the boil, turn the heat down to low and
cover tightly. Simmer gently for 1½ hours or

until the meat is tender. Add the mushrooms. Cook for a further 5 minutes then add the tamarind paste. Stir to mix and bring to a simmer. Adjust the seasoning and serve.

Jude Sequeira's Pork Vindalho

PORK WITH VINEGAR AND GARLIC

A DISH OF PORTUGUESE ancestry, *vindalho* (or *vindaloo* as it is known throughout the world) got its original name from two of its main seasonings: *vinho* or wine (actually wine vinegar) and *alhos* or garlic. This dish has now been thoroughly Indianized with the use of enormous amounts of dried red chillies brought, ironically enough, from the New World, as well as cumin, ginger and peppercorns.

A word about the chillies. The red ones that are used in Goa are Kashmiri chillies known more for the colour they impart than their heat. I use a combination of ordinary red chillies and paprika to achieve the same effect.

A *vindalho* is made by Goan families on festive occasions – birthdays, weddings and even at Christmas. The dish, an unusual combination of a curry and a preserve, can be made up to a week in advance and often is. The vinegar acts as a preservative, making it an ideal party dish. Goans do take the precaution of bringing it to a boil once a day in the earthen vessel used for cooking. We in the West can also make it a few days in advance but I would keep it, well covered, in the refrigerator.

It is generally served with the local 'red' rice, plain white rice or a Basmati rice pilaf. A simple salad of tomatoes, lettuce and cucumber, dressed with lemon juice and salt, may be served on the side.

❧

1 kg/2¼ lb boneless pork from the shoulder, cut into 5 cm/2 inch cubes
1½ teaspoons salt
6 tablespoons red wine vinegar

FOR THE SPICE PASTE:
4–10 dried hot red chillies
1 tablespoon bright red paprika
½ teaspoon cumin seeds

6 cm/3 inch cinnamon stick, broken up into smaller pieces
10–15 cloves
½ teaspoon black peppercorns

5–6 cardamom pods
10–12 garlic cloves, peeled
2.5 cm/1 inch piece of fresh
 ginger, peeled and coarsely
 chopped
½ teaspoon ground turmeric

YOU ALSO NEED:
3 tablespoons vegetable oil
3–4 garlic cloves, peeled and
 lightly crushed
3 medium-sized onions
 (250 g/9 oz), peeled and
 finely sliced

2 large tomatoes, chopped
6 fresh hot green chillies,
 sliced lengthways in half
1 teaspoon sugar

Sprinkle the pork with 1 teaspoon of the salt. Add 3 tablespoons of the vinegar. Rub in well and set aside for 2–3 hours.

Make the spice paste: Combine the red chillies, paprika, cumin seeds, cinnamon, cloves, peppercorns and cardamom pods in a clean coffee grinder and grind as finely as possible. Put the 10–12 garlic cloves and the ginger in the container of an electric blender along with 2 tablespoons of the vinegar and the turmeric. Blend well. Add the dry ground spices to the garlic mixture and blend again to mix. Rub the pork cubes with half of the spice paste, cover and refrigerate overnight. Cover and refrigerate the remaining spice paste.

Heat the 3 tablespoons oil in a wide, preferably non-stick pan over medium-high heat. When hot, put in the 3–4 garlic cloves. Stir and fry until they begin to pick up a little colour. Put in the onions and continue to fry until browned. Now add the tomatoes and 3 of the green chillies. Stir for a minute. Add the remaining spice paste, the sugar and the remaining 1 tablespoon vinegar. Stir and fry until the paste begins to brown a little. Now add the marinated meat and all the spice paste clinging to it. Turn the heat to medium-low and cook, stirring, until the pork begins to exude its own liquid. Add 300 ml/10 fl oz/1¼ cups water and the remaining salt and bring to a boil. Cover, turn the heat to low and simmer gently until the meat is tender and the sauce has thickened somewhat, about 40 minutes.

If necessary, raise the heat to reduce the sauce to a medium-thick consistency towards the end. Add the remaining 3 green chillies and stir once.

S E R V E S   4 – 6

Sophie Gonsalves' Sorpatel

PORK COOKED WITH VINEGAR AND SPICES

A FAVOURITE PARTY DISH, this is frequently cooked at Christmas-time and eaten with *sannas*, the spongy, crumpet-like breads on page 127. They are perfect for picking up the small-diced meat and soaking up the red-red sauce. *Sorpatel* is traditionally made up of various pig parts, including the tail and ears, but these days many families just use shoulder meat and liver. That is what I have done here. *Sorpatel*, rather like *vindalho*, is often made a few days ahead. The vinegar preserves it and the waiting period helps flavours to ripen.

~

675 g/1½ lb boneless, lean pork shoulder, cut into 1 cm/½ inch cubes
225 g/8 oz pork liver, cut into 1 cm/½ inch cubes
4 tablespoons vegetable oil

FOR THE SPICE PASTE:
1 teaspoon cumin seeds
1 teaspoon black peppercorns

Two 4 cm/1½ inch cinnamon sticks, broken up
10 cloves
½ nutmeg
5–6 dried hot red chillies
1 teaspoon ground turmeric
1 tablespoon bright red paprika
150 ml/5 fl oz/⅔ cup cider vinegar

YOU ALSO NEED:
1 medium-large onion (100 g/4 oz), peeled and sliced into fine half-rings
6–7 garlic cloves, peeled and finely chopped
2 cm/1 inch piece of fresh ginger, peeled and very finely chopped
3 fresh hot green chillies, slit lengthways into 3–4 pieces
1½ teaspoons salt or to taste

~

Put the cubed pork shoulder and liver into 2 separate pans. Add enough water to each pan to just cover the meats. Place over medium-high heat and bring both pans to the boil. Turn the heat down to low, cover both pans and simmer gently for 20 minutes until the meats are cooked through. Drain, saving the stock from the shoulder, and allow to cool separately.

Put half of the liver into an electric blender. Blend briefly until it forms a paste.

When the shoulder meat and remaining liver are cool, heat 1 tablespoon of the oil in a non-stick frying-pan over medium-high heat. When hot, add the cooled shoulder meat and liver. Toss and fry until lightly browned. Remove with a slotted spoon and set aside.

Put the cumin seeds, peppercorns,

cinnamon, cloves, nutmeg and red chillies for the spice paste into a clean coffee grinder and grind to a fine powder. Empty into a small bowl. Add the turmeric, paprika and vinegar. Mix well and set aside.

Heat the remaining 3 tablespoons oil in a large, wide, preferably non-stick pan over medium-high heat. When hot, add the onions. Stir and fry until well browned. Add the garlic and ginger. Stir and fry for 2 minutes. Add the green chillies and the spice paste. Stir and fry until the spice paste browns a little. Put in the browned shoulder meat and liver cubes. Stir and toss until they are well coated with the spice paste. Add 500 ml/18 fl oz/2¼ cups of the stock, the salt and the liver paste. Stir and bring to a boil. Turn the heat to low, cover and simmer gently for about 30 minutes, or until the meat is very tender, adding more stock or water if necessary. Allow to cool. Empty into a bowl, cover and refrigerate overnight to let the flavour develop. Re-heat gently before serving.

SERVES 4

Jude Sequeira's Xacuti
CHICKEN WITH A ROASTED COCONUT SAUCE

THERE ARE PROBABLY AS many recipes for this as there are Goan homes. Here is a fairly traditional Catholic one. *Xacuti* (pronounced 'sha-koo-tee') may be made out of rabbit, field heron, lamb or even with vegetables. What distinguishes a *xacuti* from other dishes is that all the seasonings in it are roasted before they are ground to a paste. It is supposed to be so spicy that it exorcizes all sniffles and coughs in the rainy monsoon season when farmers spend long hours knee-deep in the paddy fields. (For more on *xacuti*, see page 105.)

Today, many small neighbourhood stalls serve it to truck-drivers and passers-by, in small saucers. Traditionally it is eaten with local breads such as the butterfly-shaped Goan bread *poee* (see page 128) or the bun-like *pao* or with rice. You may serve this chicken *xacuti* with a pilaf, plain rice or even a crusty bread. A salad or any Goan vegetable may be served on the side.

If you wish to substitute unsweetened, desiccated coconut for fresh coconut use 115 g/4 oz/1¼ cups. Roast it in the same way as the fresh coconut, then soak it in 175 ml/6 fl oz/¾ cup water for 1 hour. Process the coconut and water together.

FOR THE SPICE PASTE:
225 g/8 oz/2 cups freshly grated coconut (page 265)
½ teaspoon ground turmeric
5–6 dried hot red chillies
4 tablespoons coriander seeds
1 teaspoon cumin seeds
1 teaspoon fennel seeds
½ teaspoon black peppercorns
5–6 cardamom pods
½ teaspoon cloves
2 star anise

5 cm/2 inch cinnamon stick, broken
A curl of mace
⅓ nutmeg
2 tablespoons white poppy seeds
1 tablespoon vegetable oil
1 medium-sized onion (75 g/3 oz), peeled and cut into fine half-rings
5 cm/2 inch piece of fresh ginger, peeled and thinly sliced
6–7 garlic cloves, peeled and coarsely chopped

YOU ALSO NEED:
1.5 kg/3 lb chicken pieces, cut into small serving pieces (whole breasts into 6 and whole legs into 4 parts)
1½ teaspoons salt
2 tablespoons lemon juice
4 tablespoons vegetable oil
2 medium-sized onions (175 g/6 oz), peeled and finely sliced into half-rings
About 15–20 fresh curry leaves, if available

Make the spice paste: Heat a cast-iron frying-pan over medium-high heat. When hot, put in the coconut. Stir and roast until it is medium-brown. Add the turmeric and stir once or twice. Remove and set aside. Put the chillies, coriander seeds, cumin seeds, fennel seeds, peppercorns, cardamom pods, cloves, star anise, cinnamon, mace and nutmeg into the same hot pan. Stir until the spices are almost roasted. Add the poppy seeds. Keep roasting until the spices are lightly browned. Remove all the spices and let them cool slightly. Put the spices into a clean coffee grinder, in several batches if necessary, and grind to a fine powder.

Put the 1 tablespoon oil into the same pan and heat over medium-high heat. When hot, put in the onion, ginger and garlic. Sauté until medium-brown. Remove.

Put the coconut, ground spices and onion mixture in an electric blender. Add 350 ml/12 fl oz/1½ cups water or more and blend to a paste, in more than one batch, if needed.

Put the chicken pieces in a single layer on a large plate. Sprinkle on both sides with ¾ teaspoon of the salt and the lemon juice. Rub this in. Set aside for 20 minutes.

Heat the 4 tablespoons oil in a wide, preferably non-stick pan over medium-high heat. When hot, put in the sliced onions. Stir and fry until browned. Put in the spice paste. Stir and cook for 2–3 minutes. Put in the chicken and all accumulated juices as well as the remaining salt and 300 ml/10 fl oz/1¼ cups water. Stir and bring to a simmer. Cover, turn the heat to low and cook for about 25 minutes or until the chicken is tender. Add the curry leaves and stir them in.

SERVES 6

Maria Fernanda Sousa's Carangrejo Recheado
STUFFED CRAB

RECHEADO IS THE PORTUGUESE word for 'stuffed' and these are whole crabs stuffed with what would be a very mild Mediterranean stuffing were it not for the use of hot green chillies. Serve with a simple green salad. On Goa's many beaches the stuffed crab often comes with chips but that, I suspect, is a more recent addition. Smaller-sized crabs make an excellent first course.

---

2 large crabs and their cooked meat
4 tablespoons olive oil
2 medium-sized onions (175 g/6 oz), finely chopped
4 garlic cloves, peeled and finely chopped

2 medium-sized tomatoes, cut into small dice
2–3 fresh hot green chillies, finely chopped
4 tablespoons finely chopped, fresh green coriander

2 tablespoons lemon juice
¾ teaspoon salt or to taste
Freshly ground black pepper
About 6 tablespoons dried breadcrumbs

Pre-heat the oven to 180°C/350°F/Gas 4.

Open up the crabs by pulling off their lower shells. Remove all the crabmeat, break it up into small lumps and save. Save the back, it will be used for serving.

Heat 3 tablespoons of the oil in a frying-pan over medium-high heat. When hot, put in the onions and garlic. Stir and fry until they turn golden. Put in the tomatoes. Stir and fry until the tomatoes are soft. Add the chillies. Stir once or twice. Now put in the coriander, crabmeat, lemon juice and salt (put ½ teaspoon first, mix and taste) and pepper. Turn off the heat and mix well.

Spoon the crabmeat into the two crab backs. Spread the breadcrumbs over the top, dribble over the remaining 1 tablespoon olive oil and bake in the oven for 10–15 minutes until heated through. Brown the top quickly under the grill (broiler).

SERVES 2

Jude Sequeira's
'RECHAD' SPICE PASTE

EVERY HOUSEHOLD IN GOA, however humble, has a big jar of what is called
rechad masala sitting in the kitchen. It looks very red, the colour coming from the
generous use of Kashmiri chilli which has some of the same properties as the
paprika pepper – it releases a lot of bright red dye. The other spices in the paste,
all of which are ground in vinegar, include cumin, cinnamon and black pepper
Vinegar helps it to last.

The name of the paste comes, of course, from the Portuguese 'recheado', meaning
'stuff', and while the paste is mainly used to stuff local fish, it is also used to curry
squid and other creatures of the sea.

Here is a recipe for the paste. What is not used should be put in a jar, covered and
refrigerated. It will keep for months.

∾

30 g/1 oz dried hot red
  chillies (about 45)
½ teaspoon cumin seeds
2.5 cm/1 inch cinnamon
  stick, broken up
1 teaspoon cardamom pods
1 teaspoon cloves
1 tablespoon black
  peppercorns

2 tablespoons bright red
  paprika
1 tablespoon vegetable oil
1 small onion (25 g/1 oz),
  peeled and coarsely
  chopped
½ head garlic (60 g/2 oz),
  peeled and coarsely
  chopped

Two 5 cm/2½ inch pieces of
  fresh ginger, peeled and
  coarsely chopped
1 teaspoon salt
100 ml/3½ fl oz/½ cup cider
  vinegar

∾

Put the chillies, cumin seeds, cinnamon,
cardamom pods, cloves and peppercorns into a
clean coffee grinder and grind them to a
powder. Put into the container of an electric
blender. Add the paprika. Heat the oil in a
small frying-pan over medium-high heat.
When hot, put in the onion, garlic and ginger.

Cook, stirring, until the onion has softened a
bit. Empty the contents of the pan into the
electric blender. Add the salt and vinegar.
Blend thoroughly.

M A K E S   A B O U T
8   T A B L E S P O O N S

Pomfret 'Rechad'
STUFFED POMFRET

THE BEST FISH TO stuff with the 'Rechad' Spice Paste (opposite) is the Indian pomfret. It is flat and meaty with very white flesh. Two large pockets are cut into it with a sharp knife that slides along both sides of the backbone. The stuffing is shoved inside and then the fish is sautéd. A light weight is sometimes put on top of the fish so that it does not open up. Other fish such as red snapper, plaice, sole and small turbots may be used. Mackerel is also good; because of its shape it is better to make several diagonal slits across its sides rather than pockets, and use those for the stuffing.

Serve with boiled potatoes and a salad or with any vegetables of your choice.

Four 340 g/12 oz pomfret (or whole plaice, sole, small turbot, red snapper or mackerel), cleaned

4 tablespoons lime or lemon juice
1 teaspoon salt
About 3 tablespoons 'Rechad' Spice Paste (opposite)

About 4 tablespoons vegetable oil
4 lemon quarters, to serve

Pre-heat the oven to 180°C/350°/Gas 4.

Make 2 deep slits on either side of the backbone of each fish. Rub each fish, inside and out, first with 1 tablespoon of the lime or lemon juice and then with ¼ teaspoon of the salt. Set aside for 10 minutes. Using about 2 teaspoons of the 'rechad' paste for each fish, stuff the pockets, making sure you get deep inside the fish. (You could use more paste if you like.)

Alternatively, if you are using mackerel, instead of making deep pockets make 3 deep slashes diagonally across the body and stuff these with the paste.

Heat the oil in a large, preferably non-stick frying-pan over medium-low heat. When hot, put in as many fish as the pan will hold in one layer and fry gently for about 5 minutes on each side. As the fish get fried, put them in a big baking tray in a single layer. When all the fish are done, put them in the oven and bake for 10 minutes. Serve with lemon quarters.

S E R V E S 4

Maria Fernanda Sousa's Guisado de Peixe

FISH ON A BED OF POTATOES, ONIONS AND TOMATOES

THIS IS ANOTHER VERY Portuguese dish, enlivened with green chillies. Serve with a green salad. Mrs Sousa adds her precious wine at the end, but I have taken the liberty of putting it in a little earlier.

～

4 tablespoons virgin olive oil

3 medium-sized onions (250 g/9 oz), cut into fine half-rings

3 medium-sized tomatoes, cut into small dice

5 garlic cloves, finely chopped

Salt

A generous pinch of sugar

1 teaspoon black peppercorns

4 small-medium potatoes (about 450 g/1 lb), peeled and cut into 1 cm/½ inch thick slices

3 thinnish 175 g/6 oz swordfish steaks

Freshly ground black pepper

150 ml/5 fl oz/⅔ cup dry white wine or dry vermouth

1–2 fresh hot green chillies, split into halves

～

Heat the oil in a large, preferably non-stick frying-pan over medium-high heat. When hot, put in the onions. Stir and fry until golden. Add the tomatoes, garlic, ¾ teaspoon salt, sugar and peppercorns. Stir and fry until the tomatoes are soft. Put in the potatoes. Stir gently a few times. Cover and cook gently over low heat, shaking occasionally, until the potatoes are almost tender.

Meanwhile, sprinkle the fish steaks lightly with salt and pepper on both sides and set aside.

When the potatoes are almost done, pour the wine or vermouth over them. Stir gently and cook for a minute. With a spoon, remove a little of the soft onion-garlic-tomato mixture. Then lay the fish steaks over the potatoes in a single layer. Spoon some of the onion-garlic-tomato mixture over them. Lay the green chillies over the top, cover and cook for 5–10 minutes or until the fish is just cooked through and the potatoes are tender.

SERVES 3

Chicken with a Roasted Coconut Sauce (page 105), Potatoes with Mustard Seeds (page 118) and Goan Bread (page 128).

Jude Sequeira's Squid Ambot Tik

SOUR AND SPICY SQUID

SQUID IS FOUND IN abundance in the waters of the Arabian Sea. The locals enjoy it but almost none is sent inland to the heart of the nation which, more is the pity, has not yet developed a taste for this excellent seafood. What the locals do not want is shipped to Japan.

There are many ways of cooking squid here, but perhaps the best is *ambot tik*, a sour and hot dish using what is locally called 'Rechad' Spice Paste (page 108), a red spice paste that is found sitting promisingly in every kitchen, ensconced in a large jar.

Ambot tik is generally served with the Goan, half-milled 'red' rice, but it could also be served with plain rice enriched perhaps by a dollop of butter. A salad and some vegetables on the side would be ideal.

---

3 tablespoons vegetable oil
2 medium-sized onions
   (175 g/6 oz), peeled and
   cut into fine half-rings
3 garlic cloves, peeled and
   finely chopped
1 medium-sized tomato,
   finely chopped

2–6 fresh hot green chillies,
   sliced lengthways into
   3–4 strips each
2 tablespoons 'Rechad'
   Spice Paste (page 108)
450 g/1 lb cleaned squid
   (page 285), opened up and
   cut crossways into
   5 mm/¼ inch wide strips

4 pieces of *kokum* (page
   272) or 1 tablespoon
   tamarind paste (page 278)
   or 1½ tablespoons lemon
   juice
½–¾ teaspoon salt or to
   taste

Heat the oil in a frying-pan over medium-high heat. When hot, add the onions. Stir and fry until golden. Add the garlic. Continue frying until the onions pick up brown edges. Add the tomatoes and chillies. Stir and fry until the tomatoes are soft and pulpy. Add the 'Rechad' Spice Paste. Stir and cook for a minute. Then add 450 ml/15 fl oz/2 cups water. Bring to a boil. Lower the heat and simmer gently until the liquid is reduced by half. Now add the squid, the *kokum* or tamarind paste or lemon juice and the salt. Stir to mix. Cook, stirring, over medium-low heat until the squid has turned white, about 2–4 minutes.

S E R V E S   4

Jude Sequeira's Prawns Caldin

COCONUT AND GREEN CHILLI PRAWNS (SHRIMP)

A SLIGHTLY SWEET (from the coconut milk) and slightly sour (from the tamarind) dish, this is generally eaten with the local 'red' rice which helps to soak up the excellent and generous sauce. In the West, it would be best served with any plain white rice – Basmati or another long-grain variety. Red Spinach (page 119) or a salad may be served on the side.

❧

- 397 g/14 fl oz can coconut milk
- 5–10 fresh hot green chillies, coarsely sliced
- 1 teaspoon ground turmeric
- 2 tablespoons finely chopped, fresh green coriander
- 1 teaspoon freshly ground black pepper

- 3 tablespoons ground coriander
- 1½ teaspoons ground cumin
- 2 tablespoons white poppy seeds
- 4 tablespoons vegetable oil
- 2 medium-sized onions (175g/6 oz), peeled and sliced into fine half-rings
- 2 garlic cloves, peeled and cut into fine slivers

- 1 cm/½ inch piece of fresh ginger, peeled and cut into fine slices and then into fine slivers
- 1 tablespoon tamarind paste (page 278)
- 1 teaspoon salt
- 900g/2 lb uncooked, unpeeled, medium-sized headless prawns (shrimp), peeled

❧

Open the coconut can without shaking it. Remove the cream at the top. Save it. Now add enough water to the can to fill it to the top again. Put this thin coconut milk into a bowl.

Put the chillies, turmeric, fresh coriander, pepper, ground coriander and ground cumin into the container of an electric blender along with 4 tablespoons of the thin coconut milk. Blend. Pour this spice mixture into the bowl with the thin coconut milk.

Put the poppy seeds into a clean coffee grinder and grind as finely as possible. Add to the thin coconut milk.

Heat the oil in a deep frying-pan over medium-high heat. When hot, put in the onions, garlic and ginger. Stir and fry until they brown at the edges. Now pour in the seasoned thin coconut milk and add the tamarind, salt and 120 ml/4 fl oz/½ cup water. Cover and simmer gently for 10 minutes. Add the prawns (shrimp) and the reserved thick coconut cream. Mix well and bring to a simmer. As soon as the prawns (shrimp) turn opaque all the way through, they are done.

SERVES 6

Sophie Gonsalves' Samar Codi
PRAWN (SHRIMP) CURRY

WHEN I ARRIVE IN Goa, the first dish I order is this simple prawn (shrimp) curry! It uses no oil as nothing in it requires frying or sautéing. In many ways, it is the humblest of curries and may be made with very cheap fish cut into chunks, fish steaks or fillet pieces.

I like it made with juicy prawns (shrimp), fresh from the sea. With a spicy, red, coconutty sauce flowing over a bed of white, pearly rice – what else can one want? I rarely order this dish in the hotel that I stay in. I find a small beach shack covered with palm thatching, generally owned by real fishermen, and order it there. All I need with it is a cold glass of beer.

If you buy unpeeled, headless prawns (shrimp) you will need 675 g/1½ lb. Peel and devein them (page 285), then wash them and pat them dry.

~

1 teaspoon cayenne pepper
1 tablespoon bright red
  paprika
½ teaspoon ground turmeric
4 garlic cloves, peeled and
  crushed to a pulp
2.5 cm/1 inch piece of fresh
  ginger, peeled and grated
  to a pulp

2 tablespoons coriander
  seeds
1 teaspoon cumin seeds
397 g/14 oz can coconut
  milk, well stirred
¾ teaspoon salt or to taste

3 pieces of *kokum* (page
  272) or 1 tablespoon
  tamarind paste (page 278)
450 g/1 lb peeled and
  deveined, medium-sized
  uncooked prawns
  (shrimps)

~

In a bowl, combine 300 ml/10 fl oz/1¼ cups water with the cayenne pepper, paprika, turmeric, garlic and ginger. Mix well. Grind the coriander seeds and cumin seeds in a clean coffee grinder and add to mixture.

Put the spice mixture into a pan and bring to a simmer. Turn the heat to medium-low and simmer for 10 minutes. The sauce should reduce and thicken. Add the coconut milk, salt, *kokum* or tamarind paste and bring to a simmer. Add the prawns (shrimp) and simmer, stirring now and then, until they turn opaque and are just cooked through.

Pork with Vinegar and Garlic (page 102) and Okra with Dried Prawns/Shrimp (page 116).

SERVES 4

Rita Themudo's Bhindi Bhaji

OKRA WITH DRIED PRAWNS (SHRIMP)

DRIED PRAWNS (SHRIMP) ARE required here. Those used in Goa are very tiny and flat. I tend to get the larger, pinkish ones sold by most Chinese grocers, and then grind them in a clean coffee grinder to get a powder which works quite beautifully with okra. Serve this dish with any Indian meal.

450 g/1 lb okra
3 tablespoons vegetable oil
1 teaspoon cumin seeds
1 medium-sized onion (75 g/3 oz), finely chopped
4 garlic cloves, finely chopped

2 large tomatoes, finely chopped
1 teaspoon ground cumin
1 teaspoon ground coriander
½ teaspoon ground turmeric

½ teaspoon cayenne pepper or to taste
¾–1 teaspoon salt or to taste
2 tablespoons dried prawns (shrimp), see above

Wipe the okra pods with a damp cloth. Cut them crossways into 1 cm/½ inch wide segments.

Heat the oil in a large, preferably non-stick frying-pan over medium-high heat. When hot, put in the cumin seeds. Let them sizzle for a few seconds. Now put in the onion and garlic. Stir and fry until they start to brown. Put in the okra. Stir and fry until lightly browned. Add the tomatoes. Stir and cook until the tomatoes are soft. Add the ground cumin, coriander, turmeric, cayenne pepper and salt. Stir to mix

and toss for a minute. Add about 150 ml/ 5 fl oz/⅔ cup water and bring to a simmer. Cover, turn the heat to low and cook for 15–20 minutes, stirring now and then, until the okra is tender.

Meanwhile, rinse the prawns (shrimp) and pat them dry. Put them into a clean coffee grinder and grind to a powder. When the okra is tender add the prawn (shrimp) powder and stir it in.

SERVES 3 – 4

Jude Sequeira's Cashew Nut Bhaji

ⓥ CASHEW NUTS WITH COCONUT

CASHEW NUTS ARE GROWN all over the south-west coast of India. They are harvested in winter, roasted lightly to rid them of their reddish-brown skins and then eaten out of hand or used in hundreds of cakes, puddings and *halvas*. The Hindus of Goa also serve them as a vegetable. Indian breads are the traditional accompaniment to this *bhaji*.

It is best to use fresh coconut in this dish.

---

450 g/1 lb/3 cups raw
  cashew nuts
2 tablespoons vegetable oil
1 teaspoon brown mustard
  seeds
1 teaspoon cumin seeds
1 teaspoon *urad dal*
  (page 261)

2–3 dried hot red chillies,
  broken up
1½ teaspoons salt
½ teaspoon ground turmeric
100 g/4 oz/1 cup freshly
  grated coconut (page 265)

2 fresh hot green
  chillies, slit
  lengthways
1 teaspoon Goan five-spice
  mix (page 101)
1 tablespoon chopped,
  fresh green coriander

Soak the cashew nuts in water to cover for 8 hours or overnight. Drain.

Heat the oil in a large frying-pan over medium-high heat. When hot, put in the mustard seeds. As soon as they start to pop, a matter of seconds, add the cumin, *urad dal* and red chillies. Stir and fry for a few seconds until the *dal* turns reddish and the chillies darken. Add the cashew nuts and salt. Stir for a minute. Add the turmeric. Stir once and add 85 ml/3 fl oz/⅓ cup water. Cover and turn the heat to low. Simmer gently for 10 minutes. Remove the cover and add the coconut, green chillies and five-spice mix.

Mix well, sprinkle with the fresh coriander and serve.

SERVES 4–6

Sookhi Bhaji
ⓥ POTATOES WITH MUSTARD SEEDS

A HINDU DISH, THIS is served with the Goan bread 'pao', or with fluffy pooris at most neighbourhood stalls. It is generally ladled out into small saucers which serve as plates. You just dip your bread into it and eat. A popular place to find this combination of 'bhaji-pao' is in the heart of Mapusa market at Café Corner, where local vendors, itinerant tribespeople and tourists all seem to want to come and eat. The place is jammed – and with good reason. The price is good (very cheap) and the taste of the food quite excellent.

Sookhi bhaji is eaten for breakfast, for lunch and even at tea-time! In fact, a cup of steaming milky tea tastes particularly good with it.

❧

3 tablespoons vegetable oil
1 teaspoon cumin seeds
1 teaspoon brown mustard seeds
1 medium-sized onion (75 g/3 oz), peeled and finely chopped

2–4 fresh hot green chillies, split into halves lengthways
4 small-medium waxy potatoes (450 g/1 lb), boiled, peeled and cut into 1 cm/½ inch dice
1 teaspoon ground cumin

1 teaspoon ground coriander
½ teaspoon ground turmeric
1 teaspoon salt
¼ teaspoon cayenne pepper
1 tablespoon finely chopped, fresh green coriander

❧

Heat the oil in a wide pan over medium-high heat. When hot, put in the cumin seeds and mustard seeds. As soon as the mustard seeds begin to pop, a matter of a few seconds, put in the onion and chillies. Turn the heat to medium. Stir and cook until the onion is quite soft but not brown. Put in the potatoes, ground cumin, coriander, turmeric, salt and cayenne pepper. Stir gently once or twice. Add

150 ml/5 fl oz/⅔ cup water and cook over medium-low heat for 8–10 minutes, stirring now and then, until all the spices have been absorbed by the potatoes. There should be just a hint of sauce at the bottom of the pan. Sprinkle the fresh coriander over the top, stir it in and serve.

S E R V E S   4

Rita Themudo's Tamari Bhaji
ⓥ RED SPINACH

THIS IS NORMALLY MADE with the heart-shaped 'red spinach' leaves that are sold fresh in many of the 'China Towns' of the West. Trim away the tough roots and stalks and coarsely slice the leaves. I have used green spinach as that is what is most easily available. Serve with any Indian meal.

If you wish to substitute unsweetened desiccated coconut for fresh coconut use 2 tablespoons. Just soak it in 4 tablespoons warm water and leave for 1 hour, then proceed with the recipe.

---

900 g/2 lb washed, trimmed spinach
3 tablespoons vegetable oil
2 medium-sized onions (175 g/6 oz), cut into fine half-rings

2–3 fresh hot green chillies, cut into fine slivers
2 pieces of *kokum* (page 272) or 1 teaspoon tamarind paste (page 278) or 1 tablespoon lemon juice

¾–1 teaspoon salt
4 tablespoons freshly grated coconut (page 265)

Cut the spinach leaves into thin strips.

Heat the oil in a wok or large, wide pan over medium-high heat. When hot, put in the onions. Stir and fry until they turn slightly brown. Put in the spinach, chillies and *kokum* or tamarind paste or lemon juice. Stir and fry briskly until the spinach has completely wilted and cooked through. Add the salt and mix. Put in the coconut and stir once (The *kokum* is not usually eaten.)

S E R V E S   4

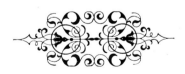

Sophie Gonsalves' Osanay Samaray

Ⓥ BEANS WITH ROASTED SPICES

OSANAY ARE SPECIAL BEANS, pinkish-green in colour, that look like small kidney beans. When cooked with roasted spices the Goan way, they become rich and meaty. The best substitute is black-eyed beans, though pinto beans may also be used.

The souring is traditionally provided by the dried pit of an unripe green mango, a seasoning that is very common in Goa, especially for dried beans. What a creative way to use up what most of us just throw away! Not being able to procure this sour, dried pit easily, I have used lemon juice instead.

This dish may be eaten with the Goan bread 'poee' (page 128) or with any crusty French or Italian bread. It is also excellent with *chapatis* or pitta bread or even with rice. It may be served as part of a Goan or a general Indian meal.

If you wish to substitute unsweetened desiccated coconut for fresh coconut use 115 g/4 oz/1¼ cups. Roast it first following the directions for fresh coconut, then soak in 250 ml/8 fl oz/1 cup warm water for 1 hour. Grind the liquid and coconut together.

∾

450 g/1 lb/2½ cups black-eyed beans or Goan *osanay* **beans**
2–2¼ teaspoons salt

FOR THE SPICE PASTE:
About 225 g/8 oz/2 cups finely grated fresh coconut (page 265)
1 tablespoon vegetable oil

4 garlic cloves
2.5 cm/1 inch piece of fresh ginger, peeled and thinly sliced
2 fresh hot green chillies, coarsely sliced
4–6 dried hot red chillies
1 teaspoon cumin seeds
2 teaspoons coriander seeds
2 cloves

2 star anise
1 tablespoon white poppy seeds

YOU ALSO NEED:
4 tablespoons vegetable oil
2 medium-sized onions (175 g/6 oz), finely sliced
1–2 tablespoons lemon juice

∾

Pick over the beans and wash and drain them. Soak overnight in plenty of water. Drain. Cover with water by 5–7.5 cm/2–3 inches and bring to the boil. Cook for 30 minutes or until the beans are just tender, adding about 1½ teaspoons salt during the last 5 minutes of cooking. Drain, saving the bean water, and set aside.

Make the spice paste: Put the coconut in a cast-iron frying-pan over medium-high heat. Stir and roast until lightly brown. Remove the coconut and put it into the container of an electric blender. Put the 1 tablespoon oil into a small frying-pan and heat over medium-high heat. When hot, put in the garlic, ginger and green chillies. Stir and fry until lightly browned. Remove and put with the coconut in the electric blender. Add about 250 ml/8 fl oz/ 1 cup water or more as needed, and blend to a smooth purée. You may need to do this in more than one batch.

Now put the red chillies, cumin seeds, coriander seeds, cloves and star anise into the small frying-pan and set over medium-high heat. Stir until very lightly roasted. Put in the poppy seeds, and roast for another minute. Remove and allow to cool. Grind just these dry spices in a clean coffee grinder. Combine with the coconut mixture. Mix and set aside.

Heat the 4 tablespoons oil in a large, wide pan over medium-high heat. When hot, put in the sliced onions. Stir and fry until lightly browned. Put in the spice paste. Stir and fry for 1 minute. Put in the beans and 1 litre/ 1¾ pints/4½ cups water (use up the bean water adding water to make up the necessary quantity). Bring to a simmer. Cook over low heat for 15–20 minutes, stirring gently now and then. Stir in the lemon juice. Check the salt, adding another ½–¾ teaspoon as needed.

SERVES 6–8

Sophie Gonsalves' Pilau

ⓥ GOAN STYLE PILAF

GOANS TEND TO EAT their own partially milled, plump-grained 'red' rice for everyday meals. For festive occasions, however, they invariably make a pilaf using the more expensive Basmati rice. Here is a typical recipe.

Basmati rice measured to the 450 ml/15 fl oz/2 cup level in a measuring jug
4 tablespoons *ghee* or vegetable oil
8 cloves
6 cardamom pods
Two 4 cm/2 inch cinnamon sticks
2 medium-sized onions (175 g/6 oz), peeled and sliced into thin half-rings
2 medium-sized tomatoes, peeled and chopped (peel after dropping into boiling water for 15 seconds)
600 ml/1 pint/2⅔ cups chicken stock
1 teaspoon salt

Wash the rice in several changes of water. Drain. Put in a bowl with water to cover and leave for 30 minutes. Drain well and leave in the strainer.

Heat the *ghee* or oil in a wide, heavy pan over medium-high heat. When hot, put in the cloves, cardamom pods and cinnamon. Stir for a few seconds. Now put in the onions. Stir and fry until browned. Put in the tomatoes. Stir and fry until they too are lightly browned and turn soft and pulpy. Put in the drained rice. Fry gently for a minute, being careful not to break the grains. Turn the heat down a bit if the grains start to stick. Add the stock and salt. Bring to a boil. Cover tightly, turn the heat to very low and cook for 25 minutes.

SERVES 4

Prawn (Shrimp) Curry (page 115).

Maria Fernanda Sousa's Arroz de Pato
DUCK RISOTTO

WHERE THERE IS A lot of fresh water, there are, invariably, ducks. Goa, apart from its coastal sea, has rivers, ponds and, perhaps most important, paddy fields where ducks can splash and feed. The local populace feels free to turn them into *vindaloos* and risottos.

This is what Maria Fernanda, an aristocratic Goan with much Portuguese blood, serves on Christmas Day, along with a dozen other dishes that come in a steady stream, starting off with a soup of potatoes and dill called *Caldo Verde*. Many of the dishes, such as this one and the soup, are not at all 'spicy'. Instead, they harken back to Maria Fernanda's Portuguese connection, to southern Europe and gentle seasonings such as garlic and onion and tomatoes.

Rice risottos, known as *arroz refogado*, are really crosses between pilafs and risottos and may be made with meat, peas, saffron or local sausages. This '*arroz*' requires Basmati rice and a nice duck. On advising us on which kind of duck to buy, Maria Fernanda said firmly, 'Make sure that it is a nice, plump, local duck. I do not want one that has walked all the way from Kerala, eating fish from every paddy field along the way!' It is best to make the stock a day in advance as it can then be refrigerated and degreased.

This rice dish may be eaten as a meal by itself, with a salad. It is a perfect lunch or light supper. You could also serve it as part of a grand banquet.

FOR THE STOCK:
1 duck (about 2 kg/4½ lb)
2 medium-sized onions
  (175 g/6 oz), peeled and
  halved
2–3 garlic cloves, peeled and
  lightly crushed
½ teaspoon ground turmeric
1 teaspoon salt
1 celery stick, cut into
  3 pieces

YOU ALSO NEED:
Basmati rice measured to
  the 750 ml/1¼ pint/3 cup
  level in a measuring jug
3 tablespoons vegetable oil
2 medium-sized onions
  (175 g/6 oz), peeled and
  finely chopped
6 garlic cloves, peeled and
  finely chopped
2 medium-sized tomatoes,
  peeled and chopped
  (page 289)

1 teaspoon salt
Freshly ground black pepper
A generous pinch of sugar
1 tablespoon lemon juice
4 large pork sausages (sweet
  Italian, Spanish *chorizos* or
  Portuguese *chouricos*),
  boiled, covered, in a little
  water until cooked through
  and cut into 1 cm/½ inch
  thick slices
15–20 black Mediterranean
  olives

Put the duck and all the other ingredients for the stock in a large pan. Add water to cover and bring to a boil. Turn the heat to medium-low and simmer gently for 1 hour, or until the duck is very tender. Strain and save the stock. Save the duck. When the stock has cooled, cover and refrigerate it.

When the duck is cool enough to handle, remove all the meat. Cut the meat into neat pieces (or pull it into coarse shreds). Set aside the meat pieces with skin.

Degrease the stock. It should measure 1 litre/1¾ pints/4 cups. If there is more, reduce it over high heat. If less, add water.

Meanwhile, wash the rice in several changes of water and then soak in water to cover for 30 minutes. Drain and leave in the strainer.

Heat the oil in a heavy, wide, preferably non-stick pan over medium-high heat. When hot, put in the onions. Stir and fry until the onions are lightly browned. Put in the garlic and tomatoes, salt, pepper and sugar. Stir and fry until the tomatoes are soft and reduced. Put in the drained rice. Stir it gently for 2–3 minutes, making sure not to break the grains. Add the stock and bring to a boil. Add the lemon juice and cover tightly. Turn the heat to very low and cook for 25 minutes or until the rice is cooked through. Do not uncover the pan during this period.

Pre-heat the oven to 180°C/350°F/Gas 4. In an ovenproof dish, put a layer of rice, then a layer of duck meat without skin. Continue this until all the lean duck meat is used up. End with a layer of rice. For the top layer, put some pieces of duck meat with skin and the sliced sausages in a neat design. Cover the rice entirely. Bake for 10–15 minutes until heated through and browned lightly at the top. Scatter the olives over the top and serve.

S E R V E S   6 – 8

Sannas

☺ STEAMED RICE 'CRUMPETS'

SANNAS ARE CRUMPET-LIKE, steamed breads about 7.5–10 cm/3–4 inches across and about 1 cm/½ inch high, that are made with a batter of soaked, ground rice and finely ground coconut. The rice is the partially milled 'red' rice that grows in most paddy fields here and the coconut is, of course, fresh, straight off the palm. The liquid in the batter is toddy, a sap taken from palms, that bubbles and ferments within a few hours of leaving the tree. It allows the batter to flow but acts as the yeast. Once the batter is made, it is allowed to rise before it is poured into moulds and steamed into *sannas*.

Not being able to get many of the ingredients, I have used substitutes – a mixture of ordinary yeast, ground rice, plain (all-purpose white) flour and desiccated coconut. To steam the *sannas*, you may use *idli* moulds, sold by many Indian grocers, or you may pour the batter into medium-sized saucers or use crumpet-sized or smaller ramekins. For general steaming instructions, see page 287. *Sannas* are traditionally eaten with Pork with Vinegar and Spices (page 104), but they may be served with any curry. Their pliable, spongy texture is ideal for soaking up hot and spicy meat sauces.

---

1 teaspoon sugar	285 g/10 oz/1½ cups ground rice (also called rice flour)	½ teaspoon salt
2 teaspoons dried yeast	4 teaspoons plain (all-purpose white) flour	A little vegetable oil for greasing
40 g/1½ oz/scant ½ cup unsweetened desiccated coconut	4 teaspoons sugar	

Let the sugar dissolve in 2 tablespoons warm water. Then sprinkle over the dried yeast. Set aside to allow the yeast to activate and froth.

Put the coconut into a clean coffee grinder and grind until fine. Empty into the container of an electric blender. Add the ground rice, flour, sugar, salt and 300 ml/10 fl oz/1¼ cups warm water. Blend until you have a smooth paste. You may need to scrape down with a rubber spatula a few times. Add the yeast mixture and blend well. The batter should

Coconut Pancakes (page 131).

have the consistency of double (thick heavy) cream. Pour into a bowl, cover with a cloth and leave in a warm place for about 15 minutes or until the batter has doubled in size.

Grease flattish ramekins or saucers or *idli* moulds. Ladle in enough batter to come three-quarters of the way up the sides. Leave for another 10 minutes to rise again.

Meanwhile, prepare your steaming equipment. Half-fill the lower part with water and bring it to a boil. Rest the steaming tray on top. Place the ramekins or saucers or moulds in the steaming tray – you may be able to fit in more than one layer. Cover and steam for 15 minutes. Repeat if necessary to use up all the batter. Allow to cool slightly before gently easing the *sannas* out by running a knife around the sides.

S E R V E S 4 – 6

Poee
ⓋGOAN BREAD

POEE IS SOMEWHAT LIKE pitta bread only it is butterfly-shaped and very spongy inside, full of large, airy holes. It can be bought in most Goan markets but it is best to go straight to the local baker and buy it just as it comes out of the oven. There is one such bakery, with a huge beehive oven made of clay, glass pieces and salt, in the tiny town of Parra. Large, wooden paddles push dough in and pull breads out. Breads line the room. Huge blobs of very soft dough rise in another room. The smell is heavenly.

'*Poees*' can be eaten with all Goan and many other Indian meals.

1 teaspoon sugar
1 teaspoon dried yeast

450 g/1 lb/3½ cups strong, plain (all-purpose white) flour, plus extra flour for dusting

A pinch of salt

Let the sugar dissolve in 100 ml/3½ fl oz/ ½ cup warm water. Then sprinkle over the dried yeast. Mix until smooth. Set aside for 10 minutes until the yeast is frothy.

Place the flour and salt in a large bowl. Pour in the yeast mixture and 350 ml/12 fl oz/ 1½ cups water. Mix well, using your hands or a fork. When all the liquid has been incorporated into the flour, turn the dough out on to a well-floured board (it will be very soft) and knead well for 5 minutes, dusting with flour frequently to prevent it from sticking to the surface. When it has become smooth and elastic, place it in a bowl and cover with a clean cloth. Put the bowl in a warm place for about an hour, or until the dough has doubled in size.

Pre-heat the oven to 220°C/425°F/Gas 7.

Turn the dough out and knead briefly again on a well-floured board. Cut into 6 equal pieces and knead these into slightly flattened rounds (see *figure 1*). Slash each over the t centre with a sharp knife or blade (see *figure 2*) and spread out both to the right and left, as if you were opening a book (see *figure 3*). Place the buns on a greased baking sheet and allow to rise for at least 30 minutes – they should now look like fat butterflies (see *figure 4*).

Sprinkle the breads with flour and place them in the oven for 15–20 minutes, until they are golden-brown.

M A K E S   6   B R E A D S

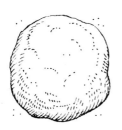

figure 1

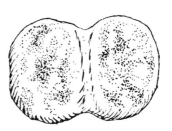

figure 2

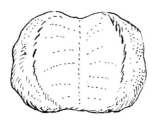

figure 3

figure 4

Sophie Gonsalves' Chutney
☉ GOAN COCONUT CHUTNEY

A SWEET, SOUR AND hot chutney that is mellow and pungent at the same time, this may be served with all Goan meals, indeed, with all Indian meals. It also makes a superb dip (just thin it out with a little water), and is quite delicious spread out on bread and eaten as a sandwich.

If you wish to substitute unsweetened, desiccated coconut for fresh coconut use 75 g/3 oz/scant 1 cup plus 1 tablespoon. Soak it in 175 ml/6 fl oz/¾ cup warm water for 30 minutes, then blend using the soaking water. You may also use 75 g/3 oz coconut cream mixed with 3 tablespoons warm water. The texture of the chutney will be different, but it will still be good.

❧

115 g/4 oz/1 cup freshly grated coconut (page 265 and above)
100 g/4 oz/3 cups fresh green coriander, chopped
1 small onion or 2 shallots (25 g/1 oz), peeled and coarsely chopped

2.5 cm/1 inch piece of fresh ginger, peeled and coarsely chopped
2 garlic cloves, peeled and coarsely chopped
2 fresh hot green chillies, coarsely chopped

2 tablespoons lemon juice
1 teaspoon coriander seeds
2 cloves
1 cm/½ inch piece of cinnamon stick
1 teaspoon salt
1 teaspoon sugar

❧

Put the coconut, coriander, onion or shallot, ginger, garlic, chillies and lemon juice in a food processor. Blend, adding 4 or more tablespoons water as needed to get a thick, coarse paste. You may, if you wish, put this mixture into the container of an electric blender in several batches to get a much finer paste, adding a little water as needed.

Put the coriander seeds, cloves and cinnamon into a clean coffee grinder and grind them to a fine powder. Mix the powder with the coconut mixture. Add the salt and sugar. Stir to mix and taste for the blend of sweet and sour. Cover and refrigerate until needed.

The chutney lasts 24–36 hours. It may also be frozen.

S E R V E S   6 – 8

Alebele
ⓥ COCONUT PANCAKES

THIS DESSERT COMBINES THE crêpe of the Western world with a delicious cardamom-flavoured coconut-cashew filling which could only come out of the tropical East. Normally, the sweetening comes from jaggery (page 272) but dark muscovado sugar or any dark brown sugar may be used in its place. Only fresh coconut should be used for the filling.

FOR THE BATTER:
115 g/4 oz/1 scant cup plain (all-purpose white) flour
A pinch of salt
1 large egg plus 1 egg yolk
300 ml/10 fl oz/1¼ cups milk
1 tablespoon melted butter

¼ teaspoon ground cardamom

FOR THE FILLING:
180 g/6 oz/1½ cups freshly grated coconut (page 265)
115 g/4 oz/¾ cup chopped, roasted, unsalted cashews
8 tablespoons muscovado (dark brown) sugar

¼ teaspoon ground cardamom
2 tablespoons sultanas (golden raisins)

YOU ALSO NEED:
3–4 tablespoons vegetable oil
1 juicy lemon

Put all the ingredients for the batter in the container of an electric blender. Blend until smooth. Set aside for at least 30 minutes. Empty into a bowl. Have ready a ladle that will pick up about 4–5 tablespoons of batter.

Combine all the ingredients for the filling. Set aside.

Brush an 18 cm/7 inch crêpe pan or a non-stick frying-pan with a little oil and set over medium heat. When smoking hot, pour in 4–5 tablespoons of the batter. Quickly tilt the pan in all directions so that the batter flows to the ends and forms a thin film. (Any extra batter may be poured back into the bowl.)

Cook the pancake for a few minutes until the bottom has some brown spots and the edges can be lifted. Turn the pancake over with a spatula and cook for another minute. Remove and put on a plate. Start to make the second pancake as you made the first. As it cooks, put 2–3 tablespoons of filling on the first pancake, squeeze a generous amount of lemon juice over that and roll it up. Keep it in a covered dish. Make all the pancakes this way, keeping them in a single layer. When they are all made, you could re-heat them briefly in a warming oven.

SERVES 6

Bebinca
ⓥ PANCAKE CAKE

THIS IS THE FESTIVE cake Goans make for Christmas. Come December even the humblest of housewives sets about the task of making her *bebinca*. First one pancake is made. Then, batter for the second is poured over it and cooked from the top. Then comes the batter for the third and then the fourth... and so on until she ends up with a caramelized confection that tastes like a rich, dense fruit cake. For anyone who wants high cakes of many layers, it can take all day. This particular cake has only 5–6 layers. A *bebinca* can be made several days in advance. Store, covered, in a cool spot.

❧

225 g/8 oz/1 generous cup brown sugar
5 cardamom pods, crushed
150 g/5 oz/ 1 generous cup plain (all-purpose white) flour

5 egg yolks
250 ml/8 fl oz/1 cup coconut milk, well stirred from a can or thick fresh milk (page 266)

½ tablespoon *ghee* or melted butter

❧

Make a syrup by putting the sugar and the crushed cardamom pods in a small pan and adding 250 ml/8 fl oz/1 cup water. Heat gently until all the sugar has dissolved and then allow to cool. Strain to remove the cardamom pods (it is fine if a few traces remain).

Combine the flour, egg yolks, coconut milk and cooled syrup in a medium-sized bowl. Beat well to make a smooth batter. Set aside to rest for 30 minutes.

Turn the grill (broiler) to high. Take a 20 cm/8 inch crêpe pan or sturdy non-stick frying-pan and set it over medium-high heat. Pour in the *ghee* or butter. When hot, ladle in 120 ml/4 fl oz/½ cup of the batter, making sure that it spreads to the edges by tilting the pan in all directions. Cook over medium heat until the bottom is golden. Place the pan under the grill (broiler) and allow the pancake to turn golden-brown on the top. You may need to adjust your grill (broiler) by turning the heat down slightly. The pancake should not burn. Now ladle a further 120 ml/4 fl oz batter over the first pancake, spread it around and place under the grill (broiler) until the second layer, too, is golden-brown. Continue this way until all the batter is used up. Allow the *bebinca* to cool overnight before turning it out of the pan.

Cut into thin wedges when serving.

SERVES 6–8

WEST BENGAL

THE BABY, HIS EYES lined with kohl, sits on his mother's lap, staring with surprise and some apprehension at all the fussing adults. He is six months old and the ceremony of *annaprasan* will mark one of his first rites of passage – the gentle leap from a liquid diet to the eating of solids, which, in West Bengal, consist mainly of rice, fish and vegetables.

Two families, his mother's and his father's, have braved the capital city's chaotic traffic to get here – and Calcutta's traffic is truly chaotic! There are double-decker buses, rusted through and through, that tilt wildly as they careen along, slow-moving, exhaust-spewing trucks piled high with green coconuts, rickshaws carrying demure nymphet students who hold up umbrellas against the sun (or rain) and trams from which people jump on and off in a speeded-up game of musical chairs. Waves of bicycles keep ringing their shrill bells hoping, vainly, that something, anything, in front of them will move and wooden bullock carts tote – would you believe it – freshly printed books. And, of course, there are cars upon cars. Some are spit-and-polished, chauffeur-driven, with lethargic, fashionable, be-pearled ladies sitting at the back on their way to 'the Club' (whichever hard-to-get into, high-priced, exclusive club they – really their husbands – have managed to get into).

Other cars, barely held together with tape, string and plastic, are driven by harassed, bespectacled intellectuals on their way to lowly jobs on some Bengali newspaper.

The families have also braved Calcutta's weather, which Mark Twain described as hot and humid enough 'to make a door knob mushy', weather which once inspired very rich Bengalis to build flat, all-marble beds on which they could roll whenever they needed to cool themselves. Only these (and not the more conventional four-poster, mattressed beds, even those with fans) provided a cool enough surface.

West Bengal sits just above the Bay of Bengal in eastern India and its main river, the mighty Ganges, breaks up here into dozens of rivers and rivulets before it flows into the sea. These encourage the proliferation of many kinds of edible fish. They also make the air so moisture-laden that every form of greenery from bananas, jackfruit and gourds to aubergines (eggplants), marrows, flat beans and rice, grows with pleasing generosity.

A *thali* is placed in front of the six-month-old baby who, if he is going to be anything like Calcutta's other ten million inhabitants, will grow to love his idiosyncratic capital city with a justifiable passion, traffic and weather notwithstanding. In the *thali* there is rice (the grain or *anna* in the name of the ceremony) in two forms: plain rice with peas and *payesh*, a sweet rice

pudding. The baby is given a spoon of *payesh*. He likes it and opens his mouth for more. He will eat rice every day of his life as it is the premier grain that lies at the heart of Bengali cuisine. With it, as he grows older, he will have some of the other dishes that are also on the *thali*.

There is a fish head, fried to a crisp with an initial rubbing of salt and turmeric, there is a dish of green plantains and yet another of potatoes cooked with *kalonji*. There is *moong dal* that has been roasted and then cooked with spinach and there is *shukto*, a very Bengali vegetable stew. The staple starter at lunchtime, *shukto* is pale in colour, lightly bitter in flavour (this bitterness can come from bitter greens or any bitter vegetable), thickened with powdered ginger and ground mustard seeds and spiced with the traditional regional mixture, *panch phoran*, a five-spice combination which contains fennel seeds, cumin seeds, *radhuni* (somewhat like a celery seed, this has now given way to mustard seeds), fenugreek seeds and *kalonji*.

Most elements of Bengali cuisine are represented in these dishes. There is the use of *panch phoran*, which originated in the region; the fennel it contains gives food a sweet, anise-like accent while the *kalonji* gives it a deeper peppery quality.

Then there is the use of mustard oil, now as synonymous with Bengali food as olive oil is with the cuisine of the Mediterranean. Deep yellow in colour, it is pungent when it leaves the bottle but turns disarmingly sweet when heated. It is used in both its forms: pungent and sweet. At times fish – such as prawns (shrimp) or the shad-like *hilsa* – are rubbed with a thin paste of ground mustard seeds, ground turmeric, salt, chillies and the pungent mustard oil, then steamed until cooked (*chingri* or *elish bhapey*). Mashed potatoes are enjoyed with a simple dressing of the pungent oil, salt and chopped green chillies (*alu bharta*). Both these dishes are spectacular.

When a milder form of mustard oil is required it is first set to heat until it is almost smoking. Its sharp fumes rise into the air, swirl around the kitchen for a bit and vanish. The oil turns sweet, while retaining its mustardy smell and taste. It can now be used to cook any vegetable or fish. It is much milder this way.

There is also the use of bitter vegetables which, although not unique to Bengal, has been refined here to become an essential taste in the daily diet. Aubergines (eggplants) may be cooked with bitter *neem* leaves (*neem begun*) and the *shukto* mentioned earlier often contains a little bitter gourd or some bitter leaves of a small local gourd (*patol*). The blending of the bitter with the other ingredients is done with the same care a clever European baker shows in adding just the right number of bitter almonds to an almond cake. Many bitter greens in India come with ancient reputations. They have, we are told, cleansing, healing properties and can, with judicious use, counteract intestinal mucus, keep smallpox at bay and even prevent cancer. Children resist the taste in their early years but soon succumb.

Crushed mustard seeds also have their own special bitterness. When used with care they add a most inviting pungency to many Bengali sauces. Bengalis sometimes grind together both the Indian brown and the European yellow mustard seeds for the same dish. This is an effort to tame the sharpness of the first with some of the mellowness of the second. I have seen Bengalis add a chilli or a little salt when they are grinding the mustard seeds. 'It keeps the bitterness under control,' they explain knowingly.

There are pulses (legumes) in one of the *batis* (small bowls, the same as North Indian *katoris*) on the *thali*. Although they are an essential part of the Bengali diet today, this was not always the case. Bengalis, like their neighbours to the east, the Burmese, Thais and Malays, thrived mostly on rice, fish and vegetables. It was the vegetarian movements coming out of the Indian heartland that prompted the addition of split peas to the local diet (not that the Bengalis gave up their fish!). But here, too, the Bengalis have put a unique twist to the taste. They often roast the split peas before they cook them, giving them a special nutty flavour and use *kalonji* or *panch phoran* for their final seasoning (*tarka* or *phoran*, as they say here). This makes the split peas taste unlike anything else in the rest of India.

And then there is the fish. The auspicious fish head, sitting straight up in the *thali*, stares at the baby and the baby, unfazed, stares back at it. Fish and rice will be there to mark many more rites of passage in his life. They will be there when, as a teenager, a holy thread is placed across his chest (only if he is of the high brahmin caste, of course); when he marries, his wife will hold a live fish as she is welcomed into his house; and at his death, balls of cooked rice and fish will be offered to his deceased ancestors.

As the baby grows older, he may find tiny prawns (shrimps) in his vegetables and his split peas may be cooked with a fish head or with large fish bones (rather like a pea soup is cooked with a ham bone in the West). His fish may be fried (*bhaja*), steamed with ground mustard seeds and coconut (*bhapey*), cooked in yoghurt (*dohi machh*), cooked with tamarind (*tetul ilish*) wrapped inside banana leaves and smoked (*paturi*) or, for everyday lunches, cooked in mustard oil with a simple sauce (*jhol*) of coriander, cumin, turmeric, cayenne pepper and whole green chillies. Rice – reliable, amenable rice – will always be the accompaniment.

Strangely enough, none of the fish the growing child eats will come from the sea. Some may come from brackish estuary waters and some (such as the mackerel-like *hilsa* or *elish*) will be fish that spend part of their time in the sea but come inland to spawn, but most will be from the rivers, lakes, tanks and ponds that pit the land. Why this is is hard to know. When asked the question, Bengalis always get a look on their faces which seems to say, 'Isn't the answer obvious?' When pressed further, they manage, 'But freshwater fish is so much sweeter.' The Bay of Bengal is a wild body of water, throwing up mad typhoons at short notice. Could some ancient fear of the sea be the reason?

To see the fish and how it is bought, dressed and sold, I decide to visit the Manik Tala market in north Calcutta. This is the older part of town.

Palaces, dozens of them, many built by wealthy Indian feudal lords who made their fortunes in opium, jute and indigo during the British Raj, lie crumbling – vast Palladian monuments scattered about like so much decaying rubble. It is easy to see why Calcutta was known as the 'City of Palaces' in the eighteenth and nineteenth centuries. By now the humid weather and pigeons, acting as the greatest of levellers, have gnawed many of the buildings to the bone. But their skeletons, fleshed out here and there by memories of past glory, still stand. And people still live in them.

I decide to visit one such palace, now owned by several members of a prominent West Bengal family. Their last name is Basu. The octogenarian patriarch studied at Oxford University. Much of the furni-

A street scene in Calcutta, West Bengal.

138

ture is made of finely carved mahogany. The chandeliers and lamps are made with European glass. It is that sort of family.

Smoke, followed by the heavenly smell of food being cooked by loving hands, seems to be coming from . . . a corridor? The dusty ruin looks like a set from one of Satyajit Ray's films about Bengali aristocracy. Little boys are playing cricket in one of the larger courtyards.

Two retainers seem to have pitched their 'tent' in a corridor already blackened with smoke and are cooking their dinner over a charcoal brazier. 'What are you making?' I yell at them – they are old and do not hear too well. '*Mangshor jhol*' one answers as he stirs the pot, a simple stew of goat meat and potatoes cooked in mustard oil with lots of black pepper, cumin, coriander, green chillies and a touch of sugar.

Goat meat is well liked and eaten by many Hindu Bengalis. Indeed, the patron goddess of the city, Kali, the one with a black face and sticking out tongue, has a temple dedicated to her in south Calcutta where goats are sacrificed on a daily basis. Some of her devotees make do with offerings of red hibiscus garlands (red being the colour of the blood she likes) but others, with more money or deeper anxieties, offer live goats. The animals are led to a marble enclosure, their necks are stretched over a kind of guillotine, the all-important wish of the devotee whispered into the goat's ear and the creature is then swiftly dispatched, carrying the message straight to the god-

dess Kali. The meat, now considered holy food, is then cooked and served.

There are other meat-eaters. In 1690 Muslims, with a diet similar to that found in the rest of North India, ruled Bengal. Those local people they converted to Islam continued to eat the traditional Hindu diet of rice, fish and vegetables but added to it meat *pullaos* (pilafs), lamb and goat cooked with plenty of onions and garlic, and chickens cooked slowly with cinnamon and cloves. By the twentieth century, they had evolved unique dishes like the *rezala* (lamb cooked in milk and yoghurt). Cubes of lamb are first marinated in milk, yoghurt, ginger, garlic, cardamom, cloves and nutmeg. The meat is then removed and lightly browned. The marinade goes back in and the meat stews gently. A few red and green chillies are thrown in and a few drops of aromatic *kewra* (screwpine essence). This exquisite dish is then ready to be eaten with flat yeast breads such as the *naan*.

At the Basu palace, I taste some of the retainers' dinner, enjoy its spicy simplicity and jot down the recipe. I am really looking for Mrs Sonali Basu who is to take me to the fish market. She is not in the main palace but in a more modern structure on her husband's share of the family property.

The daughter of a film director and herself once an actress, Sonali informs me that it is too late to go to the fish market – we really needed to have left around dawn – but will I not stay and have some *jalkhabar* with her.

Bengalis tend to have five meals a day. There is breakfast which could consist of puffed rice eaten either wet with milk and liquid palm jaggery or dryish in combination with green chillies, coconut, onion and a little mustard oil. Then there is a mid-morning snack. This is followed by lunch which, if it is formal, would have several courses, all served with rice. It would probably start with the bitter *shukto*, then go on to a split pea dish with some fried vegetable fritters (such as *alu bhaja* made with potato slices and a chick pea flour batter) on the side. Then a vegetable dish would be served, followed by a fish and vegetable combination. Next, a dish using small fish would appear, then one using large fish. This would be followed by meat or chicken (perhaps a chicken cooked with mustard seeds or fresh green coriander), then a sweet chutney course and finally the dessert, generally made with milk or yoghurt. After a siesta, another snack appears. Then there is dinner which would consist perhaps of white flour breads (*loochis*), a marrow dish, a pulse, a green vegetable and a chicken or meat dish. There would invariably be some sweetmeats as Bengalis cannot seem to live without them.

It is the mid-morning and late afternoon snacks that are known as *jalkhabar*. They could comprise a simple cold coffee served with a *singhara* (a kind of *samosa* – savoury pastry – filled with minced meat or potatoes and peas) but Sonali's *jalkhabar* threatens to be much more generous. She

wants to make a whole meal of it. Even as I demur, she brings me *begun bhaja* (aubergine (eggplant) slices dipped in batter and fried), *koraishuti kachori* (a deep-fried, puffed-up bread stuffed with green peas), some *alu dum* (small new potatoes cooked with cumin, cardamom, cinnamon, ginger and tomatoes), a cup of steaming milky tea ('Would you prefer a cold Coca-Cola? Or Limca?') and then, to end, she offers *mishti doi*, a marvellous, creamy yoghurt made with sweetened milk ('We always get ours from the same shop in north Calcutta'). I am told to come back early the next day if I want to go to the fish market.

I arrive at 6.30 a.m. The market, entered through a covered alley, is already in full swing. Men carrying cloth bags crowd around every shop. It is an accepted tradition that heads of households, always male, do the morning shopping.

I have never before seen such large quantities of such fresh fish, eyes gleaming, gills all red, skins shimmering. The silvery *hilsa*, with hints of gold, could have come straight from a jeweller. The striped tiger prawns are equally attractive and even more pricey. Many small fish such as the *koi* or climbing perch are sold live. Bengalis will not buy them any other way. They hop around on the scales.

It is here that I can watch how the fish is cut. Bengalis are as idiosyncratic about dismembering their fish as they are about everything else. First of all, traditionally, no knife is used. Instead, there is a *bonti*. A plank of wood, held down by the squatting fishmonger's foot, has attached to it, like the prow of a haughty boat, a large lethal blade that curves inwards. The fishmonger takes a 5.5 kg (12 lb) *rui* (a kind of carp) and first cuts off its head and then a fair section of its tail by pushing them against the blade with both hands. The rest of the fish is split into two, laterally. There is the bony, upper back section, the *daga*, and the fattier, more desirable stomach section or *peti*. These are now cut crossways into 2.5 cm (1 inch) thick chunks. These meaty pieces will disappear into millions of pans within the next few hours.

Calcutta's origins do not go far back in Indian history. In the late seventeenth century what is now Calcutta consisted of three small villages – Sutanati, Govindpur and Kalikata – on the banks of the Hooghly River. Job Charnock, an agent for the British East India Company, leased them from Aurangzeb, the emperor in Delhi, with the intention of establishing a trading port. From then onwards both the East India Company and the city grew and prospered until Calcutta became the formal capital of the British Empire in India. It remained the capital until 1911.

With the British came a whole slew of new foods. The potato was one of them. The Bengalis, quite literally, gobbled it up, inventing hundreds of new recipes to accommodate its starchy texture: potatoes in a poppy seed paste, potatoes with fish, potatoes with cardamom and cinnamon,

potatoes encrusted with black pepper . . .

By the nineteenth century the East Indiamen had settled into a fairly luxurious routine. The most modest of families had dozens of servants, including those whose sole job was to cool the water, watch the kettle, lift the palanquin or pull the fan. The day for most of the Company men began with an early morning ride, when the air was still cool, followed by a nap to recover from the exercise. Then, on to a breakfast of 'tea, muffins and pillaw at half-past nine'. Tiffin or lunch at 2.00 p.m. consisted of 'a rich hash or hot curry, followed by a well-cooled bottle of claret or Hodgson's pale ale, with a variety of eastern fruit'. Dinners might call for more claret, sherry, Madeira, port, perhaps champagne, soups, ducks, chickens, steaks, hams, Indian curry and rice, with puffs on the *hookah* (hubble-bubble pipe) afterwards.

Britishers could buy their food from taverns if they so desired. One tavern advertised in 1785: 'Ladies and gentlemen will be furnished with Dinners, Suppers, or Cold Collation, on the shortest notice. Biscuits of all kinds, tarts and tartlets fresh every day.' The same caterer also supplied 'the following articles for Sea, or to take Up-country, which he will warrant for six months: viz. Potted Beef, Veal, Muttons, Ducks, Geese, Pigeons, Collard Beef, Pork, and small pigs, Mince Meat, Plumb Cakes, Jams and Marmalades of all kinds, preserved butter, eggs, milk, milks punch etc.'

In the late seventeenth and early eighteenth centuries, few women accompanied the male 'writers' or clerks of the East India Company. The men, quite reasonably, acquired Indian mistresses. Some even married their Indian sweethearts. The children of such unions – and their descendants – are known in India today as Anglo-Indians. Errol O'Brien, a tea-taster and buyer (Darjeeling, where the colonial British government had its summer offices, is West Bengal's premier hill station) defines Anglo-Indians this way: 'Anyone with British ancestry on the father's side is an Anglo-Indian. The mother could be Bengali, Punjabi . . . from anywhere in India.'

With Calcutta the seat first of the British East India Company and then of the British government in India, it naturally followed that there were more Anglo-Indians here than anywhere else in the country. Their mixed race origins were reflected in their food. A look at an Anglo-Indian, turn-of-the-century cookbook, printed by one of the many small presses that still abound in this bookish city, reveals a fish pie prepared with fish, mashed potatoes, green chillies, ginger, mint and cinnamon, a rolled mutton with *ghee* in it, steaks cooked with ginger, garlic and turmeric, and a duck that looks fairly English until you notice the mustard oil. While there are recipes for Shrewsbury biscuits and plum pudding, there is also a mango fool and a jaggery toffee.

Indian independence brought with it a scurry of migrations by Anglo-Indians to England and Australia. Today their numbers in Calcutta are greatly reduced. Living in high-rise flats like the rest of Calcutta's citizens, they still preserve their own, unique culinary traditions. For lunch they might indulge in 'ball curry' and yellow rice (meatball curry and turmeric rice), or 'country captain' (chicken cooked with onions, green peppers, ginger and chillies) which they might serve with *bhuna khichuri* (rice and split peas flavoured with *garam masala*) and tomato *bharta* (a spicy salad of fresh tomatoes). Dinner could be thin beefsteaks cooked with ginger and mustard seeds and eaten with *chapatis* (flat, unleavened breads) or even a hot sausage curry served with slices of white bread.

At a country picnic with Errol's family, a gingham tablecloth is unfolded and spread out on the grass. Baskets are opened, cloth bundles untied and flasks uncorked. A world of Anglo-Indian creations is neatly set out by ladies in demure Western clothes. There are potato patties (called 'potato chops') stuffed with minced meat. We can eat them with a mint chutney or would we prefer them with ketchup? There is a large platter of spicy sausages. 'I prefer to have them made up in front of me,' Errol says. 'I have to say "Put in just *so* much *garam masala* and just *so* many chillies" otherwise who knows what those people might do!' There are puff pastry 'patties' stuffed with spicy potatoes, fried meatballs, a bread pudding made in a pressure cooker and, best of all, tall glasses of cool, fairly liquid mango fool made with the boiled pulp of sour green mangoes, sugar and milk.

Whether Hindu, Christian or Muslim, all Bengalis seem to be agreed on one thing. They love sweets. Today, a sweet shop like Chhappan Bhog (this translates as '56 offerings') carries at least a few dozen varieties of *sandesh* alone. This sweetmeat is made with a very fresh cheese (*chhana*) that is squeezed of all whey, kneaded into a dough and then pressed into a mould. *Sandesh* is probably *chhana* in its simplest, purest form. Bengalis love it but are very fussy about where they buy it.

Chhappan Bhog can sell them *sandesh* made with strawberries (very modern), *sandesh* made with saffron (very traditional and expensive), *sandesh* 'sandwiches' filled with reduced milk (very popular), pistachio *sandesh* and many others.

Once the cheese 'dough' is made, the magician sweetmakers transform it into all manner of other sweetmeats as well. It can be rolled into balls and boiled in syrup until it puffs up and becomes spongy (*rossogolla*); it can be shaped into diamonds, boiled in syrup and then 'iced' with dollops of reduced milk (*chum chum*); mixed with reduced milk, rice flour and rose attar then fried and put into syrup, it becomes Lady Kenny (named after Lady Canning, the wife of a nineteenth-century governor-general of India).

With Calcutta's heavy and torpor-inducing air that moves listlessly around decaying buildings, a never-ending Metro construction project that not only snarls traffic but is known to swallow up whole buildings and permanent settlements of discontented refugees, a first-time visitor to the city might well think that it would be nothing short of madness to live here. But after a brief stay, even the first-time visitor is infected by its intellectual passions, its eccentric brown Englishmen, its quirky publishers, gallery owners, film directors and actors. And the first-time visitor falls deeply in love with its bitter-sweet foods. Then the first-time visitor begins to think, 'How can I extend my stay?'

Sonali Basu's Begun Bhaja
⊘ DEEP-FRIED AUBERGINES (EGGPLANTS) IN BATTER

CRISP FRITTERS AND SOFT, malleable rice are often offered as one of the first courses at formal meals in Bengal. The fritters may be made out of potato skins or aubergines (eggplants) or whatever else happens to be in season. I find that the fritters, served by themselves, are also quite perfect with tea and with drinks. White poppy seeds are frequently substituted for *kalonji*.

❧

FOR THE BATTER:
225 g/8 oz/1½ cups chick pea flour, sifted
1 teaspoon cayenne pepper
1 teaspoon salt
A pinch of ground turmeric
½ teaspoon bicarbonate of soda (baking soda)

YOU ALSO NEED:
Oil for deep-frying
350 g/12 oz aubergines (eggplants), cut into 1 cm × 1 cm × 7.5 cm (½ inch × ½ inch × 3 inch) fingers; use any slim variety or the large purple ones

Salt
Freshly ground black pepper
1¼ teaspoon *kalonji* (page 272)

❧

Put the ingredients for the batter into a bowl. Mix well. Slowly add 300 ml/10 fl oz/1¼ cups water, whisking constantly to produce a smooth, thick batter. You may leave the batter this consistency – many people prefer a thick coating – or you could thin it further by adding up to 120 ml/4 fl oz/½ cup water.

Heat the oil for deep-frying in a wok or deep frying-pan over medium heat. The oil is sufficiently hot when a cube of bread sizzles nicely and turns golden.

Meanwhile, put the pieces of aubergine (eggplant) on to a plate in a single layer. Sprinkle each piece with a little salt and pepper on all sides. When the oil is hot, use one hand to dip the aubergines (eggplants) into the batter, only as many pieces as the wok or pan will hold in a single layer. Shake off the excess batter, sprinkle some *kalonji* over the top with the fingers of your second, clean hand, and put straight into the hot oil. Deep-fry for 5–7 minutes, turning the fritters half-way through. They should turn golden and crisp. Remove with a slotted spoon and drain on kitchen paper (paper towels). You may need to do the frying in several batches. Serve immediately. (Any remaining batter can be refrigerated and kept for 2 days.)

S E R V E S   4 – 6

Christine Ward's Masala Steak

SPICY STEAK

HERE IS AN ANGLO-INDIAN speciality. Even though it is called 'Masala Steak', it really contains no steaks as we know them in the West. Rather, it consists of flat, rectangular pieces of meat (lamb or beef), much smaller and thinner than official steaks, cooked with very Indian seasonings. Traditionally it is served with bread or *chapatis*. I also love it with Stir-Fried Rice with Split Peas (see page 166) or with a crusty French or Italian loaf. Serve a green salad on the side.

FOR THE PASTE:
7.5 cm/3 inch piece of fresh ginger, peeled and roughly chopped
7–8 garlic cloves, peeled and chopped
1 medium-sized onion (75 g/3 oz), finely chopped

FOR THE SPICE POWDER:
1 tablespoon ground coriander

1 tablespoon cumin seeds
1 tablespoon brown mustard seeds
½ teaspoon ground turmeric
1 teaspoon cayenne pepper

YOU ALSO NEED:
3 tablespoons vegetable oil
1 kg/2¼ lb boneless lamb, cut into 7.5 cm × 2.5 cm × 5 mm (3 inch × 1 inch × ¼ inch) pieces

2 medium-sized red onions (175 g/6 oz), cut into thin rings
2 medium-sized potatoes (275 g/10 oz), peeled and cut into 5mm/¼ inch thick rounds
1¾–2 teaspoons salt

Put the ginger, garlic and onion for the spice paste into the container of an electric blender along with 100 ml/3½ fl oz/½ cup water. Blend to a fine paste. You may need to push the mixture down with a spatula from time to time to achieve this. Set aside.

Put the ingredients for the spice powder into a clean coffee grinder. Grind to a fine powder. Set aside.

Heat the oil in a large, wide, preferably non-stick pan or wok over high heat. When hot, put in the lamb. Stir and fry for 10–15 minutes

or until the lamb pieces brown. Reduce the heat to medium and add the ginger-and-garlic paste and the spice powder. Stir once or twice to mix well. Add 500 ml/17 fl oz/2 cups water and bring to the boil. Cover, turn the heat to low and cook for 45 minutes. Add the onion rings, potato slices and salt to taste. Stir to mix. Cover and cook for a further 15–20 minutes, until the potatoes are cooked and the sauce is thick enough to just coat the lamb.

SERVES 4–6

Mrs Dasgupta's Rezala
LAMB COOKED IN MILK AND YOGHURT

REZALA, WHICH CAN BE made with both lamb and chicken, is a speciality of the Muslims of Bengal. It is eaten at celebratory meals. It is almost always made with rather fatty rib chops. I prefer to use boned lamb shoulder.

When the dish has almost finished cooking, many Muslim families add a sprinkling of *kewra* water. This has a marvellously flowery aroma. Most serious Indian grocers sell it. Use rose water or orange blossom water as substitutes.

Serve with *naans*, *chapatis*, pitta breads or any rice dish of your choice.

༽

FOR THE MARINADE:
7.5 cm/3 inch piece of fresh ginger, peeled and finely chopped
8–9 garlic cloves, peeled and coarsely chopped
350 ml/12 fl oz/1½ cups rich yoghurt, lightly beaten
250 ml/8 fl oz/1 cup milk
3–4 bay leaves

8–10 cardamom pods
8–10 cloves
1 teaspoon ground mace
½ teaspoon ground nutmeg

YOU ALSO NEED:
1 kg/2¼ lb boned lamb from the shoulder
1 tablespoon vegetable oil
3 tablespoons *ghee* or vegetable oil

1½–1¾ teaspoons salt
½ teaspoon sugar
10 fresh hot green chillies, each with a small slit at one end
6–8 dried hot red chillies, soaked in warm water for 10 minutes
1 teaspoon *kewra* water (page 272)

༽

Make the marinade: Put the ginger and garlic into the container of an electric blender. Add 4 tablespoons water. Blend to a fine, frothy paste. Put the paste into a large bowl. Add the remaining marinating ingredients and mix well. Add the lamb. Leave to stand unrefrigerated for 3–4 hours. (You may marinate the meat overnight. Cover and refrigerate and bring to room temperature before cooking.)

Remove the meat from the marinade and put the marinade to one side.

Heat the oil and *ghee* in a large, wide, preferably non-stick pan or wok over high heat. When hot, add the lamb, salt and sugar. Stir and fry for 8–10 minutes until the meat is lightly browned. Reduce the heat to very low. Add the marinade. Cover and cook for 1 hour or until the meat is tender. Add the green and red chillies. Cook for a further 5–10 minutes. Add the *kewra* water, stir and serve.

S E R V E S   4

Rakhi Dasgupta's Murgi Dhuniya Patta Diya
CHICKEN IN FRESH GREEN CORIANDER

A WONDERFUL CHICKEN DISH to serve with rice. You may use the more traditional thick coconut milk (see page 266) instead of cream.

❧

FOR THE MARINADE:
4 cloves
4 cardamom pods
2–3 bay leaves
2.5 cm/1 inch cinnamon stick
2 tablespoons ground coriander
A pinch of salt

250 ml/8 fl oz/1 cup natural (plain) yoghurt, lightly beaten
One 1 kg/2¼ lb chicken, skinned and cut into 7.5 cm/3 inch pieces

YOU ALSO NEED:
5 tablespoons mustard oil or any other vegetable oil
A pinch of ground asafetida

100 g/4 oz/2½ cups fresh green coriander, finely chopped, plus extra for garnishing
1½ teaspoons salt
1 teaspoon sugar
6–8 fresh hot green chillies, split into halves
150 g/5 oz/⅔ cup single (light) cream

❧

Put the cloves, cardamom pods, bay leaves, cinnamon and ground coriander for the marinade into a clean coffee grinder. Grind to a fine powder. Empty the ground spices into a bowl. Add the salt and yoghurt. Stir to mix. Add the chicken. Mix well to coat all the chicken pieces. Refrigerate and leave to marinate for 1–2 hours (overnight will not hurt). Take the chicken pieces out of the marinade and put the marinade to one side.

Heat the oil in a large, wide, preferably non-stick pan or wok over medium heat. When hot, add the asafetida. Let it sizzle for 4–5 seconds. Turn the heat to high and immediately add the chicken. Stir and fry for 15 minutes until the

chicken is browned. Add the marinade, 100g/4 oz fresh coriander, salt and sugar. Stir and fry over medium heat for a further 5–10 minutes until the chicken is almost tender. Add the chillies. Stir and fry for 2–3 minutes until the chillies soften. Add the cream. Stir to mix. Reduce the heat to low and allow to simmer for a further 5–8 minutes or until the sauce is thick. It should coat the chicken pieces and leave a little extra at the bottom of the pan.

Serve garnished with the remaining fresh coriander.

SERVES 4 – 6

Christine Ward's
COUNTRY CAPTAIN

I HAVE YET TO find two explanations for the name of this dish that agree! But there it is, an Anglo-Indian name, however obscure, for an Anglo-Indian dish that may well have originated in Calcutta. It is delicious and easy to prepare, tending to disappear as soon as it is made! Serve with plain rice or with Stir-Fried Rice with Split Peas (page 166) and Stewed Tomato Relish (page 168).

FOR THE PASTE:
7.5 cm/3 inch piece of fresh ginger, peeled and finely chopped
5 garlic cloves, peeled and coarsely chopped
1 small red onion (50 g/2 oz), roughly chopped

YOU ALSO NEED:
2 tablespoons vegetable oil
1 medium-large red onion (100 g/4 oz), finely sliced
One 1 kg/2¼ lb chicken, skinned and cut into 5 cm/2 inch pieces
1 teaspoon cayenne pepper
1¼–1½ teaspoons salt
¼ teaspoon sugar

1–2 tablespoons white wine vinegar
2 large, ripe tomatoes, chopped into 2.5 cm/1 inch pieces
5–6 fresh hot green chillies, each with a small slit at one end
2 green peppers, cored, seeded and finely sliced

Put the ginger, garlic and onion for the paste into the container of an electric blender. Add 100ml/3½ fl oz/½ cup water. Blend to a fine paste. You may need to push the mixture down with a spatula from time to time to achieve this.

Heat the oil in a large, wide, preferably non-stick pan or wok over high heat. When hot, add half the sliced onion. Stir and fry for 2–3 minutes until the onion begins to soften. Add the chicken. Stir and fry for 8–10 minutes until browned. Reduce the heat to medium and add the paste from the blender, and the cayenne pepper, salt, sugar and vinegar to taste. Stir and fry for a further 10–15 minutes until the chicken is tender. The spicy sauce should be thick enough to coat the chicken pieces. Add the tomatoes, remaining onion, chillies and peppers.

Stir and fry for 3–4 minutes so that the flavours blend but the peppers remain green and crisp.

SERVES 4

Sorse Murgi
CHICKEN WITH MUSTARD SEEDS

ANOTHER, VERY MUSTARDY, VERY typically Bengali creation to be eaten with
plain rice.

❧

1¼–1½ teaspoons salt
1 teaspoon ground turmeric
One 1 kg/2¼ lb chicken, cut
  into serving pieces (each
  leg into drumstick and
  thigh and the breast into
  6 pieces)

1 tablespoon brown mustard
  seeds
4–5 fresh hot green chillies,
  roughly chopped

4½ tablespoons mustard oil
  or any other vegetable oil
3 tablespoons chopped,
  fresh green coriander

❧

Rub 1 teaspoon of the salt and ½ teaspoon of
the turmeric over the chicken.

Put the mustard seeds into a clean coffee
grinder. Grind to a fine powder.

Put the ground mustard seeds, chillies and
¼ teaspoon of the turmeric into the container
of an electric blender. Add 4 tablespoons
water. Blend to a smooth paste. Set the paste
aside.

Heat 3 tablespoons of the oil in a large,
wide, preferably non-stick pan or wok over
high heat. When hot, add the chicken. Stir and
fry for 12–15 minutes until golden. Remove
from the pan.

Add the remaining oil to the pan. When hot
add the mustard-and-chilli paste and turn the
heat to low. Stir and fry for 3–4 minutes until
the oil bubbles at the surface. Add the chicken
and the remaining salt and turmeric. Stir to
mix. Add 300 ml/10 fl oz/1¼ cups water.
Bring to the boil over medium heat. Cover and
cook for 10–15 minutes or until the chicken is
tender and the sauce has reduced to just coat
the pieces.

Sprinkle the fresh coriander over the top
before serving.

S E R V E S   4

Country Captain (page 149) with Stir-fried Rice
with Split Peas (page 166) and Stewed Tomato
Relish (page 168).

Mrs Dasgupta's Dohi Machh
YOGHURT FISH

CHUNKS OF FISH – USUALLY freshwater *rui* – are cooked in yoghurt with cardamom and cloves. When there are special guests to entertain, raisins are added, especially by the Ghoti community who like a touch of sweetness in all their foods. Carp may be substituted for the *rui*. If that, too, is unavailable use halibut, grey mullet, haddock or cod. Serve with plain rice. For a true Bengali taste, you should use mustard oil but you may substitute any other vegetable oil. I find that a good virgin olive oil, with its different but equally strong taste, makes for a very pleasant alternative.

∾

FOR THE PASTE:
1 medium-large red onion (100 g/4 oz), roughly chopped
2.5 cm/1 inch piece of fresh ginger, peeled and coarsely chopped
6–7 garlic cloves, peeled and coarsely chopped

YOU ALSO NEED:
750 g/1½ lb halibut, grey mullet, haddock or cod steaks with bone, cut into 7.5 cm × 2.5 cm/3 inch × 1 inch pieces
1½ teaspoons salt or to taste
½ teaspoon ground turmeric
5 tablespoons mustard oil or any other vegetable oil
5 cardamom pods
4–5 cloves
2.5 cm/1 inch cinnamon stick

4 bay leaves
1 medium-large red onion (100 g/4 oz), finely sliced
1 teaspoon cayenne pepper
250 g/9 oz/1 cup plus 2 tablespoons rich Greek-style (whole milk) yoghurt, lightly beaten with 250 ml/8 fl oz/1 cup water
6 fresh hot green chillies
4 dried hot red chillies

∾

Put the onion, garlic and ginger for the paste into the container of an electric blender. Add 100 ml/3½ fl oz/½ cup water. Blend to a smooth, frothy paste. You may need to push the mixture down from time to time with a spatula to achieve this. Set aside.

Rub ½ teaspoon of the salt and the turmeric over the fish. Set aside.

Heat 4 tablespoons of the oil in a large, wide, preferably non-stick pan or wok over high heat. Add the fish. Fry on both sides for a total of 3–4 minutes until lightly browned. Remove from the pan using a slotted spoon, leaving as much oil behind as possible. You may have to do this in 2–3 batches, remembering that the second and third batches will take less time to cook. If the fish is very delicate and breakable, leave the centre slightly uncooked. This will hold it together. Remove the fish with a slotted spoon, leaving the oil behind.

Add the remaining oil to the pan that the fish was cooked in. Set over medium heat. When hot, add the cardamom pods, cloves, cinnamon and bay leaves. Stir and fry for 15 seconds or until the bay leaves start to darken. Add the sliced onions. Stir and fry for 3–4 minutes until lightly browned. Add the onion-and-garlic paste, cayenne pepper and remaining salt. Stir and fry for 10 minutes. The oil will rise to the surface and the sauce will turn a reddish-brown colour. Remove the pan from the heat. Allow to cool for 5 minutes. Add the yoghurt. Set the pan over low heat. Add the fish and the green and red chillies. Stir very gently to mix. Poach gently for 8–10 minutes, spooning the sauce over the fish, until it is just cooked through.

S E R V E S   4 – 6

Rakhi Dasgupta's Tetul Ilish

TAMARIND FISH

HILSA, A BEAUTIFUL SILVERY fish, is found in the estuaries of Bengal's rivers where it comes in from the sea to spawn. It is much loved. As it is very expensive, it is almost revered and reserved for special occasions. Shad, if available, makes a good substitute and so does salmon.

---

450 g/1 lb *hilsa* or salmon steaks, 2.5 cm/¾ inch thick
¾ teaspoon ground turmeric
¾–1 teaspoon salt

100 ml/3½ fl oz/½ cup mustard oil or any other vegetable oil
3 tablespoons thick tamarind paste (page 278)

½ teaspoon cayenne pepper
½ teaspoon sugar
½ teaspoon brown mustard seeds

Rub ½ teaspoon of the turmeric and ½ teaspoon of the salt over the fish steaks. Set aside for 10 minutes.

Heat the oil in a large, wide, preferably non-stick frying-pan over medium-high heat. When hot, put in the fish. Fry each side for 2–3 minutes until golden. Remove the fish from the pan using a slotted spoon, leaving the oil behind. Set aside.

Meanwhile, put the tamarind paste, cayenne pepper, sugar, remaining salt, remaining turmeric and 200 ml/7 fl oz water into a bowl. Mix well.

Take 2 tablespoons of the oil used for frying the fish and heat in a clean, large frying-pan over medium-high heat. When hot, put in the mustard seeds. As soon as they pop, a matter of seconds, add the tamarind mixture. Bring to the boil over medium-high heat. Turn the heat to low and allow to simmer for 10–12 minutes, stirring regularly, until the oil bubbles at the surface and the sauce becomes very thick. Return the fish to the pan. Continue to simmer for 5–8 minutes, turning the fish pieces once very gently during this time. The sauce should just coat the fish.

SERVES 4

Yoghurt Fish (page 152) and Cooling Mango Chutney (page 169).

Rakhi Sarkar's Maccher Sorse Diye Jhol

EASY FISH FILLETS IN A TRADITIONAL MUSTARD SAUCE

THERE IS, ON THE one hand, very traditional Bengali food that can be found only in Bengal and in Indian cities where there are Bengali markets. There is also the food of the Bengali who travels abroad and has learnt to adjust his needs to available raw ingredients and to the capabilities of modern kitchens. Rakhi Sarkar lives in Calcutta but travels frequently to the West where she cannot get the fish or the chunky, bone-in cuts of fish that Bengalis like. That does not seem to slow her down one bit. She just substitutes the fillets of salmon or any firm-fleshed white fish. Instead of deep-frying it first as 'grandmother used to do' (a fillet would just break up), she grills (broils) it and then douses it with a very traditional sauce. She has worked out a unique technique with exquisite results. Here is what she showed me in her very modern Calcutta kitchen, using fillets of a very popular freshwater fish, *bekti*. Serve this dish with plain rice.

❧

FOR THE MUSTARD PASTE:

4 tablespoons brown mustard seeds

1 dried hot red chilli

FOR THE TURMERIC PASTE:

1 teaspoon ground turmeric

¼ teaspoon cayenne pepper

FOR MARINATING THE FISH:

500 g/18 oz skinless fillets of salmon or any white-fleshed fish such as haddock, sole, turbot or red snapper

½ teaspoon ground turmeric

½ teaspoon salt

2 teaspoons mustard oil

FOR THE FINAL COOKING OF THE SAUCE:

3 tablespoons mustard oil

1½ teaspoons *panch phoran* (page 275)

¼ teaspoon salt or to taste

7–8 fresh hot green chillies, with their very tips pinched off

❧

Put the mustard seeds and dried chilli for the mustard paste into a clean coffee-grinder. Grind to a coarse powder. Put the powder in a bowl. Add 150 ml/5 fl oz/⅔ cup water and stir to mix. Set aside. Do not stir again, allowing the coarse part of the seeds to settle at the bottom.

To make the turmeric paste, combine the turmeric, cayenne pepper and 2 tablespoons water in a small cup. Stir to mix. Set aside

Pre-heat the grill (broiler).

Marinate the fish next. Arrange the fillets in a single layer in a shallow baking tin (or shallow cake tin), just large enough to hold the fish. Rub the fillets with the turmeric, salt and mustard oil. Set aside for 10 minutes. Place the fish under the grill (broiler) and grill (broil) for about 5–6 minutes or until the fish is just cooked through. Remove.

While the fish is grilling (broiling), do the final cooking of the sauce. This will all happen quite fast. Heat 2 tablespoons of the oil in a wok or pan over medium-high heat. When hot, put in the *panch phoran*. As soon as the mustard seeds in the spice mixture begin to pop, a matter of seconds, put in the turmeric paste. Stir quickly once or twice and put in 3 tablespoons water. Stir the mustard paste once and carefully pour in only the thin part, leaving all the coarse seeds behind. Bring to the boil. Add the ¼ teaspoon salt and the green chillies. Stir once or twice. Turn off heat.

Pour this sauce over the fish fillets. Place the baking tin over medium heat. Bring to a simmer. Simmer for 2 minutes. Turn off the heat and serve.

S E R V E S   3 – 4

Rakhi Dasgupta's Chingri Bhapey
PRAWNS (SHRIMP) STEAMED WITH MUSTARD SEEDS AND COCONUT

BENGALIS ARE AMONG THE few Indians that delight in steamed fish. Fish is rubbed with seasonings – mustard oil and crushed mustard seeds are frequently essential – put into a *bati* (a bowl), covered and then steamed, often in the pot that is cooking rice. Vegetables may be added to the fish – par-boiled potatoes, even cauliflower or mixed vegetables.

Serve with plain rice.

If you wish to use unsweetened, desiccated coconut instead of fresh coconut use 2–3 tablespoons. Just cover with warm water and leave for 30 minutes, then proceed with the recipe.

½ tablespoon brown mustard seeds
½ tablespoon yellow mustard seeds
340 g/12 oz peeled, deveined and washed medium-sized prawns (shrimp) or 450 g/1 lb unpeeled, headless,

medium-sized prawns (shrimp), peeled, deveined and washed (page 285)
1 medium-sized red onion (75 g/3 oz), finely chopped
4–5 tablespoons freshly grated coconut (page 265)

6–7 fresh hot green chillies, each with a 1 cm/½ inch slit at one end
4 tablespoons mustard oil or any other vegetable oil
¼ teaspoon cayenne pepper
½ teaspoon ground turmeric
½ teaspoon salt
½ teaspoon sugar

Put the brown and yellow mustard seeds into a clean coffee grinder. Grind to a fine powder. Put the mustard powder into a small bowl. Add 100 ml/3½ fl oz/½ cup water. Mix well.

Put all the remaining ingredients and the mustard paste into a large, heat-resistant bowl. Mix well. Cover the bowl (foil may be used). Put the bowl in a pan of boiling water – the water should come half-way up its sides – or inside a wok containing 7.5 cm/3 inches of boiling water. Cover. Steam over medium heat for 10–15 minutes or until the prawns (shrimp) turn opaque. Stir once half-way through the steaming, making sure that you cover the bowl and the steaming utensil afterwards. The cooking time will vary with the bowl's shape.

SERVES 4

Rakhi Sarkar's Prawn Malai Curry

PRAWN (SHRIMP) CURRY

THIS SEEMS TO BE universally called 'Prawn Malai Curry' in Calcutta. 'Malai' means 'cream' and there is coconut milk in the dish to justify the name. However, there is a theory that this dish actually came from what was once Malaya and that the correct name is 'Prawn Malay Curry'. Whatever the correct name and whatever its origin, this curry is in Calcutta to stay. It is exceedingly popular and because prawns (shrimp) are expensive, there is a cachet attached to cooking it.

Coconut milk from a well-mixed can is perfectly acceptable.

Serve with plain rice.

❧

FOR THE PASTE:

4 medium-sized red onions (350 g/12 oz), finely chopped

3 garlic cloves, peeled and roughly chopped

2.5 cm/1 inch piece of fresh ginger, peeled and finely chopped

YOU ALSO NEED:

1 kg/2¼ lb peeled, deveined and washed large prawns (shrimp) or 1.5kg/3½ lb unpeeled, headless large prawns (shrimp), peeled and deveined (page 285)

1 teaspoon salt

1 teaspoon ground turmeric

4 tablespoons mustard or any other vegetable oil

2 tablespoons *ghee* or vegetable oil

6 cardamom pods

4 cloves

2.5 cm/1 inch cinnamon stick

1 bay leaf

1 teaspoon cayenne pepper

2 tablespoons natural (plain) yoghurt

300 ml/10 fl oz/1¼ cups coconut milk, well stirred from a can, or thick fresh milk (page 266)

❧

Put the onions, garlic and ginger for the paste into the container of an electric blender. Add 100 ml/3½ fl oz/½ cup water. Blend to a smooth paste. Set aside.

Rub the prawns (shrimp) with ½ teaspoon of the salt and ½ teaspoon of the turmeric.

Heat 2 tablespoons of the oil in a large,

wide, preferably non-stick pan or wok over high heat. When hot, add the prawns (shrimp). Stir and fry for 2–3 minutes until just golden. Remove with a slotted spoon and set aside.

Add the remaining oil and the *ghee* to the pan or wok, turning the heat to medium. When hot, add the cardamom pods, cloves,

159

cinnamon and bay leaf. Stir and fry for 10–15 seconds or until the spices just turn colour. Add the onion-garlic-ginger paste. Stir and fry over medium-high heat for 3–4 minutes until the oil bubbles at the surface and the paste is light brown in colour. Add the remaining turmeric, the remaining salt and the cayenne pepper. Stir to mix. Gradually add the yoghurt, a teaspoon at a time, stirring continuously until it is incorporated into the sauce. Add the prawns (shrimp) and coconut milk. Stir and gently simmer over medium-low heat for a further 4–5 minutes until the prawns (shrimp) are just cooked through.

The sauce should have the consistency of a puréed soup.

SERVES 6

Maya's Sabji Jhol
ⓥ STRING BEANS WITH POTATOES

AN EVERYDAY DISH, THIS may be served with Deep-Fried Stuffed Breads (page 167) or with rice. It can also be a part of any Indian meal.

❀

4 tablespoons mustard oil or any other vegetable oil	1 medium-sized red onion (75 g/3 oz), finely chopped	450 g/1 lb string beans, cut on the diagonal into
1 tablespoon ground cumin	1 large potato (200 g/7 oz), peeled and cut into 1 cm/	4 cm/1½ inch pieces
3–4 dried hot red chillies	½ inch pieces	¾–1 teaspoon salt

❀

Heat the oil in a large, wide, preferably non-stick pan or wok over high heat. When hot, add the cumin. Stir for a second and add the chillies. Stir for a second and add the onion. Stir and fry over high heat for 2 minutes, until the onion is just beginning to soften. Add the potato. Stir to mix. Reduce the heat to medium low, cover and cook for 4–5 minutes. Add the beans, and salt to taste. Turn the heat up and stir and fry for 3–4 minutes. Reduce the heat and stir and simmer for 2–3 minutes. Remove from the heat and serve.

The beans should be slightly crisp and retain their green colour.

SERVES 4–6

Alu Tikki
ⓥ STUFFED POTATO PATTIES

WITHIN BENGAL THERE IS a vegetarian tradition where no garlic and onions are used and certain vegetables and pulses (legumes) are forbidden. Such food is supposed to be eaten by widows. While many women have followed these rules, they have created from this adversity some of Bengal's most delicious dishes. This is one of them. Serve with a salad or as part of an Indian meal.

❧

4 small-medium (450 g/1 lb) peeled potatoes
1¼ teaspoons salt
1 teaspoon black peppercorns
¼ teaspoon fennel seeds
2.5 cm/1 inch piece of fresh ginger, peeled and finely chopped

5–6 fresh hot green chillies, finely chopped
About 5 tablespoons vegetable oil
50 g/2 oz/½ cup shelled peas (frozen peas, defrosted well, may be used)
50 g/2 oz/⅓ cup grated carrot

50 g/2 oz red pumpkin, peeled and cut into 1 cm/ ½ inch dice
50 g/2 oz/½–¾ cup cauliflower, cut into 1 cm/ ½ inch pieces
½ teaspoon sugar
150 g/5 oz/1 cup plain (all-purpose white) flour

❧

Boil the potatoes until cooked. Mash well with ¾ teaspoon of the salt.

Put the peppercorns and fennel seeds into a clean coffee grinder. Grind to a fine powder.

Put the ginger, chillies and the ground black pepper mixture into the container of an electric blender. Add 100 ml/3½ fl oz/½ cup water. Blend to a fine paste.

Heat 1 tablespoon of the oil in a small pan over medium heat. When hot, add the vegetables, spice paste, remaining salt and the sugar. Stir and fry for 6–8 minutes over medium-low heat until the vegetables are tender. Add a sprinkling of water, if needed, to prevent them sticking. Remove from the heat.

Put the mashed potatoes and cooked vegetables into a bowl. Mix well. Divide the mixture into 4 cm/1½ inch balls. With lightly floured hands flatten each ball to roughly 7.5 cm/3 inch rounds. Coat with the flour.

Heat 3 tablespoons of the oil in a large, wide frying-pan over medium heat. When hot, put in as many of the potato patties as the pan will hold easily in a single layer. Fry for 2–3 minutes on each side until golden and hot in the centre. Make all the patties this way, adding more oil as needed. Serve immediately.

M A K E S   1 0 – 1 2
P A T T I E S

Sonali Basu's Alu Dum

ⓥ WHOLE POTATOES WITH TOMATOES

A SIMPLE, EVERYDAY DISH, eaten both as a snack with Deep-Fried Stuffed Breads (page 167) and as part of a regular lunch, this is made with small, whole potatoes. New potatoes about 2 cm/¾ inch in diameter are ideal. Larger ones may be cut to size. This recipe belongs to the Ghoti tradition of West Bengal.

2 teaspoons mustard oil or any other vegetable oil
¼ teaspoon cumin seeds
3–4 cardamom pods
2.5 cm/1 inch cinnamon stick
1 bay leaf

8–9 small new potatoes (250 g/9 oz), boiled, peeled and left whole
2.5 cm/1 inch piece of fresh ginger, peeled and very finely grated to a pulp

2 large tomatoes, roughly chopped
½–¾ teaspoon salt
1 teaspoon sugar
2 tablespoons finely chopped, fresh green coriander

Heat the oil in a small, preferably non-stick pan over medium heat. When hot, add the cumin, cardamom pods, cinnamon and bay leaf. Stir and fry for 10–20 seconds or until the spices just turn colour. Add the boiled potatoes. Stir to mix. Add the ginger, tomatoes, salt, sugar and 1 tablespoon water.

Reduce the heat to low, cover and cook for 8–10 minutes, shaking the pan occasionally to prevent the potatoes from sticking.

Remove from the heat and garnish with the coriander.

SERVES 2–4

Prawns (Shrimp) Steamed with Mustard Seeds and Coconut (page 158).

Maya's Phulkopir Posto

CAULIFLOWER ENCRUSTED WITH POPPY SEEDS

EAT THIS WITH DEEP-FRIED Stuffed Breads (page 167) as a snack or at lunchtime, or with any Indian meal. When cooking this dish, remember to dry up all the sauce. You may need to adjust your heat to achieve this.

❧

FOR THE SPICE PASTE:
3 dried hot red chillies,
  roughly broken
5 tablespoons white poppy
  seeds

YOU ALSO NEED:
½ teaspoon ground turmeric

1 teaspoon salt
1 teaspoon sugar
1 medium-sized cauliflower,
  cut into chunky 4–5 cm/
  1½–2 inch wide florets
  with minimal stalk (net
  weight 450 g/1 lb)

7 tablespoons mustard oil or
  any other vegetable oil
½ teaspoon *kalonji*
  (page 272)
2 bay leaves
3–4 dried hot red chillies

❧

Put the chillies and poppy seeds for the spice paste into a clean coffee grinder. Grind to a fine powder. Put the powder into a small bowl. Add 6 tablespoons water. Mix well. Set aside.

Rub the turmeric, ½ teaspoon of the salt and ½ teaspoon of the sugar over the cauliflower florets. Set aside.

Heat 4 tablespoons of the oil in a large, wide, preferably non-stick frying-pan or wok over medium-high heat. When hot, add the cauliflower. Stir and fry for 4–5 minutes until the cauliflower just starts to brown. Remove the florets from the pan with a slotted spoon, leaving as much oil behind as possible. Gently shake the florets in kitchen paper (paper towels) to remove the excess oil. Set aside.

Add the remaining oil to the pan and set over medium heat. When hot, add the *kalonji*, bay leaves and chillies. Stir once or twice. Quickly add the spice paste. Stir and fry for 2–3 minutes or until the mixture turns a reddish-brown colour. Add the cauliflower and the remaining salt and sugar. Stir gently to coat the cauliflower with the spices. Add 150 ml/5 fl oz/⅔ cup water. Stir to mix and bring to the boil. Cover, reduce the heat and allow to simmer gently for 10–12 minutes. Stir occasionally to prevent sticking, adding a sprinkling of water when necessary. The sauce should be absorbed and the florets should remain slightly crunchy and be evenly coated with the spices.

SERVES 4–6

Sonali Basu's Tak Dal

⊘ SWEET AND SOUR RED LENTILS

THE GHOTI COMMUNITY OF West Bengal uses a fair amount of sugar in its food. Many of its dishes, such as this *dal*, are sweet and sour. The sourness may be provided by thin slices of raw green mangoes in season or tamarind. Eat this with plain rice and a selection of vegetables and fish.

250 g/9 oz/1¼ cups red lentils
¼ teaspoon ground turmeric
2 tablespoons mustard or any other vegetable oil

½ teaspoon brown mustard seeds
½ teaspoon *panch phoran* (page 275)
4 hot dried red chillies
1 bay leaf

1¼–1½ teaspoons salt
2 tablespoons thick tamarind paste (page 278) or to taste
1 tablespoon sugar or to taste

Wash the lentils in several changes of water until the water runs clear. Put them in a medium-sized pan with the turmeric and mix. Cover with 1 litre/1¾ pints/4½ cups water. Bring the lentils to the boil over medium-high heat. Reduce the heat to low, cover partially and simmer for 40 minutes or until the lentils are tender. Stir now and then during the last 10 minutes. When the lentils are cooked, mash with a spoon to a pulp-like consistency.

Heat the oil in a large, wide, preferably non-stick pan or wok over medium-high heat. When hot, add the mustard seeds. As soon as they pop, a matter of seconds, add the *panch phoran*, chillies and bay leaf. Stir and fry for 5–6 seconds or until the chillies darken in colour. Add the cooked lentils, 150 ml/5 fl oz/⅔ cup water and the salt. Stir to mix. Add the tamarind paste, a little at a time to get the sourness you desire. Add just enough sugar to balance the sourness. Bring to the boil. Turn the heat to low and simmer for 8–10 minutes. The finished *dal* should have the consistency of a thick purée.

SERVES 4

Christine Ward's Bhuna Khichuri
ⓥ STIR-FRIED RICE WITH SPLIT PEAS

KHICHURI, A NOURISHING MIXTURE of rice and split peas, is one of India's oldest dishes, recorded in ancient texts. The Anglo-Indians have also adopted it and this is their version. It may be served with Spicy Steak (page 146), Country Captain (page 149) or with any combination of meat and vegetarian dishes.

∾

Moong dal **measured to the 85 ml/3 fl oz/½ cup plus 1 tablespoon level in a measuring jug**
Basmati rice or any long-grain rice measured to the 450 ml/15 fl oz/2 cup level in a measuring jug

3 tablespoons *ghee* **or vegetable oil**
2 bay leaves
2 cloves

3 cardamom pods
2.5 cm/1 inch cinnamon stick
1 medium-sized red onion (75 g/3 oz), finely sliced
1 teaspoon salt

∾

Wash the *moong dal* in several changes of water until the water runs clear. Soak in water to cover by roughly 10 cm/4 inches for 3–4 hours. Drain.

Wash the rice in several changes of water until the water runs clear. Soak in water to cover by roughly 5 cm/2 inches for 30 minutes. Drain.

Heat the *ghee* in a heavy, medium-sized pan over medium-high heat. When hot, add the bay leaves, cloves, cardamom pods and cinnamon. Stir for a few seconds, until the bay leaves turn colour. Add the onion. Stir and fry over medium heat for 4–5 minutes until the onion is nicely browned. Add the rice, *moong dal* and salt. Stir and fry gently for 1–2 minutes.

Add 600 ml/1 pint/2⅔ cups water. Bring to the boil over high heat. Cover tightly, reduce the heat to very low and allow to cook for 20–25 minutes or until the rice is tender.

Stir gently before serving.

S E R V E S   4 – 6

Sonali Basu's Koraishuti Kachori
⑰ DEEP-FRIED STUFFED BREADS

BENGALIS LIKE THEIR DEEP-FRIED breads made out of white flour. While other northerners eat *pooris* made out of wholewheat flour, Bengalis make very similar breads that they call *loochis* out of plain white flour. Sometimes, these *loochis* are stuffed with crushed peas. They are then called *koraishuti kachori* and are eaten at breakfast or as a mid-morning snack with a vegetable such as Whole Potatoes with Tomatoes (page 162). There are many recipes for both dishes. I like this version of the bread.

FOR THE STUFFING:
100g/4 oz/1 cup shelled green peas (frozen, defrosted peas may be used)
2 cm/¾ inch piece of fresh ginger, peeled and finely sliced
2 fresh hot green chillies, roughly chopped
1½ teaspoons sugar
1 teaspoon salt
4 tablespoons vegetable oil
1 teaspoon *ghee* or vegetable oil
1½ tablespoons plain (all-purpose white) flour
1 tablespoon cumin seeds
1 bay leaf

FOR THE DOUGH:
250 g/9 oz/2 scant cups plain (all-purpose white) flour, plus extra for rolling
½ tablespoon vegetable oil
½ teaspoon salt
½ teaspoon sugar
A pinch of *kalonji* (page 272)
Oil for deep-frying

Make the stuffing: Put the peas, ginger, chillies, sugar and salt into the container of an electric blender. Add 3 tablespoons water. Blend to a purée.

Heat the 4 tablespoons oil and the *ghee* in a large, wide, preferably non-stick pan or wok over medium heat. When hot, add the puréed peas. Stir and fry for 6–8 minutes. Add the 1½ tablespoons flour. Stir and fry for 2 minutes and remove from the heat.

Set a small pan over low heat. When hot, dry roast the cumin seeds and bay leaf for 2 minutes until the cumin seeds turn golden.

Remove from the heat. Put the roasted cumin and bay leaves into a clean coffee grinder. Grind to a fine powder. Add the ground bay leaves and cumin to the puréed peas. Stir to mix. Set aside to cool.

Make the dough: Put the flour, oil, salt, sugar, *kalonji* and 150 ml/5 fl oz/⅔ cup water into a bowl. Mix and knead, using your hands, for about 5 minutes to make a smooth dough. Divide the dough into 15 equal-sized balls. Flatten each ball to a 5 cm/2 inch round. Put 1 teaspoon of the pea purée into the centre of each round. Close the dough around the pea mixture and squeeze the edges to seal the opening well, so that no pea purée will escape. On a lightly floured surface, roll the stuffed dough balls to 13 cm/5 inch circles.

Meanwhile, heat the oil for deep-frying in a wok or frying-pan over medium heat. Let the oil get really hot. Drop in one of the breads carefully, making sure that it does not double over. It should start sizzling immediately. Baste the bread with quick motions, pushing it gently into the oil. It should puff up in seconds. Turn it over and cook for another 30 seconds. Remove with a slotted spoon. Make all the breads this way. Either eat them immediately or stack them on a plate and keep them covered with an inverted plate.

M A K E S   1 5

Christine Ward's Tomato Bharta
Ⓥ STEWED TOMATO RELISH

THIS IS REALLY A kind of tomato salad that is made with very lightly cooked tomatoes. Like a Mexican *salsa* or a North Indian onion and tomato relish, it may be eaten with all Indian meals.

To peel the tomatoes, bring 900 ml/1½ pints/3 cups water to a rolling boil in a pan over high heat. Meanwhile, score the skin of each tomato with a cross at the bottom end. Put the tomatoes into the pan of water for 10 seconds. Remove from the water with a slotted spoon. The skins will be easy to peel.

---

4 large, red-ripe tomatoes, peeled and roughly chopped
1 medium-sized red onion (75 g/3 oz), finely chopped

3 fresh hot green chillies, finely chopped
1 tablespoon finely chopped, fresh green coriander

¼ teaspoon salt
¼ teaspoon sugar

Put the tomatoes into a small, preferably non-stick pan. Stew over medium-low heat for 4–5 minutes, stirring continuously, until a bit soft. Mash lightly with a spoon. Remove from heat. Add the onion, chillies, coriander, salt and sugar. Stir to mix. Check the seasoning.

Cool. The chutney will keep for 3–4 days in a clean air-tight jar in the refrigerator.

3 0 0   M L / 1 0   F L   O Z / 1 ¼   C U P S

Mrs Dasgupta's Aam Jhol
ⓥ COOLING MANGO CHUTNEY

A CROSS BETWEEN A drink and a chutney, this is served in bowls at the end of
a meal in the summer months when green, unripe mangoes are in season.
Unripe, green mangoes can be bought from Indian grocers. Ask for green
pickling mangoes.

**450 g/1 lb green, unripe
mangoes, unpeeled**
1 teaspoon vegetable oil

A generous pinch of *panch
phoran* **(page 275)**

1½ tablespoons sugar
½ teaspoon salt

Cut 2 thick slices, as close to the pit as
possible, off the 2 flatter sides of each mango.
Now cut the side slices off as well. Discard
the pit. Without peeling, cut the slices,
crossways, at 2 cm/¾ inch intervals into thick
slices.

Heat the oil in a large, wide, preferably non-
stick pan or wok over medium heat. When hot,
add the *panch phoran*. Stir for a few seconds.
Add the mangoes. Stir once or twice. Add

300 ml/10 fl oz/1¼ cups water and the sugar
and salt. Bring to the boil. Reduce the heat to
medium and simmer gently for 4–6 minutes
until the mangoes are tender, but not pulp-
like. Remove from the heat. Serve chilled. The
chutney will keep for 48 hours.

M A K E S   9 0 0   M L /
1 ½   P I N T S / 3   C U P S
A N D   S E R V E S   4 – 6

Bhapa Doi
ⓥ STEAMED YOGHURT

ONE OF THE SIMPLEST of Bengali sweets, this is really a yoghurt enriched with
raisins and almonds. Serve it at the end of a meal. It is cool and refreshing.

200 ml/7 fl oz/1 cup canned
  condensed milk
200 ml/7 fl oz/1 cup natural
  (plain) yoghurt

2 tablespoons brown sugar
2 tablespoons raisins,
  soaked in hot water for
  40 minutes and drained

2 tablespoons flaked
  (sliced) almonds

Pre-heat the oven to 150°C/300°F/Gas 4.

Put the condensed milk and yoghurt into a medium-sized bowl. Beat to mix well using a fork. Pour the beaten mixture into a 450 ml/ 15 fl oz/2 cup ovenproof mould or suitable serving dish. Put the dish into a large, deep baking tray. Put enough water into the baking tray to cover the bottom by 5–7.5 cm/ 2–3 inches.

Put the baking tray into the pre-heated oven. Bake for 40–45 minutes or until the steamed yoghurt has just set but has not browned. Sprinkle the top with the sugar, raisins and almonds. Bake for another 3–5 minutes until the sugar caramelizes. Serve hot or chilled.

S E R V E S   4

Rakhi Dasgupta's Aam Kheer

⑦ MANGO PUDDING

A DELIGHTFUL DESSERT, PERFECT after a spicy meal.

1.2 litres/2 pints/5 cups milk
200 g/7 oz/1 cup sugar
100 ml/3½ fl oz/½ cup
  canned condensed milk

4 medium-sized ripe man-
  goes, peeled and with their
  pits removed, cut into
  1 cm/½ inch cubes

Bring the milk to the boil in a thick-bottomed pan over medium-high heat. As soon as it starts to bubble up, turn the heat down a bit to medium. Cook for 30 minutes, stirring regularly. The quantity of milk should reduce

by half. Add the sugar. Stir and boil for a further 5 minutes. Add the condensed milk. Stir and boil for 3–4 minutes. Remove the pan from the heat. Leave to cool. Add the mangoes. Stir to mix. Serve chilled.

Pancakes in Syrup (page 172).

S E R V E S   6

Sunlay Basu's Malpua
ⓥ PANCAKES IN SYRUP

PANCAKES PROBABLY ORIGINATED IN India which has had sugar and wheat flour since ancient times. The *malpua* is one of our oldest sweet pancakes. It is best to use the semolina (*sooji*) that is sold by Indian grocers and not the supermarket semolina used for puddings.

∾

2 teaspoons fennel seeds
150 g/5 oz/1 generous cup plain (all-purpose white) flour

50 g/2 oz/⅓ cup plus 1 tablespoon semolina (page 277)
275 ml/9 fl oz/1 cup plus 2 tablespoons milk

250 g/9 oz/1⅓ cups sugar
300 ml/10 fl oz/1¼ cups oil for deep-frying

∾

Put the fennel seeds into a clean coffee grinder. Grind to a fine powder.

Put the flour, semolina, ground fennel seeds and milk into a medium-sized bowl. Whisk to a smooth batter.

Meanwhile, put the sugar and 200 ml/ 7 fl oz/1 cup water into a heavy-bottomed pan. Boil over medium-high heat, stirring continuously, for 4–5 minutes. The syrup will thicken so that it forms a single thread when a little is dropped from a spoon into a cup of cold water.

Heat the oil for deep-frying in a wok over medium heat. The oil is sufficiently hot when a cube of bread sizzles nicely and turns golden.

Using a ladle, pour roughly 4 tablespoons batter into the hot oil. Allow the batter to sink to the bottom. It will form a circular shape. When it rises to the surface, turn it over and cook for 1–2 minutes until golden. Remove the pancake with a slotted spoon and place it on a large plate.

Repeat the process with the remaining batter, arranging the pancakes in a single layer on a large plate or 2 large plates. Pour the syrup over them. Leave to soak for 1–2 minutes or longer. Serve at room temperature or warmed.

SERVES 4 – 6

Sandesh

FRESH CHEESE SWEETS

THIS IS A VERY basic Bengali sweet, much loved by all and generally bought from sweet-sellers who specialize in it. It is sometimes made with sugar and sometimes with palm jaggery. These days it comes in many flavours, including fresh strawberry! Milk is first curdled into soft curds. These are hung up to drip. The resulting *chhana* is then kneaded, cooked with sugar and finally pressed into pretty moulds shaped like leaves or diamonds.

---

2 litres/3½ pints/8¾ cups full cream (whole) milk

2 tablespoons lemon juice
300 g/11 oz/1⅔ cups sugar

2 tablespoons *ghee*

Bring the milk to a boil. Add the lemon juice and stir. Turn off the heat and leave the milk to curdle. Put a sieve over a large bowl. Line the sieve with a doubled-up piece of cheese-cloth, large enough to tie into a bundle later. Empty the curdled milk – the curds and whey – into the sieve. Let the whey drain into the bowl. You will not need it. Tie the 4 corners of the cheesecloth in such a way that you form a bundle that can be suspended over a sink or bowl. Leave to hang for 7–8 hours until the curds drain and acquire the texture of cottage cheese.

Put the sugar and drained milk on a large plate or chopping board. Mix and knead, using the heels of your hands, for 10–15 minutes. This will break down the lumps and the mixture will become smooth and moist.

Heat a large, wide, preferably non-stick pan or wok over low heat. When hot, add the sugar and milk mixture. Stir and fry for 10–12 minutes. The mixture will cling to the side and have a consistency similar to that of porridge. Spoon the mixture into a tray. Spread it out and leave it to cool.

Using a pastry brush, lightly grease 16 confectioners' sweet moulds or cookie-cutters with the *ghee*. Put a little of the mixture, enough to just fill, into each of the moulds or cutters. Press down firmly. Leave to set in the refrigerator for 15–20 minutes. Remove the sweets from the moulds.

The sweets will keep for up to 2 days in the refrigerator.

MAKES 16 SWEETS

TAMIL NADU

WESTERNERS WHO COME TO Madras, Tamil Nadu's capital city, expecting its cuisine to be a living endorsement of 'Madras' curry powder, will be in for a surprise. Curry powders are indeed manufactured here, mixed in huge machines that look and sound like cement mixers, but they are strictly for export. Not an ounce is for home consumption. It never has been, even though some families have, over several generations, become wealthy on its sale to foreign nations.

The superb foods of southern India are little known in the Western world and nor are its true seasonings, which are quite different from those used in northern India. The highly aromatic mixture of roasted coriander seeds, roasted red chillies and roasted fenugreek, the startling use of *urad dal*, a pulse (legume), as a spice, and its combination with fresh curry leaves and mustard seeds to perk up the simplest of vegetables, the use of fennel seeds in the cooking of meats, the use of fresh coconut to give body and a slight sweetness to sauces and the use of yoghurt, almost as a dressing, for steamed vegetables and rice salads is all very, very southern.

South Indian traders, with easy access to the sea, have carried their foods to the East with more ease than they have to the West. Since ancient times they have had businesses in Singapore, Malaysia and the ports along the South China Sea. Here their foods still flourish as they do at home:

crisp pancakes (*dosas*) sometimes 60 centimetres (2 feet) in diameter, that come all rolled up like precious parchment; fluffy *idlis*, steamed rice cakes whose delicacy is compared to jasmine flowers and whose name can be expressed in the elegant hand gestures of classical South Indian dance; spicy semolina 'polenta' dotted with cut vegetables; young shark's meat that is shredded, sautéed with ginger, shallots and green chillies; soupy *rasams* made with crabs; lamb cooked with fennel seeds and coconut; chicken sautéed with poppy seeds and peppercorns – these are just some of the glories of Tamil Nadu's kitchens.

While meat, poultry and seafood are all eaten, what lies at the very heart of the cuisine of Tamil Nadu are pulses (legumes) and rice. Especially rice.

In a small village west of Madras city, on the way to the ancient temples and rich silks of Kanchipuram, is a long, modest shed. It has been here since the 1930s, performing a crucial function. Using techniques as old as those used to make the rich, gold-threaded silks further along the road, the men and women inside prepare 'boiled' rice. No, this is not rice that is ready to eat. It is par-boiled or 'converted' rice that is crucial to the diet of Tamil Nadu (and, indeed, much of the south) where many people, perhaps as many as one-third of its population, are vegetarian.

Previous page: Hindu temples in Madurai, Tamil Nadu.

When ordinary rice is husked and hulled, it loses a great many of its nutrients. However, if it is par-boiled before it is milled, the B vitamins in the bran and germ get pushed into the grain itself. How this was known 2000 years ago is anybody's guess, but known it was and this ancient treatment of rice, which prevents diseases like beri-beri that plague other rice-eating nations, continues to this day. The methods that are used to par-boil the rice do not seem to have changed much.

The British, under the protection of the East India Company, may have settled here in 1639, building forts, churches and later colleges along the beautiful marina in Madras and the French and the Portuguese may have tried to wrest power, authority and converts from them, but even while the European powers ruled, none of them had any effect on the basic diet of the local people. Rice, mainly 'boiled' rice, remained at its core.

Behind the shed is a large open yard where stalks of rice, hand-cut with a scythe and already dried, are brought in for threshing. Women pass sheaves to the men and the men, in a continuous, fluid motion, hit the sheaves hard against tilted stones. Rice grains come spilling out.

These grains are soaked for a day in outdoor tanks after which they are dropped into a huge, smoke-blackened vat with a few inches of boiling water at the bottom. Once the water comes to a boil again, the actual cooking – steaming really – takes less than 5 minutes. The rice, now smelling like wet, sweet hay, is emptied out on to the ground with buckets. Steam rises as it starts to cool. Two men, one pulling and the other pushing a stubby wooden rake, quickly spread it out. It must dry for 4–5 hours. It is then gathered into heaps, covered with sacks and allowed to 'ripen'. This 'ripening' is essential or the grains will break during the milling. Many simple tests are done. A little rice is removed, rubbed between the palms to remove the husks and then, if the grains remain whole, heads are shaken in approval. The rice is considered ready. Only then, after some more drying, can it be milled, the only part of the process that is now done mechanically.

This par-boiling goes on in every single rice-growing village and in many private homes as well. Rice, both par-boiled and 'raw', is at the heart of every single meal and of every course in every single meal. All else is built up around it.

The gods eat it. At exactly 12 noon in the Varadharaja temple at Kanchipuram, a curtain is pulled in front of the diamond- and gold-encrusted statues of Vishnu and his consort, Lakshmi. It is time for their lunch and they must be allowed to enjoy it in privacy. What they delight in most, it seems, is the Kanchipuram *idli*, a steamed, cylinder-shaped savoury cake made from a batter of rice and *urad dal* that has been flavoured with cumin, peppercorns, ginger and asafetida. Nearby, Lord Shiva and Parvati have their own Ekambareeshwara temple built around an ancient, 3500-year-old (so it is believed) mango tree where, according to legend, they married. The tree bears sweet, sour and bitter mangoes. Shaved pilgrims come here, sacrificing their 'earthly beauty', their hair, to a greater cause. The gods can give them something in return. A child perhaps, if that is what they desire. Shiva and Parvati also dine in privacy. The curtains are drawn and they enjoy hot and tart tamarind rice or sweet 'Pongal' rice, newly harvested grains cooked with cashew nuts and jaggery, a form of raw lump cane sugar.

The Western nutritionists who suggest to us that grains and pulses (legumes) form the major part of our meals should come here to see how it is done. They should, perhaps, visit the family of Mrs A. Santha Ramanujam in Madras.

Shoes are left at the door of this simple, first floor flat. This is a traditional Ayengar family of the upper Brahmin caste, worshippers of Lord Vishnu. Mornings begin with ablutions and prayers. Sacred designs with rice flour are drawn on a part of the floor. 'If she is very good and has done all her homework, I let her make the designs,' a daughter-in-law says of her 10-year-old child. Tradition is being passed on from mother to daughter with gentle enticements. The designs are made not only because they are sacred but because they will provide food for ants and squirrels.

The women of the house have risen at dawn to prepare both breakfast and lunch.

The cooking begins at 6 a.m. when the day is still cool and is finished by 7.30 a.m. First, there are coffee beans to be roasted. People tend not to ask for just 'coffee' when they are buying but rather a specific bean or a chosen combination of beans, all of which grow in the state. This family likes Peaberry beans which sit in a jar, greyish-green and rather sad. They are thrown into a heated, cast-iron wok and roasted slowly. As they are tossed – the process takes 20 minutes – the beans begin to come to life and the come-and-get-it aroma of coffee starts spreading through the house. As soon as they turn brown, a tiny amount of sugar is thrown into the wok. This caramelizes around the beans adding both flavour and colour. The beans are removed, ground and put through a filter. The coffee is strong but it is drunk with at least an equal amount of hot milk and some sugar.

This is very much a coffee-drinking area. Coffee beans were first introduced to India's west coast by early Arab traders. From here, they filtered inland. In those days, many families in the Nilgiri Hills (in western Tamil Nadu) had a couple of coffee trees in their kitchen gardens, enough for their own needs. It was the British who later built large plantations and turned the growing of coffee into a business. It was on some of these large estates, in sprawling bungalows built for bored coffee-planters, that many of the British 'curries' were created, hybrid mixtures of East and West, the kind that contained apples, the kind

that are now found only in the Western world. Such creations could be a wonderful subject for a future book. They do not quite belong here.

Some sons of the Ramanujam household drink quick cups of coffee and dash off to their offices on motor-cycles and scooters, the wind in their faces ameliorating the effects of the heat and Madras traffic. One son opts for a glass of buttermilk (*neer mor*), actually thinned out yoghurt, flavoured with crushed ginger, green chillies, green coriander, curry leaves, ground fenugreek, asafetida and, for good measure, a few rose petals – a heavenly concoction.

Now the women in their cool saris and the children all ribboned and ready for school, sit down to the serious business of a substantial breakfast. The ceiling fan is turned on in the dining-room. Birds chirp loudly in the shady trees outside.

Look at their many choices. They could have *idi appam*, a total delight that is almost unknown in the West or, for that matter, in North India. First you make fresh rice noodles. With the right tools, it is a breeze. Rice has already been washed and dried at home and then sent off to the mill to be ground. This special flour is mixed with boiling water to make a dough with the texture of play dough. Balls of it are put into a wooden press and the press held over

Rice growing by the side of a dam in Tamil Nadu.

an oiled saucer. As you press, thin noodles ooze out. If you move the press in a circular motion, you get a small nest of noodles. Several saucers are filled this way. All are stacked in a steamer and steamed for 5–7 minutes. ('Each plate is only 1 calorie,' the youngest daughter-in-law says brightly.) You add to the calories somewhat by eating these noodles with freshly squeezed, cardamom-flavoured coconut milk or with *ghee* that has been perked up with mustard seeds, *urad dal*, curry leaves and dried red chillies, traditional Tamilian seasonings.

I have already mentioned these seasonings. South Indian cuisine is the only one I know where hulled beans and split peas are used as spices might be. Oil is heated and a mixture of whole spices and split peas are thrown in. As they are stirred around, the split peas become red and give the oil a very pleasant nutty flavour and aroma. The flavoured oil, in turn, completely changes the taste of any food that it touches.

Back to the breakfast. The noodles are one choice. You could have *rava khichri*, a spicy semolina 'polenta' chockful of fresh vegetables, or one of the two dishes for which the south is justly famous – the *idli* or the *dosa*.

Both are made out of rice and *urad dal* batters. The two main ingredients, the rice and the split peas, are soaked and ground separately and then combined and left overnight to bubble, ferment and turn into light, frothy batter. With tropical temperatures set permanently at 'balmy', much of the state uses the climate as a God-given cooking tool. Fermentation takes place easily, tenderizing foods, making them more digestible and cutting down on cooking time. Once the protein-rich batter is ready, it can be poured into a stack of steaming trays with round depressions to make the flying-saucer-shaped, everyday *idlis*; or it can be fermented a bit more and made into the lightest of pancakes, *dosas*, golden-red on one side, pale cream on the other. Both may be eaten with *sambar*, a split pea stew which is varied daily with the addition of, say, caramelized shallots or tomatoes or okra or aubergine (egg plant) poached in tamarind juice. The *dosa* itself can be varied endlessly. Add tomatoes, onions and green chillies to it and it turns into an *utthappam*. Roll it around spicy potatoes and it becomes a *masala dosa*.

The biggest meal of the day in the Ramanujam household is not breakfast but lunch. All the sons come home for it. This is a rice meal. Every course is eaten with 'boiled' (converted) rice, which is cooked just a bit softer than rice is in the North. The grains are white, short, fat and plump. 'We like to mash the other foods into the rice,' the young daughter-in-law with jasmine in her hair explains.

But first of all, a sweet is placed on the plate. This could be a square of a slightly crispy, chick pea flour brittle (*Mysore pak*) or a *halva* made with semolina. Then you are served plain rice and vegetables – cabbage and carrots stir-fried with mustard seeds and curry leaves (*mutta kose kilangu*) or mixed vegetables dressed with a stunning sauce of ground coconut and green chillies (*kurma*) or aubergines (egg plants) or okra or marrow or green plantains, whatever is in season. Then comes *sambar*, the split pea stew. More rice is put on the plate, this to be eaten with *rasam*, a very thin split pea broth. A variety of possible flavourings may be added to it such as black pepper – making it the very health-giving 'pepper-water' (*milagu tanni*), which Anglo-Indians turned into their mulligatawny soup – tomatoes and even garlic, supposed to be perfect for those who have over-indulged. The final course, considered the cleansing one, is yoghurt, rice and pickles, all mixed and eaten together. (Whenever I see Tamils doing this, I think of their similarity to the Japanese, who like to end meals with rice, pickles and tea.) Sometimes the yoghurt and rice are combined in a salad (*bhakala bhat*), with bits of green mango, cucumber, ginger, green chillies and even grapes added to it.

Dinner, like breakfast, is light. 'We generally do not eat rice for dinner,' Mrs Ramanujam explains. Instead, the easy-to-digest fermented foods such as the *idlis* and *dosas* are preferred. With the batter already made in the morning and sitting in a bowl, they take just a few minutes to prepare.

For those who do not like to cook or are too busy, there are vast, fast food restaurants serving the very dishes that vegetarians eat at home. The Hotel Saravana Bhavan in Madras is one such place. It is a sea of people. Each day 4000 customers are served. The kitchen produces 5000 *dosas*. The staff of 300 works in two shifts that go from six in the morning to ten at night.

The work is carried on with great speed. A folded banana leaf is placed before the diner plus a tumbler of water. The leaf is your plate. You unfold it, and sprinkle water on it. It is now considered washed.

Next comes the food. A round metal plate, a *thali*, holds the rice and a set of metal bowls. In the bowls are all the vegetables, *sambars*, *rasams* and freshly made chutneys. On top of all, covering the first layer and forming the basis of a second layer, is a large poppadom. On top of that is the dessert, generally a squiggly, orange *jahangiri* (similar to the northern *jalebi*) all filled with oozing syrup. This is a fast food joint and you are supposed to undo the layers and arrange the food on the banana leaf yourself. Fresh rice appears just when you are eating what seems to be the last mouthful. When you finish, you fold up your banana leaf again. It is picked up by a wandering youth and dropped into a pail. You get up. The next diner is hovering and immediately sits down in your place. A fresh banana leaf appears. Hotel Saravana Bhavan has nine branches and they all do a roaring business in the city.

What if you wish to eat at home but do not want to make, say, the scrumptious coconut rice from scratch? A shop near the

Mylapore temple sells all the spice mixtures needed to make coconut rice, tamarind rice, lime rice and all manner of crisp nibbles which Tamils like to mix in with their rice – giant poppadums the size of elephant feet as well as dozens of varieties of pickles. If you wait a while, a new vending machine is also on its way, already working feverishly in test kitchens. It will cook and serve 50 *dosas* in 75 seconds and also pour out the *sambar* – and coconut chutney! Life in Madras, for those with power or money, is on the fast track!

Not everyone in the state is vegetarian and many will never get on the fast track. Thousands of betel-nut-chewing fishermen with gleaming black skin and worn teeth go out to sea daily with the tide. Their simple catamarans, consisting of seven to eight carved, tapering logs tied up with rope, look exactly the same as they do in seventeenth-century prints and paintings. They can be seen on the waters off South Beach Road where the British built the grand Fort S't George and S't Mary's Church (Robert Clive and Elihu Yale both married here and went on to amass great wealth). The fishermen live on their humble catches – sometimes a single crab poached in spiced-up tamarind juice or a baby shark boiled up with salt and chillies, all to be eaten with rice.

Not far from them live some other non-vegetarians with fuller coffers. Just look at the Chettiars of the formerly royal state of Chettinad who eat, with great enjoyment, some of the most exquisite meat, chicken and fish dishes in the region. It is worth visiting one of their major residences in Madras.

In the choicest of locations, just where the Adyar River meets the Bay of Bengal, is a large palace. Its many acres double as a bird sanctuary. It once belonged to Rajah Sir Annamalai Chettiar. His descendants live there now, two of them served by 127 servants.

The spacious rooms are lined with Italian marble floors. The high ceilings and doors are carved from solid Burma teak, acquired in Burma, along with vast fortunes, when the Chettiar men went to work there in the last several centuries. (The women always stayed in India.) No one is allowed to forget what they were born to do. Their motto, 'Strive, save and serve', is everywhere.

What they mainly strove to do was make money. The Chettiars, a trading community, were always money-lenders and bankers. Today, they are major industrialists as well. They are canny, not only at making money but at keeping it in the family. Marriage takes place between first cousins, ensuring that the bride's dowry of diamonds, rubies and sapphires, of dozens and dozens of rich silk saris, of rooms filled with silver utensils and cut glass and carpets, never travels too far from home!

In a palace lined with photographs of racing horses and garlanded portraits of sober-faced forebears, Rajah Sir Annamalai

Banana leaves being used as plates in Tamil Nadu.

Chettiar's descendants enjoy meals served by discreet family retainers on silver *thalis* as solid as their owners' bank accounts. The food, a combination of traditional vegetarian fare as well as Chicken Pepper Fry (chicken cooked with lots of black pepper and red chillies) and egg *kurma* (hard-boiled eggs in a gorgeous coconut-chilli sauce) and *eraichi kolumbu* (lamb in a fennel-flavoured coconut sauce), is pre-pared with great care. Chettiars love to eat.

Even though wealthy Chettiars can buy every kitchen gadget ever made, they insist that their cooks grind all the spices on stone and cook over wood fires. 'Food tastes better this way,' a Chettiar housewife explains. With their wealth, the Chettiars can buy or grow the choicest ingredients.

For *meen varuval* (spicy, pan-fried fish steaks), prepared in a Chettiar kitchen, the kingfish has just came out of the Bay of Bengal that morning and the coriander seeds were grown on the home farm. The barefoot cook, his white *veshti* (sarong) doubled up for convenience so it comes only to his knees, first cuts a whole fish at a slight diagonal to get long steaks. 'I will start at the tail and stop when I reach the start of the cleaned stomach,' he says. He wants only those steaks that are perfect ovals. What the rest of the fish will be used for is hard to say.

Several fish are needed to get the requisite number of steaks. The steaks are dipped in a paste of ground coriander, cayenne, turmeric, cumin, salt and fresh lime juice, left to marinate for a few hours and then quickly pan-fried in a heavy frying-pan lightly brushed with oil. They are cooked on wood. Of course.

British buildings, such as the Ice House which stored the ice that came all the way from Boston to cool British drinks and help make English puddings, still dominate the Madras waterfront. Every educated Tamil is versed in English literature and in Western sciences. But his food remains completely South Indian. I remember one young man waxing rhapsodic about *sundal*, a spicy salad made with boiled peanuts, tomatoes and shallots. He added, with some passion. 'What can be better on a rainy day than settling down comfortably with a hot cup of home-made coffee, some *sundal* and a book by P. G. Wodehouse!'

While some Tamils may have international preoccupations, they ultimately belong to Tamil Nadu with its ancient, very Indian traditions of glorious music, sculptured temples, sensuous, energetic dance, shimmering silks and delicious local foods.

Mrs A. Santha Ramanujam's Sundal
ⓥ MUNCHABLE PEANUT SALAD

FOR MOST VEGETARIANS IN Tamil Nadu, peanuts form an important part of the diet. Plain boiled peanuts, sprinkled with just a little salt and cayenne pepper, are sold from small wooden carts by eager vendors. They are plain and good. This is a somewhat more elaborate version of the same idea. *Sundals* with variations in seasonings can be made out of soaked and boiled beans, chick peas and dried peas, even split peas. They are sold in the evenings on the beach.

I like to put a bowl out for people to nibble with drinks. I also leave several teaspoons for people to dig in with. Nothing is fried here so this makes for a nutritious snack food as well.

---

200 g/7 oz/1½ cups raw, shelled, skinless peanuts
1½–2 teaspoons salt or to taste

4 shallots (50 g/2 oz), peeled and cut into fine slivers
2 medium-sized tomatoes, finely chopped

2¼ teaspoons cayenne pepper
4 tablespoons lime juice

Soak the peanuts in warm water to cover for 1 hour. Drain. Put the peanuts in a saucepan. Add water to cover well. Add 1 teaspoon of the salt and bring to the boil. Cover, turn the heat down and cook for about 20 minutes or until the peanuts are tender. Drain.

Put the peanuts in a bowl.

Add all the remaining ingredients, using just as much salt as is needed for a good balance of salt and sour. Mix well.

S E R V E S   6

From the home of A. C. Muthiah: Eraichi Kolumbu

LAMB IN A FENNEL-FLAVOURED COCONUT SAUCE

PERHAPS ONE OF THE best lamb dishes of the south, this Chettiar speciality has a sauce with the consistency of a cream soup. Its natural thickening comes from a ground paste of ginger, garlic, coconut, onions and tomatoes as well as a host of ground spices such as poppy seeds and coriander. It is heavenly when eaten with plain rice. Any vegetables from the north or south may be served on the side, with a yoghurt relish and perhaps some poppadoms and pickles.

The original recipe called for 2½ tablespoons cayenne pepper. I have used only one and added extra paprika to give thickness to the sauce.

This dish is quite hot. If you wish to make it milder, decrease the cayenne and increase the paprika proportionately.

If you wish to subsititue unsweetened desiccated coconut for fresh coconut use 40 g/1½ oz/7 tablespoons. Barely cover with warm water and leave for 1 hour, then proceed with the recipe.

❧

FOR THE SPICE POWDER:
1 tablespoon fennel seeds
1 tablespoon poppy seeds
3 tablespoons ground
  coriander
1 tablespoon cayenne
  pepper
1 tablespoon paprika
½ teaspoon ground turmeric

FOR THE SPICE PASTE:
8–10 garlic cloves, peeled

7.5 cm/3 inch piece of fresh
  ginger, peeled and coarsely
  chopped
75 g/3 oz/¾ cup freshly
  grated coconut (page 265)

YOU ALSO NEED:
6 tablespoons vegetable oil
¼ teaspoon fennel seeds
3 bay leaves
4 cardamom pods
5 cm/2 inch cinnamon stick
20 fresh curry leaves, if
  available

2 medium-sized onions
  (175 g/6 oz), peeled and
  chopped
2 medium-sized tomatoes,
  chopped
1½–1¾ teaspoons salt
1 kg/2¼ lb lamb from the
  shoulder and neck with or
  without bone as preferred,
  cut into 4 cm/1½ inch
  pieces
2 tablespoons chopped,
  fresh green coriander

Put the fennel seeds and poppy seeds into a clean coffee grinder and grind until you have a fine powder. Empty into a bowl. Add the coriander, cayenne pepper, paprika and turmeric. Mix and set aside.

In the container of an electric blender combine the garlic, ginger and coconut. Add 200 ml/7 fl oz/1 cup water. Blend until you have a smooth paste, scraping down with a rubber spatula when necessary. This is the spice paste.

Heat the 6 tablespoons oil in a heavy, well-seasoned wok or a large, wide, preferably non-stick pan over medium-high heat. When hot, put in the ¼ teaspoon fennel seeds, bay leaves, cardamom pods and cinnamon. Stir once or twice and put in the curry leaves. Stir once and put in the onions. Stir and fry until the onions soften a bit and begin to turn brown at the edges. Put in the tomatoes. Stir and fry until the tomatoes soften. Now put in the coconut spice paste, spice powder and salt. Stir and fry for 5–6 minutes, sprinkling in a little water if it seems to stick. Put in the lamb. Stir and cook for 2–3 minutes. Now add 900ml/ 1½ pints/3¾ cups water. Bring to the boil. Cover, turn the heat down to a simmer and cook for 60–70 minutes or until the lamb is tender. If the sauce is too watery, turn the heat up and reduce it to the consistency of thick cream soup.

Sprinkle the fresh coriander on the top before serving.

S E R V E S   4 – 6

Eraichi Porial
LAMB PEPPER-FRY

THIS FRAGRANT MEAT DISH can be served with any plain or seasoned rice. If you wish to substitute unsweetened, desiccated coconut for fresh coconut use 60 g/2 oz/⅔ cup. Just cover with warm water and leave for 1 hour then proceed with the recipe.

FOR THE DRY SPICE
MIXTURE:
1 tablespoon coriander
   seeds
1 teaspoon black
   peppercorns
1 tablespoon fennel seeds
5 dried hot red chillies

FOR THE SPICE PASTE:
2 tablespoons vegetable oil
2 medium-sized onions
   (180 g/6 oz), peeled and
   chopped

6 garlic cloves, peeled and
   chopped
1 cm/½ inch piece of fresh
   ginger, peeled and chopped
4–5 fresh hot green chillies,
   coarsely chopped
115 g/4 oz/1 cup freshly
   grated coconut (page 265)

YOU ALSO NEED:
4 tablespoons vegetable oil
2.5 cm/1 inch cinnamon
   stick
1 large onion (175 g/6 oz),
   sliced into very fine half-
   rings
900 g/2 lb boned lamb from
   the shoulder, cut into
   2.5 cm/1 inch cubes
2 large tomatoes, chopped
1½ teaspoons salt

Set a small, cast-iron frying-pan over medium heat. When hot, put in all the ingredients for the dry spice mixture. Stir and fry for 2–3 minutes or until they turn a few shades darker and smell roasted. Cool a bit and then grind in a clean coffee grinder.

Heat the 2 tablespoons oil for the spice paste in a large, preferably non-stick, frying-pan over medium-high heat. When hot, put in the onions, garlic, ginger and green chillies. Stir and fry until the onions brown a bit. Put in the coconut. Continue to stir and fry until the coconut browns as well. Empty the contents of this pan into the container of a food processor. Add 100 ml/3½ fl oz/½ cup water and blend to a paste. Set aside.

Heat the 4 tablespoons oil in a large, preferably non-stick pan over medium-high heat. When hot, put in the cinnamon. Stir once and put in the large onion sliced into half-rings. Stir and fry until the onion is browned. Add the meat. Stir and fry for 10 minutes. Add the tomatoes, the dry spice mixture, the spice paste and the salt. Stir and cook for 5 minutes. Add 450 ml/15 fl oz/2 cups water and bring to the boil. Cover, turn the heat down to low and simmer gently for 60–70 minutes or until the lamb is tender. Uncover and boil away most of the liquid over high heat. The sauce should cling to the meat.

SERVES 6

From the home of A. C. Muthiah: Koli Milagu Masala
CHETTINAD PEPPER CHICKEN

ANOTHER EXQUISITE DISH FROM the Chettiar community, this is generally served with plain rice. It may also be served with Rice and Split Pea Pancakes (page 201) and Savoury Rice Cakes (page 204), even Savoury Rice Breads (page 39), but in that case it is a good idea to keep the sauce a bit thinner so it can be sopped up.

What gives the dish a very special southern flavour is the use of fennel seeds, curry leaves and, of course, the pulse (legume), *urad dal*. This is definitely a dish you will want to make very frequently.

❧

5 tablespoons oil

FOR THE SPICE PASTE:
1½ tablespoons cumin seeds
8–10 dried hot red chillies, broken into halves
3 tablespoons coriander seeds
1½ teaspoons fennel seeds
1½ teaspoons black peppercorns
1½ teaspoons white poppy seeds
5 garlic cloves, peeled and roughly chopped

4 cm/1½ inch piece of fresh ginger, peeled and roughly chopped
½ teaspoon ground turmeric
1½ –2 teaspoons salt

YOU ALSO NEED:
3 bay leaves
5 cardamom pods
2.5 cm/1 inch cinnamon stick, broken
1 teaspoon fennel seeds
3 cloves
1½ teaspoons *urad dal* (page 261)

15–20 fresh curry leaves, if available
2 medium-sized onions (175 g/6 oz), peeled and finely chopped
1 large tomato, chopped
One 1 kg/2¼ lb chicken, skinned and cut into smallish serving pieces (breast halves into 3 and legs into drumsticks and thighs)

❧

Make the spice paste: In a small frying-pan, heat 1 tablespoon of the oil over medium-high heat. When hot add the cumin seeds, chillies, coriander seeds, fennel seeds, black peppercorns and poppy seeds. Stir and fry briefly until lightly roasted. Now, put these into a clean coffee grinder and grind to a powder. Empty into the container of an electric blender. Put the garlic, ginger, turmeric and salt into the blender as well, along with 6–8 tablespoons water. Process until you have a fine paste, pushing down with a rubber spatula if needed. Set aside.

Heat the remaining 4 tablespoons oil in a

large saucepan over medium-high heat. When hot, add the bay leaves, cardamom pods, cinnamon, fennel seeds, cloves and *urad dal*. Stir and fry briefly until the *urad dal* turns red, then add the curry leaves if using. Stir once or twice and add the onions. Fry the onions until they are soft and just lightly coloured. Now add the spice paste. Continue to stir and fry for about 4–6 minutes, adding a little water to prevent sticking. Add the tomato. Stir and fry for a further 3–4 minutes.

Add the chicken pieces to the onion and spice mixture. Stir until they are well coated, then add 600 ml/1 pint/2½ cups water, just enough to cover. Bring to the boil. Turn the heat to low, cover and simmer until the chicken is almost cooked, about 20–25 minutes.

Using a slotted spoon, remove the chicken pieces. Turn the heat up to medium-high, and reduce the sauce until very thick. This should take about 6–8 minutes. Replace the chicken, fold gently into the sauce and cook for a further 5 minutes before serving.

SERVES 4 – 6

Lamb in a Fennel-flavoured Coconut Sauce (page 186).

From the Dakshin restaurant at the Park Sheraton: Koli Uppakari

GINGER CHICKEN WITH MUSTARD SEEDS

THIS CHETTIAR RECIPE, FROM chef Praveen Anand, is easy to prepare and utterly scrumptious. It does require a marination period. Overnight is ideal but 3–4 hours will do. After marinating in ginger juice, the chicken pieces are stir-fried in a wok with very South Indian seasonings such as mustard seeds, *urad dal* and fennel seeds. When it is ready, the chicken turns reddish-brown on the outside, is encrusted with spices and is meltingly tender inside.

In the south it is eaten with rice but you may serve this with any Indian bread. You may use any chicken pieces for this dish, though the thigh is ideal. Since the pieces need to be small each thigh should be cut into two pieces. It is best if you ask the butcher to do this. If you wish to do it yourself, use a sharp, heavy cleaver, aim well at the centre of the thigh bone and hit hard once.

---

550 g/1¼ lb skinned chicken
  thighs, each cut into
  2 pieces
¼ teaspoon ground turmeric
1¼–1½ teaspoons salt
7.5 cm/3 inch piece of fresh
  ginger, peeled
4–5 tablespoons vegetable
  oil
4–5 dried hot red chillies,
  each broken into
  2–3 pieces

¾ teaspoon brown mustard
  seeds
¾ teaspoon *urad dal*
  (page 261)
½ teaspoon fennel seeds
2 small cinnamon sticks
5–6 garlic cloves, peeled and
  finely chopped
1 medium-sized onion
  (75 g/3 oz), peeled and
  sliced into fine half-rings

2 medium-sized tomatoes,
  peeled and chopped
½ teaspoon cayenne pepper
Lots of freshly ground black
  pepper
Wedges of red-ripe
  tomatoes, and chopped
  fresh coriander for
  sprinkling over the top
  (optional)

Put the chicken pieces into a bowl. Add the turmeric and 1 teaspoon of the salt. Now, either grate the ginger on the finest part of the grater or else chop it finely and put it into the container of an electric blender along with 1 tablespoon water and blend to a paste. Using your hand, squeeze the juice from the ginger over the chicken. (Discard the pulp.) Mix the chicken with the ginger juice. Cover the chicken and refrigerate for 3–4 hours or overnight.

Heat the oil in a wok or a large, preferably

non-stick frying-pan over medium-high heat. When hot, put in the red chillies, mustard seeds, *urad dal*, fennel seeds and cinnamon. Stir for a few seconds or until the chillies turn dark and the mustard seeds pop. Now put in the garlic. Stir once or twice. Put in the onion. Stir and sauté until the onion is soft and just starting to turn brown. Put in the tomatoes. Stir and fry for 2–3 minutes or until the tomatoes are soft. Now put in the chicken with its marinade juices, cayenne pepper and the remaining salt. Stir and fry on highish heat

until the chicken has browned. This will take about 6 minutes. Cover, turn the heat to low and cook for another 10–12 minutes, stirring now and then until the chicken is done. Remove the cover and sprinkle in lots of freshly ground black pepper. If there is any liquid left in the pan, turn the heat up and dry it off before serving.

Sprinkle the fresh coriander over the top and serve with the tomato wedges if you wish.

S E R V E S   3 – 4

From the home of A. C. Muthiah: Koli Kurma

EGGS IN A GREEN CHILLI-COCONUT SAUCE

A CHETTIAR DISH WITH a sauce to swoon over, this can also be made with chicken or even small, halved, slightly sautéed aubergines (eggplants). Keep the sauce somewhat thicker and more paste-like for the chicken and aubergines (eggplants). This is generally served with plain rice or with Savoury Rice Cakes (page 204) or Rice and Split Pea Pancakes (page 205). It may also be served with Savoury Rice Breads (page 39).
If you wish to substitute unsweetened desiccated coconut for fresh coconut use 50 g/2 oz/⅔ cup. Just cover with warm water and leave for 1 hour, then proceed with the recipe.

FOR THE SPICE PASTE:

6 raw cashew nuts, split into halves lengthways

2 tablespoons fennel seeds

2 teaspoons roasted *chana dal* (page 260)

5–8 fresh hot green chillies, coarsely sliced

4 garlic cloves, peeled

5 cm/2 inch piece of fresh ginger, peeled and coarsely chopped

100 g/4 oz/1 cup freshly grated coconut (page 265)

YOU ALSO NEED:

4 tablespoons vegetable oil or *ghee*

2 bay leaves

Two 2.5 cm/1 inch cinnamon sticks

5 cardamom pods

1 fresh hot green chilli, cut into 3 segments

2 medium-sized onions (175 g/6 oz), peeled and finely chopped

1¼–1½ teaspoons salt

6–8 hard-boiled eggs

2 tablespoons chopped, fresh green coriander

Make the spice paste: Put the cashew nuts, fennel seeds and roasted *chana dal* into a clean coffee grinder and grind finely. Empty the contents of the coffee grinder into the container of an electric blender. Add the chillies, garlic, ginger, coconut and 100 ml/3½ fl oz/½ cup water. Grind to a paste.

Heat the 4 tablespoons oil in a large, wide, preferably non-stick pan over medium-high heat. When hot, put in the bay leaves, cinnamon and cardamom pods. Stir and fry for 10 seconds. Put in the green chilli. Stir and fry until it softens. Add the onions. Stir and fry until they begin to soften and brown at the edges. Add the spice paste. Stir and fry for

2–3 minutes. Add the salt and 250 ml/8 fl oz/1 cup water. Bring to the boil. Reduce the heat to medium-low and simmer for 7–8 minutes.

Meanwhile, make a 5 cm/2 inch incision arching over the top of each egg and going only as deep as its yolk. Do the same around the tip of each egg but at a right angle to the top incision.

When the sauce has finished cooking, drop the eggs into it and bring to the boil. Turn off the heat. Let the eggs sit in the sauce for at least 2 hours before serving. Sprinkle the fresh coriander over the top.

SERVES 3 – 4

From the home of A. C. Muthiah: Meen Varuval
SPICY, PAN-FRIED FISH STEAKS CHETTINAD

KINGFISH STEAKS ARE ENCRUSTED with simple spices – coriander and chillies mixed into a paste with salt and lime juice – and then quickly pan-fried. Nothing could be simpler or better. It helps if the coriander seeds are freshly ground and sifted as they have a wonderful aroma. A fresh packet of ground coriander from your Indian grocer will also be very good.

You may serve this as part of a rice-based meal, as they do in Chettiar homes, or you may serve it Western style, with plain boiled potatoes and a vegetable or a salad. You might like to try it with Potatoes with Mustard Seeds and Onions (page 200) and a green salad. In spite of the rather large quantity of cayenne pepper, this dish has medium heat.

Seer fish – kingfish – is commonly used for this dish. You could also use swordfish steaks or mackerel steaks cut at a diagonal. (The steaks look much larger this way. They are traditionally cut from between the tail and the stomach.)

❧

2½ tablespoons ground coriander

2½ tablespoons cayenne pepper

½ teaspoon ground turmeric

1 teaspoon ground cumin

2 teaspoons salt

5–6 teaspoons lime juice or lemon juice

Four 1 cm/½ inch thick kingfish steaks

About 3 tablespoons vegetable oil

Extra lime or lemon wedges for serving

❧

Combine the coriander, cayenne pepper, turmeric, cumin, salt and lime or lemon juice on a large plate and mix. Add about 6 table-spoons water to make a thick paste. Taste for balance of sour and salt. The paste should be fairly salty at this stage. Rub the fish steaks on both sides with the paste and set aside for 15 minutes. (You could marinate them for up to 3 hours. Refrigerate in that case.)

Rub the bottom of a heavy frying-pan with a little of the oil and set over medium-high heat. When hot, put in as many steaks as the pan will hold in a single layer. Cook the steaks for about 6–8 minutes on each side, or until they are nicely browned and just cooked through. Do all steaks this way, adding more oil as needed.

Serve with the lime or lemon wedges.

SERVES 4

From the home of A. C. Muthiah: Sora Puttu

SHARK WITH SPICES AND FRESH CORIANDER

THIS RECIPE COMES FROM the kitchen of a princely Chettiar home. The flaked flesh of baby sharks can be cooked so that it remains moist but it can also be stirred and stirred until the flakes turn crisp. This recipe is the second version. Generally, it is mixed with plain rice and eaten with a *sambar* (see Split Peas with Shallots, page 202). If you cannot get shark, use fresh tuna or swordfish. If you wish to substitute unsweetened, desiccated coconut for fresh coconut use 50 g/2 oz/⅔ cup. Barely cover with warm water and leave for 1 hour. Squeeze dry and proceed with the recipe.

---

450 g/1 lb shark, the younger the better, cut into thick steaks
2 teaspoons salt
1 teaspoon ground turmeric
5 tablespoons vegetable oil
2.5 cm/1 inch cinnamon stick, broken
8–10 shallots (125 g/5 oz), finely chopped

½ teaspoon fennel seeds
2 cm/1½ inch piece of fresh ginger, finely chopped or grated
4–5 fresh hot green chillies, cut into fine half-rounds
5 garlic cloves, finely chopped

20 fresh curry leaves, if available
100 g/4 oz/1 cup freshly grated coconut (page 265)
2 tablespoons chopped, fresh green coriander, plus extra for garnishing
2 teaspoons lemon juice

Put the shark, 1 teaspoon of the salt and the turmeric in a large saucepan with 1 litre/1¾ pints/4½ cups water. Bring to the boil over medium heat. Reduce the heat to a gentle simmer. Cook for 15–20 minutes until the shark is tender. Drain and allow to cool. Remove the skin and cartilage of the shark and flake. Put in a large bowl and set aside.

Heat the oil in a large frying-pan over medium-high heat. When hot, add the cinnamon, shallots and fennel seeds. Stir and fry for 4–5 minutes or until the shallots are golden. Add the ginger, chillies and garlic. Stir and fry until lightly browned and softened. Add the remaining salt and the flaked shark. Stir and fry briskly for 10–15 minutes.

Add the curry leaves, coconut and 2 table-spoons coriander. Cook until dry. Just before serving, add the lemon juice. Serve hot, garnished with the remaining coriander.

SERVES 4–6

Mrs A. Santha Ramanujam's Mutta Kose Kilangu

STIR-FRIED CABBAGE AND CARROTS

STRANGELY ENOUGH, WHEN TAMILS speaking English refer to a curry they mean a dry dish, totally devoid of any sauce. This is one such 'curry'. You could cook the cabbage plain, or with carrots as I have done here, or with the addition of shelled peas. A similar dish can be made out of green beans, boiled beetroots and the pear-shaped green vegetable called 'chow chow' and known more correctly as the chayote or sayote.

If you wish to substitute unsweetened, desiccated coconut for fresh coconut use 30 g/1 oz/5 tablespoons. Barely cover with warm water and soak for 1 hour, then proceed with the recipe.

This dish may be served with all Indian meals.

❧

3 tablespoons vegetable oil
1½ teaspoons *chana dal* (page 260)
1½ teaspoons *urad dal* (page 261)
1 teaspoon mustard seeds

20 fresh curry leaves, if available
2–4 fresh hot green chillies, cut into long slivers
200 g/7 oz dark green cabbage, finely shredded

2 medium-sized carrots (200g/7 oz), coarsely grated
¾–1 teaspoon salt
50 g/2 oz/½ cup freshly grated coconut (page 265)

❧

Heat the oil in a large frying-pan over medium-high heat. When hot, add the *chana dal, urad dal* and mustard seeds. Stir and fry until the mustard seeds pop and the *dals* turn reddish, a matter of seconds. Add the curry leaves. Stir for a few seconds. Add the chillies and stir once. Now add the cabbage and carrots. Stir once to mix. Add the salt and mix again.

Cover, turn the heat to low and cook for 5–6 minutes or until the cabbage is wilted and just tender.

Remove the cover. Add the coconut and mix it in with the cabbage, stirring vigorously for a minute or so.

SERVES 4

Shoba Ramji's Vendaka Pakoda

ⓥ DEEP-FRIED OKRA IN BATTER

CRISP, DEEP-FRIED CLUMPS OF sliced okra in batter are often served as part of a meal. Crunchy foods are enjoyed here with the blander rice. I like to serve them with drinks or with tea. The rice flour in the batter keeps them very crisp.

❧

225 g/8 oz fresh okra
100 g/4 oz/¾ cup chick pea
  flour
1½ tablespoons rice flour
  (also called ground rice)

1 tablespoon cayenne
  pepper
1¼ teaspoons salt
1 teaspoon ground turmeric

1 tablespoon vegetable oil
  plus extra vegetable oil for
  deep-frying
¼ teaspoon *ajwain* seeds
  (page 259), optional

❧

Gently wipe the okra with a lightly dampened cloth and cut into 1 cm/½ inch thick rounds. Set aside.

Sift the chick pea flour, rice flour, cayenne pepper, salt and turmeric into a medium-sized bowl. Rub in the 1 tablespoon oil to get a coarse breadcrumb consistency. Add the *ajwain* seeds, if you are using them, and mix them in. Add about 100 ml/3½ fl oz/½ cup water, a little at a time, to make a paste about the consistency of double (thick, heavy) cream. Make sure there are no lumps.

Heat the oil in a deep frying-pan or wok over medium-low heat. When it is hot enough for a cube of bread to sizzle nicely and turn golden-brown, fold the okra gently into the batter. With a tablespoon take small dollops of the okra and batter and gently drop into the oil. Fry, turning now and then, until the fritters are crisp and golden. This will take about 6–7 minutes.

Serve immediately.

SERVES 4

Chettinad Pepper Chicken (page 189).

Shoba Ramji's Urala Kilangu
Ⓥ POTATOES WITH MUSTARD SEEDS AND ONIONS

EACH HOUSEHOLD IN TAMIL Nadu – indeed in all of India – must have several dozen potato recipes, each one better than the next. This particular dish has onions and tomatoes in it. Serve it with any Indian meal. I even love to serve it with a Sunday leg of lamb or with grilled (broiled) sausages.

❧

3–4 tablespoons vegetable oil

1 teaspoon brown mustard seeds

2 tablespoons *urad dal* (page 261)

2–3 dried hot red chillies, broken into halves

20–25 fresh curry leaves, if available

2 medium-sized onions (175g/6 oz), peeled, quartered and finely sliced

1–1¼ teaspoons salt

½ teaspoon ground turmeric

¼–½ teaspoon cayenne pepper

450 g/1 lb potatoes, peeled and cut into 1 cm/½ inch dice

1 medium-sized tomato, chopped

A pinch of ground asafetida

❧

Heat the oil in a well-seasoned wok or a large, preferably non-stick frying-pan over medium-high heat. When hot, put in the mustard seeds, *urad dal* and chillies. Stir until the mustard seeds pop and the *dal* turns red, a matter of seconds. Put in the curry leaves. Stir once or twice. Now put in the onions. Stir and fry until the onions just begin to turn brown at the edges. Put in the salt, turmeric and cayenne pepper. Stir for 5 seconds. Add the potatoes. Stir and fry for a minute. Add the tomato and asafetida. Stir and fry for a minute. Now put in about 275 ml/9 fl oz/1 cup plus 2 tablespoons water and bring to a boil. Cover, turn the heat to medium and cook fairly vigorously for about 10 minutes or until the potatoes are just tender and the water is absorbed. You may have to adjust the heat. Remove the cover. Stir and fry the potatoes on medium-low heat for 4-5 minutes to get a rich reddish-yellow colour.

SERVES 6

Mrs A. Santha Ramanujam's Kurma

☞ MIXED VEGETABLE CURRY

NOTHING COULD BE SIMPLER or, for that matter, more delicious. Vegetables, whatever happens to be in season, are lightly par-boiled or steamed and then 'dressed' with a ground paste of fresh coconut, poppy seeds and green chillies. The 'dressing' is not just poured over the top. Instead, it is cooked briefly with the vegetables so that it is absorbed by them. This is best with plain rice. You could serve it as part of a larger meal with Ginger Chicken with Mustard Seeds (page 192) and a relish, such as Sweet Beetroot (Beet) Chutney (page 209). If you wish to substitute unsweetened, desiccated coconut for fresh coconut use 30 g/1 oz/5 tablespoons. Barely cover with warm water and leave for 1 hour, then proceed with the recipe.

❧

½ medium-sized (100 g/4 oz) aubergine (eggplant) cut into 2 cm × 1 cm (¾ inch × ½ inch) sticks
2 small carrots (100 g/4 oz), peeled and cut into 2 cm × 1 cm (¾ × ½ inch) sticks
100 g/4 oz/1 cup peas
100 g/4 oz French beans, cut into 2.5 cm/1 inch pieces

1 medium-sized potato (100 g/4 oz), peeled and cut into 2 cm × 1 cm (¾ × ½ inch) sticks
50 g/2 oz/½ cup freshly grated coconut (page 265)
4 fresh hot green chillies
2 tablespoons white poppy seeds

1¼ teaspoons salt
3 medium-sized tomatoes, roughly chopped
1 tablespoon natural (plain) yoghurt
1 teaspoon *garam masala* (page 270)
2 tablespoons chopped, fresh green coriander

❧

Place the aubergine (eggplant), carrots, peas, French beans and potato in a medium-sized saucepan. Add 250 ml/8 fl oz/1 cup water. Bring to the boil. Cover, turn the heat to medium and cook for 4 minutes or until the vegetables are just tender.

Meanwhile put the coconut, chillies, poppy seeds and salt in the container of an electric blender. Add 150 ml/5 fl oz/⅔ cup water and grind to a fine paste. Set aside.

When the vegetables are cooked, add the spice paste and another 150 ml/5 fl oz/⅔ cup water. Stir and simmer gently for 5 minutes. Now add the tomatoes, the yoghurt and the *garam masala*. Stir gently to mix well. Bring to the boil and simmer gently for 2–3 minutes. Turn into a serving dish and garnish with the fresh coriander.

S E R V E S   4 – 6

Mrs A. Santha Ramanujam's Vengayam Sambar

ⓥ SPLIT PEAS WITH SHALLOTS

SAMBAR AND RICE ARE the meat and potatoes of Tamil Nadu. Plain *toovar dal* is first boiled. It is then made deliciously sour with tamarind paste and exquisitely spicy with the addition of a special *sambar* powder that contains a mixture of roasted spices (page 276). This basic *sambar* can be varied daily with the addition of different vegetables. One of my favourites is shallot *sambar*. The shallots are lightly sautéd before being added to the *sambar*, giving them a sweet, glazed quality. Pickling onions may be substituted.

Serve with plain rice or Savoury Rice Cakes (page 204) or Rice and Split Pea Pancakes (page 205).

~

140 g/5 oz/¾ cup *toovar dal* **(page 261), picked over and washed in several changes of water**
3 tablespoons vegetable oil
1 fresh hot green chilli, split into half lengthways

12–14 even-sized shallots (200 g/7 oz), peeled
2 tablespoons tamarind paste (page 278)
2–2½ tablespoons *sambar* **powder (page 276)**
1½ teaspoons salt

½ teaspoon ground turmeric
½ teaspoon brown mustard seeds
15–20 fresh curry leaves, if available
1 tablespoon finely chopped, fresh green coriander

~

Place the *toovar dal* in a medium-sized saucepan with 600 ml/1 pint/2½ cups water. Bring to the boil. Cover partially, turn the heat to low, and simmer for 45 minutes – 1 hour or until the *dal* is tender. When cooked, stir with a spoon to mash up the *dal*.

Heat 2 tablespoons of the oil in a medium-sized frying-pan over medium-high heat. When hot, put in the chilli. Stir for a few seconds until the chilli softens. Add the shallots. Stir and fry until the shallots are very lightly browned. Turn the heat down and cook until the shallots soften and cook through.

Add the tamarind paste, *sambar* powder,

salt, turmeric and 450 ml/15 fl oz/2 cups water to the saucepan of *toovar dal*. Also add the contents of the frying-pan. Mix and bring to a simmer. Simmer gently, uncovered, for 10 minutes, stirring now and then.

Meanwhile, heat the remaining 1 tablespoon oil in a small saucepan or small frying-pan over medium-high heat. When hot add the mustard seeds. As soon as the mustard seeds pop, a matter of seconds, throw in the curry leaves. Stir once and quickly pour over the *sambar*. Sprinkle the fresh coriander over the top.

S E R V E S   4

Mrs A. Santha Ramanujam's Tengai Sadam
⊘ COCONUT RICE

THIS IS AN EXCELLENT RICE dish, perked up with lightly roasted coconut and a very South Indian spice combination that includes split peas, chillies and mustard seeds. Eat as part of any meal, northern or southern. If you are stir-frying fresh prawns (shrimp) or scallops, serve this on the side.

If you wish to substitute unsweetened, desiccated coconut for fresh coconut use 100 g/4 oz/1¼ cups. Barely cover with warm water and leave for 1 hour. Squeeze dry and proceed with the recipe.

❧

Patna rice or any long-grain rice, measured to the 450 ml/15 fl oz/2 cup level in a measuring jug
3 tablespoons coconut oil or any other vegetable oil
7 dried hot red chillies, broken into 1 cm/½ inch pieces

1½ teaspoons *chana dal* (page 260)
1½ teaspoons *urad dal* (page 261)
1 teaspoon brown mustard seeds
10–15 curry leaves, if available

1 teaspoon salt
¼ teaspoon ground asafetida
200 g/7 oz/1¾ cups freshly grated coconut (page 265)
2 tablespoons chopped, fresh green coriander

❧

Wash the rice in several changes of water, until the water runs clear. Cover well with water and soak for 30 minutes. Drain. Put the rice in a saucepan and cover with 600 ml/1 pint/2⅔ cups water. Bring to the boil. Cover tightly, turn the heat to very low and cook gently for 25 minutes.

Meanwhile, heat the oil in a medium-sized saucepan or wok over medium-high heat. When hot, add the chillies, *chana dal*, *urad dal* and mustard seeds. Stir and fry until the chillies darken and the *dals* turn reddish. Now add the curry leaves, salt, asafetida and, finally, the coconut.

Stir and fry over high heat for a minute or so, then turn the heat down and cook gently until the coconut is a light reddish-brown and quite crisp. Turn the mixture out on to a large wide dish (such as a *thali*, page 283), spread out and allow to cool.

When the rice is cooked, take it out of the pan and spread it evenly over the coconut mixture. As soon as it is cool enough to handle mix the two together, preferably using your hands or otherwise a spoon. Garnish with the fresh coriander and serve.

SERVES 4

Mrs A. Santha Ramanujam's Idlis

ⓥ SAVOURY RICE CAKES

THESE STEAMED CAKES ARE eaten rather as rice might be, with pulses (legumes) and vegetables. Because they are light, they are a very popular breakfast and snack food. Rice and *urad dal* are soaked and ground into a creamy paste. This batter is left to ferment overnight, by which time it increases in volume by about 1½ times. Now all airy and bubbly, it is poured into egg-poacher-type moulds and quickly steamed. The *idlis* that come out of the steamer are fat in the middle and tapering at the ends. They may be eaten with Coconut Chutney (page 212) or with a *sambar* such as Split Peas with Shallots (page 202).

Idli steamers may be bought from many Indian grocers. They come in all sizes and basically consist of a central trunk on which several discs may be fitted at intervals. Each disc has several depressions for individual *idlis*. The discs are oiled lightly before batter is poured into them. The entire tree is then put inside a steaming vessel that has boiling water at the bottom. The vessel is covered and the *idlis* are allowed to steam for 15 minutes. If you cannot find these moulds, you can improvise. Use a steaming tray (Chinese grocers sell them) that is about 15 cm/6 inches in diameter. Put the tray inside a colander. Line the tray and sides of the colander with a double layer of wet cheesecloth. Pour a 1 cm/½ inch thickness of batter into the cheesecloth, cover the colander and then fold the overhanging edges of cheesecloth over the lid. Set the colander over a pan of boiling water in such a way that the water stays below the level of the *idli*. You will end up with a large *idli* which you can cut into squares or diamonds.

---

400 g/14 oz/2 cups Patna rice or any long-grain rice, washed in several changes of water

200 g/7 oz/1 cup *urad dal* (page 261), picked over and washed in several changes of water

1 teaspoon salt
About 3 tablespoons refined sesame seed oil or any other vegetable oil

---

Soak the Patna rice and *urad dal* in separate bowls for 2 hours. Water should cover them by about 2.5 cm/1 inch. Drain. Put the *urad dal* into the container of an electric blender. Add

175 ml/6 fl oz/¾ cup water and blend until the mixture is smooth, pale, light and airy, almost like a meringue mixture. This will take 5–8 minutes. Empty into a large bowl. Put the

drained rice into the container of the blender. Add 6 tablespoons water and blend until the rice turns into a fine but granular paste. Add to the bowl with the *dal*. Add the salt and mix gently.*

Leave the batter to ferment for 12-15 hours in a warm place (such as a pilot-lit oven or airing cupboard) with a temperature that hovers around 27°C/80°F. The batter should ferment to 1½ times its original volume.

Prepare your steaming apparatus and bring the water to a rolling boil. Grease the *idli* moulds with the oil and fill each with the batter. Remove the batter very carefully from its bowl to preserve its bubbly lightness. Cover the steaming vessel and steam for 15 minutes. Ease each *idli* out with the help of a knife and serve hot with its smoother side up.

20-25 CAKES

Mrs A. Santha Ramanujam's Dosas
ⓥ RICE AND SPLIT PEA PANCAKES

THESE WONDERFULLY NUTRITIOUS PANCAKES can be eaten for breakfast, as a light lunch and for dinner. They may be eaten plain with Coconut Chutney (page 212) or else they may be folded over potatoes (see Potatoes with Mustard Seeds and Onions, page 200) to make what is called *masala dosas*.
The batter used here is exactly the same as that for the *idli* in the preceding recipe, only it is allowed to ferment longer. It should double in volume.
Ideally, *dosas* should be eaten as soon as they are made. If you wish to make them ahead of time, keep them covered with a second upturned plate as they are made, then wrap the stack of cooked pancakes in foil and place in a moderate oven (160°C/325°F/Gas 3) for 15 minutes to re-heat. They will not stay crisp but will be very good. Left-over batter may be refrigerated and used the following day. Get everything ready to make your *dosas* before you start. You will need a 20 cm/ 8 inch well-seasoned frying-pan – a larger one will be just as good – with a spatula, nearby should be your batter and a ladle that can easily pick up 120 ml/4 fl oz/ ½ cup, a teaspoon for the oil, a rounded soup spoon for spreading the batter and a plate to put the cooked *dosas* on as they get made.

∿

Batter for Savoury Rice Cakes (opposite), made up to the * mark

About 300 ml/10 fl oz/ 1¼ cups vegetable oil

Once the batter is made, cover it and leave it to ferment in a warm place such as an airing cupboard or a pilot-lit oven for 24–26 hours. The batter should double in volume. Add 200 ml/7 fl oz/1 scant cup water to it and fold it in gently. Cover and leave in a warm place for another 1½ hours.

Put 1½ teaspoons of the oil in the frying-pan and set over medium-low heat. When the oil is hot, pick up 120 ml/4 fl oz/½ cup of the batter and drop it in the centre of the pan. Put the rounded bottom of the soup spoon very lightly in the centre of the batter. Using a slow, gentle and continuously spiral motion, spread the batter outwards with the back of the spoon until you have a pancake 18 cm/7 inches in diameter. Dribble ½ teaspoon of the oil over the pancake and another ½ teaspoon around its edges. Cover and cook for 1½–2 minutes or until the *dosa* turns reddish-brown. Turn the *dosa* over and cook it, uncovered, for another minute or until the second side develops reddish spots. Make all the *dosas* this way.

MAKES 15–16 PANCAKES

Mrs A. Santha Ramanujam's Bhakala Bhat

ⓥ RICE WITH YOGHURT

YOU COULD CALL THIS a salad. It is generally served at the end of a meal. Light and clean-tasting, it leaves the palate wonderfully refreshed.

Patna or other plain long-grain rice measured to the 450 ml/15 fl oz/2 cup level in a measuring jug
2–3 tablespoons milk
500 ml/17 fl oz/2 cups plus 2 tablespoons natural (plain) yoghurt, beaten lightly
50 g/2 oz cucumber, seeded and cut into 5 mm/¼ inch dice
50 g/2 oz green mango or green apple, cut into 5 mm/¼ inch dice
75 g/3 oz seedless green grapes, halved if large
1 tablespoon *ghee* or vegetable oil
½ teaspoon *urad dal* (page 261)
½ teaspoon brown mustard seeds
1 fresh hot green chilli, sliced into fine rounds
1 cm/½ inch piece of fresh ginger, peeled and very finely chopped
1½ teaspoons salt or to taste
1–2 tablespoons chopped, fresh green coriander

Rice and Split Pea Pancakes (page 205) with Coconut Chutney (page 212) and Split Peas with Shallots (page 202).

Wash the rice in several changes of water, until the water turns clear. Drain and cover well with water. Soak for 30 minutes. Drain again and place in a medium-sized saucepan. Cover with 750 ml/1¼ pints/3 cups water. Bring to the boil. Cover tightly and turn the heat down to very low. Simmer gently for 30 minutes. The rice will be very soft. Heap it in the pan or a larger bowl and mash with a wooden spoon.

Add 2 tablespoons of the milk and the yoghurt. Stir to a porridge-like consistency, pouring in a little more milk if needed. Add the cucumber, mango and grapes. Gently mix in.

Heat the *ghee* or oil in a small frying-pan over medium-high heat. When hot, add the *urad dal* and mustard seeds. As soon as the mustard seeds start to pop and the *urad dal* turns golden – a matter of seconds – add the chillies and ginger. Stir briefly and then pour over the rice. Mix in well. Add the salt and mix. Sprinkle with the fresh coriander before serving.

S E R V E S   6

Mrs A. Santha Ramanujam's Rava Khichoi
ⓥ SEMOLINA WITH VEGETABLES

THERE IS NO OTHER way to describe this dish other than as a spiced 'polenta' dotted with vegetables. It is not made with cornmeal but with a semolina sold by Indian grocers as *sooji* – the only kind of semolina that is suitable. You may eat this plain, at breakfast, with Coconut Chutney (page 212), or as a snack or with yoghurt relishes and pickles or as the starch in a full meal. You could also treat it exactly like polenta and serve it, Western style, cut into squares and rectangles, with roast duck, quails and chicken.

ॐ

8 tablespoons vegetable oil
400 g/14 oz/2 cups semolina
  (page 277)
1 teaspoon *chana dal*
  (page 260)
1 teaspoon *urad dal*
  (page 261)
1 teaspoon brown mustard
  seeds
4 raw cashew nuts, split into
  halves lengthways

1–3 fresh hot green chillies,
  split into halves
10–12 curry leaves, if
  available
8–10 shallots or 2 medium-
  large red onions (100 g/
  4 oz), finely sliced
2 small carrots (100 g/4 oz),
  peeled and cut into 2.5 cm
  × 5 mm (1 × ¼ inch) sticks

100 g/4 oz French beans, cut
  into 2.5 cm/1 inch
  segments
2 teaspoons salt
2 medium-sized tomatoes,
  chopped
½ teaspoon ground turmeric
1 tablespoon lemon juice
1–2 tablespoons *ghee* or
  butter

Heat 4 tablespoons of the oil in a large, wide, preferably non-stick frying-pan over medium heat. When hot, add the semolina and sauté gently, stirring continuously until golden, about 9-10 minutes. Remove and set aside.

Clean the pan and dry it off. Heat the remaining oil in it over medium-high heat. When hot, add the *chana dal*, *urad dal*, mustard seeds, cashew nuts, chillies and the curry leaves if using, in that order. Stir and fry until the *chana dal* and *urad dal* become reddish. Add the shallots or red onions. Stir and fry until they become soft but not coloured. Add the carrots and French beans and 300 ml/10 fl oz/1¼ cups water, just enough to cover. Add ½ teaspoon of the salt. Cover and boil over a high heat for 5–7 minutes or until the vegetables are just tender.

Now add the tomatoes, turmeric, 750 ml/ 1¼ pints/3 cups water, the remaining 1½ teaspoons salt and the semolina. Stir and cook over medium heat, breaking up any lumps as you do so, for about 8–10 minutes, until you have a smooth consistency and the semolina is cooked. Finally add the lemon juice and *ghee* or butter. Stir and serve.

S E R V E S   6

Hotel Saravana Bhavan's Beetroot Pachhadi
⦾ SWEET BEETROOT (BEET) CHUTNEY

SWEET CHUTNEYS CONTRAST WELL with the spicy foods of South India. This one, made with beetroots (beets), is as unusual as it is colourful.

❧

2 small beetroots (beets), 100 g/4 oz, peeled and grated

75 g/3 oz/¾ cup sugar
1 tablespoon honey

¼ teaspoon ground cardamom

❧

Put the beetroots (beets) and their juices in a small pan. Add 200 ml/7 fl oz/¾ cup plus 2 tablespoons water and bring to the boil over high heat. Turn the heat down to medium and cook, stirring frequently, for 5–7 minutes until the beetroots (beets) are tender. Add the sugar. Cook over medium heat, stirring, for 6–7 minutes. The texture of the mixture should be almost jam-like. Reduce the heat to low. Add the honey. Stir and cook for 4–5 minutes. Add the cardamom. Stir once and remove from the heat. Cool and bottle. The chutney will keep for a week.

1 0 0   M L / 3 ½ F L   O Z /
½   C U P

Shoba Ramji's Alimucha Oorga
① LIME PICKLE

TAMILS LIKE TO END their meals with plain rice, yoghurt and pickles. This is one of the many pickles they like to eat.

❧

4 limes (225 g/8 oz), cut into 2 cm/¾ inch pieces
1 teaspoon plus 4 tablespoons oil
1½ teaspoons brown mustard seeds

½ teaspoon fenugreek seeds
15–20 curry leaves, if available
100 ml/3½ fl oz/½ cup lime juice

1 teaspoon ground turmeric
2 teaspoons cayenne pepper
½ teaspoon ground asafetida
1 tablespoon salt

❧

Put the limes in a small stainless steel pan with water to cover and bring to the boil. Boil vigorously for 1 minute. Discard the water and repeat the process once more. Put the limes in fresh water and boil again, this time for 20–25 minutes. The limes should become tender and discolour. Drain them and put them to one side.

Meanwhile, heat the 1 teaspoon oil in a frying-pan over medium-high heat. When hot, put in ½ teaspoon of the mustard seeds and the fenugreek seeds. Stir and fry until the mustard seeds pop, a matter of seconds. Remove from the heat and put into the container of a clean mortar. Pound into a powder.

Put to one side.

Heat the 4 tablespoons oil in a medium-sized stainless steel pan over medium-high heat. When hot, add the remaining 1 teaspoon mustard seeds. As soon as they start to pop, a matter of seconds, add the curry leaves if using. Stir once or twice. Remove the pan from the heat. Add the limes, lime juice, turmeric, cayenne pepper, asafetida, mustard powder and salt. Mix well.

When cool, put into a very clean glass jar or plastic container. Cover the pickle and leave, unrefrigerated, for at least a week before using. Refrigerate after 2 weeks.

This pickle will keep well for up to 1 year.

600 ML/1 PINT/
2½ CUPS

Mixed Vegetable Curry (page 201) and Deep-fried Okra in Batter (page 199).

Thengay Chutney
ⓥ COCONUT CHUTNEY

THIS CHUTNEY GOES PARTICULARLY well with Rice and Split Pea Pancakes
(page 205) and Savoury Rice Cakes (page 204) but it may be served with all South
Indian meals.

Freshly grated coconut
   (page 265) measured to the
   340 ml/12 fl oz/1½ cup
   level in a measuring jug
   (no substitutes here)

1 tablespoon tamarind paste
   (page 278)
2 teaspoons vegetable oil
1 teaspoon brown mustard
   seeds

1½ tablespoons *urad dal*
   (page 261)
1–2 dried hot red chillies
A generous pinch of ground
   asafetida
½ teaspoon salt

Put the coconut, tamarind paste and 150 ml/
5 fl oz/⅔ cup water into the container of an
electric blender. Blend as finely as possible.
Leave in the blender.

   Heat the oil in a small frying-pan over
medium-high heat. When hot, put in the
mustard seeds. As soon as the mustard seeds
pop, a matter of seconds, put in the *urad dal*.
Stir and roast until the *dal* just begins to pick
up a little colour. Add the chillies. Continue to
roast until the *dal* turns reddish and the chillies

become dark. Add the asafetida and remove
from the heat.

   Let the spices cool a bit.

   Empty the spices into a clean coffee grinder
and grind to a powder. Add this to the coconut
mixture with the salt and blend again, thinning
the chutney out with more water if needed. It
should have the consistency of a thick batter. It
will keep for 48 hours.

S E R V E S   6

Mrs A. Santha Ramanujam's Mysore Pak
ⓥ CHICK PEA FLOUR BRITTLE

THESE RICH, BRITTLE SQUARES are generally offered in Tamil Nadu at the start of a meal. You may, of course, serve them with coffee at the very end. My desserts often consist of individual plates of fruit. I like to put one or two small squares of *Mysore pak* on each plate for added interest and a new taste.

---

340 g/12 oz/1½ cups *ghee*, divided into 2 equal portions, plus a little extra for greasing

100 g/4 oz/1 scant cup chick pea flour, sifted

300 g/12 oz/1¾ cups sugar

Grease a 28 cm/11 inch *thali* (see page 283) or a similar-sized baking tray. (A smaller baking tray will give you a thicker brittle.)

Heat one half-portion of the *ghee* in a large, preferably non-stick, pan over medium heat. When hot, add the sifted chick pea flour. Stir and fry for about 3 minutes until it is a shade darker and is golden. (The raw taste should go away.) Remove the flour from the pan and set aside. Clean the pan.

Put the remaining *ghee* in a smaller pan and heat over medium-low heat. Keep hot over low heat. At the same time, put 300 ml/10 fl oz/1¼ cups water into the cleaned first pan and set it over a high heat. Bring to the boil. Add the sugar and cook over high heat until the syrup forms a single thread when a little is dropped from a spoon into a cup of cold water. This should take about 4–5 minutes. Stir the fried chick pea flour and add. Stir continuously for about 6 minutes on high heat, adding small ladlefuls of the hot *ghee* and stirring them in.

Time this so that the last ladleful of *ghee* goes in just as the frothy, lava-like mixture is turning a rich caramel colour.

Quickly pour this mixture into the greased *thali* or baking tray, tilting and tapping the utensil gently so that the mixture is evenly thick all over. Using a wet knife cut into 2.5 cm/1 inch squares but allow to cool completely in the *thali* or baking tray before removing.

SERVES 8–10

PUNJAB

THERE IS NOTHING MORE important to a Punjabi man's diet than bread. He usually eats *rotis* (flat, round, wholewheat breads), which he embellishes with beans and vegetables, but when he is in the mood for something richer he opts for the flakier, wholewheat *paratha*, where each layer is separated with a generous layer of *ghee*. Indeed, in the towns and villages of this north-western state, if a wife has a pot of rice on the stove many a husband walking into the home has been known to take a deep sniff and complain, '*Eh purabiya kithhon aa gaya?*' ('Did some easterner show up?') Rice may do for special occasions or for making rice pudding (*kheer*) but the only food that makes a Punjabi feel that he has eaten a proper meal is his bread.

There has been wheat in the Punjab as long as anyone can remember and the earth has been known to yield grains of wheat that are 7000 years old. There is also evidence of ancient fields where wheat was planted in neat rows. The Punjab, named after the five generous rivers that flowed through the undivided state before it was partitioned to become a part of both India and Pakistan, has always been a rich, fertile plain with wheat for breads, sugar cane for sugar and milk for the much beloved dairy products. It was the site of the thriving Indus Valley civilization in 2000 BC and today the section of the Punjab that has fallen to India's lot is its most prosperous state and its breadbasket.

As about 85 per cent of the Punjab is under cultivation and 70 per cent of its people work in agriculture, it is best to visit a village in its heartland in order to understand the rhythms of its daily life. Gandiwind is only about an hour and a half away from Amritsar.

It is the end of the monsoon season and a soft mist hangs over the still darkened fields. Electric lights – in the Punjab every village has electricity – begin to glow, one by one, in all the houses. It is only four o'clock but Tarlok Singh and his brothers are already up, tumblers of sweet, milky tea in hand.

The first task of the day is the milking. If you expect to see the hallowed Indian cow here, much prized by the Aryan ancestors of these turbaned Sikh villagers, you will be in for a surprise. Tethered in the walled courtyard of the enclosed family compound are a dozen water buffaloes, dark horns arcing over their heads, eyes in pleasant contemplation of the cud they are constantly chewing.

In a state where richness in foods is unabashedly desired and the dreaded Western 'cholesterol' is considered but an invention of the effete, buffalo milk, with its 3 per cent higher fat content, is thought to be far superior to that of the cow.

The milking is done by men who squat beside the buffalo and, with their powerful

hands, squeeze the fresh milk rhythmically into a pail. The frothy milk will now have a short or long journey, depending upon what is to happen to it. Most of the milk is emptied into narrow-necked brass pots, tied to motor cycles and bicycles, covered with dampened burlap to protect it from the heat which is already building up and sent off to various markets in the neighbouring towns and cities. The remainder is kept for home consumption.

Some of it is just boiled and used for tea or for drinking. A goodly amount is poured into a round-bottomed earthenware pot, covered with a well-perforated lid and placed in a *bhadoli*. This is a simple but unique contraption. It looks like a huge, deep earthen bowl lined with India's most old fashioned fuel – dried patties made with buffalo (or cow) dung. On top of the gently smouldering fuel goes the pot of milk. Here it sits for many hours, evaporating slowly, thick layers of clotted cream forming at the top. Many Punjabis living away from their villages dream of this thick, rich milk, this *kadiya hoya dudh* which smacks of home, of parents and comfort.

It is the walled family courtyard with the tethered water buffaloes that bustles with all this early morning activity. There is an indoor kitchen but much of the cutting, chopping and cooking seems to be done under the cool shade of the banyan tree which spreads its ample branches over half of the courtyard and certainly over the many outdoor stoves and ovens that work

Previous page: A Sikh priest in the Golden Temple in Amritsar, Punjab.

their magic from morning to night. On one ledge sits the *bhadoli*, the rich milk in it getting richer by the minute. Some of this milk will later be set into yoghurt. Layers of thick cream will then be removed from the top of the yoghurt pot and churned into white butter. A portion of the white butter will be saved to put on breads and vegetables, the rest will be cooked slowly until it turns into *ghee*. All of the buffalo milk, every last ounce of it, will, in some form or other, be used with the greatest of enjoyment. Buttermilk will be drunk at midday, yoghurt will be eaten at breakfast, *ghee* will be used in the cooking at lunch, white butter will be put on the breads at night – and surely no member of the household will consider going to bed without a tall glass of hot milk? Does it not make everyone sleep better?

Breakfast is relatively simple but wholesome. First, *rotis* need to be made. A *tava* could be used and often is but today the family has decided on an oven – a special, very effective, Punjabi oven. A large clay vat that sits near the trunk of the banyan tree is lit with wood. This is the *tandoor*, now known throughout the world. When its walls are very hot, a dough is made of wholewheat flour and water. This is divided into balls. Using the palms of their hands, the women of the house flatten these balls into discs and slap them against the hot inside walls of the vat. Here the discs cook for a few minutes, puffing up slightly as they do so. Then they are pulled

out, smeared with white butter and eaten with fresh yoghurt and pickles.

By this time farmhands are beginning to arrive. (The Singhs are prosperous farmers who can afford to hire help.) The water buffaloes need to be taken to the pond so that their dark sensitive skins may get a much-needed soaking, and work needs to be done to harvest the rice and cut the fodder for the animals. Oddly enough, in this land of wheat and sugar cane, the water table of the soil has been rising as more and more canals have been built to distribute the waters of the rivers. The soil can now grow rice. And so the farmers plant it. The fields – with the help of many fertilizers and new seeds – are in constant use. Plain rice is being harvested now. By November basmati, the queen of rices with its aristocratic jade green leaves that stand out from the rest, will have ripened as well. It is always the last rice to ripen. But what else can you expect of the queen?

That will end the rice season. Mustard greens, peas and chick peas will be next, only to be followed by the all-important wheat which will be ready to harvest by the time of the Baisakhi festival in April. Harvest-time may be hard and busy but it will also be gay with all the males collecting to dance the vigorous *bhangra*.

After the men leave for work in the fields the women start the preparation of lunch. It is a tradition in the Punjab that the women of the house cook not only for their men but for all the farmhands as well. The food is the same. What their husbands, brothers and sons eat, so will the field-workers.

The *loh* is lit up. Rather like a large *tava*, it is made out of cast-iron and tends to be slightly concave. The one here is about 1.5 m (5 ft) long and 1.2 m (4 ft) wide, and is raised off the ground by two walls of bricks about 30 cm (1 ft) high. It too is lit with wood, a mixture of brush and small branches. Three or four women in long shirts (*kameez*) and loose trousers that narrow at the ankles (*salwars*) and with their heads covered with long scarves (*chunnis*) sit on one side. They are going to make *parathas* today. One woman with spectacles makes the ball of dough. She then flattens it out with her hands, puts melted *ghee* on the disc and folds it in thirds twice until she has a square. She dips the square in flour and hands it to a second woman. The second woman rolls it out into a large *paratha* and slaps it on to the *loh*. A third woman turns it over every 30 seconds, brushing it with *ghee* when needed. As soon as it is done, she throws it into a basket and covers it with a cloth. Ten to fifteen *parathas* cook at the same time. It is very much an assembly line at work, only this work is being done at home.

As the *parathas* pile up in the basket, a man who is perhaps too old to work in the fields stands over a huge pot just a few feet away. He stirs the onions in it with a massive metal paddle. When they are lightly browned he puts in some garlic and ginger.

He stirs some more. Now in go the turmeric, cayenne pepper, *garam masala*, tomatoes, green chillies and salt and then finally, potatoes and some water. These will all cook slowly over a wood fire. When they are done huge pails will be filled up and taken to the fields together with the baskets of bread. All work will stop as workers are handed two *parathas* each. Some potatoes are put on the top *paratha* which acts as a medieval trencher – plate and bread in one. Sometimes there is some raw onion which is smashed with a fist before it is eaten. For drinking, there is fresh water from the tube wells.

The women will eat the same food, though they may also draw on the many pickles sitting in neat jars. There is the sour lime pickle and what about grandmother's green mango pickle – or how about the cauliflower and carrot pickle left over from the winter?

Meanwhile, the children are all at the village school. The older ones are learning English but the little three-year-olds learn of an idyllic life by rote. They repeat these words, line by line:

> There is water in the well
> My mummy is a queen
> My daddy is a king
> I have fresh fruit to eat
> My windows are made of silver
> My doors are made of gold
> I am dancing with joy

Chapatis being cooked in a camp on the road to Amritsar.

By late afternoon all the buffaloes are back. There is another milking in the evening. Again, the milk must be dealt with immediately. The men may now start drinking the local booze distilled from sugar cane juice or from oranges – which they have with yoghurt or some radishes and salt.

Dinner, like lunch, is simple – and vegetarian. With the breads may be served whole beans: small black *ma di dal* (whole black *urad*) and kidney beans cooked to-

gether slowly in the hot ashes of the *tandoor*. When they are tender onions, ginger and garlic are sautéd, some tomatoes are thrown in and this mixture is added to the pot of beans. Nothing more is needed for the dish other than a dollop of white butter! There may also be whole bitter gourds stuffed with a paste of ground onions, dried pomegranate seeds, turmeric, cayenne pepper and salt and then sautéd gently until brown and slightly crisp on the outside. Or there may be *bharta*, for which whole aubergines (eggplants) are roasted in ashes and their pulp sautéd with onions, ginger, hot green chillies and tomatoes. Of course, there will be the glass of milk before retiring.

The motor cyclists who left Gandiwind with the narrow-necked brass pots may well roar into Amritsar, bearded and turbaned easy riders bearing milk. They may deliver their milk to Munim di Hatti. This café specializes in *lassi* (a yoghurt drink) and in *paneer* (fresh cheese). One side window serves nothing but *lassis* to a waiting line of customers. Pramod Singh, the *lassi*-maker, uses a kidney-shaped disc to remove some thick yoghurt from a deep metal dish. He puts it into a bowl. He adds more such scoops until the bowl is full. He empties all this into an electric mixer. Next he adds some sugar, cold milk and ice, mixes it all and then lets it pour out from a spigot into a tall glass. It is consumed just about as fast as it is made.

It is in the back of the café, in an open courtyard, that the yoghurt and *paneer* are made. For the yoghurt, the milk is first boiled in a huge pot then allowed to cool slightly in deep dishes. Diluted yoghurt is added and the yoghurt is left to set for 5 hours. Making the *paneer* is just as simple. Jugs of whey are added to the boiled milk to make it curdle. The curds are poured into a basket lined with cheesecloth. Once

the whey has drained away, the cheesecloth is lifted up, tied into a loose bundle and put under a weight for 5 minutes. The weight is removed and the very fresh *paneer*, still warm to the touch and now in the shape of a wheel, is ready to be cut to order and sold.

Since *paneer* is so easy to make, many people buy buffalo milk from the market and prepare the cheese at home. This is what Promila Kapoor does. When her husband returns from his work at the flour mill he owns, he likes to relax with a drink. To accompany it she sometimes buys crispy, flaky *mutthries* (savoury biscuits/crackers), all made with pure *ghee*, from the little lanes of the old city and sometimes she makes little snacks with *paneer*. For the second, she quickly boils up some milk in a pot, curdles it with lime juice and empties the contents of the pot into a strainer. The whey drains away. She pats the curds into the shape of a cake, lets the cake sit in the strainer for 5 minutes and then cuts this fresh cheese into slices. Next, she puts some chopped onions, tomatoes, ginger, green chillies and fresh green coriander into a bowl. To this she adds salt, pepper, cayenne pepper, lime juice and *chaat masala*, a spice mixture that contains *amchoor* (sour mango powder). She mixes all these ingredients and puts spoonfuls of the mixture on the cheese pieces. The snack is as refreshing as it is quick to prepare.

Paneer is used to make dozens of main dishes as well. To see them turned out in rapid succession, it is best to visit a *dhaba*. A *dhaba* is a cheap, fast food joint and there is no better one to go to than one on the Grand Trunk Road near the small town of Kartarpur. The road has many *dhabas*. But there are *dhabas* and *dhabas*. Many develop reputations. Truck drivers whoosh to a stop at this one and jump out to have a quick, nourishing bite. The food here is good. Some of them may be driving all the way to Calcutta and who knows where the next good food stop might be!

There are some rough tables with benches or cots to sit on. A truck driver walks in. His order is taken: one *paneer bhurji* with three *rotis*. The 'kitchen', all outdoors under a rough canopy, consists of an aisle between two simple, earthen counters. The man on the right counter cooks the breads while the man on the left one does the main dishes. 'Three *rotis*,' the man on the right is told. 'One *paneer bhurji*,' is barked at the man on the left. Both work fast. While breads get slapped on a *loh* on the right, a wok is heated on the left. Into the wok goes a little oil and some onions. They are quickly and noisily stirred about. In go some green chillies, ginger, tomato. They are stirred about. Now some *paneer*, made here earlier, is crumbled in. The scrambled-egg-like *paneer* dish is ready. For an order of *paneer* with tomatoes, lots more tomatoes are put in and the cheese is cut into larger cubes. A dollop of white butter is added as a bonus. If *paneer* with spinach is required, puréed spinach is added to the tomato mixture to be followed by the cubes of *paneer* and the dollop of butter. *Paneer* can even be made into fritters with a chick pea flour batter.

Dhabas specialize in different foods. Some have *chana-bhatura* (spicy chick peas served with deep-fried, puffed, slightly leavened breads). Others specialize in *tandoori* chicken or all manner of kebabs known as *tikkas*, or in batter-fried, crisp on the outside and meltingly tender inside Amritsari river fish.

Many Indian restaurants in the West serve Punjabi-style foods and as there is a preponderance of meat at these eating-places, it may be hard to believe that more than half the people of the Punjab are vegetarians, a percentage that can compare only with the state of Gujarat where more than 60 per cent are vegetarians. Much of rural Punjab eats no meat at all. The cities, however, are a different story. An excellent creation made with lamb chops might feature in one house while another might serve a royal chicken, rich with cream and nuts. Nevertheless, some of the Punjab's most popular non-vegetarian dishes seem to be found in the *dhabas* that specialize in them.

Surjit's Chicken House is on Lawrence Road in Amritsar, a much sought after *dhaba* on a popular thoroughfare. An expensive car pulls up. A man alights and walks up to the front counter over which dozens of marinated chickens hang like red bunting. He orders two of them. At

Rs 100 each, they are not such a bargain. He waits as Amarjit, the owner's young son, splits each chicken into four parts, skewers them and thrusts them into the single large *tandoor* in front of him. Every now and then he pulls the skewers up and bastes the chickens with *ghee*.

Meanwhile, the ladies in the expensive car are fanning themselves and looking impatient. The man returns to the car and makes reassuring noises. After about 20 minutes the chicken is done. It is pulled out of the *tandoor* and expertly chopped into smaller pieces which are put into a shallow bowl. A great deal of *chaat masala* is sprinkled over the top and the chicken tossed around with much acrobatic flair. It is now put into a piece of old newspaper and tied up with string. The man now has parcel A. Parcel B, which comes a bit later, consists of sliced radishes, some pieces of lime and a coriander-spinach-green-chilli chutney that is offered in tiny polythene bags. The man makes for the car, clutching his goodies. He and his male friends will eat the juicy, luscious chicken with cold glasses of beer. The women will have soft drinks.

While the origins of the freestanding, vat-like *tandoors* remain unclear, the fact that they have been around in the Punjab for centuries is not. They may even have developed here. If examined closely, they are seen to be primitive, yet most effective, ovens. Some are made right by the bus station in Amritsar.

A woman takes some good clay and kneads it with water until it is pliable. She adds some shredded coir rope to the clay 'dough' and kneads some more. Then, free hand, she begins to form the sides of a vat. There is no bottom as the *tandoor* must stand on a clear, non-flammable surface – usually the earth. She only raises the sides to about 15–20 cm (6–8 inches) as they are wet and would collapse if she went higher. At this stage she also puts in an opening through which ashes can be cleared. This much of the *tandoor* must dry in the hot sun for at least half a day before she can proceed. She then builds up the vat bit by bit, doing its neck and top opening last. *Tandoors* are made in all sizes, from very small ones for single families to very large ones for restaurants. Once sold, the buyer needs to do more work on them. A paste of mustard oil, jaggery, yoghurt and ground spinach is rubbed generously on the inside to harden it up. Then, just before breads are cooked, salted water is sprinkled on the inside walls to make sure the flat breads adhere to them and do not fall into the fire below.

If *tandoori* foods are associated with the Punjab, so are corn breads and mustard greens. Corn probably came to India with the Portuguese. Nowhere did it find more welcoming a home than in the Punjab. The Punjabis honoured it by using it for bread. They learned to make flat breads (*makki di roti*) by hand – a neat trick as the dough cracks easily. They also discovered

A farmer in a mustard field in the Punjab.

that, as wine goes with cheese and champagne with caviar, they had, growing in their own backyards, delicious mustard greens (*sarson da saag*) that would help make an equally immortal pairing. They learned to add a few green chillies to the greens and cook them very slowly, until even the stems were buttery-soft. They knew that they should then beat the greens into a thick purée and thicken it slightly with cornmeal flour, finally adding to it a sautéd mixture of onions, garlic, tomatoes and lots of ginger. And, of course, they knew that before a bowl of these mustard greens was put on the table a big piece of white butter just had to be floated over the top of them.

Nobody goes hungry in the Punjab. If nothing else, there is always free food at the Sikh *gurdwaras* (temples). On festival days it is considered an honour to eat there. At the Golden Temple in Amritsar the mass feedings seem almost miraculous. The many doors of the dining hall open in unison and people rush in, sitting down instantly in neat rows that face each other. When 3000 have been seated the doors close. The rest must wait for the next seating. Young boys, all volunteers, now put metal plates before each diner. More volunteers come in with baskets of *rotis*. Two are dropped on each plate. Next comes the beans, the *ma di dal*, which is ladled out from buckets. There are stewed chick peas and some semolina *halva*. The volunteers keep moving. The turbans of the diners – reds, yellows, pinks and purples – nod and wave. There are chants and cries of '*Bolay so nihal, Sat Sri Akal*' ('Whoever takes the name of God will be in ecstasy'). Old toothless men break their bread up into small pieces which they mix with the beans, hoping to soften them. They must eat fast. A sitting lasts but half an hour. After the half-hour, doors open and everyone leaves. The doors close and the entire hall is swept from one end to the other by a row of women. Then the doors open again and the next batch of 3000 diners comes in. This goes on all day. Every last person who desires it is fed. Such is the tradition of the Punjab.

Promila Kapoor's Paneer Chat

ⓥ SPICY FRESH CHEESE SNACK

THIS ABSOLUTELY DELIGHTFUL DISH may be served as a snack, as an accompaniment for drinks or as a first course at a more formal meal. The cheese (*paneer*) is very like the Italian mozzarella.

❧

FOR THE CHEESE:
1.75 litres/3 pints/7½ cups
full-fat (whole) milk
4 tablespoons white wine
vinegar or more as needed

YOU ALSO NEED:
2.5 cm/1 inch piece of fresh
ginger, peeled and cut into
minute dice

4 tablespoons finely
chopped onion
4 tablespoons finely
chopped tomato
1–2 fresh hot green chillies,
finely chopped
2 tablespoons finely
chopped, fresh green
coriander or mint or a
mixture of the two

1 teaspoon salt
Freshly ground black pepper
½–1 teaspoon *chaat masala*
(page 263)
2–3 tablespoons lemon juice

❧

Make the cheese: Bring the milk to the boil in a heavy saucepan. As soon as it begins to froth, add vinegar, stir it in and turn off the heat. The curds should separate from the whey – if they don't do so completely, bring the milk to the boil again and add another tablespoon or so of vinegar. Stir and turn the heat off.

Line a strainer with a large, doubled-up piece of cheesecloth. Set the strainer over a large bowl. Pour the contents of the saucepan into the strainer. Let the whey drain away. Lift up the 4 corners of the cheesecloth. Using one of the corners tie up the cheese in the cheesecloth into a bundle. Put this bundle on a board set in the sink. Put a plate on the bundle. Now put a weight – such as a medium-sized pan filled with water – on top of the plate. Remove the weight after 3–4 minutes. Untie the bundle. The cheese is ready It can be refrigerated if necessary.

Combine in a bowl the ginger, onion, tomato, chillies, coriander or mint, salt and black pepper, *chaat masala* and lemon juice. Toss. Taste for the balance of the seasonings.

Cut the cheese into 3 mm/⅛ inch thick slices. Arrange the slices in a single layer on a serving dish or on several individual plates. Put a generous dollop of the onion-tomato mixture on top of each piece and serve immediately.

SERVES 4

Hoshiyar Singh at the Mohan International Hotel: Mutton Tikka

LAMB KEBAB

TINY KEBAB STALLS ARE scattered all over the city of Amritsar. People either eat the kebabs on the street or take them home for dinner or to accompany drinks. They can be rolled up in any Punjabi bread or eaten with a salad and rice.

❧

175 ml/6 fl oz/¾ cup thick, Greek-style (whole milk) yoghurt

6 tablespoons mustard oil or any other vegetable oil

5 cm/2 inch piece of fresh ginger, peeled and grated to a pulp

2 garlic cloves, peeled and mashed to a pulp

1 tablespoon Punjabi *garam masala* (page 270)

1 teaspoon cayenne pepper

2 teaspoons Kashmiri chilli powder (page 264)

2 teaspoons salt

1 kg/2¼ lb lamb from the leg, cut into 2 cm/¾ inch cubes

3 tablespoons *ghee*, melted unsalted butter or vegetable oil

1 teaspoon *chaat masala* (page 263)

3–4 tablespoons chopped, fresh green coriander

½ medium-sized red onion (40 g/1½ oz), cut into very fine rings

Lime wedges

❧

Place a strainer in the sink and line it with cheesecloth. Empty the yoghurt into it and let it sit for 10 minutes. Put the drained yoghurt into a bowl and add the mustard oil, ginger, garlic, *garam masala*, cayenne pepper, chilli powder and salt. Beat well with a whisk or eggbeater. Put in the cubes of meat and mix well. Cover and marinate overnight in the refrigerator.

Pre-heat the grill (broiler). Lift the lamb pieces out of the marinade and divide equally between 4–6 skewers. Brush with the *ghee* or the butter or oil and place under the grill (broiler) about 10–13 cm (4–5 inches) from the source of heat. Grill (broil) for 3–4 minutes on one side until lightly browned. Turn the pieces over and grill (broil) for another 3–4 minutes until the lamb is browned and just cooked through to your liking. Remove from the skewers and spread out on a serving plate. Sprinkle the *chaat masala*, fresh coriander and onion rings over the top and serve with the lime wedges.

S E R V E S 6

Spicy Fresh Cheese Snack (page 225) and Mint and White Radish Chutney (page 251).

Kheema Cholay
MINCED (GROUND) LAMB WITH CHICK PEAS

FOR A FAMILY DINNER or gathering of friends, I can imagine nothing better than this dish with a plate of Puffed Leavened Breads (page 243) or Flaky Breads (page 244), a yoghurt relish, sliced raw onions and some pickles!

❧

FOR THE CHICK PEAS:
100 g/4½ oz/¾ cup dried chick peas
1 bay leaf
¼ teaspoon ground asafetida
2 cloves
1 cm/½ inch cinnamon stick
1 teaspoon salt
2 tablespoons vegetable oil
1 tablespoon peeled and finely grated fresh ginger
1 tablespoon finely chopped garlic

½–1 teaspoon cayenne pepper

FOR THE MINCED (GROUND) MEAT:
4 tablespoons *ghee* or vegetable oil
800 g/1¾ lb minced (ground) lamb
1 large onion (175 g/6 oz), finely chopped
1 tablespoon peeled and finely grated fresh ginger

1 tablespoon finely chopped garlic
1 tablespoon ground coriander
4 very finely chopped plum tomatoes (400 g/14 oz)
2–4 fresh hot green chillies, finely chopped
1½–2 teaspoons salt
2 teaspoons ground *amchoor* (page 259)
2–3 tablespoons coarsely chopped, fresh green coriander

❧

Prepare the chick peas: Soak the chick peas in water overnight. The water should cover them by 13 cm (5 inches). Drain. Put 1.2 litres/2 pints/5 cups water into a saucepan. Add the chick peas, bay leaf, asafetida, cloves, cinnamon and 1 teaspoon salt. Bring to the boil. Cover, turn the heat to low and simmer gently for 2–3 hours or until the chick peas are very tender. Drain, saving the liquid, and set aside.

Heat the oil for the chick peas in a large wok or frying-pan over medium-high heat. When hot, add the 1 tablespoon ginger and 1 tablespoon garlic. Stir-fry for a minute. Add the drained chick peas. Stir and cook for 2 minutes. Add 120 ml/4 fl oz/½ cup of the drained chick pea liquid (or a mixture of water and chick pea liquid) and the cayenne pepper and bring to the boil. Turn the heat to low and simmer gently for 15–20 minutes or until all the liquid is absorbed. Check for salt. If you add more, stir and cook for another 2 minutes.

Cook the mince: Heat the *ghee* or oil in a separate wok or large frying-pan over medium-high heat. When hot, add the minced lamb.

Stir and fry for 5–8 minutes or until the mince turns brown and is sealed. Add the onion, ginger and garlic. Stir and fry for 2–3 minutes. Add 500 ml/18 fl oz/2¼ cups of the chick pea liquid (or water or a mixture of the two) and the coriander, tomatoes, chillies and salt. Bring to the boil. Cover, turn the heat to low and simmer gently for about 45 minutes. Most, but not all, of the liquid should be absorbed by the meat. If it is not, turn the heat up and dry it off. Add the *amchoor* and stir.

Spoon the chick peas into a shallow serving dish. Layer the cooked meat on top of the chick peas. Garnish with the fresh coriander.

SERVES 6–8

Mrs Chadda's Chaamp Masala

LAMB CHOPS MASALA

SERVE THIS WITH ANY Punjabi bread and Mustard Greens (page 236).
Note: In the Punjab tomatoes are grated to make a purée.

∽

- 7.5 cm/3 inch piece of fresh ginger, peeled and coarsely chopped
- 3 tablespoons peeled and coarsely chopped garlic
- 6–8 lamb chops (800 g/ 1¾ lb) from the ribs, each about 2 cm/¾ inch thick; remove all extra fat
- 250 ml/8 fl oz/1 cup grated or finely chopped tomatoes
- 2 medium-sized onions (175 g/6 oz), very finely chopped
- 1 tablespoon cayenne
- 400 ml/14 fl oz/1¾ cups thick, Greek-style (whole milk) yoghurt, beaten
- 1½ teaspoons salt or to taste
- 1 teaspoon ground, roasted cumin seeds (page 269)
- 1–2 teaspoons Punjabi *garam masala* (page 270)
- 3 tablespoons lemon juice
- 2–3 tablespoons chopped, fresh green coriander

∽

Put the ginger and garlic into the container of an electric blender with 2–3 tablespoons water and blend to a paste.

Put the chops, tomatoes, onions, cayenne pepper, yoghurt, salt and the ginger–garlic paste into a large wok or large, heavy-bottomed saucepan. Stir and bring to the boil. Turn the heat to low, cover and simmer for 50 minutes or until the chops are almost cooked. Add the ground, roasted cumin seeds and simmer for 10–15 minutes or until the meat is tender and the sauce is thick. Add the *garam masala* and lemon juice. Stir. Sprinkle the fresh coriander over the top serve.

SERVES 3–4

Hoshiyar Singh at the Mohan International Hotel: Murgh Tikka

CHICKEN KEBABS

THIS DISH IS WELL known and well liked in the West. It may be served with drinks, as a first course or as a main dish with a salad and flavoured rice.

❧

500 ml/18 fl oz/2¼ cups thick, Greek-style (whole milk) yoghurt
175 ml/6 fl oz/¾ cup single (light) cream
4 teaspoons salt
1 teaspoon cayenne pepper
2½ teaspoons Kashmiri chilli powder (page 264)
2.5 cm/1 inch piece of fresh ginger, peeled and grated to a pulp

2 garlic cloves, crushed to a pulp
1 teaspoon cardamom seeds
1 teaspoon cumin seeds
1 teaspoon black peppercorns
¼ nutmeg
5 cm/2 inch cinnamon stick
7–8 cloves
1 kg/2¼ lb boned, skinned chicken, cut into 2.5 cm/ 1 inch cubes

2 tablespoons white vinegar
2–3 tablespoons *ghee*, melted unsalted butter or vegetable oil

FOR THE FINAL FLAVOURING:
1 teaspoon *chaat masala* (page 263)
Lime or lemon wedges

❧

Place a strainer in the sink and line it with cheesecloth. Empty the yoghurt into it and let it sit for 10–15 minutes. Put the drained yoghurt into a large bowl. Add the cream, 2 teaspoons of the salt, cayenne pepper, chilli powder, ginger and garlic. Mix. This is the marinade.

Put the cardamom, cumin, peppercorns, nutmeg, cinnamon and cloves into the container of a clean coffee grinder and grind to a fine powder. Add to the marinade. Beat well with a whisk or eggbeater.

Rub the chicken pieces with a solution of the remaining 2 teaspoons salt and the vinegar. Let them sit for 5 minutes. Pat them dry with kitchen paper (paper towels). Drop the chicken pieces into the marinade. Marinate for 2 hours or even overnight.

Pre-heat the grill (broiler). Lift the chicken pieces out of the marinade and divide them equally between 4 skewers. Brush with the *ghee* or the butter or oil. Grill (broil) about 10–13 cm (4–5 inches) from the source of heat for 3–4 minutes on one side until lightly browned. Turn over and grill (broil) for another 3–4 minutes or until the chicken is browned and cooked through. Remove from the skewers and place on a serving plate. Sprinkle the *chaat masala* over the top and serve with the lime or lemon wedges.

SERVES 4–6

Hoshiyar Singh at the Mohan International Hotel: Murgh Patiala

CHICKEN PATIALA

MOST RICH DISHES ARE given royal names. Whether they have any real connection to royalty is often questionable. Such is the case with this dish. Patiala was once an important princely state in the Punjab. Whatever its origins, *murgh Patiala* is quite worthy of being served at a grand dinner with a pilaf and a selection of vegetables. It is fairly mild and gentle.

Skinned melon seeds are sold by Indian grocers. If you cannot get them, use more poppy seeds or chopped raw cashews.

---

6 tablespoons white poppy seeds

7 tablespoons skinned melon seeds

4 tablespoons *ghee* or vegetable oil

1 medium-large onion (100 g/4 oz), peeled and finely chopped

2 medium-sized tomatoes, finely chopped

150 ml/5 fl oz/⅔ cup thick, Greek-style (whole milk) yoghurt

One 1 kg/2¼ lb chicken, cut into about 8 serving pieces

1 tablespoon Punjabi *garam masala* (page 270)

1 teaspoon ground white pepper

¼ teaspoon cayenne pepper

1 teaspoon Kashmiri chilli powder (page 264)

1½ teaspoons salt

120 ml/4 fl oz/½ cup single (light) cream

2 tablespoons sultanas (golden raisins)

2 tablespoons blanched, slivered almonds

Put the poppy seeds and melon seeds into a clean coffee grinder and grind as finely as possible. Put in a bowl and add 5–6 tablespoons water to make a paste. Set aside.

Heat the *ghee* or oil in a heavy, wide saucepan over medium-high heat. When hot, put in the onion and brown lightly. Add the tomatoes and continue to brown until you can see the oil separating from the sauce. Add the poppy and melon seed paste and continue to stir and fry for 2–3 minutes. Put in the yoghurt a tablespoon at a time, stirring and frying each

time until it is incorporated in the sauce. Add the chicken pieces, the *garam masala*, white pepper, cayenne pepper, chilli powder, salt and 200 ml/7 fl oz/1 cup water. Stir and bring to a simmer. Cover, turn the heat to low and cook until the chicken is tender, about 20 minutes. Add the cream, sultanas (golden raisins) and almonds. Mix and bring to a simmer. Cook very gently without covering for another 5 minutes.

SERVES 3 – 4

Surjit's Chicken House on Lawrence Road, Amritsar: Tandoori Murgh

TANDOORI CHICKEN

SURJIT'S CHICKEN HOUSE – in reality it is a tiny stall – is reputed to sell the best *tandoori* chicken in town and has become quite an institution in Amritsar. Over the last 40 years, I have watched and monitored the changes in this simple, oven-roasted chicken dish from the north-west frontier of what is now Pakistan. Originally, it had no seasonings other than the very simple ones in the marinade itself. Today, with North India's passion for sour and spicy foods, a great deal of the flavour comes from *chaat masala*, a mixture of seasonings used mainly for snack foods, which is sprinkled over the top. Here is the new version of the dish. (*Chaat masala* may be bought from any Indian grocer or made at home using the recipe on page 263.)

For those of us who do not have clay *tandoors* (ovens) in our homes, it is best to use an oven heated to its maximum temperature.

This chicken may be enjoyed with sliced white radishes and beer, as it is by the men of Amritsar, or eaten as part of a meal with a salad and any bread, Indian or Western.

❧

THE DRY SEASONINGS IN THE MARINADE:
1½ tablespoons cumin seeds
1½ tablespoons black peppercorns
Seeds from 3 black cardamom pods
Seeds from 1 tablespoon green cardamom pods
1 teaspoon cloves

THE REMAINING SEASONINGS IN THE MARINADE:
3 fresh hot green chillies, coarsely chopped
2 garlic cloves, peeled and coarsely chopped
4 cm/1½ inch piece of fresh ginger, peeled and coarsely chopped
1½ teaspoons salt
1 tablespoon Kashmiri chilli powder (page 264) or paprika

2 tablespoons double (heavy) cream
4 tablespoons vegetable oil

YOU ALSO NEED:
1 kg/2¼ lb chicken pieces, skinned
2–3 tablespoons *ghee* or melted unsalted butter or vegetable oil
1–2 tablespoons *chaat masala* (see above)
4 lime or lemon wedges for squeezing over the chicken pieces before serving

❧

Combine all the dry ingredients for the marinade in a clean coffee grinder and grind to a powder.

Combine the remaining ingredients for the marinade and 120 ml/4 fl oz/½ cup water in the container of an electric blender and blend to a paste. Empty the dry marinade spices into the blender and blend to mix. Empty into a large bowl.

Cut deep, diagonal slits in the fleshy parts of the chicken pieces.

Rub the marinade all over the chicken pieces, making sure that you go deep into the slits. Put the chicken into the marinade bowl, cover and refrigerate overnight or for up to 48 hours.

Remove the chicken pieces from the marinade. Shake off as much marinade as possible. If you have a *tandoor*, pierce the chicken pieces on to a sturdy skewer and cook for 15–20 minutes, depending on the thickness of the flesh. If you do not have a *tandoor*, put one shelf in the upper third of the oven and pre-heat the oven to its highest temperature. Lay the chicken pieces in a single layer in a very shallow baking tray. Brush with the *ghee* or the butter or oil. When the oven is very hot, put in the tray. The breast pieces will probably cook in 10–12 minutes. Legs and thighs may take 15–20 minutes. Take the chicken out of the oven, sprinkle with the *chaat masala* and lime or lemon juice and serve immediately.

S E R V E S   4

Amritsari Macchi

AMRITSARI FISH

THIS IS SOLD ALL over Amritsar: fish, either filleted or in steaks, that has been marinated, rubbed with a spicy chick pea flour paste and then deep-fried. It is crunchy on the outside and very sweet and tender inside. Local river fish such as *rahu*, a kind of carp, or *singhara*, a slimmer, long fish, are generally used but you may substitute sea fish like grey mullet, which is superb cooked by this method. Serve it with Mint and White Radish Chutney (page 251).

∽

1 kg/2¼ lb fish steaks, cut into 2 cm/¾ inch thick slices; use any fleshy, round fish such as grey mullet, salmon (sea) trout or a smallish cod
1 tablespoon salt plus 2 teaspoons

3 tablespoons cider vinegar
150 g/7 oz/1⅓ cups chick pea flour
1½ tablespoons peeled and very finely grated fresh ginger
1½ tablespoons crushed garlic

1 teaspoon cayenne pepper
½ teaspoon ground turmeric
½ teaspoon freshly ground black pepper
1½ tablespoons *ajwain* seeds (page 259)
Oil for deep-frying
Lime wedges

∽

Wash and clean the fish steaks and pat them dry on kitchen paper (paper towels). In a shallow ceramic bowl mix the 1 tablespoon salt and the vinegar. Add the fish steaks in a single layer, turning them so that they are coated with this marinade. Marinate for 30 minutes. Remove the fish steaks from the marinade and place on kitchen paper to get rid of any excess marinade.

Put the chick pea flour into a bowl. Slowly add 300 ml/10 fl oz/1¼ cups water to make a smooth paste of coating consistency. Add the ginger, garlic, cayenne pepper, turmeric, *ajwain* seeds, black pepper and 2 teaspoons salt to the paste and mix them in. Rub the fish with this mixture and place in a flat dish in a single layer to marinate for 30 minutes.

Heat the oil in a wok or deep frying-pan over high heat. When hot, put in as many pieces of fish as will fit in a single layer. Fry for a minute and turn the heat to medium-high. Cook, turning now and then, until the fish is golden-brown and cooked through. Remove with a slotted spoon and drain on kitchen paper (paper towels). Do all the fish this way. Serve with the lime wedges.

SERVES 4–6

Chicken Patiala (page 231) with Puffed Leavened Breads (page 249).

Jatinder Kaur's Sarson Da Saag

Ⓥ MUSTARD GREENS

IF YOU CAN IMAGINE a buttery, meltingly soft, mustard-greens-flavoured polenta, this is it. It is Punjab's very own winter speciality, made nowhere else in India. Something of a cross between a dish of greens and polenta, it is always eaten with Flat Corn Breads (page 250) lathered generously with home-made white butter. If a Punjabi farmer comes in for lunch after a hard morning's work in the cold fields to find that his wife has prepared a big warming bowl of these greens, butter glistening at the top, a stack of flat corn breads and a tall glass of *lassi* (yoghurt drink), he tends to return to the fields a very happy man. For most Punjabis, this meal is as much yearned for as roast beef and Yorkshire pudding are in England.

The greens must cook slowly and for a long time. The fairly tough stems of the leaves need to turn very soft. If your greens are still a bit watery when you finish cooking them, you can increase the cornmeal flour by 1–2 tablespoons. The coarse purée of greens should be fairly thick, but still soft and flowing.

It is best to use the cornmeal flour sold by Indian grocers. It has just the right texture for this dish and the breads.

In the Punjab a special wooden tool is used to mash the greens in the pan in which they are cooked. Called a *saag ghotna* (greens masher!), it looks somewhat like a wooden potato masher, with a long straight handle attached to a chunk of wood with a rounded base. A whisk, not an electric blender, is the best substitute.

~

500 g/18 oz spinach, very finely chopped

500 g/18 oz mustard greens (just leaves with their stems), very finely chopped

5 tablespoons coarsely chopped garlic

4–6 fresh hot green chillies

1½–2 teaspoons salt

About 5–6 tablespoons cornmeal flour

3 tablespoons *ghee* or vegetable oil

1 medium-large onion (115 g/4 oz), finely chopped

5 cm/2 inch piece of fresh ginger, peeled and cut into thin, long slivers

2 medium-sized tomatoes, finely chopped

A generous dollop of unsalted butter

~

Combine the spinach, mustard greens, garlic, chillies, salt and 800 ml/1⅓ pints/3⅓ cups water in a large, heavy pan. Set over high heat and bring to the boil. Cover, turn the heat to low and simmer gently for 1¾ hours or until even the stems of the mustard green leaves have turned buttery soft. With the heat still on, add 5 tablespoons of the cornmeal flour, beating constantly with a whisk or a traditional greens masher as you do so. Using the same whisk or masher, mash the greens until they are fairly smooth (a little coarseness is desirable). The greens will thicken with the addition of the cornmeal flour. If they remain somewhat watery, add another tablespoon or so. Leave on very low heat.

Heat the *ghee* or oil in a separate pan or wok over medium-high heat. When hot, put in the onion. Stir and fry until it turns golden-brown. Add the ginger. Keep stirring and frying until the onion is medium-brown. Put in the tomatoes. Stir and fry until the tomatoes have softened and browned a little. Now pour this mixture over the greens and stir it in.

Empty the greens into a serving dish, top with a dollop of butter and serve.

SERVES 6

Mrs Kapoor's Baigan Bharta
Ⓥ AUBERGINE (EGGPLANT) PÂTÉ

AUBERGINE (EGGPLANT) *BHARTAS* ARE much loved all over the Punjab. In villages whole aubergines (eggplants) are put into hot ashes and left to roast. When they are completely cooked through and quite pulpy inside the charred skin is removed and the pulp stir-fried with ginger, garlic, onions, green chillies and tomatoes. Here it is eaten with Punjabi breads, pickles and tall glasses of cool *lassi* (a yoghurt drink) but you may serve it with any Indian meal. It may also be served as a dip with potato crisps or as a first course, on slices of thin toast. The aubergines (eggplants) are best roasted over a gas flame but may, if necessary, be baked in the oven.

1.5 kg/3½ lb aubergines
  (eggplants)
3 tablespoons vegetable oil
1 teaspoon cumin seeds
1 large onion (175 g/6 oz),
  finely chopped

1 tablespoon peeled and
  very finely grated fresh
  ginger
1 tablespoon very finely
  chopped garlic
4 peeled plum tomatoes
  (500 g/18 oz), finely
  chopped

3–5 fresh hot green chillies,
  finely chopped
1 teaspoon cayenne pepper
2 teaspoons salt
85 g/3 oz/2 cups fresh green
  coriander, finely chopped

Prick a few holes in the aubergines (eggplants). Stand one directly on top of a medium-low gas flame. Hold it with a pair of tongs until the bottom has charred. Lie it down on the flame and move it back and forth until one section is completely charred. Keep turning the aubergine (eggplant) until it is charred on the outside and soft on the inside. Do all the aubergines (eggplants) this way. Hold one aubergine at a time under running water and peel off the charred skin. Collect all the pulp in a bowl and mash it lightly.

If you wish to use the oven to do this roasting, you may, though the *bharta* will not have its traditional smoky taste. Pre-heat the oven to 240°C/475°F/gas 9. Cut the aubergines (eggplants) in half lengthways and place them, cut side down, on a lightly oiled baking tray. Bake in the oven for 10–15 minutes or until the aubergines (eggplants) have collapsed slightly. Remove from the oven and spoon out the flesh. Discard the skin. Roughly chop up the flesh and set it aside.

Heat the oil in a wok or wide, preferably non-stick pan over medium-high heat. When hot, put in the cumin seeds. Let them sizzle for 20 seconds. Put in the onion. Stir and fry until the onion is translucent. Add the ginger and garlic. Stir and fry for another 2–3 minutes. Add the tomatoes, chillies, cayenne pepper and salt. Stir and fry for 2 minutes. Turn the heat to medium-low and continue to cook for another 7–8 minutes or until the tomatoes are soft. Put in the aubergine (eggplant) pulp. Stir and fry for 5 minutes or until the vegetables are melded together.

Add the fresh coriander, stir and remove from the heat.

SERVES 4 – 6

Mustard Greens (page 236) with Flat Corn Breads (page 250).

Promila Kapoor's Gobi Aloo
⊘ CAULIFLOWER WITH POTATOES, BANQUET STYLE

CAULIFLOWER AND POTATOES ARE cooked together throughout the Punjab and there are many recipes for this delightful combination. Here is one that is used for parties and banquets. Serve it with Flaky Breads (page 244) and a yoghurt relish or as a part of any North Indian meal.

∽

1 large cauliflower (to yield 500 g/18 oz florets)
2–3 medium-sized potatoes (225–350 g/8–12 oz), peeled
8 tablespoons vegetable oil
3 medium-sized onions (250 g/9 oz), finely chopped

5 cm/2 inch piece of fresh ginger, peeled and cut into very fine slices and then into very fine slivers
2 medium-sized tomatoes, grated or very finely chopped
¼–½ teaspoon cayenne pepper

½ teaspoon ground turmeric
1½ teaspoons ground coriander
1–1½ teaspoons salt
½ teaspoon Punjabi *garam masala* (page 270)
½ teaspoon ground roasted cumin seeds (page 269)

∽

Break the cauliflower into medium-sized florets. Cut the potatoes lengthways into halves and then cut each half lengthways into roughly 3 pieces to get chunky chips.

Heat the oil in a wok or frying-pan over medium heat. When hot, add the potatoes and fry them until they are medium-brown and just barely cooked through. Remove with a slotted spoon and drain on kitchen paper (paper towels). Put the florets into the same oil and fry until golden and just barely cooked through. Remove with a slotted spoon and drain on kitchen paper. Remove all but 3 tablespoons of the oil from the wok or frying-pan. Put in the onions and stir until they

are light brown. Put in the ginger and continue to stir and fry until the onions are medium-brown. Add the tomatoes and keep frying until they turn soft and darker and the oil seems to separate from the sauce. Add the cayenne pepper, turmeric, coriander and salt. Stir and fry for a minute. Put in the potatoes and florets. Stir to mix gently. Sprinkle a tablespoon of water over the vegetables. Cover. Turn the heat to low and cook gently for 3–5 minutes. Uncover. Add the *garam masala* and ground roasted cumin seeds. Stir gently to mix and turn off heat.

S E R V E S   4 – 6

Karele Pyazaa
ⓥ STUFFED BITTER GOURDS

I HAVE NEVER NEEDED any special incentive to eat bitter gourds (*karela*), having loved them since I was a little girl. They are, indeed, bitter, as their name suggests, but that is part of their attraction. Of course, everyone in India (and much of East Asia as well) believes that they cleanse the blood and help fight off cancers but that is part of folklore and I can only pass this information on, not substantiate it. The gourds are, perhaps, an acquired taste, like olives, but once you fall under their spell there is no getting away. The gourds are sold by Indian grocers. Serve these gourds with any Indian meal.

---

1 kg/2¼ lb small bitter gourds (*karela*), page 261
6 tablespoons salt
3–4 medium-sized onions (250–350 g/9–12 oz), peeled and coarsely chopped

2 teaspoons *amchoor* (page 259)
1 teaspoon freshly ground black pepper

1 teaspoon cayenne pepper
½ teaspoon ground turmeric
200 ml/7 fl oz/1 cup vegetable oil

Scrape the skins of the bitter gourds so thoroughly with a sharp knife that all the ridges are removed. Pick up a gourd and, using a small, sharp knife, make a slit lengthways down one side from top to bottom, being careful not to cut it in half. Do all the gourds this way. Rub salt inside the slits and all over the skin. Leave in a colander for 30 minutes. Rinse thoroughly, squeeze out excess moisture and pat dry on kitchen paper (paper towels).

Put the onions into the container of an electric blender and blend to a smooth paste. Add the *amchoor*, black pepper, cayenne pepper and turmeric to the onion paste. Blend for a second to mix. With a teaspoon, stuff the gourds with this mixture and tie a string around each one in 2 or 3 places, depending on size, to hold in the stuffing.

Heat the oil in a wok or large frying-pan over medium-low heat. When very hot, lay down the gourds, stuffed sides up, and fry one side for 7–9 minutes or until browned. Turn the gourds over and fry gently until the opposite side, too, is brown. This will take another 7–10 minutes. With a slotted spoon, lift the gourds out of the oil and drain them on kitchen paper (paper towels). Cut off the strings before serving.

SERVES 4–6

Ma Di Dal/Dal Makkhani
⦵ CREAMY SPICED BEANS

MORE THAN HALF OF the Punjab's population is vegetarian and for them, after wheat, nothing is more important than beans. This dish in a simpler form (without the cream, garlic and tomatoes as well as the final *tarka* of onions) is served with plain breads (*rotis*) at Sikh *gurdwaras* (temples) to any one who asks for food. In this simple form, it also bubbles away for hours in all *dhabas* (fast food joints), in monstrous, narrow-necked pots, stirred every now and then with huge paddles. It can be enriched as orders come in. This enrichment can consist of a simple *tarka* of onions and cayenne pepper in *ghee*, in which case it is called *ma di dal* with *tarka* or it can have cream added to it as well as the *tarka* or a generous dollop of butter, in which case it is called *dal makkhani* (buttery beans).

White butter is butter that is churned at home or on farms and is without additives or colouring. Good, unsalted butter is the best substitute.

Serve with a Punjabi bread, any meat in this chapter, a Punjabi vegetable, a yoghurt relish and a pickle or chutney.

❧

200 g/7 oz/1 cup whole black *urad* beans (page 261)

60 g/2 oz/⅓ cup red kidney beans (page 260)

4 teaspoons peeled and very finely grated fresh ginger

4 teaspoons crushed garlic

2 medium-sized tomatoes, grated or finely chopped

2 teaspoons cayenne pepper or to taste

2–3 teaspoons salt or to taste

85 g/3 oz/⅓ cup freshly made white butter, if available, or any unsalted butter

120 ml/4 fl oz/½ cup single (light) cream

2 teaspoons Punjabi *garam masala* (page 270)

FOR THE FINAL FINISH OR *TARKA*:

A generous dollop of unsalted butter

or

3 tablespoons *ghee* or vegetable oil

1 smallish onion (25 g/ 1 oz), cut into very fine half-rings

1 teaspoon cayenne pepper

2–3 tablespoons chopped, fresh green coriander (optional)

❧

Wash the 2 types of beans and drain. Cover with water and leave to soak overnight. Drain. In a large pan, combine the beans with 2.75 litres/5 pints/2½ quarts water and bring to the boil. Cover, turn the heat to low and simmer gently for 3–4 hours or until the beans are quite tender. With a potato masher, beat or mash about half of the beans lightly until they form an exceedingly coarse purée. Half the beans should remain whole. Add the ginger, garlic, tomatoes, cayenne pepper, salt, butter, cream and *garam masala*. Cook very gently for another 30 minutes, stirring occasionally.

The beans may be served just this way with a final dollop of butter at the top. They are also very good with a *tarka*. For this, heat the *ghee* or oil in a small pan or small frying-pan over medium-high heat. When hot, put in the onion. Stir and fry. When the onion is a rich, reddish-brown, put in the cayenne pepper. Immediately lift up the pan and empty its contents into the pot with the beans.

Garnish with the fresh coriander, if desired, before serving.

S E R V E S   6

Amritsari Dal

ⓥ AMRITSARI BEANS

THIS IS ANOTHER BEAN and split pea dish that is served at Sikh *gurdwaras* (temples) and in all Punjabi homes as part of everyday meals. In villages it is often cooked slowly and gently in dung-cake-fuelled clay ovens where it sits in covered earthen pots for 4–5 hours. It is gentle and soothing. Two types of beans are combined here in equal proportions, one whole and the other split. There is whole *urad*, or *ma di dal* as it is called here, which has a slightly glutinous texture, and *chana dal*, which is more crumbly. Because all the green chilli seeds are removed, the dish is quite mild. If you wish to make it more fiery, leave the seeds in. This is best eaten with a Punjabi bread and a selection of vegetables and pickles. If meat is desired, any of the lamb or chicken dishes in this chapter may be served.

❧

140 g/5 oz/¾ cup whole
  black *urad* beans (page 261)
115 g/4 oz/generous ½ cup
  chana dal (page 260)
1½ teaspoons salt or to taste
2 tablespoons very finely
  chopped garlic
2 tablespoons peeled and
  very finely chopped fresh
  ginger

3 tablespoons *ghee* or
  vegetable oil
1 teaspoon cumin seeds
1 medium-large onion
  (120 g/4 oz), finely
  chopped
4–5 fresh hot green chillies,
  seeded and finely chopped
2 medium-sized tomatoes,
  finely chopped

1 teaspoon Punjabi *garam
  masala* (page 270)
A generous dollop of
  unsalted butter to garnish
  (optional)
A handful of coarsely
  chopped, fresh mint or
  green coriander (optional)

❧

Wash the combined *urad* beans and *chana dal* and drain. Cover with water and leave for 2–3 hours. Drain and put in a large, heavy pan with the salt and 2 litres/3½ pints water. Bring to the boil. Turn the heat to low and skim any scum off the surface. Add 1 tablespoon each of the garlic and ginger. Cover and simmer for 2 hours or until the *urad* beans and *chana dal* are soft. Whisk them until they are smooth.

Heat the *ghee* or oil in a separate wok or large pan over medium-high heat. When hot, put in the cumin seeds. Let them sizzle for 15 seconds. Put in the onion. Stir and fry until the onion is golden-brown. Add the remaining ginger and garlic and continue to fry for another 5–6 minutes. Add the chillies and tomatoes and stir and fry until the tomatoes are soft. Add this spice mixture to the *urad* beans and *chana dal*, stir and continue to cook over low heat for another 30 minutes or until the *dal* is fairly thick and smooth. Sprinkle the *garam masala* over the top and mix it in. Garnish with a dollop of butter and the fresh mint or coriander, if desired.

S E R V E S   4 – 6

Parathas
ⓥ F L A K Y   B R E A D S

THESE PAN-FRIED BREADS ARE very simple to make and are quite a staple in the Punjab. They may be served with almost any meat, vegetable or bean dish in this chapter. Many villagers have them for breakfast with pickles and yoghurt or a glass of freshly churned buttermilk. *Chapati* flour is sold by Indian grocers.

∾

450 g/1 lb/4 cups *chapati*
   flour or a combination of
   225 g/8 oz/2 cups sifted
   wholewheat flour and
   225 g/8 oz/2 cups plain
   (all-purpose white) flour

2 teaspoons salt
8 tablespoons *ghee*, melted
   unsalted butter or
   vegetable oil for cooking
   the *parathas*

∾

Sieve the flour with the salt into a large, shallow bowl. Make a well in the centre and slowly pour in about 300 ml/10 fl oz/1¼ cups water. Mix. When all the water is incorporated, knead to form a soft, pliable dough. Cover with a damp cloth and leave to rest in a cool place for 45 minutes. This is the basic *paratha* dough.

Divide the dough into 8 equal portions and form into balls. Dust with flour.

Set a *tava* or a large heavy frying-pan over high heat.

Meanwhile, flatten one ball between the palms of your hands to make a disc. Put the disc on a lightly floured surface and, with a rolling pin, roll it out into a circle about 15 cm (6 inches) in diameter.

When the *tava* is hot, grease it lightly with a little *ghee* or the butter or oil and slap on the *paratha*. Cook for about 30 seconds. Flip the *paratha* over and cook the second side for 30 seconds. Flip over again and brush about 1½ teaspoons of the *ghee* over the top. Cook for 30 seconds, pressing down all over the surface with a spatula. Flip over again and brush the second side with 1½ teaspoons of the *ghee*. Cook for another 30 seconds, again pressing down with a spatula. Flip over a few more times, leaving the *paratha* to cook for about 10 seconds at a time. It should now be a nice golden-brown with a couple of dark spots. Remove and keep covered. Repeat the process with the remaining balls of dough. Keep the stack of *parathas* covered as you make them.

Note: *Parathas* are best when they are freshly made, but if you wish to make them ahead of time wrap the stack in foil and place the entire wrapped bundle in a moderate (160°C/325°F/Gas 3) pre-heated oven for 15 minutes to re-heat.

You may also place one *paratha* in a microwave oven for 1 minute to re-heat.

M A K E S   8   B R E A D S

Kheema Paratha
FLAKY BREADS STUFFED WITH SPICY MINCED (GROUND) LAMB

PARATHAS MAY BE STUFFED with dozens of fillings. Here is a very festive one. Eat it as part of a grand Indian meal or have it with a yoghurt relish and pickles.

❧

FOR THE DOUGH:
450 g/16 oz/4 cups *chapati* **flour or a combination of 225 g/8 oz/2 cups sifted wholewheat flour and 225 g/8 oz/2 cups plain (all-purpose white) flour**
2 tablespoons *ghee*, **melted unsalted butter or vegetable oil**

FOR THE MINCED (GROUND) LAMB:
2 tablespoons *ghee* **or vegetable oil**
2 tablespoons peeled and finely grated fresh ginger
6 garlic cloves, finely chopped
1 teaspoon cayenne pepper
1 medium-sized tomato, finely chopped
2 fresh hot green chillies, finely chopped

200 g/7 oz/1 cup finely minced (ground) lamb
¾–1 teaspoon salt
180 g/6 oz/4½ cups fresh green coriander, chopped

YOU ALSO NEED:
4 tablespoons *ghee*, **melted unsalted butter or vegetable oil for cooking the** *parathas*

❧

Make the basic Flaky Breads dough (page 245) but with this difference: incorporate the 2 tablespoons *ghee* or butter or oil into it as you knead. Cover with a damp cloth and set aside in a cool place for 45 minutes.

Make the minced (ground) lamb: Heat the *ghee* or oil in a large wok or pan over medium-high heat. When hot, add the ginger, garlic and cayenne pepper. Stir and fry for about 2–3 minutes. Add the tomato and chillies. Stir and fry for 5 minutes. Add the lamb. Stir and fry for 2–3 minutes. Add 25 ml/1 fl oz/2 tablespoons water, stir again and bring to a simmer.

Cover and cook on low heat for 40 minutes, stirring occasionally, until the liquid is fully absorbed. Add the salt and fresh coriander. Stir to mix. Divide this lamb mixture into 4 portions.

Knead the dough once again, divide it into 4 equal portions and form into balls. On a lightly floured surface, flatten each ball and, with a rolling pin, roll it out into a disc that is approximately 10 cm (4 inches) in diameter. Place a portion of the lamb mixture in the centre of one of the discs. Lift the edges of the dough to cover the filling completely and then give the gathered edges a slight twist to seal the bundle shut. Put the bundle on your floured work surface, sealed side down. Flatten the bundle slightly and roll it out again to form a disc about 19 cm (7½ inches) in diameter.

Set a heavy, cast-iron frying-pan or large *tava* over high heat. When very hot, lift up the rolled *paratha* and slap it on. Let it cook for about 1½ minutes. Flip it over and cook the second side for another minute. Brush the top with 1½ teaspoons of the *ghee* or butter or oil and quickly flip the *paratha* over again. Brush 1½ teaspoons of the *ghee* over the top, press down gently all over the surface with a spatula and cook for 30 seconds. Flip over. Cook for about 15 seconds and flip over. Keep flipping over at 15-second intervals a few more times, until the *paratha* is golden with a few dark brown spots. It should also cook through. Remove to a plate. Keep it covered while you make the remaining *parathas*.

To re-heat, see Flaky Breads (page 245).

MAKES 4 LARGE BREADS

Aloo Aur Anardana Paratha

FLAKY BREADS STUFFED WITH
ⓥ POTATO & POMEGRANATE SEEDS

ANOTHER STUFFED *PARATHA*, THIS time with a filling of lightly mashed, seasoned potatoes and tart, dried pomegranate seeds (*anardana*). Eat it for breakfast with plain yoghurt as the Punjabis do or serve it as part of a grand, North Indian meal. Wrapped in foil, it may also be taken on picnics.

∾

FOR THE DOUGH:
450 g/1 lb/4 cups *chapati* flour or a combination of 225 g/8 oz/2 cups sifted wholewheat flour and 225 g/8 oz/2 cups plain (all-purpose white) flour
2 tablespoons *ghee*, melted unsalted butter or vegetable oil

FOR THE STUFFING:
1 medium-large potato (200 g/7 oz), boiled and roughly mashed
2 tablespoons peeled and finely grated fresh ginger
2 fresh hot green chillies, finely chopped
2 teaspoons cayenne pepper
115 g/4 oz fresh green coriander, chopped

2 teaspoons dried pomegranate seeds (*anardana*, page 259), lightly crushed in a mortar
1 teaspoon salt

YOU ALSO NEED:
4 tablespoons *ghee*, melted unsalted butter or vegetable oil for cooking the *parathas*

∾

Make the dough as you did for the Flaky Breads stuffed with Minced (Ground) Lamb (page 246). Set aside.

In a large mixing bowl, combine the potato, ginger, chillies, cayenne pepper, fresh coriander, pomegranate seeds and salt. Mix well, and divide this mixture into 4 portions.

Make the breads following the instructions for Flaky Breads Stuffed with Minced (Ground) Lamb.

MAKES 4 BREADS

Bhatura
☺ PUFFED LEAVENED BREADS

RATHER LIKE NORTH INDIAN *pooris*, these are puffed, deep-fried breads. The difference is they are made with white flour and have leavening and yoghurt in the dough making them slightly spongy. They may be eaten with any split peas, beans and vegetables and are also delightful with kebabs inside them and with Minced (Ground) Lamb with Chick Peas (page 228).

~

400 g/14 oz/3 cups plus 2 tablespoons plain (all-purpose white) flour, plus extra for dusting
100 g/3½ oz/scant ½ cup semolina (*sooji*), page 277

½ teaspoon baking powder
¼ teaspoon bicarbonate of soda (baking soda)
1 teaspoon salt
2 tablespoons thick, Greek-style (whole milk) yoghurt

2 teaspoons sugar
2 tablespoons *ghee* or unsalted butter
Vegetable oil for deep-frying

~

In a large, shallow bowl, mix together the flour, semolina, baking powder, bicarbonate of soda (baking soda) and salt. Whisk the yoghurt, 175 ml/6 fl oz/¾ cup water and sugar in a separate bowl. Make a well in the centre of the flour mixture and slowly pour in the yoghurt mixture, mixing as you do so, until it is fully absorbed. Knead this dough until it is pliable but firm. Cover with a damp cloth and let it stand for 15 minutes.

Melt the *ghee* or butter and mix it into the dough. Knead for another 5 minutes. Cover with a damp cloth and let the dough rest for 45 minutes. Break the dough into 3 cm/ 1¼ inch wide balls. There should be about 18.

Heat the oil in a wok or large frying-pan over high heat. While it heats, dust your rolling surface with flour. Flatten one ball in the flour.

Roll the ball out with a rolling pin, dusting it with flour when needed, until you have a disc about 13 cm (5 inches) in diameter. Lift up the disc carefully, without allowing it to fold up, and slip it into the hot oil. It should sink to the bottom and rise immediately. Quickly flip it over. Keep tapping it lightly with a slotted spoon, pushing it down gently into the oil as you do so. It should puff up within seconds. Turn it over after 30 seconds and fry for a further 20–30 seconds or until it is golden and crisp. Remove with a slotted spoon. Rest briefly on kitchen paper (paper towels) to drain and then put on a plate. Cover with a domed lid or inverted bowl. Make all the *bhaturas* this way and serve immediately.

MAKES ABOUT 18 BREADS

Jatinder Kaur's Makki-Di-Roti

⑰ FLAT CORN BREADS

IN THE SMALL TOWNS and villages of the Punjab all the women and many of the men can form these flat corn breads by hand in seconds. For those not used to it, this is quite an art – but one well worth learning. I have described the method below. You may, if you prefer, roll them out with a rolling pin, as you would any other Indian flat breads, into 16 cm/6½ inch rounds. Just keep your rolling surface well dusted with flour. The edges of the breads may crack a little but that does tend to happen with the rolled version.

These breads are always served with Mustard Greens (page 236) and are a winter delight. They are best enjoyed with a nice layer of butter slathered on them while they are still hot! Punjabis like to pinch the thinner top layer of the bread before applying the butter so that it cracks open in places, allowing the butter to be properly absorbed. The amount of butter you put on is up to you. I have watched, with the usual Western trepidation, Punjabi women put as much as 2 tablespoons on to each bread. And I have watched Punjabi men devour four or five of the breads at a single sitting. I find that just cutting down on the butter eases my conscience, yet does not interfere too much with the demands of my palate!

Cornmeal flour is sold by Indian grocers.

---

400 g/14 oz/3 cups cornmeal flour plus extra for dusting
1 teaspoon salt

About 425 ml/14½ fl oz/ 1¾ cups plus 1 tablespoon warm water (it should be just bearable to the touch)

Unsalted butter for putting on top of breads (about 2–3 teaspoons per bread)

Mix the cornmeal and salt in a large, shallow bowl. Gradually add as much warm water as you need (aim for the texture of playdough), mixing the water until it is incorporated into the flour. Knead for 10 minutes, or until the dough is pliable. Divide the dough into 8 equal portions and form into balls. Flatten the balls to form patties and keep them covered.

Set a cast-iron frying-pan or *tava* over high heat. Wait for it to get really hot.

Take one patty and dip it in the extra flour. Roll the edges of the patty in the flour as well, as if it were a wheel. Put the patty down on a floured work surface. Press down repeatedly on the patty with the palm of one hand, in quick succession, all the while turning the patty a little. This will keep flattening it and thinning it out. Keep your other hand at the edge of the patty and push in slightly to prevent the edges from breaking. Dip the patty in the flour a second time if you need to. When you have a disc about 16 cm (6½ inches) in diameter, lift it up carefully and slap it on to the hot frying-pan or *tava*. Let it sit for 1 minute. Turn it over. Let it cook on the second side for 40 seconds. Turn it over again and cook for 30 seconds. This time, using a bunched-up cloth, press down on the bread in different spots to help it puff up slightly.

Now turn it over again. Cook for another 30 seconds, pressing down with the cloth. Turn it again and cook for 30 seconds. The bread should have attractive brown spots and be cooked through. If not, turn one more time. Take it off the heat. Pinch it in a few spots and put a generous dollop of butter all over it. Make all the breads this way.

Keep them in a covered dish as you make them and eat them while they are hot with a lathering of unsalted butter.

M A K E S   8   B R E A D S

Hoshiyar Singh at the Mohan International Hotel: Pudina Mooli Chutney
ⓥ M I N T & W H I T E R A D I S H C H U T N E Y

THIS CHUTNEY IS SERVED in the Punjab with fried fish and all manner of kebabs. You may serve it with any Indian meal. The radish flavour makes it very unusual and appealing.

❧

250 g/9 oz/10 cups fresh mint leaves, coarsely chopped
115 g/4 oz peeled white radish or red radishes, coarsely chopped

10–12 fresh hot green chillies, coarsely chopped
1 small onion (25 g/1 oz), chopped

2½ teaspoons salt or to taste
2–3 tablespoons fresh lime or lemon juice

❧

Combine all the ingredients in the container of an electric blender and blend, adding 2 or more tablespoons of water as needed.

S E R V E S   4

From Kesar-da-Dhaba, Amritsar: Ghiya Raita

COURGETTE (ZUCCHINI) RAITA

THIS VERY SIMPLE YOGHURT relish is offered at one of the oldest fast food joints in the walled city of Amritsar. Serve it with any Indian meal or eat it by itself. It is made with *ghiya* (bottle gourd) in Amritsar but I find that very lightly cooked courgettes make a good substitute.

❧

2 medium-sized courgettes (zucchini)

300 ml/10 fl oz/1¼ cups natural (plain) yoghurt
½ teaspoon salt or to taste

2 tablespoons finely chopped, fresh mint leaves

❧

Peel the courgettes (zucchini) and cut them in half lengthways. Scrape out the seeds with a spoon and grate the remaining flesh.

Bring 600 ml/1 pint/2½ cups water to the boil in a small pan. Put in the grated courgettes (zucchini). Boil rapidly for 10 seconds then drain thoroughly in a strainer. Let the courgettes (zucchini) sit in the strainer until they are cool enough to handle. Squeeze out as much moisture as you can. Set aside.

Put the yoghurt into a bowl. Beat lightly with a fork or whisk until it is smooth and creamy. Add the salt and mix it in. Add the fresh mint and the courgettes (zucchini). Stir to mix, making sure that all the courgette (zucchini) strands are well separated.

S E R V E S   4

Shalgham, Gajar Aur Phoolgobi Aachar
CAULIFLOWER, TURNIP & CARROT PICKLE

AT ITS SIMPLEST this may be eaten with Flaky Breads plain or stuffed (pages 244–8), but you may also serve it with grand Indian meals.

❧

- 250 ml/8 fl oz/1 cup mustard oil
- 1 small onion (25 g/1 oz), finely chopped
- 1 tablespoon fresh ginger that has been peeled and cut into very fine strips
- 1 teaspoon finely chopped garlic
- 200 g/7 oz cauliflower, cut into large, chunky florets
- 1 medium-sized turnip (150 g/5½ oz), peeled and cut into 2.5 cm/1 inch cubes
- 2 carrots (150 g/5½ oz), peeled and cut into 2.5 cm/1 inch sections and then halved lengthways; if too thick, quarter lengthways
- 2 teaspoons Punjabi *garam masala* (page 270)
- 1½–2 tablespoons cayenne pepper
- 4 teaspoons ground cumin
- 2 tablespoons brown mustard seeds, lightly ground in a clean coffee grinder
- 1 tablespoon salt
- 150 g/5 oz/⅔ cup sugar
- 120 ml/4 fl oz/½ cup white vinegar

❧

Heat the mustard oil in a wok or large frying-pan over medium-high heat. When hot, add the onions. Reduce the heat to medium and cook until the onions are light brown. Add the ginger and garlic and stir and fry for 1 minute. Put in the cauliflower, turnip and carrots. Stir and fry for 30 seconds. Add the *garam masala*, cayenne pepper, cumin, mustard seeds and salt. Stir for 1 minute. Mix the sugar with the vinegar and add to the vegetables. Stir and fry for another 30 seconds. Remove from the heat and leave to cool.

Transfer the pickle to sterilized jam or pickling jars. Cover the lids with cheesecloth, secured with rubber bands, and keep the jars in a dry and if possible sunny place for 2 days to allow the pickle to breathe, and so that any excess moisture is dried up. Shake the pickle jars every now and then.

On the third day remove the cheesecloth and seal the jars with tight fitting lids. Leave unrefrigerated in a warm, sunny spot in the house. The pickle should be ready in 4–7 days. It is ready when it has turned sour. It can now be refrigerated.

Stir well before removing from the jar.

900 ML/1½ PINTS/3¾ CUPS

Radha Anand's Seviyan
ⓥ VERMICELLI PUDDING

A MUCH LOVED DESSERT made with what Punjab has in abundance: milk.

---

1 tablespoon *ghee* or melted
unsalted butter
85 g/3 oz fine vermicelli,
broken up into 7.5 cm/
3 inch pieces

1.2 litres/2 pints/5 cups full-
fat (whole) milk
30 g/1 oz/¼ cup blanched
and slivered almonds
140 g/5 oz/⅔ cup sugar

8 green cardamom pods
2 tablespoons sultanas
(golden raisins)
2–3 drops *kewra* water
(page 272)

Heat the *ghee* or butter in a large wok or
frying-pan over medium heat. When hot, add
the vermicelli and stir-fry until it is golden-
brown. This should take about 5–6 minutes.
With a slotted spoon, remove the vermicelli
and place on kitchen paper (paper towels) to
absorb excess fat.

Bring the milk to the boil in a heavy based
saucepan. Add the vermicelli. Turn the heat to
low, add the almonds and sugar and stir.
Meanwhile, peel the cardamom pods, discard
their skins, and add the seeds to the milk as
well as the sultanas (golden raisins). Simmer
for 30 minutes, stirring often, until the mixture
is thick. Remove from the heat and add the
kewra water. Serve warm.

SERVES 4

Cauliflower with Potatoes, Banquet Style (page 240)
and Amritsari Beans (page 243).

Sunil Vijayakar's Rabadhi

ⓥ CREAMED MILK PUDDING

THIS DELICIOUS INDIAN DESSERT quite justifies the time taken to prepare it.

❧

3 litres/5¼ pints/3 quarts
  full-fat (whole) milk
340 g/12 oz/⅔ cup sugar
4 tablespoons shelled,
  unsalted pistachio nuts,
  skinned and roughly
  chopped

2 cardamom pods, lightly
  crushed
2–3 drops *kewra* water
  (page 272)
2–3 drops rose water
Fresh rose petals (optional)

❧

Bring the milk to the boil in a large, heavy saucepan, over medium-high heat. Turn the heat down slightly so that the milk does not bubble over and continue to boil for another 30 minutes, stirring constantly. Continue to cook the milk, stirring every 3–4 minutes, for another 45 minutes. The consistency should now be grainy and thick. Add the sugar, pistachio nuts, and cardamom pods. Continue to stir and cook for another 10–15 minutes. The mixture should be fairly thick by now. Remove from the heat and add the *kewra* and rose waters.

Place in a bowl. Cover and refrigerate for a couple of hours before serving. Garnish with rose petals, if desired.

S E R V E S   4 – 6

SPECIAL INGREDIENTS

AJWAIN (OR AJOWAN) SEEDS

These small seeds look like celery seeds but taste more like a pungent version of thyme. (A student of mine compared it to a mixture of anise and black pepper!) Used sparingly, as their flavour is strong, they are sprinkled into Indian breads, savoury biscuits and numerous noodle-like snacks made with chick pea flour. They also add a pleasant thyme-like taste to vegetables such as green beans and potatoes and to roast meats.

AMCHOOR (GREEN MANGO POWDER)

Unripe green mangoes are peeled, sliced and their sour flesh sun-dried and ground to make *amchoor* powder. (The dried slices are also used in Indian cookery but not needed for recipes here.) The beige, slightly fibrous powder, rich in vitamin C, is tart but with a hint of sweetness and is used as lemon juice might be. It is particularly useful when sourness is required but the ingredients need to be kept dry, such as when sautéing spiced potatoes. As the powder can get lumpy, crumble it well before use.

ANARDANA (POMEGRANATE SEEDS)

Sour, dried pomegranate seeds used mainly in Punjabi cooking to give sourness to foods. They are sometimes crushed or ground before use. You may do this in a mortar or else grind them for a second or two in a clean coffee grinder.

ASAFETIDA

The sap from the roots and stem of a giant fennel-like plant dries into a hard resin. It is sold in both lump and ground form. Only the ground form is used here. It has a strong fetid aroma and is used in very small quantities both for its legendary digestive properties and for the much gentler, garlic-like aroma it leaves behind after cooking. (James Beard compared it to the smell of truffles.) Excellent with dried beans and vegetables. Store in a tightly closed container.

ATA
See *Chapati flour*.

BAY LEAVES
These dried leaves are added to scores of Indian rice and meat dishes for their delicate aroma. Sometimes they are lightly browned in oil first to intensify this aroma, using the '*tarka*' technique (page 256).

BEANS AND PEAS, DRIED
All beans should be picked over and washed in several changes of water. Store in tightly closed jars.

Chana dal: The Indian version of yellow split peas but with better texture and a very nutty flavour. Comes hulled and split. It may be cooked by itself or it can be soaked and cooked with rice or vegetables or meat. In the south, it is used as a spice. It also goes into many Indian snacks of the 'Bombay Mix' variety.

Chana dal, roasted: This is *chana dal* that has been roasted. It is actually edible at this stage. It is often ground and used to bind all manner of minced (ground) meat kebabs. It can also be fried and put into snack foods or used to thicken sauces.

Kidney beans, red: Known as *rajma* in the Punjab where they are eaten most, these are the red kidney beans that are sold by most supermarkets.

Masoor dal (red split lentils): A hulled, salmon-coloured pea that turns yellow after cooking.

Moong (or mung) dal: These yellow split beans are sold both with and without skin by almost every Indian grocer. The skins are green, the flesh yellow.

Mung beans, whole: The same bean as above, only whole. It is these beans that are sprouted and sold as bean sprouts. Indians half-sprout them and also cook them whole.

Toovar dal (also called arhar dal): A dull yellow split pea with an earthy taste. It is sold in its plain form and in an 'oily' form which is darker. The latter is rubbed with castor oil. This oil needs to be washed off.

Urad beans, whole black: Small, black-skinned oval beans that are pale yellow inside. Their texture is somewhat glutinous. You can buy them from all Indian grocers. Ask for whole *urad* or *sabut urad*. In the Punjab, where they are much loved, they are known as *ma di dal*.

Urad dal: A small, pale yellow split pea that is used, among other things, to make all manner of South Indian pancakes. It has a slightly viscous texture. It is also used as a seasoning. It is South Indians who seem to have discovered that if you throw a few of these dried, split peas into hot oil, using the 'tarka' method, the seeds will turn red and nutty. Anything stir-fried in the oil afterwards will pick up that nutty flavour and aroma.

BITTER GOURDS (KARELA IN MOST OF NORTH INDIA)
One of the many bitter vegetables loved in India, these look like members of the marrow family except that their green skins are ridged like that of an alligator. To prepare *karela*, the ridges are first scraped off leaving a smooth skin, and the gourd is then rubbed with salt and set aside. Some of the bitterness flows out with the salty water. Indians consider them very good for cleansing the blood and for diabetes.

BLACK PEPPER
Native to India, whole peppercorns are added to rice and meat dishes for a mild peppery-lemony flavour. Ground pepper was once used in large amounts, sometimes several tablespoons in a single dish, especially in South India where it grows. The arrival of the chilli pepper from the New World around 1498 changed that usage somewhat, though it still exists. In some South Indian dishes peppercorns are lightly roasted before use to draw out their lemony taste.

BLACK SALT (KALA NAMAK)
This fairly strong-smelling rock salt is used in many of North India's snack foods. It is sold both ground and in lump form by Indian grocers. If you

buy the lump form, grind what you need in a clean coffee grinder. Store in a tightly lidded jar.

CARDAMOM

Cardamom pods: Small green pods, the fruit of a ginger-like plant, hold clusters of black, highly aromatic seeds smelling like a combination of camphor, eucalyptus, orange peel and lemon. Whole pods are put into rice and meat dishes and ground seeds are the main flavour in *garam masala* (page 270). This versatile spice is the vanilla of India and used in most desserts and sweetmeats. It is also added to spiced tea and sucked as a mouth-freshener.

Cardamom seeds that have been taken out of their pods are sold separately by Indian grocers. If you cannot get them, take the seeds out of the pods yourself. The most aromatic pods are the ones that are green in colour. White ones sold by supermarkets have been bleached and therefore have less flavour.

Cardamom pods, black: Somewhat like the smaller cardamom in flavour, these large black pods have seeds with a cruder, heavier flavour and aroma.

Cardamom seeds, ground: The seeds of the cardamom pods are sold by themselves in both their whole and ground forms. This powder can be put into rice dishes, desserts and Indian-style meat dishes.

CASHEW NUTS

These nuts travelled from the Americas via Africa and India all the way to China. It might be useful for you to know that all so-called 'raw' cashews have been processed to remove the prussic acid in their outer shells. They are grown commonly on India's west coast and are used in pilafs, desserts and even made into *bhajis* and curries.

CAYENNE PEPPER

This hot powder is made today by grinding the dried, red skins of several types of chilli peppers. In India, and in Indian grocer shops in the West, it is simply called chilli powder. But since that name can be confused with the Mexican-style chilli powder that also contains cumin, garlic and oregano, I am using the name 'cayenne pepper' in all recipes. Even though chillies came from the New World, India today is the largest producer and one of the largest exporters and consumers. When adding to recipes, use your discretion.

CHAAT MASALA

There are many versions of this throughout North India. Here is a Punjabi version.

Makes about 5 tablespoons

4 teaspoons lightly roasted and ground cumin seeds

1½ tablespoons *amchoor*

2 teaspoons cayenne pepper

1 teaspoon finely ground black pepper

¾ teaspoon finely ground black salt

1 teaspoon salt

Mix all the ingredients thoroughly, breaking up any lumps. Store in a tightly lidded jar.

CHAPATI FLOUR

Very finely ground wholewheat flour used to make *chapatis*, *pooris* and other breads. Sold by all Indian grocers.

CHAROLI NUTS

A tiny nut that tastes a bit like hazelnut. Used in rich meat sauces and in sweets and stuffings.

CHHANA

A fresh cheese made by curdling milk. Used for making many Bengali sweets. See the recipe on page 173.

CHILLIES, WHOLE, DRIED, HOT, RED

When whole dried chillies are added to Indian food, it is generally done through the 'tarka' method (page 286). A quick contact with very hot oil enhances and intensifies the flavour of their skins. It is that flavour that Indians want. (Mexicans traditionally do this by roasting their chillies.)

Then, if actual chilli-heat is desired, the chillies are allowed to stew with the food being cooked. The most commonly used dry chilli is a cayenne type. To remove seeds from dried chillies, break off the stem end and shake the seeds out. Rotating a chilli between the fingers can help. Sometimes it is necessary to break the chilli in order to get all the seeds out.

There is a variety of red chilli, known frequently as the 'Kashmiri chilli', that is known for the bright red colour it imparts, rather like good paprika. Since it is not always easy to get in the West, I often use a combination of cayenne pepper and paprika in my recipes.

CHILLIES, WHOLE, FRESH, GREEN AND RED

The fresh green chilli used in Indian cooking is of the cayenne type, generally about 7.5 cm/3 inches long and slender. Its heat can vary from mild to fiery. (Stupid bees, it seems, unthinkingly cross-pollinate different varieties that grow in proximity to each other.) The only way to judge the heat is by tasting a tiny piece of skin from the middle section. (Keep some yoghurt handy!) The top part of the chilli with more seeds is always the hottest, the bottom tip, the mildest. The hot seeds of the chilli are never removed in India but you may do so. Use whatever chilli you can find. The *jalapeno* is thicker skinned and hotter than the Indian chilli. Use discretion. Also wash your hands well after handling chillies. If you touch your eyes, mouth or nose without washing, they may burn.

Red chillies are just ripe green chillies. However, their flavour is slightly different, though their intensity can be exactly the same.

Chillies are a very rich source of iron and vitamins A and C. To store fresh red or green chillies wrap them first in newspaper, then in plastic and store in the refrigerator. They should last several weeks. Any that begin to soften and rot should be removed as they tend to infect the whole batch.

CHILLI POWDER, KASHMIRI

This is powder made from a long Kashmiri chilli that is relatively mild in taste but which, like paprika, gives off a lovely, deep red colour.

CINNAMON

Used mainly for desserts in the West, cinnamon, often in its 'stick' form, is added to many Indian rice and meat dishes for its warm, sweet aroma.

This inner bark from a laurel-like tree is also an important ingredient in the aromatic mixture *garam masala* (page 270).

CLOVES

Indians rarely use cloves in desserts but do use them in meat and rice dishes and in the spice mixture *garam masala* (page 270). They carry the pungently aromatic cloves as well as cardamom pods in tiny silver boxes, to use as mouth-fresheners when needed. For the same reason cloves are always part of the betel leaf paraphernalia that is offered as a digestive at the end of a meal.

COCONUT, FRESH

When buying a coconut, look for one that shows no signs of mould and is free of cracks. Shake the coconut. If it contains a lot of water it has a better chance of being good. People generally weigh a coconut in each hand and pick the heavier of the two. In the West it is always safer to buy an extra coconut just in case one turns out to be bad.

To break open a coconut, use the unsharpened side of a cleaver and hit the coconut hard all around its equator. You can hold the coconut in one hand over a large bowl while you hit with the other. Or you can rest the coconut on a stone while you hit it and then rush it to a bowl as soon as the first crack appears. The bowl is there to catch the coconut water. Some people like to drink it. I do. This coconut water, by the way, is not used in cooking. But it is a good indication of the sweetness and freshness of the coconut.

You should now have two halves. Before proceeding any further, cut off a small bit of the meat and taste it. The dreaded word here is 'rancid'! Your coconut should taste sweet. If it is lacking in sweetness, it can be endured. But it must never be rancid or mouldy inside. Now remove the tough outer shell by slipping a knife between it and the meat and then prising the meat out. Sometimes it helps to crack the halves into smaller pieces to do this. This meat now has a thin brown skin.

To grate fresh coconut: If your recipe calls for freshly grated coconut, peel the skin off with a vegetable peeler or a knife, cut the meat into small cubes and throw the cubes into the container of a food processor or blender.

When you blend you will not get a paste. What you will get is something resembling grated coconut. You can freeze what you don't use. Grated coconut freezes very well and it is a good idea to keep some at hand.

As a substitute for freshly grated coconut, you can use unsweetened, desiccated coconut which is sold in most health food stores. Here is how you do this: To get the equivalent of 2 oz/60 g/8 tablespoons of freshly grated coconut, take 1 oz/30 g/5 tablespoons unsweetened, desiccated coconut and soak it in 4 tablespoons water for about an hour.

COCONUT MILK

This is best made from fresh coconuts but is also available canned or may be made using powdered milk, unsweetened, desiccated (shredded) coconut or blocks of creamed coconut. No prepared coconut milk keeps well – this includes canned coconut milk after the can has been opened. Its refrigerated life is no longer than two days.

Using fresh coconut: First you prise off the flesh as suggested above. Whether you peel the brown skin or not depends on the dish. It if needs to look pale and pristine, remove the skin. If not, leave it on and grate the meat in a food processor or blender (see page 265). To make about 350 ml/12 fl oz/1½ cups coconut milk, fill a glass measuring jug to the 450 ml/ 15 fl oz/2 cup mark with grated coconut. Empty it into a blender or food processor. Add 300 ml/10 fl oz/1¼ cups very hot water. Blend for a few seconds. Line a sieve with a piece of muslin or cheesecloth and place it over a bowl. Empty the contents of the blender into the sieve. Gather the ends of the cloth together and squeeze out all the liquid. For most of my recipes, this is the coconut milk that is needed. It is sometimes referred to as thick coconut milk. If a recipe calls for thin coconut milk, the entire process needs to be repeated using the squeezed-out coconut and the same amount of water. If you let the thick coconut milk sit for a while, cream will rise to the top. That is why I suggest that you always stir the coconut milk before using it. If just the cream is required, then spoon it off the top.

Canned coconut milk: This is available at most Asian grocer shops but the quality varies. There is a brand which I like very much and use frequently.

It is *Chaokoh* and is a product of Thailand. It is white and creamy and quite delicious. As the cream tends to rise to the top in a can as well, always stir it well before using it. Sometimes, because of the fat in it, tinned coconut milk tends to get very grainy. You can either whir it for a second in a blender or else beat it well.

I find that whereas you can cook a fish, for example, in fresh coconut milk for a long time, canned coconut milk, which behaves differently is best added toward the end. Canned coconut is very thick, partly because it has thickeners in it. As a result, many of my recipes require that canned coconut milk be thinned before use.

Powdered coconut milk: You can now buy packets of powdered coconut milk from Oriental grocers and supermarkets. Their quality varies from good to poor, the poor ones containing hard-to-dissolve globules of fat. Emma brand from Malaysia is acceptable. Directions for making the milk are always on the packets. The process usually involves mixing an equal volume of powder and hot water and stirring well. Unwanted lumps should be strained away. This milk is best added to recipes towards the end of the cooking time.

Using unsweetened, desiccated coconut: Put 115 g/4 oz/2 cups unsweetened, desiccated coconut into a pan. Add 600 ml/1 pint/2½ cups water and bring to a simmer. Now pour the contents into the container of a blender or food processor and blend for a minute. Strain the resulting mixture through a double thickness of cheesecloth pushing out as much liquid as you can. You should get about 350 ml/12 fl oz/1½ cups of thick coconut milk. If you repeat the process with the same amount of water again, using the left-over coconut, you can get another 450 ml/15 fl oz/ 2 cups of thin coconut milk.

Using creamed coconut: Available in block form, this can also be turned into coconut milk. I do not advise that you do this if you need large quantities of milk. However, if just a few tablespoons are required you can, for example, take 2 tablespoons creamed coconut and mix them with 2 tablespoons hot water. The thick coconut milk that will result should only be put into dishes at the last moment.

CORIANDER, FRESH GREEN

This is the parsley of India. It is ground into fresh chutneys, mixed in with vegetables, cooked with chicken and used as a garnish.

Generally just the delicate, fragrant, green leaves are used though South Indians often throw the stems into soupy *dals* for extra flavour. The coriander should be very well washed first. When fresh green coriander is called for, chop up the top of the plant where the stalks are slender. From the lower half, where the stalks are thicker, you will have to pick off the leaves.

When you buy fresh green coriander, the best way to keep it is to stand it in a glass of water, cover it with a plastic bag and refrigerate the whole thing. Break off the leaves and stems as you need and keep the rest refrigerated. The water should be changed daily and dead leaves removed.

CORIANDER SEEDS

These beige, ridged seeds are sweetly spicy and cheap. As a result they are very commonly used in a great deal of Indian cookery. They are often the major part of many spice mixtures. In Maharashtra in western India, they are combined with cumin, shredded coconut and other spices, then dry roasted and ground to make a delicious 'black *masala*' that is used with both meat and vegetables. In the southern state of Kerala, they are combined with fenugreek seeds, black peppercorns and red chillies, dry-roasted and used to flavour dishes of prawns (shrimps) and lobster. In the north, coriander, cumin and turmeric are a common trinity used in hundreds of dishes.

To dry-roast coriander seeds: Put the required quantity into a small, heated cast-iron frying pan. Stir and roast for 2–3 minutes until the seeds turn a few shades darker and emit a roasted aroma. To grind the seeds, it is best to use a clean coffee grinder or other spice grinder.

CORNMEAL FLOUR

There are many grades of cornmeal flour. The one used for tortillas is perhaps the closest to the Indian variety. It is really best to buy this flour from Indian grocers where it is called *makki ka ata*. Store as you would any flour, in a tightly closed tin.

CUMIN SEEDS

These look like caraway seeds but are slightly larger, plumper and lighter in colour. Their flavour is similar to caraway, only gentler and sweeter. They are used both whole and ground. When whole, they are often subjected to the 'tarka' technique (page 286), which intensifies their flavour and makes them slightly nutty. When ground, they are used in meat, rice and vegetable dishes. Cumin seeds can also be dry-roasted first and then ground. This version is sprinkled over many snack foods, relishes and yoghurt dishes.

Ground roasted cumin seeds: Put 3–4 tablespoons cumin seeds into a small, heated, cast-iron frying-pan. Keep over medium heat. Stir the cumin until it is a few shades darker and emits a distinct roasted aroma. Grind in a clean coffee grinder and store in a tightly lidded jar.

CUMIN SEEDS, BLACK

A rare and therefore more expensive form of cumin with sweeter, smaller and more delicate seeds. Their mild pungency is perfect for the aromatic mixture of spices known as *garam masala* (page 270). The seeds can also be lightly dry-roasted and sprinkled whole over rice pilafs.

CURRY LEAVES, FRESH AND DRIED

These highly aromatic leaves are used in much Indian coastal and southern cookery. They are always used in their fresh form. They are now increasingly available in the West. You could use the dried leaf if the fresh is unavailable. Its aroma is very limited. Indian grocers sell both fresh and dried curry leaves. They come attached to stalks. They can be pulled off their stalks in one swoop. Keep curry leaves in a flat, plastic bag. They last for several days in the refrigerator. They may also be frozen, so when you do see them in the market, buy a lot and store them in your freezer.

FENNEL SEEDS

They look a bit like cumin seeds but are much plumper and greener. Their flavour is decidedly anise-like. In Kashmir they are often ground and used in conjunction with asafetida and powdered ginger for a host of fish and vegetable dishes. In north and western India, the whole seeds are used in pickles and chutneys and snack foods. Using the 'tarka' technique, they are also used in the stir-frying of vegetables, particularly in Bengal (eastern India), where they are part of the five-spice mixture called *panch phoran* (page 275). Fennel seeds can be dry-roasted and then eaten after a meal as both a digestive and mouth-freshener. To grind fennel seeds, just put 2–3 tablespoons into a clean coffee grinder or other spice grinder and grind as finely as possible. Store in an air-tight container.

FENUGREEK SEEDS

It is these angular, yellowish seeds that give many commercial curry powders their earthy, musky 'curry' aroma. In most of northern India they are used mainly in pickles, chutneys and vegetarian dishes. In western, southern and eastern India, they are used in meat and fish dishes as well (such as the *vindaloo* from Goa). They are a part of the Bengali spice mixture, *panch phoran*.

GARAM MASALA

This spice combination varies with each household though the name seems constant. *'Garam'* means 'hot' and *'masala'* means 'spices' so the spices in this mixture were traditionally those which 'heated' the body according to the ancient *ayurvedic* system of medicine. They all happened to be highly aromatic as well. Commercial mixtures tend to cut down on the expensive cardamom and fill up with the cheaper coriander and cumin. Here is how you make a classic ground mixture: Combine in a clean coffee grinder 1 tablespoon cardamom seeds, 1 teaspoon cloves, 1 teaspoon black peppercorns, 1 teaspoon black cumin seeds, a 5 cm/ 2 inch cinnamon stick, 1/3 nutmeg and a curl of mace. Grind to a fine powder. Store in a tightly closed jar and use as needed. Many people add a bay leaf to the mixture. Generally, though not always, *garam masala* is sprinkled towards the end of the cooking time to retain its aroma. The *garama masala* spices can also be used whole. If two or more of them are used together, they are still loosely referred to as *garam masala*.

Punjabi garam masala: *Garam masalas* vary in different parts of India. Here is one that is commonly used in the Punjab.

5 tablespoons coriander seeds

3 tablespoons cumin seeds

2½ tablespoons black peppercorns

2½ tablespoons black cardamom seeds

1½ teaspoons green cardamom seeds

5 cm/2 inch cinnamon stick

4–5 cloves

About ⅙ nutmeg

Put the coriander and cumin into a cast-iron frying-pan over medium heat. Stir until very lightly roasted. Empty on to a plate. Allow them to cool slightly, then put them and the remaining ingredients into a clean coffee grinder and grind as finely as possible. You may need to do this in more than one batch. Store in a tightly lidded jar.

GARLIC

Some Indians (Kashmiri Hindus, the Jain sect) do not touch garlic but the rest of the country eats it with pleasure. It is an important ingredient in meat sauces which often require that onion, garlic and ginger, the 'wet' trinity of seasonings, be ground into a paste and then be fried in oil until dark and thick. In parts of Saurashtra in western India, garlic, salt and dried red chillies are pounded together to make an everyday condiment.

GHEE (CLARIFIED BUTTER)

This is butter that has been so thoroughly clarified that it can even be used for deep-frying. As it no longer contains milk solids, refrigeration is not necessary. It has a nutty, buttery taste. All Indian grocers sell it and I find it more convenient to buy it. If, however, you need to make it, put 450 g/ 1 lb unsalted butter in a pan over low heat and let it simmer very gently until the milky solids turn brownish and cling to the sides of the pot or else fall to the bottom. The time that this takes will depend on the amount of water in the butter. Watch carefully toward the end and do not let it turn. Strain the *ghee* through a triple layer of cheesecloth. Home-made *ghee* is best stored in the refrigerator.

GINGER, FRESH

This rhizome has a sharp, pungent, cleansing taste and is a digestive to boot. It is ground and used in meat sauces (see *Garlic*) and in drinks. It is also cut into slivers or minute dice and used when stir-frying potatoes, green beans, spinach and other vegetables. When finely grated ginger is required, it should first be peeled and then grated on the finest part of a grater so it turns into pulp. When a recipe requires that 2.5 cm/1 inch of ginger be grated, it is best to keep that piece attached to the large knob. The knob acts as a handle and saves you from grating your fingers.

Ginger should be stored in a dry, cool place. Many people like to bury it in dryish, sandy soil. This way they can break off and retrieve small portions as they need them while the rest of the knob generously keeps growing.

JAGGERY

A form of raw, lump, cane sugar. It is sold in pieces that are cut off from larger blocks. You should look for the kind that crumbles easily and is not rock-hard. It can be found in Indian grocer shops.

KALONJI (NIGELLA)

Most Indians associate these black, tear-drop-shaped seeds with *tandoor* oven breads (they are sprinkled over the top), with pickles, with Bengali food and the Bengali five-spice mixture, *panch phoran* and with certain North Indian vegetarian dishes. Their oregano-like taste is quite strong so they should be used with some discretion.

KEWRA ESSENCE

This flowery essence comes from a variety of the screwpine plant. In Muslim Indian cooking it is used in banquet-style dishes of rice and meat and in desserts. It may even be sprinkled on breads though this is usually done not with the concentrated essence but with the lighter *kewra* water which is sold in larger bottles. *Kewra* is also available as a syrup which is mixed with ice and water to make a summer drink.

Kewra water: This is a more diluted version of *kewra* essence.

KOKUM

This is the pliable, semi-dried, sour and astringent skin of a mangosteen-like fruit (*Garcinia indica*) that grows along India's coast. It is used for souring, rather like tamarind. It can sometimes be a bit salty as well so use a little care. Store in an air-tight container to prevent drying out. When *kokum* is used in a dish, it is rarely eaten. It is left either in the pan or in the serving dish.

MACE, SEE NUTMEG

MELON SEEDS, PEELED
These are used to thicken sauces, especially for meat dishes.

MUSTARD OIL
This oil has the same characteristics as the seeds it comes from. When raw, it smells hot and pungent. When heated, the pungency goes into the air (you can smell it in your kitchen) and the oil turns sweet. It is used in Bengali and Kashmiri cookery, and in most oil pickles. It is also good for a massage!

MUSTARD SEEDS, BROWN
Of the three varieties of mustard seeds, white (actually yellowish), brown (a reddish-brown) and black (slightly larger, brownish black seeds), it is the brown that has been grown and used in India since antiquity. To confuse matters, the brown seeds are often referred to as black. When shopping, look for the small, reddish-brown variety although, at a pinch, any will do. All mustard seeds have Jekyll and Hyde characteristics. When crushed, they are nose-tinglingly pungent. However, if they are thrown into hot oil and allowed to pop using the '*tarka*' method (page 286), they turn quite nutty and sweet.

In India, both these techniques are used, sometimes in the same recipe. Whole mustard seeds, popped in oil, are used to season vegetables, pulses (legumes), yoghurt relishes, salads and rice dishes. Crushed seeds are used to steam fish, in sauces and in pickles.

MUSTARD SEEDS, HULLED AND SPLIT
Brown mustard seeds are hulled and split and made into what Indians call a *dal*. This spice is mainly used for pickling. The best substitute is coarsely ground brown mustard seeds.

MUSTARD SEEDS, WHOLE, YELLOW

The European mustard seeds are also used by Indians when a milder flavour is desired. Sometimes brown and yellow mustard seeds are mixed for a special effect.

NUTMEG AND MACE

Nutmegs are the dried seeds of a round pear-like fruit. Mace is the red, lacy covering around the seeds that turns yellowish when dried. Both have similar warm, sweetish and slightly camphorous flavours though mace has a slightly bitter edge. Both nutmeg and mace are used here in the *garam masala* mixture (page 270). A nutmeg breaks easily. Just hit it lightly with a hammer to get the third needed for the *garam masala* recipe. Indians almost never use nutmeg for desserts and drinks.

OIL

For most of the recipes in this book, I would recommend using ground-nut/peanut or corn oil. If oil is used for deep-frying, it can be re-used. Skim off all extraneous matter with a skimmer and then drop a chunk of ginger or potato into it and let it fry. This chunk will absorb many of the unwanted flavours. Strain the oil when it is cool enough to handle through a triple thickness of cheesecloth or a large handkerchief. Let it cool completely and then store it in a bottle. When re-using, mix half old oil with half fresh oil.

Olive oil: This is only found in Goan recipes because of that area's Portuguese heritage. Its use is now quite rare as almost no foreign oil is imported.

PALM SUGAR

This is a delicious, raw, honey-coloured lump sugar used in much of coastal India. It is sold by South-east Asian grocers both in cans and in plain plastic containers. It comes in lump or fairly flowing forms. The best substitute for it is either Indian sugar cane jaggery (make sure it is not rock-hard) or brown sugar. It keeps well if tightly covered. Refrigeration is not needed.

PANCH PHORAN (5-SPICE MIXTURE)

This very Bengali spice mixture consists of fennel seeds, mustard seeds, fenugreek seeds, cumin seeds and *kalonji* mixed in equal proportions.

PAPRIKA

Not generally used in Indian food. I use it frequently in place of red chillies in order to give the dishes their traditional red colour. Paprika tends to darken as it sits in glass bottles. Since I use it only for the colour, it is important that you use good quality paprika that is bright red.

POPPADOMS

Also called *papar*, these Indian wafers are made out of dried split peas and are sold either plain or studded with black pepper (or garlic or red pepper) by Indian grocers. They should be deep-fried for a few seconds in hot oil or toasted. They are served with most Indian vegetarian meals. They are also good with drinks.

POPPY SEEDS, WHITE

Only the white seeds are used in India, mainly to thicken sauces.

PRAWNS (SHRIMP), DRIED

These are sold in plastic packets at Chinese and all South-east Asian grocer shops and are best when pinkish in colour. Price is often an indication of quality. They should be rinsed off and then soaked for 5–10 minutes in hot water before being lifted out of the water and ground. They add a tremendous amount of concentrated flavour to the dishes to which they are added. They last well if kept in a well-closed plastic container in the refrigerator. I have used these prawns (shrimp) instead of the very tiny ones found in Goan markets.

RICE

Many varieties of rice are used in Indian cookery. There is the protein-rich, partially milled 'red' rice used along the Konkan coast south of Bombay. Then there is 'boiled' rice. This is the original par-boiled rice that predates Uncle Ben and must have been the inspiration for the rice Uncle Ben produced in 1943. Along India's southern coasts, 'boiled' rice has been produced for centuries. The process of boiling the rice before it is husked and milled not only makes the grains tough and indestructible but it also pushes the B complex vitamins into the inner kernel. This rice is used not only for everyday eating in the south but also to make a variety of pancakes, cakes and snacks.

Then there is Basmati rice, the pearls of the north. It is a very fine, long-grain, highly aromatic rice grown in the foothills of the Himalaya mountains. The better varieties are generally aged a year before being sold. This rice is now being grown in America as well.

RICE FLOUR

This is made from ground rice and is sold by most East Asian, South-east Asian, Indian and Pakistani grocers.

SAFFRON

I have only used leaf saffron in this book. These are the whole, dried saffron threads, the stigma of the autumn crocus. Look for a reliable source for your saffron as it is very expensive and there can be a great deal of adulteration. Indians often roast the saffron threads lightly before soaking them in a small amount of hot milk to bring out the colour. This milk is then poured over rice, in dishes such as *biryani*, to give it its orange highlights.

SAMBAR POWDER

Fills a 300 ml/10 fl oz/1¼ cup jar.

This powder, which uses split peas as spices, is used to make the South Indian dish called *sambar*. It can be stored in a tightly closed jar for several months.

1 teaspoon vegetable oil

5 tablespoons coriander seeds

1 teaspoon mustard seeds

1 teaspoon *moong dal*

½ tablespoon *chana dal*

½ tablespoon *urad dal*

1 teaspoon fenugreek seeds

1 teaspoon black peppercorns

¼ teaspoon ground asafetida

1 teaspoon cumin seeds

20 fresh curry leaves, if available

12 dried hot red chillies

Heat the oil in a large, heavy frying-pan or a heavy wok over medium heat. Put in the coriander seeds, mustard seeds, *moong dal, chana dal, urad dal,* fenugreek seeds, black peppercorns, asafetida and cumin seeds. Stir and roast for 3–4 minutes. Add the curry leaves if using. Stir and roast for another 5 minutes. Add the dried chillies and continue stirring and roasting for 2–3 minutes or until chillies darken. Remove spices to a plate. When the spices have cooled, put them into a coffee grinder in small batches and grind as finely as possible. Store in a tightly closed jar.

SEMOLINA

This is wheat ground to the texture of grain cornmeal or polenta. It is sold by Indian grocers as *sooji* and really has no good substitute. The supermarket semolina tends to be far too fine for Indian pilafs and *halvas*.

SESAME SEEDS

You may use white sesame seeds or the beige ones for all the recipes in this book.

To roast sesame seeds: Put a small, cast-iron frying-pan to heat over medium-low heat. When hot, put in 1–3 tablespoons sesame seeds. Stir them around until they turn a shade darker and give out a wonderful roasted aroma. Sesame seeds to tend to fly around as they are roasted. You could turn down the heat slightly when they do this or cover the pan loosely. Remove the seeds from the pan as soon as they are done. You may roast sesame seeds ahead of time. Cool them and store them in a tightly lidded jar. They can last several weeks this way though I must add that they are best when freshly roasted.

To roast and lightly crush sesame seeds: Roast the seeds as suggested above. Now put them into the container of a clean coffee grinder or spice grinder and whir it for just a second or two. The seeds should *not* turn to a powder. You may also crush them lightly in a mortar.

SHALLOTS

These are used routinely in South India in place of the larger onion common to the north. In places like Goa, they hang in kitchens like long ropes, to be plucked at will.

STAR ANISE

A flower-shaped collection of pods. Brownish-black in colour, this spice has a decided anise flavour. It is used frequently along India's western coast where the trade with China started in ancient times. Store in a tightly lidded jar. If a pod of star anise is called for, think of a pod as a petal of the flower and break off one section.

TAMARIND

The fruit of a tall shade tree, tamarinds look like wide beans. As they ripen, their sour green flesh turns a chocolate colour. It remains sour but picks up a hint of sweetness. For commercial purposes, tamarinds are peeled, seeded, semi-dried and their brown flesh compacted into rectangular blocks. These blocks need to be broken up and soaked in water. Then the pulp can be pushed through a strainer. This is tamarind paste.

To make your own tamarind paste: Break off 225 g/8 oz from a brick of tamarind and tear into small pieces. Put in to a small non-metallic pot and cover with 450 ml/15 fl oz/2 cups very hot water, and set aside 3 hours or overnight. (You could achieve the same result by simmering the tamarind for 10 minutes or by putting it in a microwave oven for 3–5 minutes.) Set a sieve over a non-metallic bowl and empty the tamarind and its soaking liquid into it. Push down on the tamarind with your fingers or the back of a wooden spoon to extract as much pulp as you can. Put whatever tamarind remains in the sieve back into the soaking bowl. Add 125 ml/ 4 fl oz/½ cup hot water to it and mash a bit more. Return it to the sieve and extract as much more pulp as you can. Some of this pulp will be clinging to the underside of the sieve. Do not fail to retrieve it. This quantity will make about 350 ml/12 fl oz/1½ cups of thick paste. All the calculations for my recipes have been done with this thick, chutney-like paste, so do not water it down too much. Whatever paste is left over may either be put into the refrigerator where it will keep for 2–3 weeks or it can be frozen. It freezes well.

TURMERIC

A rhizome like ginger, only with smaller, more delicate 'fingers', fresh turmeric is quite orange inside. When dried, it turns bright yellow. It is this musky yellow powder that gives some Indian dishes a yellowish cast. As it is cheap and is also considered to be an antiseptic, it is used freely in the cooking of pulses, vegetables and meats. Both the fresh and the dried form are used in India. In the West, we generally get the dried powder. If you have access to Indian grocers, try using the fresh rhizome. A 2.5 cm/ 1 inch piece of fresh turmeric is equal to about ½ teaspoon of ground turmeric. Just like ginger, it needs to be peeled and ground. This grinding is best done with the help of a little water in an electric blender.

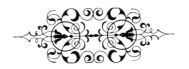

EQUIPMENT

WOK

Known in India as a *karhai*, this is an all-purpose utensil that may be used for steaming, simmering, stir-frying or deep-frying.

A wok is traditionally a round-bottomed pan. Because of its shape, flames can encircle it and allow it to heat quickly and efficiently. It is most economical for deep-frying as it will hold a good depth of oil without needing the quantity a straight-sided pan would require. It is ideal for stir-frying as foods can be vigorously tossed around in it. As they hit nothing but well-heated surfaces, they cook fast and retain their moisture at the same time.

Choosing a wok: What kind of wok should you buy? A traditional Indian wok is generally made out of cast-iron but any wok will do. Advances are being made all the time and every year seems to bring new woks into the market place. Traditional woks of good quality are made either of thin tempered iron or carbon steel. The ideal wok is 35 cm/14 inches in diameter and fairly deep. (Saucer-shaped shallow woks are quite useless.) A round-bottomed wok works well on a gas hob (burner). A new, somewhat flat-bottomed wok has been invented for people who have electric hobs (burners). I cannot say I love it. Instead I have opted for a yet newer invention in my country house in the USA which has an all-electric kitchen. This is an electric wok – but a very special one. It is the only electric wok I know which heats very quickly, becomes *very* hot and allows foods to be both stir-fried and simmered, though I must add that it is better for stir-frying than it is for simmering.

Seasoning a wok: The iron and carbon steel woks leave the factory coated with oil. This needs to be scrubbed off with a cream cleanser. Then a wok needs to be seasoned. Rinse it in water and set it over a low heat. Now brush it all over with about 2 tablespoons vegetable oil. Let it heat for 10–15 minutes. Wipe the oil off with a piece of kitchen paper (paper towel). Brush the wok with more oil and repeat the process 3–4 times.

The wok is now seasoned. Do not scrub it again; just wash it with hot water and then wipe it dry. It will *not* have a scrubbed look. It will, however, become more and more 'non-stick' as it is used.

Wok accessories: For use on a gas hob (burner), a wok needs a stand that not only stabilizes it but allows air to circulate underneath. The perfect stand is made of wire. The collar variety with punched holes seems to kill free circulation of heat and should not be used on gas hobs (burners).

When you buy a wok, it is also a good idea to invest in a curved spatula, a steaming tray and a lid.

CAST-IRON FRYING-PANS

I find a 13 cm/5 inch cast-iron frying-pan ideal for roasting spices and a large one perfect for pan-grilling (pan-broiling) thin slices of meat. All cast-iron frying-pans can be heated without any liquid and they retain an even temperature. Once properly seasoned, they should never be scrubbed with abrasive cleaners.

BLENDER AND COFFEE GRINDER, MORTAR AND PESTLE

In India, pestles and grinding-stones of varying shapes, sizes and materials are used to pulverize everything from cumin seeds to dried hot red chillies. I find it much easier to use an electric blender for wet ingredients and a clean electric coffee grinder for dry ones. For small quantities, you might still want to use a heavy mortar and pestle.

GRATER

The Japanese make a special grater for ginger and Japanese horseradish which produces a fine pulp. It has tiny hair-like spikes that are perfect for their purpose. If you ever find one, do buy it. Otherwise use the finest part of an ordinary grater for grating fresh ginger.

DOUBLE-BOILER

This is simply one pan balanced over another. The lower pan holds boiling water and allows the ingredients in the other pan to cook very gently.

Double-boilers are available from good kitchenware shops but can be easily improvised.

ELECTRIC RICE-COOKER

Its main use is to free all burners on the hob for other purposes and make the cooking of rice an easy, almost mindless task. I do have one and use it only for plain rice.

DEEP-FAT FRYER

For those who are afraid of deep-frying, this is a godsend. Because it has a lid that closes over all splattering foods, this piece of equipment also helps to make deep-frying a painless, safe and clean task.

RACKS FOR GRILLING FISH.

Hinged double racks are useful for grilling fish over charcoal. The fish lies sandwiched between the two racks and can be easily turned and basted. Many types of hinged double fish racks are available in the West, some even shaped like a fish. Most of them are sold by kitchen equipment stores. I find them exceedingly useful.

THALI

This is a round, flat metal tray with raised sides used as a plate for eating and as a tray for serving and also for other kitchen uses such as steaming.

Thalis can vary in size from about 15 cm (6 inches) to almost 90 cm (3 ft) in diameter. Stainless steel *thalis* are sold by most Indian grocers.

TECHNIQUES

TO PEEL, DEVEIN AND CLEAN PRAWNS (SHRIMP)

In the United Kingdom, these instructions and illustrations apply to the large uncooked prawns known as Pacific or king prawns. These are usually sold frozen and in the shell, but with the heads already removed. In the rest of the world, they apply to the common prawns (shrimp) that are sold, fresh or frozen, with the heads often removed in the West. If frozen, defrost. (a) First, peel off the shell and, with it, the tiny legs. (b) Pull off the tail. (c) Make a shallow cut down the back. (d) Remove the fine digestive cord which runs along the length of it.

It is always a good idea to wash off prawns (shrimp) before cooking them. I think this makes them taste sweeter. To do this, put the peeled and de-veined prawns (shrimp) into a bowl. Add about 1 tablespoon coarse or kosher salt for every 450 g/1 lb of prawns (shrimp) (unpeeled weight). Rub the prawns (shrimp) with the salt. Wash off the salt. Repeat this one more time. Drain the prawns (shrimp) well and pat them dry. They may now be covered and refrigerated and are ready for cooking.

TO CLEAN SQUID

Twist off the head (with the tentacles). The inner body sac will probably come away with it. If it does not, pull it out. Discard the sac and the hard eye area, which you may have to cut off with a knife. Retain the tentacles. If possible pull off some of the brownish skin on the tentacles. (You may safely leave this on, if you wish.) Peel the brownish skin from the tube-like body. Discard this skin and pull out the smooth inner cartilage (or pen). The squid can now be washed and used.

MARINATING

Meats are often cut up and put into marinades before they are cooked. A marinade tenderizes meat and injects it with all the flavours and aromas of its myriad ingredients. The meat can then be grilled (broiled) or quickly stir-fried while retaining the tastes of all its seasonings.

SPICE PASTES

Most curry-style dishes require that a spice paste be prepared first. To this end, fresh and dried spices are ground on grinding-stones. We in the West have to use blenders and coffee grinders to make our lives easier. Once the pastes are made, they often need to be fried in oil to get rid of their raw taste. As they fry, sprinklings of water are frequently added to prevent burning and sticking. Sometimes yoghurt and chopped tomatoes are added to the pastes to make a rich sauce.

DRY-ROASTING

Spices are often dry-roasted before use. It is best to do this in a heavy cast-iron frying-pan which has first been heated. No oil is used: the spices are just stirred around until they brown lightly. Roasted spices develop a heightened, nutty aroma. They can be stored for several months in an air-tight jar though they are best when freshly roasted.

'TARKA' (POPPING SPICES IN HOT OIL)

The 'tarka' technique, known by many other names such as *baghaar*, *chhownk* or 'seasoning in oil' is quite unique to India. First, the oil has to be very hot. Then, spices such as mustard seeds or cumin seeds are dropped into it. They pop and sizzle. Their whole character changes in an instant. They get much more intense. Their flavours change. Then, either this flavoured oil is poured over cooked foods or foods are added to the oil and cooked in it. Since four or five spices can go into a 'tarka', they are often added to the hot oil in a certain order so that those that burn easily, such as dried chillies, go in last. The flavour of each is imparted to the oil. In the case of the chillies, the flavour comes only from the browned skin of the chilli. Any food cooked in this oil picks up the heightened flavour of all the spices.

Doing a 'tarka' takes just a few seconds so it is important to have all spices ready and at hand. A 'tarka' is sometimes done at the beginning of a recipe and sometimes at the end. Pulses (legumes), for example, are usually just boiled with a little turmeric. When they are tender, a 'tarka' is prepared in a small frying-pan, perhaps with asafetida, cumin seeds and red chillies, and then the entire contents of the frying-pan, hot oil and spices, are poured over the pulses (legumes) and the lid shut tight for a few minutes to trap the aromas. These flavourings can be stirred in later. They perk up the boiled pulses (legumes) and bring them to life. Sometimes '*tarkas*' are done twice, both at the beginning and end of a recipe.

COOKING COCONUT MILK

When cooking fresh coconut milk, care must be taken that it does not curdle. Stir it constantly as it cooks. Canned coconut milk does not behave in quite the same as fresh coconut milk as it often has thickeners in it. I often add it only towards the end of the cooking period and then just bring it to a simmer and leave it at that. If I wish to simmer it for longer periods, I thin it out first with water or stock.

STEAMING

Steaming is used for cooking anything from the rice cake, *idli*, to Bengali fish. Just as every home in the West has a roasting pan, so every home in South India tends to have a steamer. Steaming cooks gently and preserves flavour.

One of the most satisfactory utensils for steaming is a wok because its width easily accommodates a whole fish, a casserole or a large plate of food. Use a wok with a flat base or set a round-based wok on a wire stand. Put a metal or wooden rack or a perforated tray into the wok. (You could use a small inverted tin can instead.)

Now pour in some water. Bring it to a gentle boil and lower in the food so it sits on the rack, tray or can. The water should stay about 2 cm/ ¾ inch below the level of the food that is being steamed. Extra boiling water should be kept at hand just in case it is needed to top up the level.

Cover the whole wok, including the food, with a domed wok lid or a large sheet of aluminium foil. The domed lids are preferable as condensed steam rolls down the sides instead of dripping on the food itself.

If you like, you can also invest in the many-tiered bamboo or aluminium steamers sold in Chinese markets.

DEEP-FRYING

You need several inches of oil in a wok or frying-pan and a good deal more in a deep-fat fryer in order to deep-fry. The oil must be heated to the required temperature before you drop in a single morsel of food. Properly deep-fried foods are not at all greasy; the outside is beautifully crisp while the inside is completely cooked.

Oil that has been used for deep-frying may be re-used. Let it cool completely and then strain it. Store it in a bottle. When you cook again, use half old oil and half fresh oil. Oil that has been used for frying fish should be re-used only for fish.

GRINDING SPICES

Many recipes call for ground spices. In India, spices are generally bought whole and then ground as needed. They have much more flavour this way. You probably already know the difference between freshly ground black pepper and ground pepper that has been sitting around for a month. The same applies to all spices. In India, the grinding of spices is generally done on heavy grinding-stones. We, in our modern kitchens, can get the same results without the labour by using an electric coffee grinder. It is best to grind limited quantities so that the spices do not lose their flavour. If you wipe the grinder carefully after use there will be no 'aftertaste' of spices to flavour your coffee beans.

Buying ground spices is perfectly all right as long as you know that they will be less potent as time goes on.

MAKING THICK SAUCES

Many of India's meat, poultry and fish dishes have thick, dark sauces. My mother always said that the mark of a good chef was his sauce which depended not only on a correct blalance of all the ingredients, but the correct frying (*bhuno*-ing) of these ingredients.

There is no flour in these sauces. The 'body' comes, very often, from onions, garlic and ginger. The rich brown colour comes from frying all these ingredients properly. Very often, a paste of one or more of these ingredients is made first. In India, this is done on a grinding-stone but in Western kitchens it can be done easily in food processors and blenders, sometimes with the aid of a little water.

Once the paste has been made, it needs to be browned or the sauce will not have the correct flavour and colour. This is best done in a heavy pan, preferably non-stick, in a *generous* amount of oil. Remember that extra oil can always be spooned off the top once the dish has been cooked.

ADDING YOGHURT TO SAUCES

Yoghurt adds a creamy texture and a delicate tartness to many sauces. But yoghurt curdles when it is heated. So when Indian cooks add it to their browning sauces, they add just 1 tablespoon at a time. After a tablespoon of yoghurt has been put in, it is stirred and fried until it is absorbed and 'accepted' by the sauce. Then the next tablespoon is added.

PEELING AND CHOPPING TOMATOES

Many of my recipes call for peeled and chopped tomatoes. To peel tomatoes, bring a pan of water to a rolling boil. Drop in the tomatoes for 15 seconds. Drain, rinse under cold water and peel. Now chop the tomatoes, making sure that you save all the juice that comes out of them. In India, tomatoes are very rarely seeded. Many people do not even bother to peel them though I do feel that this improves the texture of a sauce.

REDUCING SAUCES

Sometimes meat is allowed to cook in a fairly thin, brothy sauce. Then the lid of the pan is removed and the sauce reduced over fairly high heat until it is thick and clings to the meat. The meat has to be stirred frequently at this stage, so that it does not catch and burn.

COOKING CHICKEN WITHOUT ITS SKIN

In India the skin of the chicken is often removed before cooking. The flavour of the spices penetrates the chicken much better this way and the entire dish is less fatty. It is very easy to remove the skin. Just hold it with kitchen paper (paper towels) so that it does not slip, and pull!

BROWNING MEATS

In India, cubes of meat are not generally browned by themselves. Instead, they are browned with the sauce. However, in the West many meats release far too much water as they cook – Indian meats tend to be very fresh and have far less water in them. So to avoid this problem I brown my meat a few pieces at a time in hot oil and set them aside. Once I have made the sauce, I add the browned meat cubes (and all the good juices that come out of them) and let them cook.

MAIL ORDER SUPPLIERS

The following suppliers offer a mail order service.

THE UNITED KINGDOM
Harrods Food Hall (Pantry Department), Harrods Ltd,
Knightsbridge, London SW1X 7XL; (071) 730 1234

Selfridges Food Hall, Selfridges Ltd, 400 Oxford Street,
London W1A 1AB; (071) 629 1234

Curry Direct, P.O. Box 7, Liss, Hampshire GU33 7YS; (0730) 894949

THE UNITED STATES
Culinary Alchemy Inc., P.O. Box 393, Palo Alto, CA 94302;
(415) 598 9143

India Spice and Gift Shop, 3295 Fairfield Avenue, Bridgeport,
CT 06605; (203) 384 0666

Seema Enterprises, 10618 Page Avenue, St Louis, MO 63132;
 (314) 423 9990

Foods of India, 121 Lexington Avenue, New York, NY 10016;
(212) 683 4419

INDEX

Page numbers in *italics* refer to illustrations.

A

Aam jhol, 169
Aam kheer, 171
Ahmadabad, 52, 58, 60–1
Ahmed Shah, Sultan, 60
Ajwain (ajowan) seeds, 259
Albuquerque, Afonso de, 92
Alebele, 99, 131
Alexander VI, Pope, 18
Alimucha oorga, 211
Almonds:
    steamed yoghurt, 169–71
Aloo aur anardana paratha, 248
Alu bhaja, 141
Alu dum, 141, 162
Alu tikki, 161
Ambot tik, 98, 112
Amchoor, 259
Amritsar, 220, 221–2, 224
Amritsar macchi, 234
Amritsari beans, 243–4, *255*
Amritsari dal, 243–4
Amritsari fish, 234
Anand, Praveen, 192
Anand, Radha, 255
Anardana, 259
Anglo-Indians, 143
Anthony, E.X., 16
Apa de camarao, 98

Appams, 13, 39–40
Arabs, 60, 178
Arhar dal, 261
Arroz de pato, 124
Arroz refogado, 94
Asafetida, 259
Assado de leitoa, 94
Attarwala, Nishrin, 64, 66, 84
Aubergines (eggplants):
    aubergine pâté, 237–8
    aubergines in coconut milk, 33–4
    deep-fried aubergines in batter, 145
Aurangzeb, Emperor, 142
Avial, 12, 32

B

Baigan bharta, 237–8
Bajri no rotlo, 58
Balasundaram, Mr, 24, 32
Balchao, 98
Bananas:
    yoghurt with banana and mustard, 84–5
    see also Plantains
Basu, Sonali, 140, 141, 145, 162, 165, 167
Basu, Sunlay, 172
Basu family, 138–40
Batata nu shak, 53, 69

Batica, 99
Bavani, Mrs, 34
Bay leaves, 260
Beans:
    Amritsari beans, 243–4, *255*
    beans with roasted spices, 120–1
    creamy spiced beans, 242–3
    dried beans, 260–1
Bebinca, 98, 132
Beef:
    beef chilli-fry, 100
    beef with mushrooms, 101–2
Beef xecxec, 101–2
Beet (beetroot):
    sweet beet chutney, 209
Beetroot (beet):
    sweet beetroot chutney, 209
Beetroot pacchadi, 209
Begun bhaja, 141
Bengal *see* West Bengal
Bengal, Bay of, 136, 138, 184
Besun bhaja, 145
Bhadoli, 216, 217
Bhaja, 138
Bhakala bhat, 181, 206–8
Bhapa doi, 169–71
Bhapey, 138
Bharli vaangi, 97
Bharta, 143, 220
Bhartura, 249
Bhavani, Mrs, 36
Bhindi bhaji, 116
Bhuna khichuri, 143, 166
Bibo upkari, 97
Bife assado, 96
Bitter gourds, 261

    stuffed bitter gourds, 241
Bitter vegetables, 137
Black-eyed beans:
    beans with roasted spices, 120–1
Black pepper *see* Pepper
Black salt, 261–2
Blenders, 282
Boatman's curry, 16–17, 30
Bohris, 60, 64
Bonda, 12
Brahmin caste, 177
Breads:
    deep-fried stuffed breads, 167–8
    flaky breads, 244–5
    flaky breads stuffed with potato and
        pomegranate seeds, 248
    flaky breads stuffed with spicy minced
        (ground) lamb, 246–7
    flat breads stuffed with cabbage, 82
    flat corn breads, *238*, 250–1
    Goan bread, *111*, 128–9
    puffed leavened breads, *234*, 249
    savoury rice breads, *21*, 39–40
    steamed rice 'crumpets', 127–8
British Empire, 142
Brittle, crisp chick pea, 213
Browning meats, 289–90
Buffalo milk, 216–17
Butter, clarified *see Ghee*

C

Cabbage:
    flat breads stuffed with cabbage, 82

gingery cabbage and peas, 67
stir-fried cabbage and carrots, 197
Cake, pancake, 132
Calcutta, 135–6, 138–42, 143–4
Caldin, 98
Caldo verde, 97
Canning, Lady, 144
Carangrejo recheado, 98, 107
Cardamom pods, 18, 262
Cardamom seeds, 262
Carrots:
carrots stir-fried with green chillies, 68, *70*
cauliflower, turnip and carrot pickle, 253
mixed vegetables with coconut, 32
savoury grain cake with mustard and sesame seeds, 76–7
stir-fried cabbage and carrots, 197
stuffed potato patties, 161
Cashew nut bhaji, 117
Cashew nuts, 91–2, 262
cashew nuts with coconut, 117
coconut pancakes, 131
lamb in a cashew nut sauce, 64–5, *70*
Cast-iron frying pans, 282
Cauliflower:
cauliflower encrusted with poppy seeds, 164
cauliflower, turnip and carrot pickle, 253
cauliflower with potatoes, banquet style, 240, *255*
stuffed potato patties, 161
Cayenne pepper, 262–3
Chaamp masala, 229

Chaat masala, 263
Chadda, Mrs, 229
Chana-bhatura, 221
Chana dal, 260
Amritsari beans, 243–4
roasted, 260
savoury grain cake with mustard and sesame seeds, 76–7
Chanyacho ros, 97
Chapati flour, 263
Chapatis, 143
Charnock, Job, 142
Charoli nuts, 263
Chavadi, 16
Chaval, 84
Cheese:
fresh cheese sweets, 173
spicy fresh cheese snack, 225, *226*
Cheewra, 56
Chettiar, Rajah Sir Annamalai, 182–3
Chettiars, 182–4, 186, 189, 192, 193, 196
Chettinad pepper chicken, 189–90, *199*
Chhana, 263
Chick pea flour:
chick pea flour pancakes, 81
crisp, chick pea brittle, 213
crispy chick pea flour noodles, 62
spongy, spicy, savoury diamonds, 74–5
steamed peanut diamonds in a garlic-onion sauce, 72–3
sweet and sour chick pea flour soup, 79
Chick peas:
minced (ground) lamb with chick peas, 228–9
Chicken:
Chettinad pepper chicken, 189–90, *199*

chicken cooked in green chutney, 66
chicken in fresh green coriander, 148
chicken kebabs, 230
chicken Patiala, 231, *234*
chicken with a roasted coconut sauce,
    105–6, *111*
chicken with mustard seeds, 151
cooking without its skin, 289
country captain, 149, *151*
country chicken curry, 24–5
ginger chicken with mustard seeds,
    192–3
tandoori chicken, 232–3
Chilli powder, 262–3
    Kashmiri, 264
Chillies, 58, 263–4
    beef or lamb chilli-fry, 100
    carrots stir-fried with green chillies, 68,
        70
    chicken cooked in green chutney, 66
    coconut and green chilli prawns
        (shrimp), 113
    crispy chick pea flour noodles with
        onions and chillies, 63
    eggs in a green chilli-coconut sauce,
        193–4
    green chilli and lime pickle, 86
    lamb cooked in milk and yoghurt, 147
    pork with vinegar and garlic, 102–3
    'rechad' spice paste, 108
    stuffed crab, 107
China, 97
Chingri, 137
Chingri bhapey, 158
Chips, plantain, 17, 43
Chouricos, 96

Chum chum, 144
Chutney ni murgh, 61, 66
Chutneys:
    chicken cooked in green chutney, 66
    coconut chutney, *206*, 212
    cooling mango chutney, *154*, 169
    garlic chilli chutney, 85
    ginger chutney, *43*, 44–5
    Goan coconut chutney, 130
    green coriander and peanut chutney, *79*,
        86
    mint and white radish chutney, *226*, 251
    sweet beetroot (beet) chutney, 209
    see also Pickles
Cinnamon, 264–5
Clarified butter *see Ghee*
Clive, Robert, 182
Cloves, 265
Cochin, 17, 18
Coco pista pasand, 53, 88–9
Coconut, 12
    beans with roasted spices, 120–1
    cashew nuts with coconut, 117
    chicken with a roasted coconut sauce,
        105–6, *111*
    coconut and green chilli prawns
        (shrimp), 113
    coconut chutney, *206*, 212
    coconut pancakes, *123*, 131
    coconut pistachio sweetmeat, *86*, 88–9
    coconut rice, 203
    creamed coconut, 267
    desiccated coconut, 267
    'dry' lamb encrusted with spices, 20–1
    eggs in a green chilli-coconut sauce,
        193–4

fresh coconuts, 265–6
Goan coconut chutney, 130
lamb in a fennel-flavoured coconut
    sauce, 186–7, *190*
lamb pepper-fry, 187–8
mango curry, 36
mixed vegetables with coconut, 32
prawns (shrimp) steamed with mustard
    seeds and coconut, 158, *162*
spinach with coconut, 37, *43*
squid with coconut, 31
Coconut milk, 266–7
    aubergines (eggplants) in coconut milk,
        33–4
    coconut and green chilli prawns
        (shrimp), 113
    cooking, 287
    lamb in a cashew nut sauce, 64–5
    lamb stew, 19
    moong dal pudding, 48
    pancake cake, 132
    prawn (shrimp) curry, 159–60
    savoury rice breads, 39–40
Coconut oil, 17
Cod:
    Amritsari fish, 234
    fish stew, 25
    yoghurt fish, 152–3
Coffee, 178
Coffee grinders, 282
'Converted' rice, 176–7
Cooling mango chutney, *154*, 169
Le Corbusier, 52, 54
Coriander, 268
    chicken cooked in green chutney, 66
    chicken in fresh green coriander, 148

flaky breads stuffed with spicy minced
    (ground) lamb, 246–7
green coriander and peanut chutney, *79*,
    86
savoury grain cake with mustard and
    sesame seeds, 76–7
shark with spices and fresh coriander,
    196
stuffed crab, 107
Coriander seeds, 268
    dry-roasting, 268
Corn breads, 222
Corn oil, 274
Cornmeal flour, 268
    flat corn breads, *238*, 250–1
Country captain, 149, *151*
Country chicken curry, 24–5
Courgette raita, 252
Crab, stuffed, 107
Creamed milk pudding, 256
Creamy spiced beans, 242–3
Crisp, chick pea brittle, 213
Crispy chick pea flour noodles, 62
Crispy chick pea flour noodles with onions
    and chillies, 63
'Crumpets', steamed rice, 127–8
Cucumber:
    cucumber cooked with lentils, 34, *43*
    rice with yoghurt, 206–8
Culculs, 99
Cumin seeds, 269
    black, 269
    ground roasted, 269
Curry leaves, 269
Curry powder, 175

D

Dal dhokli, 60
Dal makkhani, 242–3
Damodaran, Mr, 16–17, 30
Dasgupta, Mrs, 147, 152, 169
Dasgupta, Rakhi, 148, 154, 158, 171
Deep-fat fryers, 283
Deep-frying, 287–8
Desserts:
    coconut pancakes, 131
    creamed milk pudding, 256
    mango pudding, 171
    mango yoghurt, 89
    moong dal pudding, 48
    pancakes in syrup, 172
    plantain roast, 47
    steamed yoghurt, 169–71
    vermicelli pudding, 255
Dhabas, 221–2
Dhoklas, 52, 74–5
Divar, 98
Dodol, 92
Dohi machh, 138, 152–3
Doongri nu shaak, 58
Dosas, 176, 180, 181, 182, 205–6
Double-boilers, 282–3
'Dry' lamb encrusted with spices, 20–1
Dry-roasting, 286
'Dry' split peas, 70
Duck:
    duck curry, country style, 23, *26*
    duck risotto, 124–5

E

East India Company, 142–3, 176
Eggplants (aubergines):
    deep-fried eggplants in batter, 145
    eggplant pâté, 237–8
    eggplants in coconut milk, 33–4
Eggs in a green chilli-coconut sauce,
    193–4
Ekambareeshwara temple, 177
Electric rice-cookers, 283
Elish bhapey, 137
Emanuel, King of Portugal, 92
Equipment, 281–3
Erachi olathu, 13, 20–1
Erachi uruga, 41
Eraichi kolumbu, 183, 186
Eraichi porial, 187–8

F

Fafra, 57
Farsan, 57, 60
Feijoada, 96
Fennel seeds, 269–70
    lamb in a fennel-flavoured coconut
      sauce, 186–7, *190*
Fenugreek seeds, 270
Fish, 13–16, 97–8, 138, 141–2
    Amritsari fish, 234
    boatman's curry, 30
    easy fish fillets in a traditional mustard
      sauce, 156–7
    fish baked in foil, 26–8

fish on a bed of potatoes, onions and
tomatoes, 111
fish stew, 25
grilling racks, 283
marinated and stewed sardines, 28–9, *34*
spicy, pan-fried fish steaks Chettinad,
195
stuffed pomfret, 109
tamarind fish, 154
yoghurt fish, 152–3, *154*
Fish moilly, 25
Five-spice mix, 101
Flaky breads, 244–5
Flaky breads stuffed with potato and
pomegranate seeds, 248
Flaky breads stuffed with spicy minced
(ground) lamb, 246–7
Flat breads stuffed with cabbage, 82
Flat corn breads, *238*, 250–1
Flour:
chapati, 263
cornmeal, 268
rice, 276
see also Chick pea flour
Foil, fish baked in, 26–8
Francis Xavier, St, 92
Fritters:
deep-fried aubergines (eggplants) in
batter, 145
Frying, deep-fat, 287–8
Frying-pans, cast-iron, 282

G

Gajar marcha no sambharo, 68
Gama, Vasco da, 16
Gandiwind, 216–20
Ganges River, 136
Garam masala, 270–1
Garlic, 271
garlic chilli chutney, 85
pork with vinegar and garlic, 102–3, *115*
steamed peanut diamonds in a garlic-
onion sauce, 72–3
Ghandi Nagar, 52
Ghee, 217, 271
crisp, chick pea brittle, 213
Ghiya raita, 252
Ghoti community, 165
Ginger, 18, 271–2
ginger chicken with mustard seeds,
192–3
ginger chutney, *43*, 44–5
gingery cabbage and peas, 67
Goa, 91–132
beans with roasted spices, 120–1
beef or lamb chilli-fry, 100
beef with mushrooms, 101–2
cashew nuts with coconut, 117
chicken with a roasted coconut sauce,
105–6, *111*
coconut and green chilli prawns
(shrimp), 113
coconut pancakes, *126*, 131
duck risotto, 124–5
fish on a bed of potatoes, onions and
tomatoes, 111
Goan bread, *111*, 128–9

Goan coconut chutney, 130
Goan style pilaf, 123
okra with dried prawns (shrimp), *115,* 116
pancake cake, 132
pork cooked with vinegar and spices, 104–5
pork with vinegar and garlic, 102–3, *115*
potatoes with mustard seeds, *111,* 118
prawn (shrimp) curry, 115, *123*
'rechad' spice paste, 108
red spinach, 119
sour and spicy squid, 112
steamed rice 'crumpets', 127–8
stuffed crab, 107
stuffed pomfret, 109
Goan bread, *111,* 128–9
Goan coconut chutney, 130
Goan five-spice mix, 101
Goan style pilaf, 123
Goat meat, 140
Gobi aloo, 240
Golden Temple, Amritsar, 224
Gonsalves, Sophie, 91, 94–5, 104, 115, 120, 123, 130
Grapes:
    rice with yoghurt, 206–8
Graters, 282
Green beans:
    mixed vegetables with coconut, 32
Green chilli and lime pickle, 79, 86
Green coriander and peanut chutney, 79, 86–8
Grey mullet:
    Amritsari fish, 234
Grilling racks, fish, 283

Grinding spices, 288
Ground rice:
    steamed rice 'crumpets', 127–8
Groundnut oil, 274
Guisado de peixe, 111
Gujarat, 8, 51–89, 221
    black pepper rice, *70,* 84
    carrots stir-fried with green chillies, 68, *70*
    chick pea flour pancakes, 81
    chicken cooked in green chutney, 66
    coconut pistachio sweetmeat, *86,* 88–9
    crispy chick pea flour noodles, 62
    crispy chick pea flour noodles with onions and chillies, 63
    'dry' split peas, 70
    flat breads stuffed with cabbage, 82
    garlic chilli chutney, 85
    gingery cabbage and peas, 67
    green chilli and lime pickle, *79,* 86
    green coriander and peanut chutney, *79,* 86
    lamb in a cashew nut sauce, 64–5, *70*
    mango yoghurt, 89
    noodles with tomato, 80, *82*
    savoury grain cake with mustard and sesame seeds, 76–7
    spicy potatoes with tomatoes, 69
    spongy, spicy, savoury diamonds, 74–5, *79*
    steamed peanut diamonds in a garlic-onion sauce, 72–3
    sweet and sour chick pea flour soup, 79
    yoghurt with banana and mustard, 84–5

H

Haddock:
  easy fish fillets in a traditional mustard
    sauce, 156–7
  fish stew, 25
  yoghurt fish, 152–3
Hakimji, Samina, 86
Halibut:
  fish stew, 25
  yoghurt fish, 152–3
Halva, 224
Handva, 51, 76–7
Hilsa:
  tamarind fish, 154
Hinduism, 56
Holi, 60
Hooghly River, 142
Hotel Saravana Bhavan, Madras, 181, 209

I

Idada dhokla, 52
Idi appam, 13, 178–80
Idlis, 176, 177, 180, 181, 204–5
Indus Valley, 215
Ingli poli, 44–5
Ingredients, 259–79
Islam *see* Muslims

J

Jaggery, 272

Jahangiri, 181
Jainism, 56–7, 58, 60
Jalebi, 181
Jalkhabar, 140, 141
Jasdan, Rajmata of, 72
Jhol, 138

K

Kachchh, 57
Kadhi, 53, 79
Kadiya hoya dubh, 216
Kaitha chaka pachadi, 45–6
Kala namak, 261–2
Kalappam, 13
Kali, 140
Kalonji, 272
Kanchipuram, 177
Kannava varitiyathu, 31
Kansara, Mrs Kumud, 62–3, 67–71, 74–85,
    88–9
Kapoor, Mrs, 237
Kapoor, Promila, 220, 225, 240
Karela, 261
  stuffed bitter gourds, 241
Karele pyazaa, 241
Kari, 61, 64–5
Karimeen fishermen, 14
Kartarpur, 221
Kassim, Mohammad, 60
Kaur, Jatinder, 236, 250
Kavi, Niranjana Row, 86
Kaya varathathu, 43

Kebabs:
    chicken kebabs, 230
    lamb kebab, 226
Kela nu raitu, 84–5
Kerala, 8, 11–48
    aubergines in coconut milk, 33–4
    boatman's curry, 30
    country chicken curry, 24–5
    cucumber cooked with lentils, 34, *43*
    'dry' lamb encrusted with spices, 20–1
    duck curry, country style, 23
    fish baked in foil, 26–8
    fish stew, 25
    ginger chutney, *43*, 44–5
    lamb stew, 19, *21*
    mango curry, 36
    marinated and stewed sardines, 28–9, *34*
    meat pickle, 41
    mixed vegetables with coconut, 32
    moong dal pudding, 48
    plantain chips, 43, *43*
    plantain roast, 47
    savoury rice breads, *21*, 39–40
    spicy pineapple-yoghurt, 45–6
    spinach with coconut, 37, *43*
    squid with coconut, 31
    vegetable rice, *26*, 38
Kesar-da-Dhaba, Amritsar, 252
Kewra essence, 272
Kewra water, 272
Khakra, 52
Khaman dhokla, 57, 74–5
Khandvi, 51, 53–4, 60
Khasi tribe, 7–8
Khasta kachoris, 57

Kheema cholay, 228–9
Kheema paratha, 246–7
Kheer, 215
Khichra, 61
Kidney beans, red, 260
    creamy spiced beans, 242–3
Kingfish:
    fish baked in foil, 26–8
    fish stew, 25
    spicy, pan-fried fish steaks Chettinad, 195
Kobi vatana nu shak, 53, 67
Kodampoli, 13
Kokum, 272–3
Koli kurma, 193–4
Koli milagu masala, 189–90
Koli uppakari, 192
Koraishuti kachori, 141, 167–8
Kunechi poee, 96
Kurma, 181, 183, 201

L

Lady Kenny, 144
Laganya sheek, 61
Lakshami, 177
Lamb:
    'dry' lamb encrusted with spices, 20–1
    flaky breads stuffed with spicy minced (ground) lamb, 246–7
    lamb chilli-fry, 100
    lamb chops masala, 229
    lamb cooked in milk and yoghurt, 147

lamb in a cashew nut sauce, 64–5, *70*

lamb in a fennel-flavoured coconut sauce, 186–7, *190*

lamb kebab, 226

lamb pepper-fry, 187–8

lamb stew, 19, *21*

minced (ground) lamb with chick peas, 228–9

spicy steak, 146

Lassi, 220

Lasun chutney, 58, 85

Leeli chai, 56

Leeli chutney, 86–8

Lentils, 260

cucumber cooked with lentils, 34, *43*

sweet and sour red lentils, 165

Lime:

green chilli and lime pickle, *79*, 86

lime pickle, 211

Liver:

pork cooked with vinegar and spices, 104–5

Loh, 218

Loochis, 141

M

Ma di dal, 219, 224, 242–3

Maccher sorse diye jhol, 156–7

Mace, 274

Madras, 175, 182–2, 184

Makki-di-roti, 222, 250–1

Malpua, 172

Manga kalan, 36

Mangoes, 52–3

cooling mango chutney, *154*, 169

green mango powder, 259

mango curry, 36

mango pudding, 171

mango yoghurt, 89

Manghor jhol, 140

Manik Tala market, Calcutta, 138

Mapusa, 96

Marchanu athanu, 52, 86

Marinades, 285, 289

Marinated and stewed sardines, 28–9, *34*

Masala dosa, 180

Masala steak, 146

Masoor dal, 260

Matthew, Mrs K.M., 37

Meat:

browning, 289–90

marinades, 285, 289

meat pickle, 41

see also Lamb; Pork *etc.*

Meen patichatu, 28–9

Meen pollichathu, 26–8

Meen varuval, 184, 195

Meen pappas, 18

Meen vevichathu, 13

Melon seeds, 273

Milagu tanni, 181

Milk:

buffalo milk, 216–17

creamed milk pudding, 256

fresh cheese sweets, 173

lamb cooked in milk and yoghurt, 147

mango pudding, 171

vermicelli pudding, 255

Milk, coconut *see* Coconut milk

Milk, condensed:
    mango pudding, 171
    steamed yoghurt, 169–71
Mint and white radish chutney, *226, 251*
Mishti doi, 141
Mohan International Hotel, 226, 230–1, 251
Moong (mung) dal, 260
    'dry' split peas, 70
    moong dal pudding, 48
    stir-fried rice with split peas, 166
Mortars, 282
Moss, Norma, 8
Mugh ni dal, 71
Mugphali noo shak, 72–3
Mulligatawny soup, 181
Munambam Harbour, 14
Munchable peanut salad, 185
Mung beans, 260
Munim di Hatti, 220
Murgh Patiala, 231
Murgh tikka, 230
Murgi dhuniya patta diya, 148
Mushrooms, beef with, 101–2
Muslims, 60, 93, 94, 140
Mustard greens, 223, 236–7, *238*
Mustard oil, 136–7, 273
Mustard seeds, 137, 273–4
    chicken with mustard seeds, 151
    easy fish fillets in a traditional mustard
        sauce, 156–7
    ginger chicken with mustard seeds,
        192–3
    potatoes with mustard seeds, *111*, 118
    potatoes with mustard seeds and onions,
        200

prawns (shrimp) steamed with mustard
    seeds and coconut, 158, *162*
yoghurt with banana and mustard, 84–5
Muthiah, A.C., 186, 189, 193–6
Mutta kose kilangu, 181, 197
Mutthries, 220
Mutton tikka, 226
Mysore pak, 180, 213

N

Naan, 140
Nadan kori kootan, 24–5
Nair community, 34
Neem begun, 137
Neer mor, 178
Neureos, 92
Neyychoru, 38
Nigella, 272
Nilgiri Hills, 178
Noodles, 58–60, 178–80
    crispy chick pea flour noodles, 62
    crispy chick pea flour noodles with
        onions and chillies, 63
    noodles with tomato, 80, *82*
Nutmeg, 274

O

O'Brien, Errol, 143
Oil, 274
    mustard oil, 136–7

Okra:
    deep-fried okra in batter, 199, *211*
    mixed vegetables with coconut, 32
    okra with dried prawns (shrimp), *115*,
       116
Olan, 17, 34
Olive oil, 274
Olives:
    duck risotto, 124–5
Onions:
    crispy chick pea flour noodles with
       onions and chillies, 63
    fish on a bed of potatoes, onions and
       tomatoes, 111
    potatoes with mustard seeds and onions,
       200
    spicy steak, 146
    steamed peanut diamonds in a garlic-
       onion sauce, 72–3
Osanay samaray, 97, 120–1

P

Palitana, 57, 58, 60
Palm sugar, 274
Panaji, 92–3
Pancakes:
    chick pea flour pancakes, 81
    coconut pancakes, *123*, 131
    pancake cake, 132
    pancakes in syrup, *171*, 172
    rice and split pea pancakes, 205–6, *206*
Panch phoran, 136, 275
Paneer, 220–1

    spicy fresh cheese snack, 225
Paneer bhurji, 221
Paneer chat, 225
Pao, 96, 97
Papar, 56
Papri, 57
Paprika, 275
Par-boiled rice, 176–7
Parathas, 215, 218, 244–8
Park Sheraton Hotel, 192
Parra, 92
Parvati, 177
Patel, Smita, 56
Patel, Surendra, 54–6
Pâté, aubergine (eggplant), 237–8
Paturi, 138
Paunk, 58
Payasam, 12, 48
Payesh, 136
Pazham roast, 47
Peanut oil, 274
Peanuts:
    green coriander and peanut chutney, *79*,
       86
    munchable peanut salad, 185
    steamed peanut diamonds in a garlic-
       onion sauce, 72–3
Peas, dried, 260
Peas, fresh:
    deep-fried stuffed breads, 167–8
    gingery cabbage and peas, 67
    savoury grain cake with mustard and
       sesame seeds, 76–7
    stuffed potato patties, 161
Peas, split, 137
    'dry' split peas, 70

rice and split pea pancakes, 205–6, *206*
split peas with shallots, 202, *206*
stir-fried rice with split peas, *151*, 166
Pepper, black, 18, 261
black pepper rice, *70*, 84
lamb pepper-fry, 187–8
Pepper, Sichuan, 98
Pestles and mortars, 282
Phulkopir posto, 164
Pickles:
cauliflower, turnip and carrot pickle, 253
green chilli and lime pickle, *79*, 86
lime pickle, 211
meat pickle, 41
see also Chutneys
Pilaf:
Goan style pilaf, 123
vegetable rice, 38
Pilau, 123
Pillau, 94
Pineapple:
spicy pineapple-yoghurt, 45–6
Pistachio nuts:
coconut pistachio sweetmeat, *86*, 88–9
creamed milk pudding, 256
Plantains:
mixed vegetables with coconut, 32
plantain chips, 43, *43*
plantain roast, 47
see also Bananas
Poee, 128–9
Pomegranate seeds, 259
flaky breads stuffed with potato and pomegranate seeds, 248
Pomfret, stuffed, 109

Poori, 53
Pootu, 13
Poppadoms, 275
Popping spices, 286–7
Poppy seeds, 275
cauliflower encrusted with poppy seeds, 164
Pork:
meat pickle, 41
pork cooked with vinegar and spices, 104–5
pork with vinegar and garlic, 102–3, *115*
roast suckling pig, 94
Pork vindalho, 102–3
Portuguese, in Goa, 92–3
Potatoes:
cauliflower with potatoes, banquet style, 240, *255*
fish on a bed of potatoes, onions and tomatoes, 111
flaky breads stuffed with potato and pomegranate seeds, 248
mixed vegetables with coconut, 32
potatoes with mustard seeds, *111*, 118
potatoes with mustard seeds and onions, 200
spicy potatoes with tomatoes, 69
spicy steak, 146
string beans with potatoes, 160
stuffed potato patties, 161
whole potatoes with tomatoes, 162
Prawn malai curry, 159–60
Prawns (shrimp), 13–14, 16
coconut and green chilli prawns, 113
dried, 275
okra with dried prawns, *115*, 116

to peel, devein and clean, 285
prawn curry (Bengal), 159–60
prawn curry (Goa), 115, *123*
prawns steamed with mustard seeds and
    coconut, 158, *162*
Prawns caldin, 113
Pudina mooli chutney, 251
Pudla, 52, 81
Puffed leavened breads, *234*, 249
Pullao, 140
Pumpkin:
    stuffed potato patties, 161
Punjab, 8, 215–56
    Amritsari beans, 243–4, *255*
    Amritsari fish, 234
    aubergine (eggplant) pâté, 237–8
    cauliflower, turnip and carrot pickle,
        253
    cauliflower with potatoes, banquet style,
        240, *255*
    chicken kebabs, 230
    chicken Patiala, 231, *234*
    courgette (zucchini) raita, 252
    creamed milk pudding, 256
    creamy spiced beans, 242–3
    flaky breads, 244–5
    flaky breads stuffed with potato and
        pomegranate seeds, 248
    flaky breads stuffed with spicy minced
        (ground) lamb, 246–7
    flat corn breads, *228*, 250–1
    lamb chops masala, 229
    lamb kebab, 226
    minced (ground) lamb with chick peas,
        228–9
    mint and white radish chutney, *226*, 251

mustard greens, 236–7, *238*
puffed leavened breads, *234*, 249
spicy fresh cheese snack, 225, *226*
stuffed bitter gourds, 241
tandoori chicken, 232–3
vermicelli pudding, 255
Punjabi *garam masala*, 270–1

Q

Quisado de peixe, 98

R

Rabadhi, 256
Rabaris, 57–8
Racks, grilling fish, 283
Radishes:
    mint and white radish chutney, *226*, 251
Raisins:
    steamed yoghurt, 169–71
Raita:
    courgette (zucchini), 252
    spicy pineapple-yoghurt, 45–6
Ramanujam, Mrs A. Santha, 177–9, 185,
        197, 201, 202–8, 213
Ramji, Shoba, 26, 28, 33, 41, 44–5,
        199–200, 211
Rasam, 176, 181
Rava khichri, 180, 208–9
Ray, Satyajit, 140
Rechad masala, 108

Rechad spice paste, 98, 108
Red kidney beans *see* Kidney beans
Red spinach, 119
Reducing sauces, 289
Relishes:
  stewed tomato relish, *151*, 168
  yoghurt with banana and mustard, 84–5
Rezala, 140, 147
Rice, 12, 176–7, 217, 275–6
  black pepper rice, *70*, 84
  coconut rice, 203
  duck risotto, 124–5
  Goan style pilaf, 123
  rice and split pea pancakes, 205–6, *206*
  rice with yoghurt, 206–8
  savoury grain cake with mustard and
    sesame seeds, 76–7
  savoury rice breads, *21*, 39–40
  savoury rice cakes, 204–5
  stir-fried rice with split peas, *151*, 166
  vegetable rice, *26*, 38
Rice-cookers, electric, 283
Rice flour, 276
  steamed rice 'crumpets', 127–8
Risotto, duck, 124–5
Rotis, 215, 217, 224, 250–1

S

Sabji jhol, 160
Saffron, 276
Salads:
  munchable peanut salad, 185
  rice with yoghurt, 206–8

Salmon:
  Amritsari fish, 234
  easy fish fillets in a traditional mustard
    sauce, 156–7
  tamarind fish, 154
Salt, black, 261–2
Samar codi, 98, 115
Sambar, 180, 181, 182, 202
Sambar powder, 276–7
Sandesh, 144, 173
Sannas, 94–6, 127
Sarabhai family, 53
Sardines, marinated and stewed, 28–9, *34*
Sarkar, Rakhi, 156, 159
Sarson da saag, 236–7
Sauces:
  adding yoghurt to, 289
  making thick sauces, 288
  reducing, 289
Saurashtra, 60
Sausages, 96
  duck risotto, 124–5
Savoury grain cake with mustard and
    sesame seeds, 76–7
Savoury rice breads, *21*, 39–40
Savoury rice cakes, 204–5
Selvaraj's stew, 19
Semolina, 277
  pancakes in syrup, 172
  semolina with vegetables, 208–9
Sequeira, Jude, 100–2, 105, 108, 112–13,
    117
Sesame seeds, 277
  roasting, 277
Sev, 57, 62
Sev masala, 63

Sev tamate, 51, 80
Seviyan, 255
Shalgham, gajar aur phoolgobi aachar, 253
Shallots, 278
    split peas with shallots, 202, *206*
Shark with spices and fresh coriander, 196
Shertha, 58
Shetrunjaya mountain, 57, 60
Shiva, Lord, 177
Shrikhand, 53, 89
Shrimp (prawns), 13–14, 16
    coconut and green chilli shrimp, 113
    dried, 275
    okra with dried shrimp, *115*, 116
    to peel, devein and clean, 285
    shrimp curry (Bengal), 159–60
    shrimp curry (Goa), 115, *123*
    shrimp steamed with mustard seeds and
      coconut, 158, *162*
Shukto, 136, 137, 141
Sichuan pepper, 98
Sikhism, 224, 243
Singh, Hoshiyar, 226, 230–1, 251
Singh, Pramod, 220
Singh, Tarlok, 216
Sookhi bhaji, 97, 118
Sopa de camarao, 98
Sora puttu, 196
Sorpatel, 94–6, 104–5
Sorse murgi, 151
Sour and spicy squid, 112
Sousa, Maria Fernanda, 107, 111, 124
Spices:
    chaat masala, 263
    dry-roasting, 286
    garam masala, 270–1

grinding, 288
    panch phoran, 136, 275
    'rechad' spice paste, 98, 108
    sambar powder, 276–7
    spice pastes, 286
    'tarka' technique, 286–7
    see also individual spices
Spicy fresh cheese snack, 225, *226*
Spicy, pan-fried fish steaks Chettinad, 195
Spicy pineapple-yoghurt, 45–6
Spicy potatoes with tomatoes, 69
Spicy steak, 146
Spinach:
    mustard greens, 236–7
    red spinach, 119
    spinach with coconut, 37, *43*
Spinach thoran, 37
Split peas *see* Peas, split
Spongy, spicy, savoury diamonds, 74–5, *79*
Squid:
    cleaning, 285
    sour and spicy squid, 112
    squid with coconut, 31
Squid ambot tik, 112
Star anise, 278
Steamers, *idli*, 204
Steaming, 287
Stepwells, 51
Stews:
    fish stew, 25
    lamb stew, 19, *21*
String beans with potatoes, 160
Suckling pig, 94
Sugar:
    jaggery, 272
    palm sugar, 274

Sundal, 184, 185
Sunil, A.R., 20, 23, 25, 31, 38, 43, 47
Surat, 58
Surjit's Chicken House, Amritsar, 221–2, 232
Sweet and sour chick pea flour soup, 79
Sweet and sour red lentils, 165
Sweet beetroot (beet) chutney, 209
Sweetmeats, 144
    coconut pistachio sweetmeat, *86*, 88–9
    crisp, chick pea brittle, 213
    fresh cheese sweets, 173
Swordfish:
    fish on a bed of potatoes, onions and tomatoes, 111
Syrup, pancakes in, *171*, 172

T

Taharava kootan, 23
Tak dal, 165
Tamari bhaji, 97, 119
Tamarind, 278–9
Tamarind paste, 278–9
    sweet and sour red lentils, 165
    tamarind fish, 154
Tamil Nadu, 175–213
    Chettinad pepper chicken, 189–90, *199*
    coconut chutney, *206*, 212
    coconut rice, 203
    crisp, chick pea brittle, 213
    deep-fried okra in batter, 199, *211*
    eggs in a green chilli-coconut sauce, 193–4

    ginger chicken with mustard seeds, 192–3
    lamb in a fennel-flavoured coconut sauce, 186–7, *190*
    lamb pepper-fry, 187–8
    lime pickle, 211
    mixed vegetable curry, 201, *211*
    munchable peanut salad, 185
    potatoes with mustard seeds and onions, 200
    rice and split pea pancakes, 205–6, *206*
    rice with yoghurt, 206–8
    savoury rice cakes, 204–5
    semolina with vegetables, 208–9
    shark with spices and fresh coriander, 196
    spicy, pan-fried fish steaks Chettinad, 195
    split peas with shallots, 202, *206*
    stir-fried cabbage and carrots, 197
    sweet beetroot (beet) chutney, 209
Tandoor, 217, 222
Tandoori chicken, 232–3
Tandoori murgh, 232–3
'*Tarka*' technique, spices, 286–7
Techniques, 285–90
Tellicherry, 18
temples, Sikh, 224
Tengai sadam, 203
Tetul ilish, 138, 154
Thali, 283
Themudo, Rita, 116, 119
Thengay chutney, 212
Thenkapal varadhiniya, 33–4
Thepla, 82

Thomas, St, 12, 14
Thoran, 12
Tikkas, 221
Toddy, 96
Tomato bharta, 168
Tomatoes:
    aubergine (eggplant) pâté, 237–8
    country captain, 149
    fish on a bed of potatoes, onions and tomatoes, 111
    lamb chops masala, 229
    noodles with tomato, 80, *82*
    peeling and chopping, 168, 289
    spicy potatoes with tomatoes, 69
    stewed tomato relish, *151*, 168
    whole potatoes with tomatoes, 162
Toovar dal, 261
    savoury grain cake with mustard and sesame seeds, 76–7
Turmeric, 18, 279
    easy fish fillets in a traditional mustard sauce, 156–7
Turnips:
    cauliflower, turnip and carrot pickle, 253
Twain, Mark, 136

U

Urad beans, 261
    Amritsari beans, 243–4
    creamy spiced beans, 242–3
Urad dal, 180, 261
    savoury rice cakes, 204–5

Urala kilangu, 200
Utthappam, 180

V

Vallamkarnanda meen kootan, 30
Varadharaja temple, 177
Vartal, 58–60
Vegetables:
    mixed vegetable curry, 201, *211*
    mixed vegetables with coconut, 32
    semolina with vegetables, 208–9
    vegetable rice, *26*, 38
    see also individual types
Vegetarian dishes:
    Amritsari beans, 243–4, *255*
    aubergine (eggplant) pâté, 237–8
    aubergines (eggplants) in coconut milk, 33–4
    beans with roasted spices, 120–1
    black pepper rice, *70*, 84
    carrots stir-fried with green chillies, 68, *70*
    cashew nuts with coconut, 117
    cauliflower encrusted with poppy seeds, 164
    cauliflower, turnip and carrot pickle, 253
    cauliflower with potatoes, banquet style, 240, *255*
    chick pea flour pancakes, 81
    coconut chutney, *206*, 212
    coconut pancakes, *127*, 131
    coconut pistachio sweetmeat, 88–9

coconut rice, 203
cooling mango chutney, *154*, 169
courgette (zucchini) raita, 252
creamed milk pudding, 256
creamy spiced beans, 242–3
crisp, chick pea brittle, 213
crispy chick pea flour noodles, 62
crispy chick pea flour noodles with
    onions and chillies, 63
cucumber cooked with lentils, 34, *43*
deep-fried aubergines (eggplants) in
    batter, 145
deep-fried okra in batter, 199, *211*
deep-fried stuffed breads, 167–8
'dry' split peas, 70
eggs in a green chilli-coconut sauce,
    193–4
flaky breads, 244–5
flaky breads stuffed with potato and
    pomegranate seeds, 248
flat breads stuffed with cabbage, 83
flat corn breads, *238*, 250–1
fresh cheese sweets, 173
garlic chilli chutney, 85
ginger chutney, *48*, 44–5
gingery cabbage and peas, 67
Goan bread, *111*, 128–9
Goan coconut chutney, 130
Goan style pilaf, 123
green chilli and lime pickle, *79*, 86
green coriander and peanut chutney, *79*,
    86–8
lime pickle, 211
mango curry, 36
mango pudding, 171
mango yoghurt, 89

mint and white radish chutney, *226*, 251
mixed vegetable curry, 201, *211*
mixed vegetables with coconut, 32
moong dal pudding, 48
munchable peanut salad, 185
mustard greens, 236–7, *238*
noodles with tomato, 80, *82*
pancake cake, 132
pancakes in syrup, *171*, 172
plantain chips, 43, *43*
plantain roast, 47
potatoes with mustard seeds, *111*, 118
potatoes with mustard seeds and onions,
    200
puffed leavened breads, *234*, 249
'rechad' spice paste, 108
red spinach, 119
rice and split pea pancakes, 205–6, *206*
rice with yoghurt, 206–8
savoury grain cake with mustard and
    sesame seeds, 76–7
savoury rice breads, *21*, 39–40
savoury rice cakes, 204–5
semolina with vegetables, 208–9
spicy fresh cheese snack, 225, *226*
spicy pineapple-yoghurt, 45–6
spicy potatoes with tomatoes, 69
spinach with coconut, 37, *43*
split peas with shallots, 202, *206*
spongy, spicy, savoury diamonds, 74–5,
    79
steamed peanut diamonds in a garlic-
    onion sauce, 72–3
steamed rice 'crumpets', 127–8
steamed yoghurt, 169–71
stewed tomato relish, *151*, 168

stir-fried cabbage and carrots, 197

stir-fried rice with split peas, *151*, 166

string beans with potatoes, 160

stuffed bitter gourds, 241

stuffed potato patties, 161

sweet and sour chick pea flour soup, 79

sweet and sour red lentils, 165

sweet beetroot (beet) chutney, 209

vermicelli pudding, 255

whole potatoes with tomatoes, 162

yoghurt with banana and mustard, 84–5

Vembanad Lake, 11, 14

Vendaka pakoda, 199

Vengayam sambar, 202

Vermicelli pudding, 255

Vijayakar, Sunil, 256

Vindalho (vindaloo), 93–4

pork, 102–3

Vinegar:

pork cooked with vinegar and spices, 104–5

pork with vinegar and garlic, 102–3, *115*

Vishnu, 177

country captain, 149, *151*

deep-fried aubergines (eggplants) in batter, 145

deep-fried stuffed breads, 167–8

easy fish fillets in a traditional mustard sauce, 156–7

fresh cheese sweets, 173

lamb cooked in milk and yoghurt, 147

mango pudding, 171

pancakes in syrup, *171*, 172

prawn (shrimp) curry, 159–60

prawns (shrimp) steamed with mustard seeds and coconut, 158, *162*

spicy steak, 146

steamed yoghurt, 169–71

stewed tomato relish, *151*, 168

stir-fried rice with split peas, *151*, 166

string beans with potatoes, 160

stuffed potato patties, 161

sweet and sour red lentils, 165

tamarind fish, 154

whole potatoes with tomatoes, 162

yoghurt fish, 152–3, *154*

Wheat, 215

Willingdon Island, 17

Woks, 281–2

accessories, 282

seasoning, 281–2

W

Ward, Christine, 146, 149, 166, 168

West Bengal, 135–73

cauliflower encrusted with poppy seeds, 164

chicken in fresh green coriander, 148

chicken with mustard seeds, 151

cooling mango chutney, *154*, 169

X

Xacuti, 97, 105–6

Y

Yale, Elihu, 182
Yoghurt, 60, 217, 220
   adding to sauces, 289
   chicken kebabs, 230
   courgette (zucchini) raita, 252
   lamb chops masala, 229
   lamb cooked in milk and yoghurt, 147
   mango curry, 36
   mango yoghurt, 89
   marinades, 289
   rice with yogurt, 206–8

   spicy pineapple-yoghurt, 45–6
   steamed yoghurt, 169–71
   sweet and sour chick pea flour soup, 79
   yoghurt fish, 152–3, *154*
   yoghurt with banana and mustard, 84–5

Z

Zacharias, Uma and Zac J., 39, 48
Zucchini raita, 252

PHOTO CREDITS

BBC Books would like to thank the following for providing photographs and for permision to reproduce copyright material. While every effort has been made to trace and acknowledge all copyright holders, we would like to apologise should there have been any errors or omissions.

All location photographs Colorific: pages   6–7, 10–11, 15, 50–51, 55, 59, 134–135, 139, 174–175, 179, 183, 214–215, 219, 223 (Raghubir Singh); 90–91, 95 (Dilip Mehta); 99 (Gianfranco Gorgoni).

ACKNOWLEDGEMENTS

KERALA:
Selvaraj, Mr A.R. Sunil, Mr Balasundaram, Shoba Ramji, Mr Damodaran, Mrs Bavani, Mrs K.M. Matthew, A.L. Shrinivasa Shenoy, Ajit Edassery, Ms Rolly Sapru, Uma and Zac J. Zacharias.

GUJARAT:
Mrs Kumud Kansara, Deepak Kansara, Nishrin Attarwala, The Rajmata of Jasdan, Niranjana Rao, Samina Hakimji, Sanjay De, N.P. Kaushal, Surendra Patel, Anand Sarabhai, Basil Joseph and Rambhai Bharwad.

GOA:
Jude Sequeira, Sophie Gonsalves, Reza, Maria Fernanda Sousa, Rita Themudo, Arnold Pinto, Anju Timblo, Lalit Mishra, Rui Madre Deus and Maria Fernandes.

WEST BENGAL:
Sonali Basu, Christine Ward, Mrs Dasgupta, Rakhi Dasgupta, Rakhi and Aveek Sarkar, Ann and Bob Wright and Maya.

TAMIL NADU:
Mrs A. Santha Ramanujam, A.C. Muthiah, Dakshin restaurant at the Park Sheraton Hotel, Shoba Ramji and her staff, Mrs C.K. Ghariyali and Hotel Saravana Bhavan.

PUNJAB:
Promila Kapoor, Shashi Mehra, Jatinder Kaur, the Tarlok Singh family, Munim di Hatti, Surjit's Chicken House, Hoshiyar Singh at the Mohan International Hotel, Mrs Chadda, Kesar da Dhaba, Radha Anand and Sunil Vijayakar.

I also wish to offer my deepest thanks to Ravissant and Damania Airways.